"The authors . . . present their findings clearl[y] P9-EGM-140
—*The Cleveland Plain Dealer*

"One of the best sources of help for Alzheimer's since Mace and Rabin's *The 36-Hour Day*. An absolute standout."
—*Kirkus Reviews*

"With Alzheimer's and the fear of it looming ever larger in a society marked by increasing longevity, good books on it are needed. . . . This is one of the best."
—*Booklist*

"Practical information on new drug therapies, alternative treatments, tips on evaluating residential facilities, as well as an appendix of other resources make this an indispensable guide for patients, caregivers, and anyone who must deal with Alzheimer's disease."
—*Publishers Weekly*

"With authority and compassion, [the authors] cover everything from the history of the disorder to its warning signs, stages, and treatments—including new pharmaceuticals and complementary therapies."
—*Healthy Living*

"The most up-to-date and complete single guide for caregivers available today."
—Soo Borson, M.D., director,
Geropsychiatry Services,
Department of Psychiatry and Behavioral Sciences,
University of Washington Medical Center

"An outstanding new guide."
—Jerome Yesavage, M.D.,
professor of psychiatry,
Stanford University

"Should inspire hope in patients and their families."
—Marcia Ory, M.P.H., chief,
Social Science Research on Aging,
Behavioral and Social Research Program,
National Institute on Aging

"This is a wonderful and important resource for families who often lack basic information about the disease and strategies that can preserve their own well-being."
—Laura N. Gitlin, Ph.D., director,
Community and Homecare Research Division,
Thomas Jefferson University, and director for Research,
Senior Health Institute, Jefferson Health System

MICHAEL CASTLEMAN

DOLORES GALLAGHER-THOMPSON, PH.D.

MATTHEW NAYTHONS, M.D.

A Perigee Book

There's Still a Person in There

∽

The Complete Guide
to Treating and Coping
with Alzheimer's

Every effort has been made to ensure that the information contained in this book is complete and accurate. However, neither the publisher nor the author is engaged in rendering professional advice or services to the individual reader. The ideas, procedures, and suggestions contained in this book are not intended as a substitute for consulting with your physician and obtaining medical supervision as to any activity, procedure, or suggestion that might affect your health. Accordingly, individual readers must assume responsibility for their own actions, safety, and health, and neither the author nor the publisher shall be liable or responsible for any loss, injury, or damage allegedly arising from any information or suggestion in this book.

*The names, dates, places, and identifying details of the profiles
in chapters 4, 8, and 11 have been changed to preserve privacy.
The profiles of Ann and Julian Davidson (chapter 1) and
Debbie and Doris Hoffmann (chapter 15) are unaltered.*

A Perigee Book
Published by The Berkley Publishing Group
A division of Penguin Putnam Inc.
375 Hudson Street
New York, New York 10014

G. P. Putnam's Sons edition: December 1999
First Perigee edition: November 2000

Perigee ISBN: 0-399-52635-8

Published simultaneously in Canada.

The Penguin Putnam Inc. World Wide Web site address is
http://www.penguinputnam.com

The Library of Congress has cataloged the G. P. Putnam's Sons edition as follows:

Castleman, Michael.
There's still a person in there : the complete guide to treating
and coping with Alzheimer's / Michael Castleman, Dolores
Gallagher-Thompson, Matthew Naythons.
p.   cm.
Includes bibliographical references and index.
ISBN 0-399-14571-0
1. Alzheimer's disease—Popular works.   2. Alzheimer's disease—Case
studies.   I. Gallagher–Thompson, Dolores.   II. Naythons, Matthew.
III. Title.
RC523.2.C386   1999   99-34745 CIP
362.1'96831—dc21

Printed in the United States of America

10   9   8   7   6   5   4   3   2

Acknowledgments

The authors gratefully acknowledge and thank:

Their agent, Susan Naythons, of The Naythons Agency, Sausalito, California.

Their editors at Putnam, Jeremy Katz and Laura Shepherd.

The caregivers who gave so generously of their time to share their stories: Ann Davidson, Anna and Jorge Flores, Deborah Hoffmann, Faith Hung, and Sandra Worthington.

The staff and affiliates of the VA Palo Alto/Stanford Older Adult and Family Center for their support and expertise, particularly Ana Menendez and David Coon, Ph.D. Also: Patricia Arean, Ph.D.; Anne Bechtle, M.S.; Erin Cassidy, Ph.D.; Joan Cook, M.A.; Pam Dal-Canto, M.A.; James D'Andrea, Ph.D.; Carla Corral; Dee Haynie, Ph.D.; Dana Iller, B.S.; Josefina Juarez, B.S.; Rebecca Kovan; Valerie Lee, M.H.S.; Maria Lorente; Christine McKibben, Ph.D.; Christopher Murphy, Ph.D.; Lidia Mena-Hermida; Christina Nichols; Lisa Oliver; Celine Ossinalde; Veronica Padilla; David Powers, Ph.D.; Kenneth Rider, Ph.D.; Jose Romero, Ph.D.; Aida Saldivar; Lynn Snow, Ph.D.; Monica Soto; Douglas Stewart; Kellie Takagi, Ph.D.; Irene Valverde; Blanca Vasquez; and Darrelle Volwiler, Ph.D.

These professional colleagues for their support and expertise: Helen Davies, R.N., psychiatric clinical nurse specialist, Stanford/VA Alzheimer's Research Center; Elizabeth Edgerly, Ph.D., program director, Alzheimer's Association of the Greater San Francisco Bay Area Chapter; William Fischer, director, Alzheimer's Association, Greater San Francisco Bay Area Chapter; Esperanza Hernandez, M.S.W., U.C. Davis Alzheimer's Disease Center; Helena Kraemer, Ph.D., Stanford University; Esther Lara, L.C.S.W., U.C. Davis Alzheimer's Disease Center; Rudolph Moos, Ph.D., Stanford University; Greer Murphy, M.D., Stanford University; Robert Phillips, M.A., CEO, Del Mar Caregivers Resource Center; Josie Romero, L.C.S.W., community consultant; Ann Steffen, Ph.D., University of Missouri, St. Louis; Joy Taylor, Ph.D., Alzheimer's Disease Clinical Research Center; Jared Tinklenberg, M.D., director, Stanford/VA Alzheimer's Research Center; Ramon Valle, Ph.D., professor, San Diego State University; Gwen Yeo, Ph.D., director, Stanford Geriatric Education Center; Jerome Yesavage, M.D., Stanford University and VA Palo Alto; Antonette Zeiss, Ph.D., VA Palo Alto.

The staffs of NetHealth and PlanetRx, publishers of Alzheimers.com (www. alzheimers.com): Peter Goggin, Martyn Harmon, Ellen Sanok, Nancy Opitz, and Michael Stroh.

Gina Monroe and Jerry Rosenberg at Bayer Corporation, Pharmaceutical Division, for the unrestricted educational grant that launched Alzheimers.com.

And Arnold Levinson for help in Denver; Anne Simons, M.D., for her support and patience; Larry Thompson, Ph.D., without whose support and encouragement this book would not have been possible; and the following sources of research support: the National Institute of Mental Health, the National Institute on Aging, the Alzheimer's Association national office in Chicago, the California Department of Health Services, and the VA Palo Alto Research Service.

*To Bernard Lazar, whose retirement passion for
stained-glass art was cut short by Alzheimer's disease*

—MICHAEL CASTLEMAN

*To my mother, Elizabeth, who inspired me to help caregivers
deal with their distress. And to my husband, Larry,
who has always been there for me*

—DOLORES GALLAGHER-THOMPSON

To my aunt Pearl, the caregiver

—MATTHEW NAYTHONS

Contents

When you've met one person with Alzheimer's disease, you've met one person with Alzheimer's.

Virginia Bell, M.S.W.,
David Troxel, M.P.H.

Introduction

New Insights, New Hope

A joke that was popular in the late 1970s asked: What are the three losses of old age? Loss of eyesight. Loss of hearing. And . . . and . . . damn, what *is* that third one? I can't recall. . . .

That joke passed out of vogue because memory loss stopped being funny in the early 1980s, when a group of caregivers and professionals incorporated the Alzheimer's Association and began educating the public about Alzheimer's disease. Today, when people over forty misplace their keys, they rarely make light of it. They are much more likely to feel a stab of concern that it might be a harbinger of The Big A.

If you've ever worried about minor memory lapses, relax. It's perfectly normal to misplace your keys now and then. The time to get concerned is when you *find* them but can't recall what to *do* with them. It's also normal—and quite common—to forget people's names occasionally. The time to get concerned is when you're reminded who they are but don't recall knowing them.

Feel reassured? Then read on. Most Americans, even many who provide care for Alzheimer's sufferers, are woefully uninformed about the disease. Alzheimer's usually inspires hopelessness. Most Americans believe that it strikes out of the blue, cannot be prevented, and that once it's diagnosed, afflicted individuals quickly sink into the quicksand of a living death.

Despite his firm commitment to "live the remainder of the years God gives me on this earth doing the things I have always done," the public reacted with hopelessness to former President Ronald Reagan's 1994 announcement that he was in the early stages of Alzheimer's. A widespread sense of doom and despair contrasted sharply with the President and First Lady's quiet courage. Whatever plans the Reagans might have had, to the American people and media, this was the beginning of the end.

Don't get us wrong; as of this writing, there is no cure for Alzheimer's. Despite medications that slow its progression, Alzheimer's sufferers currently follow an irreversible downward course. But the grim mythology surrounding the disease has kept most Americans from noticing that in the years since Ronald Reagan's diagnosis, *real progress* has been made in diagnosing, treating, managing, and preventing the disease.

Scientists now know more about the biology of Alzheimer's than ever (chapter 3). The disease may strike out of the blue, but a considerable number of risk factors have been identified (chapter 5), and some people who seem to have Alzheimer's actually have conditions that are reversible (chapter 9). Although Alzheimer's treatments are far from curative, both drug and nondrug therapies can slow its progression and enhance quality of life for those who have it and their caregivers. Drugs currently in development promise even greater benefits. Experts estimate that if the progression of Alzheimer's could be delayed just five years, the need for nursing home care would plummet 50 percent (chapter 10). Innovative approaches now allow caregivers to provide better care longer, which preserves families and can save a fortune in residential care costs (chapters 12, 13, and 14). Finally, researchers have discovered many ways that the worried well can preserve their mental acuity and greatly reduce their risk of Alzheimer's (chapters 5 and 16).

Interspersed throughout this book are a series of in-depth personal profiles (chapters 1, 4, 8, 11, and 15) that illuminate the progression of Alzheimer's and the demands of caregiving. These profiles, based on extensive interviews by Michael Castleman, serve to enhance the other, more expository chapters, and we hope the voices of these exceptional people (one of whom gave us the title for our book) will provide another level of comfort and understanding.

The hopelessness surrounding Alzheimer's has become outdated. It's still a terrible disease, of course, but today, for the first time, Alzheimer's experts are cautiously optimistic that in the not-too-distant future, we may have the tools to delay or prevent its onset, to manage it more effectively, and to slow or possibly even halt its progression.

I.

"There's Still a Person in There"

Profile of Ann and Julian Davidson

The absentminded professor. That's how Ann Davidson often thought of her husband, Julian. A handsome, quick-witted man with roots in Scotland, Julian spent virtually his entire career as a professor of physiology at Stanford University. He looked the part of the academic, with rumpled casual clothes, wire-rimmed glasses, an ambling gait, a graying beard, receding curly gray hair, a deep love of classical music, and an air of perpetual preoccupation as he pedaled his bike daily from their large, comfortable ranch home on the prestigious campus to his office and back.

During their thirty-seven years of marriage, Ann and Julian raised three children. Ann trained as a speech pathologist and worked part-time while their children were growing up. The children went off to college, and later their daughter produced three grandchildren.

Over the decades, Ann adjusted to her husband's workaholic preoccupation with his career, admiring his intellect and fretting with him over his lectures, grant applications, journal articles, committee responsibilities, and the vagaries of academic politics. Of course, she got annoyed when she realized, too frequently, that Julian was not giving her his undivided attention. She did not like to repeat herself or say, "Julian, listen," because he was off in some physiological reverie instead of focusing on her. He *was* the classic absentminded professor. Ann was forever reminding him not to forget his briefcase, or his keys, or his brothers' birthdays, or the dinner or concert date they had in the evening.

Yet their love was deep and enduring, their marriage strong, and when her moments of irritation over Julian's daydreaming passed, Ann understood that one of the things that endeared him to her was his ability to live in his imagination, and to revel in the life of the mind.

In 1986, when he was fifty-four, things started to change for Julian. "I didn't see it at first," Ann recalls, "and certainly no one else had any inkling, but Julian was convinced that he had memory problems, and he became concerned." For twenty years, Julian had had no problem delivering lectures to Stanford medical and graduate students from brief notes. Then one day he found they were no longer enough. He began outlining his lectures more thoroughly, and by the late 1980s, he felt he had to write them out and read them word for word. Julian also found it increasingly difficult to write scientific papers and grant applications. When colleagues broached new ideas, he had trouble absorbing them and giving them cogent feedback. "What you hear at many Alzheimer's workshops," Ann says, "is that in the early stages, those with the disease typically deny that they have memory problems. That happens with a lot of people, but not everyone. Julian was the first to realize that something was wrong."

For three years, with rising apprehension and anxiety, Julian complained to Ann about his memory. At first, she chalked his anxiety up to chronic career stress, but after a while she noticed that her absentminded husband seemed increasingly scattered. Still, it didn't concern her too much. "He misplaced things a little more, but that was completely in character. He'd always lost things. So he did it a little more. So what?"

Despite Ann's efforts to comfort and reassure him, Julian insisted that something was *really wrong* with him, and, true to his training, he began seeking answers as a scientist would, in an organized, systematic fashion. He consulted his family doctor, who did not suspect Alzheimer's because Julian was not yet sixty and the disease is rare in people under sixty-five. But Julian was clearly anxious, so his doctor sent him to a psychologist.

Julian had good reason to be anxious. Both of his older brothers had died a few years earlier at age fifty-nine, one from Hodgkin's disease, the other from complications of coronary bypass surgery. Julian was fifty-seven, and worried that he might fall victim to what he only half-jokingly called his "family curse." The psychologist agreed. Anxiety, confusion, and memory problems are all symptoms of depression, which was what the psychologist first diagnosed. Julian took this information to his doctor, who prescribed anti-anxiety medication along with counseling from a psychotherapist. His memory problem did not improve.

Then, Julian began using words incorrectly, often saying the opposite of what he meant. He'd mean "up" and say "down," mean "increase" and say "decrease." Ann noticed but didn't take her husband's lapses too seriously. "Who hasn't said 'left' when they meant 'right'?" But Julian's Stanford colleagues were not quite so generous. Science demands precision, and Julian's increasingly frequent errors irritated them and frustrated his students, which only increased his anxiety and growing sense of apprehension and shame.

In early 1989, Julian began forgetting appointments with Ann. "We'd have a date to meet for lunch, and he wouldn't show up, or he would agree to pick me up at a certain time and place, and then leave me hanging." Alzheimer's disease was still the farthest thing from Ann's mind. Julian was so young. No one in either of their families had ever had it, and Julian still functioned more or less competently— a far cry from the picture Ann had of the disease. Ann didn't think her husband was ill. On the contrary, he was the picture of health. She figured he was being rude or uncaring. "I was furious with him for much of the year before his diagnosis," Ann admits. Ann's anger made her less sympathetic to Julian's growing plight, and it made him feel even more anxious and ashamed.

Maybe the psychologist was right, Julian thought. Maybe anxiety *was* his underlying problem. But as the months passed, he became convinced that, independent of any anxiety or depression, his memory was going. He asked a Stanford colleague, a neuropsychologist who did memory research, to evaluate him. "His short-term memory was a bit deficient," Ann recalls, "but still in the normal range. Julian felt reassured. His memory trouble seemed to be caused by anxiety, which was the result of stress."

Then in early 1990, Julian was invited to present his latest research at a conference in Acapulco, after which he and Ann planned to tour the Yucatán for a week. "It was a disaster," Ann sighs. Julian was frantic about his lecture. By this time, notes were out of the question. He wrote his lecture word for word and carefully packed it and his slides into his briefcase. Then at the Acapulco airport, he lost the briefcase. "He panicked," Ann recalls. "It was all I could do to calm him down enough to search the airport." Eventually, Ann found the briefcase.

Julian's troubles continued. At his presentation, he mixed up his slides and answered several questions inappropriately, which elicited quizzical looks from the audience. Afterward, he forgot to pay the hotel bill, and as they drove away, the hotel's security people chased after them.

In the Yucatán, things went from bad to worse. "Julian couldn't read maps," Ann recalls. "He got lost repeatedly. He couldn't deal with Mexican currency. He couldn't find our room in several hotels."

The low point occurred in Palenque, at a hotel near some Mayan ruins. After a day of hiking around the ruins, they returned to their small room, with its one dresser. Ann put their green daypack on top of it.

"Where's my wallet?" Julian asked Ann.

"In the daypack," she replied. Julian did not understand.

"Where's my wallet?" he repeated.

"In the pack," Ann reiterated, annoyed. Again, no reaction.

"Where is my damn wallet?" Julian demanded, exasperated, anxiously scanning the room and either not understanding the word "pack" or not seeing it in front of him.

Ann recalls experiencing "a horrible sinking feeling." This was not the husband she knew.

"But when we returned home," Ann recalls, "he got better. I've heard many similar stories. People with very early Alzheimer's can function reasonably well on familiar turf, but take them anywhere new, and they fall apart. They can't learn like they used to, so they can't cope with unfamiliar surroundings."

However, by the summer of 1990, as the problems continued, Ann was convinced that Julian's difficulties went beyond anxiety and rudeness. She encouraged him to return to his Stanford colleague, the memory expert. Julian went in for testing one morning. That afternoon, the memory expert called Ann and said, "Julian needs a neurological evaluation."

"Why?" Ann asked.

The memory expert didn't answer. He just said, "Please, make the appointment."

Ann accompanied Julian to his neurological exam. In the afternoon, while Julian was still being tested, his neurologist emerged from the examination area and motioned for Ann to follow her. They wound up in the photocopying room. The neurologist said, "I wanted you to know before we meet with Julian. He has progressive dementia, probably Alzheimer's."

The diagnosis hit Ann like a slap in the face. "I'd never felt so frightened in my entire life. I had this vision of Julian's brain shriveling up and dying, turning into mush overnight."

Ann said nothing to Julian. "I could have told him any other diagnosis—a stroke, a brain tumor—more easily. Alzheimer's just seemed like the worst thing that could ever befall an intellectual like Julian. I decided to let the neurologist tell him, but I asked the doctor not to use the word 'Alzheimer's.'"

A few days later, Ann and Julian again met with the neurologist, who ran down a long list of diseases that the exam had ruled out, including a stroke, a brain tumor, diabetes, and vitamin deficiencies, among others. Then she said, "But there is a problem with your memory. You need to reduce your stress. Take it easy. Think about cutting back at work."

The neurologist did what Ann had asked. She never uttered the word "Alzheimer's." She told the truth, just not the whole truth. Ann was relieved and glad. She was still in shock over the diagnosis herself and felt she needed time to adjust, so she could support Julian effectively when he finally learned the truth.

Ann didn't get much adjustment time. Soon after that meeting, Julian received a letter from the California Department of Motor Vehicles (DMV) asking him to appear at the local DMV office. No reason, just a request to appear in person. Julian figured it was time to renew his license.

When he presented himself, the clerk hit some computer keys, then some more.

"Is anything wrong?" Julian asked.

"I can't give you a regular renewal," the clerk replied.

"Why not?"

"Because you have Alzheimer's disease."

(California doctors are required to report Alzheimer's diagnoses to the DMV. At the time of Julian's diagnosis, the DMV did not automatically revoke affected individuals' licenses but could require them to take periodic road tests to assess their competence. As this book goes to press, new research shows that driving is one of the first skills Alzheimer's sufferers lose [see chapter 3]. The American Psychiatric Association has called for immediate revocation of driver's licenses at diagnosis. But Julian was diagnosed back in 1990, and he was allowed to drive for another year.)

When Julian returned home, he began to weep, and Ann immediately realized what must have happened. "We embraced, and I began crying, too. What else could we do?"

The realization that he had Alzheimer's made Julian even more anxious, agitated, and depressed. One evening during dinner, Ann had to help him find words and finish quite a few sentences. It was hard for both of them, but she felt hopeful because despite Julian's increasing verbal difficulties, the conversation continued to flow. They still shared good communication.

Julian, however, felt differently. After dinner, he trudged into their bedroom, lay down, and pulled the covers over his head. Ann asked if he felt ill.

"Leave me alone," he mumbled.

"What's wrong? Did I say something that hurt your feelings?"

No reply.

"Tell me, please."

"I'm no good. I'm no good anymore. I can't do anything anymore. Thoughts just fly away. I think of something I want to say, and I can't remember the words."

Ann tried to comfort him. "There are many quiet people in the world. It's not bad to be a quiet person—you just haven't been one before. Being quiet is new for you. Let's try to find good images of quiet people."

Meanwhile, Ann sank into a deep depression of her own. She experienced terrifying premonitions of impending doom. "I had visions that I was trapped in a room with no exit, and the walls began closing in." This is the end, she thought. Our lives are over. "They weren't, but I didn't realize that until much later."

Ann felt overwhelmed by grief. "I was losing my husband, and the life we'd created. Alzheimer's hit like a strange kind of death sentence. Julian wasn't dying. In fact, he was very healthy, but the person I knew, the husband I loved, and our marriage—all that was dying."

She also felt overwhelmed by fear. "What would happen to Julian? To me? How would I handle things like our finances? How would I manage him?"

Despite Ann's depression and Julian's frantic anxiety, the aftermath of his diagnosis brought an unexpected gift—a rekindling of their passion for each other. "I immediately dropped all my anger at Julian's forgetfulness," Ann recalls. "In doing so, I realized how deeply I loved him, and how much precious time I'd wasted resenting his lapses." Meanwhile, Julian struggled to come to grips with what was happening to him, and he clung to Ann for support. "I was his anchor in the storm. As horrible as that period was for us, it was also a time of great love and tenderness."

When Julian was diagnosed with Alzheimer's disease, he and Ann knew nothing about the realities of the illness. All they knew were the grim stereotypes. "I imagined Julian wandering aimlessly around the neighborhood in his pajamas," Ann recalls. "I envisioned him tied into a wheelchair, drooling and staring off into space in some awful nursing home. I thought he'd be reduced to infancy, curled up in a fetal position, saying nothing and barely moving for years."

As the months passed, Ann overcame her initial fears and started getting serious about coping with her husband's illness. She visited the local office of the Alzheimer's Association. "I had to force myself to go there, and when I opened the door, I burst into tears." After the initial shock, though, she obtained some helpful literature and referrals to community caregiver resources.

Ann didn't fight Julian's diagnosis, but she decided to have him reevaluated by a different neurologist, just to make sure. "The second opinion was the same—early Alzheimer's," she recalls. "I wasn't surprised. Deep down, I knew that was what Julian had."

A friend gave Ann a copy of *The 36-Hour Day,* at the time the main resource about caring for people with dementia. "I thought, Is this what I have to look forward to? Thirty-six-hour days? I made myself read the chapter on finances because Julian had always taken care of ours, and I dreaded taking them over, but I couldn't face the rest of that book and didn't read it for two years."

Ann struggled to find something—anything—that might slow the progression of Julian's Alzheimer's. She learned of a clinical trial of an experimental drug that seemed to help, tacrine (Cognex). Three years later, in 1993, Cognex became the first medication to win Food and Drug Administration approval as a treatment for Alzheimer's. Unfortunately, Cognex helps only a fraction of those who take it. It does not reverse the disease but only slows its progression, and caregivers often fail to notice any benefit. "Cognex didn't make any difference that I could see," Ann recalls, "but it was *something,* which felt better than doing nothing. And maybe Julian would have been worse without it."

Because Julian was part of the clinical trial, Ann obtained his Cognex for free. Afterward, she was told she'd have to buy it. "It was expensive. Julian's neurologist didn't believe in it, and our insurance refused to pay for it, so eventually I stopped giving it to him."

At this time, one of Ann and Julian's sons was working at a health-food store and plied them with supplements reputed to help the mind: vitamins, minerals, and the medicinal herb ginkgo. "I've never been big on vitamins," Ann concedes. "I didn't expect any of that stuff to help. I gave Julian the supplements for a few months, mostly to support my son's efforts to help his father. After a while, I stopped them, too."

(Supplements do not work miracles for Alzheimer's sufferers, but several recent studies show that vitamin E, ginkgo, and the amino acid–based drug carnitine slow cognitive decline. See chapter 10.)

Their second son urged Ann to take Julian to a doctor of Chinese medicine. If Western medicine wasn't helping him, maybe Chinese medicine would. "The Chinese herbalist prescribed a bunch of herbs and sent us home with a huge bag of roots and twigs, but that didn't last long. Julian hated the taste of the tea, and I felt silly making it."

The best thing Ann did was to join an Alzheimer's support group for couples run by the psychiatry department at the Stanford VA Hospital. Two psychiatric nurses led the discussion at the group's monthly meetings, and about ten couples attended, each with an affected spouse and a caregiver.

On the one hand, the meetings were very sad and distressing. Ann and Julian were the youngest couple there, by at least ten years. Many of the affected individuals were much deeper into the illness than Julian was and had problems he did not yet have. They couldn't dress themselves, they wandered off, they left the stove on, or they became belligerent with the mail carrier. Is this my future? Ann wondered. Alzheimer's seemed so grim.

On the other hand, Ann found great comfort in the group. Here were people who knew *exactly* what she and Julian were going through in a way no one else did. Many of the caregivers seemed so resilient, so resourceful. When they feared that they were at their wits' end, the group leaders usually had wise, practical suggestions.

"I scream at her," one elderly husband-caregiver admitted, full of shame and guilt. "I can't help myself. She can be so infuriating!" His wife sat next to him, well dressed and looking quite normal, except that she paid no attention and incessantly mumbled nonsense.

"Every caregiver of a demented individual yells sometimes," one of the nurses said softly. "It's okay to let out your stress."

Ann absorbed the discussions. With the help of everyone here, she thought, I just might get through this.

But Julian felt differently. He hated the group, hated seeing the people in more advanced stages of the disease. "I'm not like them," he insisted after each meeting. "I'm healthy and strong." But his bravado couldn't hide his understanding of what awaited him. After six meetings, he refused to attend any more. Ann went by herself.

Although the support group diminished Ann's feelings of isolation as a caregiver, it also heightened her sense of growing distance from the close community of friends and family who knew Julian. "He went downhill right before my eyes. I could see it, day by day, week to week, but few others noticed because you had to spend a lot of time with him to see the gradual decline. Every day brought another heartache, another task he couldn't quite manage on his own, like making coffee, balancing the checkbook, dialing the phone. It was heartbreaking and very frustrating for me. I had good support, and yet I felt utterly alone in my knowledge of his deterioration."

By 1992, two years after Julian's diagnosis, Ann stopped scouring the newspaper for word of an Alzheimer's breakthrough and ignored the names and numbers of new doctors and alternative practitioners friends suggested she call. "I decided to put all my energy into caring for Julian, to help him slide as painlessly as possible into whatever Alzheimer's held for him."

To do that, Ann decided to keep his life—and their life together—as normal as possible for as long as possible. The effort was exhausting. She was losing her husband and knew that with each passing day he would be less and less the man she'd loved for more than thirty years. "I realized that I had to accept his journey and learn to let go of the husband I knew. It sounds so simple and right to say it now, six years later, but in the midst of it, there were many times I felt paralyzed with fear and grief and thought I was going insane."

In time Ann surprised herself. Little by little, she accepted Julian's losses. "There were days when the process was horrible, when his deterioration infuriated and scared me, when I sobbed and cursed in despair," she recalls. "But there were good times, too, periods of fun, and joy, and pleasure—times when Julian would hold me as tenderly as I've ever been held, or he'd see something that struck him as funny and laugh uproariously, which would start me laughing, too. Our life was going down the tubes, but it was still *our life,* and all I could do was make the best of it."

Ann was also surprised by Julian. His intellect slowly evaporated, but in some ways Alzheimer's disease highlighted the nicer side of his personality. His sarcasm disappeared, replaced by an innocent gentleness. "Julian declined steadily, but the process was not as grim as the stereotypes suggest. Even as he became increasingly confused and impaired, his fundamental personality remained. There was still a person in there."

Retiring from work terrified Julian. His work was a huge part of his identity, and Alzheimer's disease ripped it away from him long before he imagined letting it go. Julian's inability to work infuriated him. He had so many plans, so many ideas for research he wanted to do, but they all began slipping away. He and Ann had many dreams of what they would do when he retired, which, before his illness, he believed was at least a decade away. With his illness, retirement was foisted on him suddenly and cruelly.

As fate would have it, about this time Stanford was in the process of closing the entire Anatomy building, where Julian worked, to repair damage sustained during the 1989 Loma Prieta earthquake. Like the other professors, Julian was assigned a new office in another building, but as his colleagues moved, he could not tear himself away from his beloved old desk and bookcases. Eventually, he received a form letter from the Buildings and Grounds department specifying the date, several weeks away, when he had to turn in his Anatomy building keys.

In preparation, Julian went to his office every day "to sort my papers," he told Ann. She encouraged him to bring his books and files home, but each afternoon he returned empty-handed. Finally, after weeks of procrastination, Ann drove to the campus and appeared at Julian's door with several boxes.

"Get out of here!" Julian shouted. "Leave me alone! This is my stuff! You think I'm no good! This is *my* business!"

Ann tried to explain that he had to be out of the office in just a few days. That only made Julian more agitated. "Leave me alone! Get out of my business!"

Ann had been patient for weeks, but at that point she lost her temper. "You don't understand anything!"

Julian glared at her, and all at once Ann experienced an epiphany. Julian's books and files didn't matter. He couldn't use them anymore, so why fight about them? "Okay," Ann said. "You're right. It's not my job to clean out your office. I'm leaving and won't come here again. Do whatever you want."

They walked down the hall in stony silence. In the parking lot, Julian said, "You think I'm no good. You think I'm useless!"

"Darling, I never said that." Ann's eyes filled with tears, and she realized that her voice was hoarse from shouting. "I never used those words. You're saying that."

They embraced, and Julian began to cry. They cried together.

"Looking back on that period," Ann explains, "I didn't let go soon enough. I could have avoided that ugly scene—and so many others—if I hadn't tried to reason with Julian to get him to see things my way. How slowly I learned."

When Julian finally vacated his office, leaving most of his things for the custodians to discard, he had no real reason to be on the Stanford campus anymore. His lab was closed. His old familiar office was gone. His career was over. His colleagues were sympathetic to his plight, but life went on, and they let it be known that they expected him to quietly disappear. It was difficult for Julian to tear himself away. He'd commuted back and forth from his home to the campus, usually by bike, for thirty years. He grew restless and felt useless hanging around the house.

Fortunately, the Stanford Library had a comfortable faculty study. Julian loved the library and for years had gone there almost every day. His trips to the library marked the last vestige of his professional identity. Technically, Julian was no longer on the faculty and not entitled to faculty privileges, but the library staff understood his situation and made him feel welcome. "The staff people were wonderful to him," Ann recalls. "They kept an eye on him, retrieved his briefcase whenever he lost it, several times a week, and if anything seemed wrong, they called me."

As Julian struggled with relinquishing his career and leaving his productive past behind, he also wrestled with his uncertain future.

Despite his failing mind, he tried to come to grips with the person he was becoming. He retained an intense desire to lead an interesting life and do meaningful work. Over and over again, he asked Ann, "Who will I be?" The question broke her heart. She struggled to maintain her composure, to reassure him. "You'll always be you, and I'll always love you." But inside, she was asking herself the same question: Who *is* he becoming?

Julian's forced retirement may have been his biggest personal loss, but Ann's attempt to keep him from driving infuriated him. Ann was astonished that the DMV didn't revoke Julian's license the moment his neurologist reported his diagnosis. By then, he was a terrible driver. He'd make right turns from the left lane and run stop signs. "I was a basket case whenever he was behind the wheel. If I knew Julian had the car and the phone rang, I'd answer it praying that he hadn't hurt himself or someone else."

Still, Julian adamantly refused to stop driving. *"I've never had an accident!"* he bellowed whenever Ann raised the subject. "We had our biggest, most bitter fights over his driving," Ann recalls. "I couldn't forbid him to drive, so I got sneaky about it. The books all say, 'Just take the person's car keys and they won't know the difference.' But when Julian discovered that I'd removed his car key from his key ring, he became furious. I'd stripped him of his dignity. He cursed me, which was a first for us. That moment was one of my lowest points as a caregiver."

No matter how much Ann coaxed, pleaded, and railed, Julian stubbornly clung to this last freedom, even as his ability disintegrated. Ann began orchestrating their errands to accommodate Julian's insistence on driving. "I'd ask him to drive to the stores near our house during the day. There was rarely much traffic, and he never got going that fast. I had to insist on driving at night, on the freeways, and on any long trip."

Sometimes, the informal split of their driving responsibilities worked well, but Ann could never be sure that Julian would play along. Once, one of their sons flew in from New York and had to be picked up at the airport, about forty-five minutes away. It was a lovely day, and Ann suggested that Julian might like to take a little snooze while she drove to the airport. No sale. Julian marched out to the car, plopped down in the driver's seat, and would not budge, no matter how much Ann begged.

Finally she said, "If you're driving, I'm not going."

"Fine," Julian replied, and backed out of the driveway and drove off alone.

Immediately, Ann regretted her tactic. "I was a nervous wreck. I had visions of losing both my husband and my son in a freeway fireball. They finally showed up a few hours later. Those were the longest few hours of my life."

A year after Julian's post-diagnosis renewal, the DMV finally revoked his license. Ann heaved a huge sigh of relief—but prematurely. Julian was still cogent enough to understand that he'd lost his license, but he didn't care. He kept trying to drive anyway. "I was appalled, of course," Ann recalls, "but as long as he could recognize his car key, I couldn't take it away from him, and I couldn't get rid of the car because I needed it."

Time was on Ann's side. Soon after Julian lost his license, he'd declined to the point where he became less adamant about driving. If Ann confronted him about it, he became huffy, but if she was casual and tender, he would go along. Eventually, Julian's desire to drive faded and, along with it, his anger about the subject.

Unfortunately for Ann, the conflicts raised by Julian's driving did not disappear when he finally stopped. Like a recurring nightmare, they came back to haunt her over his bike riding. He was as attached to bicycling as he was to driving—and there was no DMV to order him off the road. "He got lost," Ann remembers. "The police and kindly strangers brought him home many, many times. He lost his bike more times than I care to recall. He'd wander home confused, saying he'd left it by a brown building or by a green truck—God knows where. I'd call the campus police and we'd search all over the place. Usually we'd find the bike within a block or two of the library."

Ominously, as Julian became more confused, he stopped paying attention to stop signs and traffic lights, and the inevitable happened. One afternoon, he pedaled through a red light into heavy traffic, and a German graduate student hit him. Julian was not injured, but when the student asked, "Are you okay?" Julian couldn't respond. He didn't know his name or where he lived. The poor student was frantic. Fortunately, the bewildered student found Julian's address in his wallet and brought him home.

Ann had always participated in the family checking account, but Julian paid the bills, took care of their taxes, financial planning, and record-keeping. Ann felt intimidated by those chores, especially taxes, and feared taking responsibility for them. "Early on," she recalls, "I read about how the caregiver must eventually take over the finances, but in the day-to-day chaos of Julian's decline, we never got around to discussing things like taxes."

About two years after Julian's diagnosis, Ann realized that he could no longer handle paying the bills. "He'd pay bills several times, or write checks and leave the amount blank, or forget to sign his name." Recalling the battle they'd had over Julian's driving, she began assuming the financial chores slowly and stealthily. This time her cautious approach was unnecessary. "Julian was relieved to give up the finances."

Then April rolled around, and Ann was forced to confront her deep fear of dealing with their income tax. She hoped Julian would be able to help her file their taxes, but he was too impaired to explain anything. All he could communicate was his relief at not having to fill out the forms himself. "I kicked myself for not dealing with the documents when he could still help."

On her own, full of dread, Ann began sifting though their financial papers. What she discovered in their tax files left her in despair. Julian had misfiled just about everything. Important papers were stuffed haphazardly in various desk drawers. "It was a nightmare," Ann recalls. "I remember sitting there looking at this incomprehensible jumble of papers and just sobbing."

Eventually, Ann gathered up every document that looked the least bit important, dumped them all in a big box, and took them to their accountant. Julian never mentioned their finances again.

Neatness had never been Julian's strong suit, and with three active kids, the Davidson home was comfortable but cluttered. Not long after Julian's diagnosis, Ann realized that their piles of books, magazines, personal papers, clothing, and athletic gear were becoming increasingly difficult for Julian to handle. "In all the chaos, he couldn't find things," Ann recalls, "and when he put something down, I couldn't find it." Ann began tidying up with a vengeance. "The house was neater than it had ever been." Eliminating the clutter helped.

Unfortunately, around this time, Julian became obsessed with paper. He had less and less idea what documents meant, but he felt compelled to scoop them up, carry them around the house, and usually deposit them in some out-of-the-way nook, effectively hiding them from Ann. It often took weeks for bills or invitations to turn up. "It was chaos," Ann recalls. "I felt like I was fighting chaos all the time."

There was only one way to cope—hide any significant papers from Julian. The key was to be the first one to collect the mail. Ann lay in wait for the postman, and quickly, quietly secreted everything that was important in places where Julian never looked, usually in the deep recesses of her own desk.

As he declined, Ann had to spend more and more time supervising him, which left precious little time to do things like pay bills, answer letters, or maintain their home. If she tried to do chores when Julian was around, there was always the danger that he would snatch up some paper and, like a toddler, simply refuse to let it go. "I had to be very sneaky," Ann explains. "It was exhausting. I hated it."

Ann had to watch Julian every second. He had never done much in the kitchen, but as his Alzheimer's progressed, he became a menace. "He never had any accidents with knives, thank God, but he started burning things in the toaster oven, so I had to get rid of it. While trying to make tea, he melted two kettles to the point where they looked like weird abstract sculptures." As the months passed, Ann jettisoned every nonnecessary item around the house that might injure Julian or cause some disaster. "He began cutting his lips while shaving, so I threw out his razor and bought him an electric shaver."

Dressing was another major issue. Julian became increasingly confused when deciding what to wear. By this time, Ann understood a key to Alzheimer's caregiving: limit the affected individual's choices.

She emptied his closet, leaving only three shirts and three pairs of pants, eliminating the confusion.

Once Julian decided what to wear, he found it increasingly difficult to dress himself properly. He might put his underwear on over his pants, or his shirts on backward, so Ann got creative. After Julian showered, she laid out his clothes in a trail on the floor starting at the bathroom door: first his underwear, then his socks, then his pants, pullover shirt, and shoes.

"Dressing is very complicated," Ann explains. "I had to break everything down into a string of simple tasks. After a while, I realized that I was living my life in slow motion. Taking care of Julian required patience and stamina I never thought I had. That was a gift—learning that I was more resilient than I thought I was. Julian's personal care was maddening. It's one thing when your husband can't hold up his end of the conversation. It's quite another when he can't brush his teeth." Eventually, she bathed him, fed him, and cleaned him up after he went to the bathroom.

As Julian deteriorated, Ann spent most of her time in a whirl, dealing with the hundreds of banal, exhausting details involved in caregiving. Every now and then, a moment of passage drew her up short and she experienced the full weight of what was happening to them. For example, birthday cards. "For the longest time, I automatically signed 'Ann and Julian.' Eventually, I wrote just 'Ann.'" Then there was their phone machine message. "It said, 'Neither Ann nor Julian can take your call right now. . . .' I left it that way for months after Julian lost the ability to have a meaningful conversation. Then I changed it to: 'Ann can't . . .'" Those transitions were sad because they forced Ann to realize that Julian was disappearing from the world. "But in a funny way," she recalls, "they also helped me adjust to what was happening to him, to us."

Caregiving utterly drained Ann. "Every little loss meant another demand on me. The amount of energy it required was bad enough, but the tedium got so depressing." To assist with the process, Ann attended a very helpful class, sponsored by the Alzheimer's Association, on *reframing*. "The class helped me change, or *reframe,* my reactions to Julian's behavior. Before the class, when Julian would do something weird, my first thought would be, He's so stupid, or Oh my God, he's getting worse. Afterward it changed to, He's doing the best he can. He wouldn't be this way if he had any choice in the matter. Reframing helped me accept what was happening. Not that the class changed my reactions overnight. It took time and effort. I still cried, and yelled, and felt crazy at times, but eventually I changed, and it helped."

As Julian went downhill, Ann's once busy social life became increasingly constrained. Invitations had to be declined. Friendships frayed. Movies, concerts, and many other outings were out of the question. "Many friends pulled away," she recalls, "and for a while, I resented it. Over time I realized that I haven't been there for every friend of mine who's gotten sick or had some family problem that overwhelmed them. Instead of feeling angry about the friends who withdrew, I felt very grateful for the few who hung in there with us."

One friend took Julian out to lunch and to a music appreciation class every Tuesday afternoon. Another regularly took him to the local food bank, where together they assembled food boxes for the homeless. A third took him to a singing group at the Jewish community center.

The respite was a godsend for Ann, but as the months turned into years and Julian deteriorated further, she realized that even their loyal friends could no longer handle him and that she needed more help. She turned to adult daycare.

Julian's daycare center was a dream come true. Housed in a clean, pleasant facility and staffed by caring souls who genuinely liked him, Julian reveled in the activities and liked the other clients who were there with him. He was ten years younger than the average participant, but no one seemed to notice, least of all Julian.

At first, Julian went to daycare two days a week, then increased to five. Suddenly, Ann had freedom she hadn't had in years, whole days where she could renew friendships and resume suspended activities without worrying about Julian burning down the house. As the months passed, however, Julian's attention span grew shorter and he became less cooperative with the staff. He wouldn't sit down for meals or activities. All he wanted to do was wander aimlessly around the center, sometimes escaping out the front door. The staff found him increasingly hard to handle, and asked Ann to cut him back to four days a week.

Then Julian became physically aggressive. He never punched anyone, but he began poking and shoving people. Ann and the staff tried reprimanding him, but he was oblivious. Eventually, the staff hinted that unless Ann asked Julian's doctor to medicate him, he would have to stop coming. "They never gave me an ultimatum, and they were very kind and helpful, but it was clear they thought he needed to be medicated."

Ann was not eager to put Julian on drugs. She considered hiring an in-home aide, but rejected the idea. "The center staff was better trained, and they had a good program. In-home help would have been nothing more than very expensive baby-sitting. Julian would not have liked it. Besides, I didn't want strangers in my home."

So reluctantly she took Julian to the doctor. He prescribed Mellaril, an antipsychotic drug used to treat combativeness. "It was awful for Julian," Ann sighs. "As his dose was increased, he turned into a catatonic gorilla. He'd stand in our kitchen for long periods hunched over with his arms hanging down just like an ape. He stopped talking. Not that his talking made much sense by that point, but he was always verbal, even if what he vocalized was nonsense. But on the Mellaril, he retreated into an eerie silence. When he wasn't doing his gorilla thing, he began crawling around the floor on his hands and knees more confused than ever. He had no idea where he was. He couldn't find the bathroom, so he urinated all over the house. Twice he defecated in the shower."

Meanwhile, despite the drug, Julian continued his disruptive ways at daycare. He grabbed people by the throat. The staff asked Ann to cut him back to three days a week and insisted that she ask the doctor to prescribe something stonger. "The word 'nightmare' does not even begin to describe what I went through."

With less and less time at the daycare center, Julian spent more time at home. "He never wandered away as so many people with Alzheimer's do," Ann recalls, "but he wandered around the house incessantly, aimlessly manipulating objects he no longer recognized. There were hardly any places I could take him. I was afraid he might grab someone as he was doing at daycare. It got to the point where our life shrank down to eating, taking long walks around our neighborhood, and listening to music."

Like the daycare staff, Ann also had an increasingly difficult time handling Julian. Again, she considered hiring an aide to come to the house, but again decided against it. Then Julian started urinating in any round container—wastebaskets, flowerpots. Around the same time, Julian began staying up most of the night. He would sleep from seven to eleven P.M. and then be up until morning, shuffling aimlessly from room to room for hours on end. Ann couldn't stay up to supervise him and didn't want to pay for a home aide overnight. She asked Julian's doctor to prescribe sleeping pills, but nothing worked. In the end, she locked the house so Julian couldn't leave, went to sleep in the spare bedroom, and let him wander around the rest of the house.

To make matters worse, as Julian wandered, he virtually dismantled the house. He moved furniture, emptied closets, took pictures off the walls, and dragged sheets and blankets into the kitchen. "He never got into the garbage or lit any fires, thank God," Ann explains, "but every morning, it was like a hurricane had struck. I'd get up and have to brace myself for what I'd find, including urine puddles. It was almost impossible to put things back together again and care for Julian at the same time. It drove me crazy." This continued for months.

Ann saw the writing on the wall. She knew she was approaching her physical and emotional limit as a caregiver. She also knew what that meant—residential care. "From the time Julian was first diagnosed, I understood that I'd eventually have to face up to putting him in a home," Ann recalls, "but I kept thinking, Later, later, next year." (Colloquially, residential care facilities are often called nursing homes, but there's a big difference. In nursing homes, residents are either frail or ill and require nursing care. In residential care, they don't need nursing, just supervision and help with activities of daily living.)

In the early stages of Alzheimer's, when those with the disease still understand the implications of their illness, some people exhort their families: "Don't put me in a home. I couldn't stand it." But Julian never said a word against them, which helped Ann face the fact that she had to start looking. "When Julian became disruptive at daycare, I knew that I wouldn't be able to keep him at home much longer. Fortunately, a social worker at the daycare center was familiar with the residential care facilities in the area that accepted people with Alzheimer's. She accompanied me to visit some."

The first few times Ann stepped into residential care center dementia units, she felt as though she'd had the wind knocked out of her. In some, bathroom odors were pervasive. The residents were much older than Julian, and most of them were not as healthy. Some places had no activities appropriate for Julian. Others had programs that he would like but that were too structured for him. Most of them looked like hospital units—a nurses' station in the middle of a long hall with rooms off it, and a day room/dining room. Ann imagined Julian spending the rest of his life wandering up and down some long hall, locked in, profoundly confused, a robust man jailed. It broke her heart.

Then, through an acquaintance, she heard about a refreshingly different Alzheimer's care facility about an hour away from their home. It was not built on a hospital model. "It was ranch-style, all on the ground floor, with rooms along several short halls that radiated off a central activity room. At the end of each hall was a glass door that opened out to a big enclosed yard. Residents were free to participate in organized activities or to wander around the halls and yard. I thought, Here's a place designed especially for confused wanderers like Julian. He could feel comfortable here. I liked the activities, too. They had lots of music, which was one of the few things Julian still loved."

Simply finding an acceptable residential care facility did not make it any easier for Ann to move Julian there. "Placing him was by far the hardest part of Alzheimer's for me," Ann says. "It was the hardest decision of my life."

Moving Julian marked the end of their thirty-seven years together, or so it seemed to Ann at the time. Of course, they hadn't had much of a life together for several years, but in Ann's view, as long as she was caring for her husband, she was still living her marriage vows. If she placed Julian, she felt she would be walking away from those vows, and the idea filled her with guilt and doubt. Julian was still sweet and affectionate at times. He was still deeply connected to her. He needed her. How could she send him away?

"Maybe I should keep him at home a while longer," Ann chided herself, "somehow muddle through." She thought of acquaintances who had cared for a sick parent or spouse at home until they died. She should be like them, she berated herself, but deep down she knew that placing Julian was the best alternative for both of them. "I couldn't provide good care for him any longer, and trying to was ruining my health and life."

A few months after Ann found the home, the daycare center said they couldn't handle Julian anymore. "I called the residential care center and took Julian there the next day." That was February 1996, almost seven years after Julian's diagnosis.

Within a few days, Ann knew she'd made the right decision. "I should have moved him to the home months earlier," she says. "Julian thrived there."

The first thing the staff did was take him off Mellaril, which made a tremendous difference. "He became more alert, more attentive, more alive," Ann recalls. "I hadn't realized how bad that drug had been for him until he stopped taking it."

Julian was also more relaxed. "They kept everything simple and predictable. Of course, I'd tried to do the same at home, but I couldn't do it as well as a dedicated dementia care facility. Julian enjoyed the routine, which helped keep him calm, relaxed, and happy. Julian never felt locked in. He could wander to his heart's content, in and out any door and all around the big yard as he pleased. He could also stay up all night and not disturb anyone. The night staff put him in his bathrobe and slippers and talked to him or let him wander. Most of what we hear about Alzheimer's is stereotypes," Ann explains. "The truth is that everyone with the disease is a unique individual, even as their dementia becomes severe. This home allowed each resident the freedom to be who they were, and I think Julian appreciated that. I know I did."

Julian's care cost $105 a day, about $38,000 a year. Combining their savings, Social Security, and Julian's Stanford benefits, Ann could just swing it, but Julian's care has forced some hard choices on Ann. "I can't help my kids buy homes, or send my grandchildren to summer camp, much less college. Still, I keep thinking how lucky we are to be able to afford this care center, even though it's a killer financially." Down the road, when Julian can no longer walk or eat by himself, he may need nursing care. That can cost $50,000 to $60,000 a year. Ann does not know if she can afford it, but she tries to take things one day at a time and not think too far into the future.

At first, Ann visited Julian every day, but as the months passed, she dropped back to four times a week, then three, and as this book goes to press, two. "If I thought Julian missed me, or if the staff thought so, I'd go more often, but the time interval between my visits doesn't matter to him. He lives entirely in the present. When I'm there, he's excited to see me, but when I'm not, he doesn't seem to mind."

Ann visits not out of a sense of duty but because she wants to. "We still connect. Although he is severely impaired now, our relationship endures. We continue to be deeply connected, to the extent that we can be, given his condition."

Julian no longer knows Ann's name, but he knows *her*. "When I arrive, he smiles, runs up to me, and gives me a big hug. He's very affectionate and tender. We share lots of loving eye contact. We hold hands. He strokes my hair and kisses me."

Julian has also surprised Ann with unexpected flashes of lucidity. "He spoke mostly gibberish for more than a year before he moved to the home, but after a few weeks there—once he was off the Mellaril—he told me he loved me. Some time later, he said, 'I'm okay. I'm really okay. Now you be okay, too.'" Once when Ann arrived, another resident walked up to her, took her hand, and asked to go for a walk. That was fine. Ann knew the man and was willing. "But when Julian saw it, he marched up and tapped the man on the shoulder as if cutting in at a dance. He stood up straight and said, 'Pardon me, sir.'" Months later, after Julian had declined further, Ann brought an old friend to see him, someone he hadn't seen in several years. "He smiled and greeted her by name, which was astonishing." Another old friend came from Israel and spoke to Julian in Hebrew, which he once knew. He beamed at her and said, "Finally! Someone who knows."

Flashes of cogency aside, Julian's loss of speech has been hard for Ann. "We had such a verbal marriage. It's been quite a challenge for me to feel comfortable with Julian without words. I imagine it's been very hard for him, too, but we still communicate with looks, and caresses, and smiles, and laughter. It's taken a while, but I've gotten used to it. Odd as it may sound, we still have fun together."

Long after people with Alzheimer's disease lose their language ability, they often retain the ability to sing—maybe not lyrics, but melodies, either humming along or singing la-la-la. That's been the case with Julian. "For his first year at the home, he had a repertoire of maybe forty songs: 'Clementine,' 'Oh Susannah,' 'Red River Valley,' other American standards, and quite a few Jewish folk songs. I'd start singing, and just two or three notes into the song he would recognize the song and join me. He's lost many of the words now, but he still sings with such feeling! Singing always puts him in a good mood. We sing, and laugh, and sing some more."

Before Alzheimer's, Julian and Ann were avid hikers. They hiked along the shore of San Francisco Bay and in the high Sierra. When she visits Julian, Ann often takes him to a nearby park, and they take long walks together, two or three miles. "We walk, hold hands, laugh, and sing. If you saw us, you'd never know that Julian had Alzheimer's, except for his constant humming. You'd think we were just another middle-aged couple out for a stroll, enjoying each other's company. Afterward, I take Julian to a little café and get him hot chocolate. He loves chocolate."

As this book goes to press, Julian has severe Alzheimer's, yet he retains certain skills that many others with the disease lose early on: He still buttons buttons, zips zippers, ties his own shoes, and toilets by himself. He's usually happy, and that makes Ann happy. Of course, she has hard times, too. "Sometimes, when friends tell me about their trips to Europe, their professional activities, or their summers in the mountains, I think of the life Julian and I might have had and I have moments of feeling very sad. Sometimes, I miss him terribly and feel very lonely. But this is my life. It's what I've been given. I try to count my blessings. I've had everything that's important in life, and I work to take pleasure in the connection Julian and I still share."

The mass media often describe Alzheimer's disease as a "living death." Ann disagrees. "As human beings, we're a great deal more than how we define ourselves. It's amazing how much you can lose of what you once considered essential to your *self,* and still retain your humanity. Julian can no longer take care of himself, and he's down to just a few tunes and an occasional word, yet he greets me with a warm smile and a loving hug. We take our walks. We fool around. As long as I don't expect anything from him, as long as I stay in the moment, we can have fun. It's amazing to me, impaired as he is, Julian is still with me. There's still a loving person in there."

Ann Davidson kept a journal while caring for her husband. She has collected fifty-six poignant vignettes in a deeply moving memoir, Alzheimer's: A Love Story *(Birch Lane Press/Carroll Publishing, Secaucus, NJ, 1997. $19.95). It deals with the period from the summer of 1992 through the spring of 1993, when Julian had mild to moderate Alzheimer's.*

2.

Worried About Someone?

The Warning Signs of Alzheimer's

Alzheimer's disease has what experts call "insidious onset." Like a cat, it sneaks up silently, stealthfully. Before their diagnoses, some people notice increasing memory loss, worry about it, and may become quite anxious. Others deny that anything is wrong and, when confronted, respond belligerently. Some quietly cover up their cognitive problems.

The Alzheimer's Association has compiled a list of ten warning signs of early Alzheimer's disease, adapted here somewhat:

1. **Increasing forgetfulness and confusion.** It's normal to forget people's names from time to time. It's normal to feel confused occasionally when presented with new information, but habitual forgetfulness, confusion, or indecisiveness is cause for concern.
2. **Difficulty performing familiar tasks.** Anyone can leave a button unbuttoned, but when a person becomes persistently challenged by the simple tasks of daily living, that's cause for concern.

3. **Language problems.** From time to time, anyone can have difficulty finding the right word. But when simple words present problems, or when sentences start to become incomprehensible, that might signal Alzheimer's.

4. **Time and place disorientation.** It's normal to forget the date or a destination occasionally, but people with early Alzheimer's often feel lost anywhere that's not completely familiar.

5. **Loss of judgment.** Anyone can fail to notice that an item of clothing is stained. Someone with Alzheimer's will dress inappropriately—two different shoes, or wearing pants backward.

6. **Problems with abstract thinking.** Anyone can struggle over brainteasers or have occasional problems balancing a checkbook. People with Alzheimer's can't add up the change they're carrying.

7. **Misplacing things.** Most of us misplace a wallet or lose keys from time to time, but when a person puts his wallet in the refrigerator, or her keys in the sink, that's cause for concern.

8. **Changes in mood and behavior.** Changing moods are a fact of life, but people with Alzheimer's often experience unusual mood changes that disturb family and friends. For example, they may exhibit unusual irritability or agitation. They might behave oddly by eating sloppily or emerging from the bathroom half undressed.

9. **Changes in personality.** People often become more crotchety as they become elderly. By contrast, Alzheimer's disease can make people very confused, frustrated, or fearful.

10. **Loss of initiative.** It's normal to get bored with daily activities, but when people lose much of their usual get-up-and-go, that's cause for concern.

These warning signs are valuable, but they are also maddeningly vague. Is smeared makeup twice in one week cause for concern? Or getting lost three times in three months? Or missing two dentist appointments in a row? The fact is, it's hard to tell. That's what "insidious onset" means. For each Alzheimer's sufferer profiled in this book, the disease developed differently.

Recently, researchers at the Karolinska Institute in Stockholm (the university that administers the Nobel prize) discovered that automobile accidents may signal very early Alzheimer's. Driving is the most intellectually demanding activity of daily living. It requires continual processing of an enormous amount of new information, and demands split-second decision-making based on it. These abilities are often the first to go during early Alzheimer's.

The researchers performed brain autopsies on ninety-eight drivers, aged sixty-five to ninety, who had been killed in auto accidents in Sweden or Finland. None of the victims had been diagnosed with Alzheimer's disease, but the researchers discovered the brain abnormalities characteristic of the disease (chapter 3) in *one-third* of these deceased drivers. In an additional 20 percent, they discovered changes in brain tissue that suggested the very earliest stages of Alzheimer's-type brain damage.

If an elder you love seems unusually confused or forgetful, and then has an auto accident, or if you notice an increasing number of dents or scratches on the person's vehicle, consider an Alzheimer's evaluation.

What would happen in your family if you—or anyone—suggested that a loved one might have memory problems beyond everyday forgetfulness? The insidious onset of Alzheimer's disease often triggers family conflict. Typically, someone in the family starts saying, "Something is wrong here," while others dismiss such concerns as unwarranted, cruel, or paranoid.

If you're the first in your family to raise the issue, try not to criticize relatives who take longer to see the problem. Also, try to forgive relatives who dismiss your concerns. Alzheimer's is a progressive disease. As it worsens, other family members inevitably come to the realization that the affected individual has a problem.

On the other hand, if you're not among the first in your family to recognize problems, try not to berate yourself for being "blind." No one wants to see a relative's mind deteriorate. It's natural to deny cognitive problems until they become obvious. In addition, if you criticized a relative for suggesting that your loved one might have Alzheimer's, admit your error and then move on. You're not the first person to miss the earliest signs of the disease. It's not easy for *doctors* to diagnose Alzheimer's, so forgive yourself. Work to let go of recriminations. Alzheimer's caregiving demands a great deal of teamwork among the affected individual's family members (chapter 12). Resentments and guilt are counterproductive. Focus on the challenges ahead.

3.

Dr. Alzheimer's Strange Discovery

The History, Biology, and Rising Toll of Alzheimer's

Since ancient times, it has been clear that some people lose their intellectual abilities (cognitive function) as they age, but Alzheimer's disease was not identified until 1906. That year, a German neurologist, Alois Alzheimer (1864–1915), chanced to autopsy the brain of Auguste D., a fifty-six-year-old Frankfurt woman who had died after five years of progressive mental deterioration marked by irrational jealousy, increasing confusion, and loss of memory and the ability to care for herself. Taking advantage of a then new staining technique, Alzheimer noticed bizarre disorganization of the nerve cells in her cerebral cortex, the part of the brain responsible for memory and reasoning. The cells were bunched up like a rope tied in knots. He called the strange nerve knots neurofibrillary tangles. He also noticed unexpected accumulations of cellular debris around the knotted nerves, which he called senile plaques. In a medical journal article published in 1907, Alzheimer speculated that the nerve tangles and plaques might have been responsible for the woman's dementia.

Years passed, and more autopsies of severely demented individuals showed the same cerebral abnormalities. Eventually, a prominent German psychiatrist, Emil Kraepelin (1856–1926), suggested naming the new disease in honor of his countryman, Alzheimer.

Fifty years after Alzheimer's discovery, physicians thought that the disease named for him was very rare. By the 1960s, researchers demonstrated that it was the leading cause of age-related dementia. From Kraepelin's time through the 1980s, physicians viewed Alzheimer's disease as a psychiatric disorder because of its impact on memory, reasoning, and behavior. Today, however, experts insist that Alzheimer's is a *medical* illness because it results from physical changes in the brain.

Alzheimer's Disease Terminology

Today, the condition Dr. Alzheimer discovered is known as Alzheimer's disease (AD), or dementia of the Alzheimer's type (DAT). Some experts have dropped the apostrophe s, calling the condition Alzheimer disease (paralleling the name change from Down's syndrome to Down syndrome), but most authorities continue to call the illness Alzheimer's disease, as we do throughout this book.

In the past, Alzheimer's disease was sometimes called senile dementia. In medical jargon, the word "senile" means over age sixty-five. If Alzheimer's was diagnosed before age sixty-five, the person was said to have pre-senile dementia. Today, these terms are outdated and are no longer used by those familiar with Alzheimer's disease. If a physician uses them, consider it a tip-off that the doctor is not well informed about Alzheimer's.

The word "dementia" sometimes causes problems as well. In common usage, "demented" may imply crazy. In medical jargon, it simply means a loss of cognitive function. The same problem crops up in Spanish. People with Alzheimer's are called *loco,* but it means demented, not crazy.

Who Has Alzheimer's Disease?

It's not clear how many Americans have Alzheimer's. The Alzheimer's Association estimates 4 million, but a 1998 report by the U.S. General Accounting Office, the investigative arm of Congress, put the figure at 2.1 million. Many epidemiologists estimate 2.5 million.

Many famous people have had Alzheimer's disease, including British statesman Winston Churchill, composer Aaron Copland, boxer Sugar Ray Robinson, writer E. B. White, actors Dana Andrews and Rita Hayworth, and most recently, former President Ronald Reagan and British novelist Iris Murdoch.

Occasionally, Alzheimer's develops before age fifty, but the vast majority of people are diagnosed after age sixty. According to an oft-cited study, about 10 percent of Americans sixty-five and older have Alzheimer's disease. Other studies have produced slightly lower estimates—6 to 8 percent—but overall averages obscure the fact that the risk of the disease changes considerably during the elderly years:

- Among those sixty-four to seventy-four years of age, 2 to 3 percent have Alzheimer's disease.
- In the age group from seventy-five to eighty-four, the proportion rises to about 15 percent.
- And among those eighty-five and older, Alzheimer's afflicts approximately 30 to 40 percent.
- In addition, recent research suggests that various racial and ethnic groups have different rates of Alzheimer's. This issue remains controversial, but race and ethnicity do play a role in genetic risk (chapter 5).

The U.S. population is aging. People over eighty-five have become the nation's fastest-growing age group. Because this is also the group most affected by Alzheimer's disease, experts warn that unless researchers discover how to prevent it, in the future the social and financial costs of Alzheimer's could soar, with as many as 14 million Americans affected by 2040.

A Statistical Snapshot

The Alzheimer's Association and the National Institute on Aging have compiled the following statistics:

- Some 2 to 4 million Americans have Alzheimer's disease.
- Approximately 250,000 Americans are diagnosed each year.
- An estimated 2.7 million spouses, relatives, and friends care for people with Alzheimer's.
- Some 19 million Americans say a family member has the disease.
- About 37 million Americans say they know someone with Alzheimer's.
- More than 70 percent of Alzheimer's sufferers live in their own homes or in caregivers' homes, not in residential care facilities.
- About half of all nursing home residents suffer from Alzheimer's disease or another type of dementia.
- Experts estimate that Alzheimer's disease currently costs the United States some $95 billion a year in lost productivity, medical care, and caretaking.
- For Alzheimer's sufferers cared for at home, the average out-of-pocket cost to family caregivers (excluding lost wages) is $12,500 per year.
- For Alzheimer's sufferers in residential care centers or nursing homes, the average cost is $42,000 per person per year, though in some parts of the country nursing home care may climb to $70,000 a year.
- The average cost of Alzheimer's care from diagnosis until death is $174,000, making Alzheimer's disease the nation's third most costly illness, after heart disease and cancer.
- The Alzheimer's disease research budget has grown substantially over the past decade, to more than $300 million a year, but that figure represents only a tiny fraction of what the disease costs.

Survival After Diagnosis

Most people live eight to ten years after an Alzheimer's diagnosis and spend about five years under the vigilant care of a caregiver or in residential care.

Until recently, most experts did not consider Alzheimer's disease fatal. If affected individuals were well cared for, they said, those with the disease could live with virtually complete loss of cognition. Deaths of people with Alzheimer's were attributed to the same causes as those of cognitively normal elderly Americans: heart disease, cancer, stroke, various infections, etc. In the last few years, however, this view has changed. Many experts now believe that Alzheimer's shortens life expectancy, and barring some other clear cause of death—heart attack, cancer, stroke, etc.—late-stage Alzheimer's is terminal.

The National Center for Health Statistics (NCHS) has adopted this view. In its 1997 report on the top-ten causes of death in 1995, the NCHS listed Alzheimer's disease as the eighth leading cause of death among women, accounting for 13,607 deaths, or 1.2 percent of all women's deaths. (Alzheimer's was not one of the top-ten causes of death for men.)

The Stages of Alzheimer's Disease

At New York University Medical Center's Aging and Dementia Research Center, Barry Reisberg, M.D., and colleagues have developed the Functional Assessment Staging (FAST) scale, a quick way to chart the progression of Alzheimer's disease (see page 39).

Dr. Reisberg and colleagues have also developed the Global Deterioration Scale, a more elaborate way to chart the cognitive decline of Alzheimer's, adapted here somewhat:

- **Stage 1. Cognitively Normal.** No complaints or indications of memory problems.

FAST SCALE STAGE	CHARACTERISTICS
1. Normal adult	No functional decline.
2. Normal older adult	Personal awareness of some functional decline.
3. Early Alzheimer's disease	Noticeable deficits in demanding situations.
4. Mild Alzheimer's	Requires assistance in complicated tasks such as handling finances, travel, etc.
5. Moderate Alzheimer's	Requires assistance in choosing proper attire.
6. Moderately severe Alzheimer's	Requires assistance dressing, bathing, and toileting. Experiences urinary and fecal incontinence.
7. Severe Alzheimer's	Speech ability declines to a handful of intelligible words. Progressive loss of abilities to walk, sit up, smile, and hold head up.

© 1984 by Barry Reisberg, M.D.

- **Stage 2. Very Mild Cognitive Deficit.** Forgetfulness. People continue to function competently but complain of forgetting once-familiar names and where they have put things like keys.
- **Stage 3. Mild Cognitive Decline.** Early Confusional. People have trouble remembering the names of objects, recent acquaintances, material just read. They lose keys, wallet, or checkbook. They get lost easily in unfamiliar surroundings.
- **Stage 4. Moderate Cognitive Decline.** Late Confusional. People get lost going to familiar destinations and have difficulty handling their finances and recognizing familar individuals. They forget recent events and are uncertain of the time and date.

- **Stage 5. Moderately Severe Decline.** Early Dementia. Individuals cannot survive without ongoing assistance, make significant errors in dressing, and get confused about the season and year. They forget their address, phone number, high school, and where they are.
- **Stage 6. Severe Cognitive Decline.** Middle Dementia. People forget close relatives' names but still know their own. They have little if any idea where they live, what date and year it is, what they ate at their last meal, and how to get from place to place. Their behavior changes. They seem nervous, tense, and agitated. They may pace or lose interest in doing what they used to enjoy. They may become suspicious and paranoid, and may lash out verbally or physically. They may talk to imaginary companions. They have bladder and bowel accidents.
- **Stage 7. Very Severe Cognitive Decline.** Late Dementia. They become incontinent, cannot feed themselves, and lose the ability to walk and talk.

For many years, experts described Alzheimer's as "child development in reverse." It's a tempting analogy. The skills children progressively acquire as they move from infancy to puberty—speaking, walking, dressing, toileting, etc.—are the same skills people with Alzheimer's progressively lose. Even though they appear increasingly childlike, people with Alzheimer's *are still adults.* Even with severe Alzheimer's, many people retain some of their adult personalities and continue to respond to some of the interests they enjoyed before the disease developed. Experts in caregiving warn against treating Alzheimer's sufferers as children and feel this approach can invite a patronizing attitude that upsets affected individuals and actually makes caregiving considerably more difficult (chapter 13).

The Biology of Alzheimer's Disease

Alois Alzheimer had no idea what caused the neurofibrillary tangles and senile plaques he discovered in that original brain autopsy. He assumed they had caused the woman's mental deterioration, but it might have been the other way around. The tangles and plaques might have been the *result* of the woman's cognitive deterioration. Although scientists have learned a great deal about the disease since Alzheimer's time, they are still not entirely certain whether changes in brain tissue cause the disease or whether those changes are the result of some other causative process. However, the vast majority of Alzheimer's researchers believe that the tangles and plaques are causative, and a great deal of research effort is being devoted to understanding how and why they develop. Scientists hope one day to prevent the Alzheimer's disease process, and perhaps even return damaged brain tissue to health.

Normally, nerve cells in the brain are arranged in an orderly manner. With Alzheimer's disease, they become extremely disorganized and stop functioning. As brain cells deteriorate and die, the activities they control—memory, reasoning, and the ability to care for oneself—fade away. Over time, neurofibrillary tangles and senile plaques take over an ever-larger area of the brain, which is why Alzheimer's disease is progressive.

Recent research has linked neurofibrillary tangles to an abnormal accumulation of a protein called tau. The link between tau and Alzheimer's remains unclear, but in recent years the protein has become the focus of a great deal of research. Tau can be detected in cerebrospinal fluid (CSF), and compared with unaffected individuals, those with Alzheimer's disease have elevated levels. A test for high levels of tau in CSF can help diagnose the disease (chapter 6).

Senile plaques are accumulations of cellular debris surrounding a central core of beta-amyloid peptide, a molecular fragment of a large protein found in the normal brain. Beta-amyloid peptide was first identified in the 1980s, some seventy years after Alzheimer identified senile plaques.

There are several types of beta-amyloid peptide, each with a different molecular length. The short forms tend not to form the cores of senile plaques. The one most closely linked with Alzheimer's disease is a longer form, beta-amyloid$_{42}$.

Like tau protein, beta-amyloid$_{42}$ is detectable in CSF, but as it forms senile plaques, CSF levels fall. A new test for low levels of beta-amyloid$_{42}$ can help diagnose the disease. A combination test—

simultaneously high CSF levels of tau and low levels of beta-amyloid$_{42}$ holds promise for diagnosing Alzheimer's, but as this book goes to press, many researchers remain unconvinced (chapter 6).

Where does all the beta-amyloid in the brains of Alzheimer's sufferers come from? The blood cells involved in clotting, the platelets, are an important source. Recently (1998) Steven Sevush, M.D., of the University of Miami Medical Center in Florida showed that the platelets of people with Alzheimer's are unusually active, meaning that they produce extra beta-amyloid. Sevush measured the proportion of platelets that were actively producing beta-amyloid in ninety people with probable Alzheimer's and forty age-matched controls. In the healthy individuals, 0.5 percent of their platelets were actively producing beta-amyloid, but in those with Alzheimer's, the figure was more than 30 percent. If researchers can figure out how to deactivate platelets, they might be able to prevent or delay the formation of senile plaques.

Recently, in 1998, researchers at Northwestern University showed that even before beta-amyloid begins accumulating into senile plaques, related, long, fiberlike proteins called amyloid beta-derived ligands (ADDLs) interfere with brain-cell activity and presumably pave the way for plaque development. As this book goes to press, ADDL research is in its infancy. No test can detect it in the living brain, and no treatment can eliminate it. But if scientists can figure out how to detect and eliminate ADDLs before plaques and neurofibrillary tangles form, it might be possible to prevent—or at least postpone—Alzheimer's.

Neurofibrillary tangles and senile plaques develop only in the parts of the brain that control memory and retention of learned information. Functions such as heartbeat, breathing, and digestion remain unaffected. As a result, many people with severe Alzheimer's are "healthy" for their age, except that their minds no longer function normally.

Today, the brain changes of Alzheimer's can be seen only on autopsy, not in the living. As a result, until recently physicians had considerable difficulty diagnosing the disease. During the 1970s, many people were misdiagnosed as having Alzheimer's when they actually had other conditions, some treatable (chapter 9). Today, physicians who specialize in dementing illnesses are much better at distinguishing Alzheimer's disease from other illnesses, though mistakes are still possible.

Alzheimer's Disease and Down Syndrome: Intriguing Links

Alzheimer's disease is not the only condition associated with neurofibrillary tangles and senile plaques. To some extent, their development is a part of normal, healthy aging. Many people over seventy have some evidence of tangles and plaques, yet they show none of the cognitive decline of Alzheimer's. Currently, no one knows why.

In addition, the brain changes of Alzheimer's also develop in people with Down syndrome. On autopsy, the brains of those with Down and Alzheimer's are often indistinguishable. The major difference is that in Down syndrome, the brain changes develop much earlier in life.

Down results from a genetic abnormality before birth. Instead of having twenty-three pairs of chromosomes, the double-helix repositories of genetic information coded in DNA, the cells of people with Down syndrome contain an extra copy of chromosome 21. Affected individuals develop a characteristic physical appearance and a particular form of mental retardation. If they live long enough—into their forties or fifties—they almost always develop Alzheimer's disease.

Why? Researchers are not entirely certain, but they believe the extra copy of chromosome 21 leads to the unusually early development of senile plaques. Chromosome 21 contains the gene for amyloid precursor protein (APP), which gives rise to beta-amyloid peptides, which in turn form the core of the senile plaques of Alzheimer's. People with Down syndrome produce abnormally large amounts of APP, which appears to lead to unusually high levels of beta-amyloid peptide in middle age—and Alzheimer's.

Like Alzheimer's disease, Down syndrome is currently neither preventable nor curable, but as science learns more about each condition, both may benefit mutually from the research.

A New Stain Reveals a New Type of Alzheimer's Brain Damage

Recall that Alois Alzheimer was able to visualize the neurofibrillary tangles and senile plaques of Alzheimer's disease thanks to a staining technique that was new in 1906. More than ninety years later, in 1997, another new staining technique allowed researchers to see an entirely new type of brain damage in people with Alzheimer's. The study, conducted by John Trojanowski, M.D., director of the Alzheimer's Disease Center at the University of Pennsylvania, used the new stain during brain autopsy to discover a different type of plaque that occupies as much of the brain as amyloid plaques. Dr. Trojanowski now believes that this new type of brain damage plays a crucial role in the development of Alzheimer's disease.

So far, the new plaques are called AMY, because Dr. Trojanowski used an antibody called AMY117 to visualize them. As this book goes to press, no one is sure what AMY plaques are made of since the protein that composes them has not yet been identified. Nor do we know how they form or what role they play in Alzheimer's, but the discovery has stirred tremendous interest among Alzheimer's researchers.

Animal Models for Alzheimer's Promise to Speed Research

Until recently, Alzheimer's researchers faced a major problem: There was no animal model for the disease. Promising new treatments had to be tested exclusively on people, an arduous process limited by ethical considerations.

Recently, however, veterinarians have realized that elderly dogs seem to develop a condition very similar to Alzheimer's. In the last decade, advances in veterinary care have led to a population explosion of old dogs. There are now some 7 million canines age eleven or older in the United States, the human equivalent of seventy-seven or older. Many of these old pets become disoriented in familiar surroundings, lose their house training, stop sleeping normally, become restless and agitated at night, and experience personality changes— the classic symptoms of Alzheimer's.

Veterinarian William Ruehl, D.V.M., of Overland Park, Kansas, and Benjamin Hart, D.V.M., of the University of California at Davis, surveyed owners of 140 dogs aged eleven to sixteen who considered their pets to be in good health. More than 60 percent of them showed at least one symptom of "doggie Alzheimer's."

In addition, researchers at the University of California at Irvine have discovered that old dogs develop plaque-like brain accumulations of beta-amyloid peptide, a characteristic abnormality of Alzheimer's. Oddly, though, they do not appear to develop neurofibrillary tangles, which suggests that doggie and human Alzheimer's are similar but not identical.

Nonetheless, one drug that helps treat human Alzheimer's has shown considerable benefit also in the canine version of the disease. The drug is selegiline, a potent antioxidant Parkinson's medication (chapter 10). In one study of 200 animals taking either selegiline or a placebo, the dogs given the drug showed significantly improved cognitive function. In 1997, Canada approved selegiline as a treatment for canine Alzheimer's.

Even more exciting, in 1996, a University of Minnesota research team led by Karen Hsiao, M.D., announced the creation of a mouse genetically engineered to develop Alzheimer's-type memory loss. Dr. Hsiao's team created this animal by inserting into mouse embryos a mutated human gene linked to Alzheimer's disease. The mutated gene increases production of amyloid precursor protein, which forms beta-amyloid, the core of the senile plaques found in the brains of people with Alzheimer's. Maze experiments show progressive memory loss in Dr. Hsiao's mice, similar to that of humans with the disease. As youngsters, the mice learn to navigate the mazes successfully, but as they age, they lose the ability.

It took only three years for these mice to demonstrate their value in Alzheimer's research. Shortly before this book went to press, researchers at Elan Pharmaceuticals in South San Franciso announced they had used Alzheimer's mice to test a vaccine that appears remarkably effective in preventing beta-amyloid plaques and in eliminating plaques that have already formed. The researchers injected Alzheimer's mice with beta-amyloid, the very compound that forms Alzheimer's plaques. In young mice, the injections stimulated an immune response that prevented formation of plaques as the mice aged. In older mice that already had plaques, the injections largely eliminated them.

Alzheimer's experts have hailed this research as a major breakthrough. It is the first report to show that vaccination can protect against the development of plaques, and the first to demonstrate a treatment that clears them. Elan has petitioned the Food and Drug Administration to begin human studies (clinical trials) sometime in 2000. If beta-amyloid vaccination safely produces the same benefits in people, this treatment might become widely available by 2005.

Of course, Elan's mouse vaccine may turn out to be a dead end. A great deal of animal research does not pan out in people. But this potential advance would not have been possible without mice that develop Alzheimer's disease. Even if Elan's vaccine doesn't work in humans, the new animal models for the disease should greatly benefit Alzheimer's research.

4.

"We Wanted Very Much to Take Care of Her"

Profile of Jorge, Anna, and Rosa Flores

The old resentment in a bizarre new guise. That's what then thirty-five-year-old Anna Concepcion Flores Rodriguez thought in 1985, when her parents came north from Mexico for their annual three-month visit, and out of the blue her mother accused her of stealing her purse. Anna did not steal it. She simply *moved* the purse to minimize the clutter of her parents' luggage in the one-bedroom apartment she shared with her husband, Esteban Rodriguez, in San Antonio, Texas. But Anna's mother, Rosa, refused to believe that her daughter had just moved her purse. When Anna returned it, she angrily accused her daughter of stealing *from* it, stealing from her *mama*. Rosa grabbed her purse from Anna, clutched it tightly, and withdrew into a brooding silence.

Anna felt mortified. The incident occurred in front of her husband, her father, her nine siblings, and her dozen nieces and nephews. It spoiled the family fiesta, the celebration in honor of her parents' arrival. Anna was on the verge of tears: How could her mother accuse her of such a thing? Rosa lived in Anna's home three months of the year. How could she imagine even for one moment that her devoted daughter would steal from her? Then Anna thought, My mother doesn't love me.

That terrible belief had bubbled up many times since Anna had left Mexico for San Antonio ten years before, in 1975. Her mother had opposed her move very vocally. She had castigated Anna for "abandoning her." Anna was not the first of her siblings to move to *El Norte,* The North, but she was the eldest child, and Rosa lamented—and resented—her departure the most. "An eldest daughter should stay near her parents, look after them," Rosa insisted. She'd chastised Anna almost daily before her move, and frequently after she'd settled in Texas. To make matters worse, Anna's letters home touting the better life available in the United States quickly enticed most of her other siblings to move north, which deepened her mother's resentment.

Slowly, awkwardly, the family fiesta resumed. One by one, Anna's father and siblings took her aside to comfort her. They all agreed that the ridiculous accusation of theft simply reflected Rosa's enduring bitterness over her children's move north. Never mind that Anna and the others had begged their parents to move to Texas to be with them. Never mind that they'd offered to house and care for them. Never mind that they sent money, wrote and spoke often, returned to Mexico for visits, and knocked themselves out to make their parents feel welcome, loved, and well cared for during their annual visits, especially Anna, in whose home they stayed. None of that seemed to matter to Rosa. Nothing could crack the hard shell of her resentment. Anna felt a deep sadness. She adored her mother, but Rosa apparently did not feel the same way about her.

Still, an accusation of theft was a strange way to express even bitter resentment. Everyone in the family agreed that's what it was— Rosa's old resentment in a new guise. But it didn't quite make sense to Anna. Years later, she realized that the incident marked the dawn of her fears that something beyond resentment might be troubling her mother.

Rosa Castaneda Castro was born in 1927 in the little village of Santa Rita, population three thousand, in Zacatecas, a state in the high plateau country of central Mexico some 250 miles northwest of Mexico City. She left school after the second grade to help her mother with the housework. She woke up early and did not mind cooking, cleaning, and ministering to her brothers and sisters until well into the evening. She took great pride in her cooking and home-making, and insisted that everything be done just so. Sometimes she skipped meals to get all her work done.

When Rosa was not working, she spent time with her friends in the village, including a boy two years older, Jorge Carlos Flores, who had stayed in school through the fourth grade before his family pulled him out to work with his father and uncle building and repairing adobe houses in and around Santa Rita. Rosa and Jorge married in 1950. Anna was born eleven months later. Over the next nineteen years, she was followed by nine other children, five girls and four boys.

"My mother was a very hard worker," Anna recalls, "and amaz-ingly well organized. With ten children, she had to be. She did the housework, raised us kids, and took care of my father and grandfather until he died, all with a lot of love and caring."

The Flores family was poor. They lived in a three-room adobe home with a large, lush garden that was Rosa's pride and joy, but as more children arrived, the house became increasingly cramped. When Anna was twelve, they moved five hundred miles northwest to the high desert countryside on the outskirts of San Cristobal, Sonora. Their new home was larger, but it had no garden, and there was not enough water to plant one. Rosa often spoke wistfully about the gar-den she'd left behind. To shade the house and to please his wife, Jorge planted trees and shrubs around their new home. They helped, but there was no getting around the fact that their new home was in the desert.

Jorge and Anna and her siblings worked long hours in the cotton fields. Whenever Rosa could, she worked alongside them. When she worked, she asked the girls who were too young to work in the fields to take care of the household chores. Inevitably, when Rosa returned from the fields, she redid what they'd done. No one was as fastidious about homemaking as Rosa. She was never satisfied until the house was spotless. "My mother had no real education," Anna explains, "but she had a keen mind, tremendous energy, and great powers of concentration. She had good judgment and always gave thoughtful advice. She also had an excellent memory, which made her illness especially sad for us."

Like her mother, from the time Anna was a young child, she helped with the housework and childcare. She also quit school early, in the fourth grade, to join her father in the cotton fields.

When Anna was around eighteen, her uncle, her father's brother, left Mexico for *El Norte* and wound up in San Antonio. He spoke enthusiastically about the opportunities in Texas, and two of Anna's brothers quickly followed him. Anna wanted to go, too. She wanted a better life than back-breaking field work in Sonora could offer, but her mother opposed her moving, and out of love and respect for her, Anna stayed home.

Years passed. Anna's uncle and two brothers kept urging the family to join them in the States. When Anna turned twenty-four, she finally told her parents she was moving to San Antonio. She established herself in the housecleaning business, and after a few years married Esteban, an auto mechanic who was also from Mexico—Guadalajara, Jalisco.

Anna kept in close touch with her parents by mail and by phone. Since Rosa and Jorge did not have a phone at home, they called Anna or her siblings collect from a pay phone in San Cristobal twice a month. Anna sent them money regularly, and the Texas Flores siblings chipped in every year to bring their parents north for a three-month visit. But no matter how devoted Anna was, Rosa never forgave her eldest daughter for abandoning her, and everyone in the family knew it. That was why, when Rosa made her absurd theft accusation, the family attributed it to her long-festering resentment.

After that visit, when Jorge and Rosa returned to Sonora, Anna and her siblings began receiving disturbing reports from their father. Rosa was acting odd. She was becoming forgetful. She would begin a task—washing the dishes, folding the laundry, whatever—and then wander off leaving it unfinished. When Jorge or the two daughters who were still at home mentioned her lapses, Rosa either ignored them or became verbally abusive. Anna could not believe it. Her mother had never done such things.

There was more. Increasingly, Jorge had the feeling that Rosa wasn't following him, that when he spoke to her, she had no idea what he was saying. She also repeated herself over and over again. When anyone pointed out that she'd just said the exact same thing moments earlier, either she insisted they were lying or she became abusive. If she didn't repeat herself, Rosa stopped talking in the middle of a thought, unable to finish her sentence. When Jorge or the girls asked her to continue, she couldn't. If they tried to prompt her, she yelled at them.

Jorge knew that the elderly often became forgetful. He'd seen it in his parents, but Rosa was only fifty-eight, and her forgetfulness was nothing like the memory lapses he'd seen in others. With his parents, a little prompting usually reminded them of what they'd been saying or doing, but not with Rosa. Prompting didn't help her. It just made her belligerent.

Anna found it difficult to reconcile her father's reports with the quick-witted mother she knew. It seemed inconceivable that Rosa would leave chores half-finished, or forget what she was saying, or yell for no reason. Soon after these reports, Anna encouraged her father to take Rosa to see a doctor. Jorge agreed that his wife needed professional attention. "I took her to several doctors and psychologists who were within a day's journey from San Cristobal," he recalls. "One doctor gave us a bottle of pills. He never said what they were. For as long as they lasted, Rosa was less belligerent, but no one had any idea what was wrong with her." (The pills were almost certainly mild tranquilizers.)

In 1987, two years into her memory and behavior problems, Rosa did the unthinkable: She stopped doing housework altogether. "One day," Jorge recalls, "I watched as she took a broom from the closet. She had no idea what to do with it. I could see her struggling, trying to figure out what to do with the strange stick with the straw end. It didn't take her long to become frustrated and agitated. She dropped the broom and just walked away." Rosa seemed equally lost cooking and doing laundry. She had no idea how to make tortillas or cook *frijoles,* refried beans, things she'd done since she was four years old.

Jorge was aghast. Cooking, cleaning, keeping house—homemaking—had been Rosa's life, her art, all the years they'd been together. Having her quit doing housework was as inconceivable as her being elected Pope. Jorge implored her to fix dinner, do the laundry, sweep the floor. She had no idea what he was talking about. "She's so different," he complained to Anna and her siblings. "She's no longer the woman I married. Who is she? I don't know who she is anymore." Fortunately, Inez and Cecilia, the two girls who were still at home, took over the housework. A neighbor woman helped, and Jorge pitched in.

Around this time, Rosa began pacing. She could not sit still. She walked back and forth, back and forth through the house for hours on end. She wore herself out pacing, but once she started, neither Jorge nor the girls could stop her. When they tried, she either ignored them, yelled at them, or physically resisted them. By 1990, she was wandering out of the house. By now, Rosa's eccentricities were well known in the neighborhood, and when she wandered into other people's homes, they brought her back. When she wandered out into the cotton fields, neighbors told Jorge, who ran after her.

Rosa also began talking to herself. "She muttered under her breath," Jorge recalls. "At first she said things like, 'The garden needs water,' or 'Merry Christmas.' Her words made no sense—we hadn't had a garden in years, and it wasn't Christmas, but at least I could understand her." As the months passed, however, Rosa made less and less sense. About the only place Rosa was her old self was in church. "I took her about twice a month," Jorge explains. "She sat quietly, took communion, and seemed to enjoy mass, but as soon as we were back outside, she became forgetful, stubborn, and abusive again."

In 1989, Inez and Cecilia, the last two Flores children, left home to join their siblings in San Antonio. In contrast to the contention that had preceded Anna's move north, Rosa hardly seemed to notice their departure. For Jorge, the transition was very difficult. "I never resented any of my children going north. I knew they would have more opportunity there, but without Inez and Cecilia, I was all alone with Rosa. Our neighbors helped, especially the woman who cooked for us, but I got no rest. All day long, I worked in the fields worrying about Rosa, and when I came home, I had to take care of her."

Anna and her siblings implored their father to move to San Antonio where the children could care for Rosa, but Jorge refused. "I loved the Mexican countryside. It was my country, my home. I didn't want to live in the hustle-bustle of Texas, and I was too old to learn much English."

Anna offered to pay for a housekeeper to care for her mother while her father worked, but Jorge refused to turn her care over to someone else. "She's my wife, and I love her. Caring for her is my responsibility," he told the children firmly.

Only one other alternative made sense. The children offered to support Jorge so he could stop working and care for Rosa full-time. "It was his labor of love," Anna explains, "but it wasn't easy. My father had a very rough time. While I was growing up, I remember him as calm and self-assured, even with ten kids running around the house, but as my mother got worse, he became very upset, constantly nervous and worried. Taking care of her was overwhelming." On the phone, Jorge sounded increasingly desperate, exhausted, and depressed. "We visited when we could," Anna explains, "but he was angry and disappointed when we weren't there."

Freed from working, Jorge took Rosa to more doctors. In 1990, a doctor in Hermosillo said he thought she had Alzheimer's disease. Jorge had never heard of it. The doctor explained that Rosa would get worse, and gradually lose what was left of her memory as well as her other remaining abilities. "It was terrible news," Jorge recalls. "I didn't think she would get better, but when the doctor said it, he took away my hope. I wanted to cry."

The doctor also said there was no treatment, no cure, but that he could give Jorge some medicine that would keep Rosa from wandering and getting too agitated (more tranquilizers). Jorge gave her the pills for a few days, but they just put her to sleep, so he stopped them.

Jorge asked Anna to find out more about Alzheimer's. A friend who was a nurse confirmed what the doctor had said, but Anna, newly Americanized, didn't trust the Mexican doctor. She wanted to have her mother examined in the United States. The problem was that they had no health insurance and couldn't afford to have an Alzheimer's workup.

With a little help from the neighbors and periodic visits from his children, Jorge coped as a caregiver for two years. He walked with Rosa as she paced. When she wandered into the cotton fields, he chased after her. He played music on the radio that she liked, and the two of them often sang together. Rosa could still dress herself, and eat, and toilet without assistance. Jorge helped her bathe, and he took her anywhere she had to go, for example, to the dentist.

In 1992, Rosa had to have two teeth extracted. After the anesthetic wore off, her mouth began to hurt, and she accused Jorge of torturing her. The dentist had given Jorge antibiotics to give Rosa to keep her gums from getting infected, but when he tried to give her the pills, she recoiled in terror and screamed, "You're poisoning me!" Then she slapped him hard across the face, catching Jorge off guard. He grabbed her hands to keep her from hitting him again. Although a lifetime of manual labor had made him strong, it took everything he had to subdue Rosa without hurting her. Shaken and exhausted, he dragged his wife into town and called Anna.

"He sounded awful," Anna recalls, "and hearing what had happened, I felt terrible. It wasn't easy for me to drop everything and run down to Sonora. I had a business to run, but my father needed me and I was very worried about my mother."

Anna and one of her brothers made the trip. When they arrived, Rosa seemed dimly aware that the two visitors were her children, although she had trouble recalling their names. Anna was aghast. The three of them took Rosa to the small community hospital in Hermosillo.

After talking with the family and giving Rosa a cursory exam, a hospital doctor diagnosed Alzheimer's. It was untreatable, he told them, but if she stayed in the hospital awhile, he thought he could make her less belligerent. At first Anna was skeptical, since the hospital's reputation was not stellar, but Rosa's violence appalled the family, and Jorge definitely needed some time off. Reluctantly, she agreed to have Rosa hospitalized.

Anna returned to San Antonio deeply shaken by her mother's turn for the worse but optimistic that a hospital stay would help her. It didn't. On the contrary, her father reported that Rosa was going from bad to worse. While she was no longer belligerent, she had suddenly lost most of her remaining abilities. She'd walked into the hospital on her own two feet, but within a week, she could no longer walk at all. She barely recognized Jorge. She couldn't dress. Her speech was nonsense, and she seemed perpetually dazed. She barely ate, and had become pale and thin.

Anna couldn't stand hearing about her mother's rapid deterioration secondhand. A month after taking her to the hospital, she dashed back to Sonora to see Rosa for herself. Everything her father had said was true. Barely conscious, Rosa had lost at least twenty pounds, and her legs were covered with strange bruises. Anna was shocked.

"Come on," she told her father. "We're taking her home." They said nothing to any of the nurses, and did not wait for an official discharge. They simply packed Rosa up, grabbed the pills she'd been prescribed, commandeered a wheelchair, and rolled her out.

With Rosa back home, Anna and Jorge were horrified to discover the full extent of her deterioration after just one month in the hospital. In addition to neither walking nor talking, she couldn't dress herself, eat, or use the toilet without assistance. "She was terrible," Anna recalls, "really terrible."

That evening, Anna confronted her father: "You can't stay here anymore. Come up North. Move in with me. Mom will get better medical care, and we'll all help you take care of her. I don't see any other choice."

Jorge's love for Rosa won out over his love of the Mexican countryside. Two weeks later, Anna ushered her parents into her apartment in San Antonio.

Among the ten Flores children, there was never any question who would house Rosa and Jorge. "I had no kids," Anna explains. "I was the eldest daughter, and I wanted very much to take care of my mother, to do this for her." Anna's husband wasn't so sure. It was one thing, Esteban said, to put them up for a few months a year when they visited, but he was not eager to have his in-laws live with them permanently. Couldn't Anna's nine brothers and sisters help?

"I told him how much I wanted to take care of my mother," Anna recalls. "All my brothers and sisters had kids. They could help, but it didn't seem like a good idea to have a woman in my mother's condition around little children. I also reminded Esteban how often we'd opened our home to his family when they visited or moved up from Guadalajara."

Esteban agreed that Anna had been gracious to his family. Still, none of them had ever moved in permanently. They went back and forth, Anna trying to impress her husband with how committed she was to housing her parents, and Esteban refusing.

Finally, Anna said, "I am going to care for my parents in my home. I'm going to do it with you or without you, but I *am* going to do this."

"You'd leave me over this?" Esteban was incredulous.

"Yes," Anna replied fervently. "I would leave you over this."

Esteban did not want to lose Anna. Reluctantly, he agreed to have Jorge and Rosa move in. Their apartment was large, with a lovely patio garden, but even so, it had only one bedroom. Anna and Esteban kept the bedroom and rearranged their living room to accommodate Rosa and Jorge, as they'd done when her parents had visited. Anna was worried that Esteban would resent her parents' presence and treat them poorly. "But once he adjusted to their living with us, Esteban treated them very well," Anna explains. "He even helped take care of my mother. I knew I'd married a good man."

At first, Rosa seemed to understand that she was in Texas staying with Anna as she'd done annually for so many years, but it soon became apparent that she thought she was still in Mexico, and that Anna and Esteban and her other children had come down to be with her. In Rosa's mind, the family was together again. That had been her most cherished wish ever since her children had begun moving to *El Norte*. There was no point telling her otherwise.

As soon as her parents were set up in her apartment, Anna and her siblings scraped up the money to take Rosa to a neurologist at the University of Texas Health Science Center in San Antonio, hoping to learn the answers to two questions: What was wrong with her, and why had she deteriorated so rapidly in the hospital in Hermosillo?

The doctor took one look at the pills Rosa had been prescribed in Hermosillo and knew why she'd declined so quickly. The drug was a very powerful antipsychotic tranquilizer. It would have been understandable to prescribe it for a day or two after her attack on Jorge, but not for weeks on end, and not at the dose Rosa had been given.

"The doctor threw away the pills," Anna recalls, "and pretty quickly, my mother came out of her daze. She started walking again, and regained her appetite and the weight she'd lost." (It is also likely that the medication was to blame for Rosa's bruises. Antipsychotics can cause dizziness, fainting, and loss of coordination. She had probably fallen while on her way to or from the bathroom, or bumped into things and not realized it.)

As for Rosa's memory loss and other symptoms, the neurologist recommended a series of tests that took several days and more money. Finally, he informed the family of his verdict: Alzheimer's disease.

"I wasn't surprised," Jorge explains. "I'd been told the same thing in Mexico."

The diagnosis still came as a shock to Anna and her siblings, who'd dismissed the opinions of the Mexican doctors. They felt confident that the Anglo doctors at the big university medical center would be able to cure her. "When the neurologist said there was nothing he could do, we realized what we were in for, what the rest of my mother's life would be like, and what our lives would be like taking care of her. We all felt very sad, like at a funeral, only our mother was still alive." (Rosa was diagnosed in 1992, before any drugs were available to treat Alzheimer's, and before the value of most non-drug approaches had been demonstrated.)

Of course, compared with most families struggling to care for a member stricken with Alzheimer's, the Flores clan had a major advantage—numbers. In addition to Jorge, there were ten children. They all volunteered to help, and for a few months they followed through, visiting often, giving Jorge time off during the day and Anna a break in the evenings and on weekends. "But after a few months, my brothers and sisters and their husbands and wives began to withdraw from us," Anna recalls. "Their visits became less regular and then pretty much stopped except for birthdays and holidays, or specific errands like taking my mother to the doctor. They didn't call much either."

At first, Anna and Jorge couldn't believe what was happening. Rosa was their *mother*. How could her children abandon her? How could they abandon their *father and sister?* "I was very disappointed in my brothers and sisters," Anna says. "I called them and complained that they weren't doing what they said they'd do. They reminded me they had their own families to take care of, and that *Mama* hardly recognized them, so what was the point of spending time with her?"

Anna begged and pleaded for help, but to no avail. Eventually, she became disgusted with her siblings and stopped calling them. It was all she could do to remain civil when the family got together for Christmas, Easter, birthdays, and Cinco de Mayo (May 5, a Mexican holiday). "Without their help, all the caregiving fell on my father and me and Esteban. It was very hard on us."

Hard, yes, but feasible, Anna decided, if they got themselves organized. They divided up the caregiving. Jorge watched Rosa during the day, and Anna took over at night and on weekends, with Esteban pitching in when he could.

With the antipsychotic tranquilizer behind her, Rosa perked up considerably. She regained the ability to feed and shower herself, and she could get dressed with a little assistance. Most heartening was the disappearance of the belligerence that had landed her in the Mexican hospital. As her Alzheimer's progressed, Rosa became increasingly easygoing and very affectionate. "She could still say simple things," Anna recalls, "but she couldn't express complicated ideas like telling us that she appreciated what we were doing for her. Instead, she showed it. She smiled when we came near her, and reached out and caressed our arms and faces, and she snuggled up to us when we sat with her." Rosa's new warmth buoyed Anna's spirits tremendously. Her mother had not shown her this much affection for seventeen years, since she'd announced she was leaving Mexico.

During weekdays, Jorge and Rosa spent a good deal of time puttering with the potted plants in Anna's patio garden. "Rosa was happy on the patio," Jorge says. "I think she thought she was back in her old garden in Santa Rita."

Jorge also took Rosa for long walks. Their route took them through a large park where mariachi bands often played. Rosa could sit for hours listening to mariachi music. "She cried when they played her favorite songs," Anna recalls. Jorge also played Mexican music for her on Anna's stereo, and they often danced around the apartment. Anna, who wrote songs in the style of Mexican folk music, often sang with her mother, which they both enjoyed. "But only the old songs she'd known all her life," Anna says. "She couldn't learn any of my songs. They were too new for her."

Spanish-language television was another activity Rosa enjoyed. "My mother couldn't really follow what was happening, but if a pretty girl came on the screen and my father seemed a little too interested, she got upset. She'd nudge him and give him disapproving, jealous looks. The same thing happened if my father paid any attention to women who visited our apartment. My mother would go from being all smiles to sulking and looking at him very disapprovingly. She was no longer able to say, 'He's mine,' but she could show it."

Several times a week, Jorge took Rosa to church. Just like in Mexico earlier in her illness, the solemn, candle-lit dimness and the familiar ritual seemed to calm her, and Rosa needed calming. When she wasn't occupied by a favorite activity, she paced obsessively, back and forth, around the apartment for hours on end. Several times, when Jorge or Anna was called away to the telephone or to do something in the kitchen, she walked out of the apartment and wandered off. "When she wandered in San Cristobal it wasn't so bad," Jorge observes. "All the neighbors knew that she was confused and shepherded her back home. And if she wandered into the cotton fields, I could see her and run after her, but San Antonio was different. There were more neighbors and only a few watched out for her. I was always worried that she'd wander into a busy street." Anna and Jorge kept the windows closed and the doors locked, and tried not to let Rosa out of their sight.

After a few months of sharing the caregiving with her father, Anna realized that Jorge was no longer up to being solely responsible for Rosa for ten hours a day, five days a week. Her mother was descending deeper into Alzheimer's, and her father, then sixty-seven, no longer had the stamina to deal with her. To help him, Anna hired a maid to work eight to five, Monday through Friday. The maid cooked meals and helped Rosa shower, dress, and use the toilet. Unfortunately the luxury of a maid was expensive, and Anna and Esteban strained their budget to pay for her. "I didn't even ask my brothers and sisters to chip in," she explains. "I was still disgusted with them."

The maid also gave Jorge time to rest, which he needed badly because the challenges of the daylight hours were nothing compared with what happened at night. "In 1993, after she'd been in Texas about a year, my mother stopped sleeping normally. She became very restless at night and got up and paced. She never left the apartment because we were careful about keeping the windows closed and the doors locked, but she paced all over the place for hours until she exhausted herself—and us." Neither Anna nor Jorge felt comfortable allowing Rosa to pace unsupervised, so they took turns staying up and pacing with her until the wee hours when she finally fell into fitful slumber.

Pacing half the night was torture for Anna. "I needed more than four hours of sleep a night. My business suffered. I just couldn't work as hard. My marriage suffered. I had no energy or patience for Esteban. A few times, I almost dozed off while driving. That was very scary."

As Rosa deteriorated, she continued to pace at night but increasingly lost coordination. "She started walking into the walls and furniture," Anna explains. "I had to get rid of things like end tables and other furniture that she might fall over, and anything breakable that she might knock into." Over time, Anna's apartment felt less like a home and more like a cell.

After two years of housing her parents in what once had been her living room, the apartment now felt tiny. Sleep-deprived and increasingly overwhelmed with caring for her mother, Anna felt that its walls were closing in on her. Her life had become as small as her apartment. All she did was work, care for her mother, and sleep. She felt depressed, irritable, and desperate. She couldn't remember the last time she'd had any fun.

Then a friend showed her a flier advertising classes for Alzheimer's caregivers at the Health Science Center where Rosa had been diagnosed. One was called "Coping with the Blues," the other, "Coping with Frustration and Anger." Both were given in English and Spanish. Anna signed up for the Spanish sections of both classes. They felt like a lifesaver.

Each class met one evening a week for eight weeks. While Anna went to the classes, Jorge or Esteban watched Rosa. In "Coping with the Blues," the instructors insisted that caregivers shouldn't be martyrs, and can't be if they hope to provide decent care. They urged participants to set aside time for themselves, for the other people in their lives, and for fun—without feeling guilty.

"That message was very helpful for me," Anna explains. "I knew I wasn't taking care of myself, but if I wasn't working or looking after my mother, I felt guilty. The class taught me to make time for myself. My husband and I began going out—listening to music and going to dances. I learned to communicate better, to let my husband and father know what I needed. I also began taking some time for just me—writing my songs. That class put some balance back in my life. It helped me a great deal."

She felt the same way about "Coping with Frustration and Anger." "We learned to recognize when we were getting upset, to stop ourselves before we lost control, and to relax using deep breathing and thoughts of things we liked [visualization exercises]. We learned to take things one day at a time and how to solve the problems we had as caregivers that made us feel frustrated and angry. That class gave me inner strength."

In addition to refining her coping skills, the classes also taught Anna the value of support. "At work, I had to deal with my customers' problems. At home, I had to deal with my mother's, my father's, and my husband's problems. I felt there was no place I could focus on *my* problems, no one to really listen to me." After the classes ended, she joined a support group. "It helps to talk with people who are going through the same experience."

The classes also led Anna to a realization; her apartment was too small for four people. In 1994, Anna and Esteban scraped up enough money to buy a modest home in San Antonio about a mile from their apartment. It had three bedrooms and a large fenced-in yard. "Esteban and I had a bedroom. My parents had a bedroom. The third bedroom allowed us to get away and spend some quiet time alone. There was a big garage for Esteban to work on the cars he restored, and the yard allowed my mother to pace all she wanted safely without constant supervision."

By the time of the move from the apartment to the house, Rosa still recognized Jorge and Anna and Esteban, but no longer knew their names. Sometimes she didn't recognize her other children, and she had no idea who her grandchildren were.

She also had increasing difficulty talking. "She still had words, but not sentences anymore," Anna recalls. From the time Rosa was diagnosed with Alzheimer's, Anna had dreaded her loss of speech and her eventual descent into silence. Rosa's firm, clear voice was such an integral part of Anna's experience of her. Remarkably, two years later, in 1996, when Rosa stopped speaking for good, Anna was pleasantly surprised by how little difference it made. "She didn't say much for the year before she stopped talking, so I had time to get used to her silence. We knew her likes and dislikes, and we had a routine that worked for her. If she needed something, she communicated with gestures. The adjustment wasn't easy, but somehow it worked out."

By this time, Rosa could not dress, bathe, feed herself, or use the bathroom without a great deal of help. Fortunately, the classes helped Anna adjust to her mother's accelerating deterioration. "We dressed her simply, fed her, gave her sponge baths, and used adult diapers. At each step, I had to fight thinking, What next? The classes had stressed taking things one day at a time and not getting upset about what might happen in the future, and that was good advice. As the disease progressed, it was hard, but not as hard as I'd imagined."

In the new house, Rosa continued to pace at night, but with the yard and added square footage, it wasn't as hard to handle as it had been in the claustrophobic confines of the old apartment. She also got tired sooner, so Jorge and Anna got more sleep.

Jorge continued to take Rosa to church through 1997. Then he realized that she no longer felt comfortable there. "Instead of sitting quietly and taking it all in," he explains, "she would look frightened and tug on my arm as if to say, 'Let's go.'"

Not long after her final visit to church, Rosa stopped walking.

"She forgot how," Anna explains. Anna set her mother up in a wheel-chair, and she seemed content to sit by a window that overlooked the backyard.

Rosa's loss of mobility was a mixed blessing. On the one hand, it ended her nightly pacing, allowing Jorge and Anna to get eight hours of sleep a night for the first time in several years, but it also compli-cated taking care of her. Fortunately, Rosa was a small, increasingly frail woman, and not difficult to lift.

In early 1998, Rosa suddenly became belligerent again. She grabbed Anna and Jorge, pushed them, and hit them. "At first we didn't know what to think," Anna recalls, "but then we realized that she only acted that way before mealtimes. We soon realized that it was her way of communicating that she was hungry." Instead of giving her three meals a day, they switched Rosa to six or seven snacks, and she calmed down.

By mid-1998, Rosa was clearly going downhill. "She became al-most completely inactive," Anna explains. "She just sat in her chair doing nothing, hardly looking out the window, not interested in any-thing or anyone. She stopped smiling. She looked half asleep all the time."

Then one evening, Rosa had a seizure. As her limbs and head jerked uncontrollably, Anna and her father hustled her to a nearby community hospital. Jorge wrapped his arms around his flailing wife and held her tight so that she wouldn't hurt herself, or him. Rosa was also having trouble breathing, so they decided to call the rest of the family to the hospital.

A staff doctor reassured the family that Rosa would rest comfort-ably that night, and suggested that they go home and return in the morning. Anna had to start work early and decided to leave. A few of her brothers and sisters also left. The rest spent the night on the sofas in the hallway outside their mother's room. Jorge stayed at his wife's bedside. He was holding her hand when she stopped breathing and died. Rosa Flores was seventy-one.

The children who would not care for their mother while she was alive were better about burying her once she had died. They made the funeral arrangements, giving Anna and Jorge some time to decompress from six years of caregiving in Anna's case, and for Jorge, thirteen. "I had bad feelings about my siblings, and they had bad feelings about me," Anna explains, "but we all put them aside for the funeral. My mother's death reunited us."

Three months after Rosa's death, Anna and Jorge still get choked up talking about her. Jorge says he feels sad that his other children did not do much for their mother in her final years, but he's philosophical: "They have their own lives to live in this new country."

Anna has been slower to forgive. After her mother's funeral, her resentment of her brothers and sisters welled up again, and her siblings made a conscious effort to reach out to her. At first Anna wanted little to do with them, but as the months passed, she softened. "They're my brothers and sisters," she sighs. "In spite of everything, I still love them, and can't stay angry at them forever."

Anna's support group helped her process her feelings about her siblings. "When I think about how they didn't come through when my father and I needed them, I can get very angry, but that doesn't help me, or them. Instead I try to think about my mother, and how caring for her brought me closer to my father, and taught me a lot about myself. Then I feel sorry for them. They missed that experience and most of the final years of their mother's life."

These days, Anna's brothers and sisters call and drop by regularly. Their kids enjoy visiting their grandfather, and Jorge delights in his grandchildren. Anna is slowly getting over her resentment. She doesn't want it to fester the way her mother's did when her children moved north. "We talk more now, which is good." But they don't talk much about Rosa's illness or the many hardships of caring for her. By an unspoken agreement, the siblings prefer to remember their mother as the healthy, vibrant woman who could simultaneously raise a family, keep her home spotless, and work in the cotton fields, not as the Alzheimer's sufferer she became.

"Caregiving was very hard," Anna affirms, "but I have no regrets about having done it. My mother raised me. I felt guilty leaving her when I moved to Texas. When she really needed me, I wanted very much to be there for her, and I'm glad I was."

5.

Who's at Risk?

Important New Insights into Risk Factors for Alzheimer's

The cause of Alzheimer's disease remains a mystery, but scientists have identified several risk factors that increase its likelihood. Some are well established and clearly play a role in Alzheimer's, while others are less firmly established but probably contribute to the risk. A handful of other risk profiles remain quite controversial.

Well-Established Risk Factors for Alzheimer's Disease

INCREASING AGE

This is the main risk factor. The older you get, the greater your risk.

Between the ages of sixty-five and seventy-four, an estimated 3 percent of the population has Alzheimer's. From age seventy-five to eighty-four, the figure rises to about 15 percent. And for those eighty-five and older, the disease afflicts some 30 to 40 percent.

Oddly, however, according to the Multi-Institutional Research in Alzheimer's Genetic Epidemiology (MIRAGE) project based at Boston University School of Medicine, after age ninety, the risk of Alzheimer's *declines.* Currently, no one knows why.

FEMALE SEX

The MIRAGE study also shows that at all ages, women's risk of Alzheimer's disease is somewhat higher than men's. By age ninety-three, women's risk is 13 percent higher. However, women can take something that reduces their risk—postmenopausal hormone replacement therapy (see below).

FAMILY HISTORY

Finnish researchers have found that if one member of an identical-twin pair develops Alzheimer's, the risk to the other twin is unusually high—40 to 50 percent—which points to some genetic predisposition.

In addition, having a close relative who develops Alzheimer's increases the risk. The MIRAGE project researchers tracked the lifetime risk of 12,971 people who had a first-degree relative (parent, sibling) with the condition. By age eighty, people with Alzheimer's disease in both parents had a 54 percent risk, 1.5 times the risk of people with just one affected parent, and five times the risk of people with two unaffected parents. Most people with one affected parent do not, themselves, develop Alzheimer's.

GENETICS

The genetic mechanisms of familial Alzheimer's remain largely unexplained, but a few genetic mutations (specific abnormalities on chromosomes 1, 14, and 21) have been identified that greatly increase the risk in some families. The mutations on these chromosomes cause rare clusters of unusually early-onset Alzheimer's disease in small numbers of families around the world. Along with observations about family history as a risk factor, these defects prove that Alzheimer's has a genetic component.

Chromosome 21 also causes Alzheimer's disease in people with Down syndrome. Normally, all cell nuclei (except sperm and egg cells) have two copies of each chromosome. People with Down syndrome have an extra copy of chromosome 21 and, as a result, an extra gene for a protein that plays a role in Alzheimer's, the gene that codes for production of amyloid precursor protein (APP). If people with Down syndrome survive into their forties and fifties, they almost always develop Alzheimer's because their extra APP gene causes them to produce abnormally large amounts of amyloid precursor protein, which leads to unusually high levels of beta-amyloid peptide, the major component of the senile plaques of Alzheimer's.

In addition, chromosome 19 has generated a great deal of interest among Alzheimer's researchers. A gene on this chromosome plays a significant role in late-onset Alzheimer's, the most prevalent type of Alzheimer's disease. Chromosome 19 contains a gene that codes for apolipoprotein E (APOE), a protein involved in cholesterol metabolism. There are three natural variations (alleles) of the APOE gene, known as allele 2, 3, and 4. Everyone has two alleles, meaning that there are six possible combinations (2-2, 2-3, 2-4, 3-3, 3-4, and 4-4).

Alzheimer's risk varies depending on the different allele combinations. In general, allele 2 is protective, while alleles 3 and 4 increase the risk (except when they are paired with allele 2). The highest risk is associated with the 3-4 and 4-4 combinations, though many people with one of these combinations *do not* develop the disease. Recently, a research team led by biostatistician Lindsay Farrer, Ph.D., at Boston University School of Medicine used sophisticated statistical techniques (meta-analysis) to combine the results of more than forty studies of APOE allele effects. The results show that people with Alzheimer's are two to three times more likely than the general population to have at least one copy of allele 4, and six to ten times more likely to have the 4-4 combination. The 3-4 combination also raises the risk substantially, but allele 2 is powerfully protective. Even those with the 2-4 combination had a very low risk of Alzheimer's.

APOE alleles are not evenly distributed throughout the population. In general, allele 3 is the most common (about 78 percent of all alleles), while alleles 2 and 4 are considerably less common (7 and 15 percent, respectively). The most common combination, 3-3, occurs in 60 percent of Americans. The 2-2 combination occurs in 0.05 percent (1 per 200), and the 4-4 combination occurs in 2 percent of the population.

APOE alleles also influence age at Alzheimer's diagnosis. People with the highest-risk 4-4 allele combination who develop Alzheimer's tend to get diagnosed before age seventy, while those with the lowest-risk 2-2 pair who develop the disease tend to get diagnosed near the age of ninety.

Unlike the mutations on chromosomes 1, 14, and 21 that cause Alzheimer's in anyone who has them, APOE allele status does not reliably predict Alzheimer's risk. Many people with the high-risk 3-4 and 4-4 combinations never develop the disease, and some people with the low-risk allele 2 combinations do. A test that determines APOE allele status is available to physicians, but it does not predict Alzheimer's very well. Recently, officials of the Program in Genomics, Ethics, and Society at Stanford University released a report discouraging APOE allele testing as a mass screening tool for Alzheimer's risk because of the combination of its cost, poor predictive value, and the fact that those with higher-risk combinations would suffer considerable anxiety, often unnecessarily.

Nonetheless, when doctors evaluate people with suspected Alzheimer's disease, they increasingly test for APOE allele status. Having even one copy of allele 4 can help make a diagnosis of Alzheimer's. Without allele testing, clinicians currently diagnose Alzheimer's correctly in about 90 percent of cases, but in a recent study, when people with suspected Alzheimer's had at least one allele 4, diagnostic accuracy increased to 97 percent, according to Allen Roses, M.D., the Jefferson-Pilot Corporation professor of neurology and director of the Joseph and Kathleen Bryan Alzheimer's Disease Research Center at Duke University School of Medicine. There may also be a gene involved in late-onset Alzheimer's disease on chromosome 12. Some studies suggest this, but the issue remains controversial.

ETHNICITY

The different racial and ethnic groups have slightly different genetics. One area of difference is the prevalence of high-risk APOE allele 4. African-Americans are most likely to have at least one allele 4 (19 percent), followed by whites (14 percent), Hispanics (11 percent), and Asian-Americans (9 percent).

However, even without an allele 4, African-Americans and Hispanics are two to four times more likely than whites to develop Alzheimer's by age ninety. This finding comes from a recent study by Columbia University neurologists of 1,079 elderly New Yorkers, who were tracked from 1991 to 1996. The researchers controlled for gender, education, family history, and blood pressure, so the differences in risk had nothing to do with any of those attributes.

It's not clear why African-Americans and Hispanics might be at unusually high risk of developing Alzheimer's, but researchers point to two possibilities—an as yet undiscovered gene or environmental factors.

Cherokee Indians appear to possess some as yet undetermined genetic resistance to Alzheimer's disease. Scientists from the University of Texas Southwestern Medical Center in Dallas studied fifty-two members of the Cherokee Nation who had varying degrees of Cherokee ancestry. Half of those studied had Alzheimer's disease, and half did not. Using genealogical information supplied by the Cherokee Nation Tribal Registration Department, the researchers discovered that as the participants' proportion of Cherokee ancestry increased, their Alzheimer's risk decreased.

ENVIRONMENTAL FACTORS

Ethnic differences in Alzheimer's disease rates are only one indication that environmental factors play a role in the disease. The Finnish identical-twin study mentioned earlier provides even stronger evidence. That study shows that while genetic factors play an important role in Alzheimer's, genetic identity is not destiny. Identical twins have the exact same genetic makeup, but Alzheimer's disease develops in only about half of identical-twin pairs. In addition, when both members of an identical-twin pair develop Alzheimer's, their ages at diagnosis often differ by as much as fifteen years. These findings demonstrate that environmental factors also play a role in Alzheimer's risk, even among those with clear genetic predisposition.

Additional support for environmental factors comes from a recent analysis of a long-term study of Japanese men living in Hawaii. Back in 1965, researchers from the National Institute on Aging recruited four thousand middle-aged Japanese-American men and have tracked their health ever since. Thirty years later, in 1995, 3,734 of the men, by then elderly, were still alive. The survivors had a rate of dementia from all causes of 9.3 percent, and 5.4 percent specifically had Alzheimer's. The researchers then compared the incidence of dementia and Alzheimer's in a similar group of elderly Japanese men living in Hisayama, Japan. Only 3.2 percent showed dementia, and 1.5 percent had Alzheimer's—about one-third the risk of the group from Hawaii.

The researchers did all they could to make sure that the same Alzheimer's diagnostic criteria were used in both groups of men. The genetics of Japanese-Americans and native Japanese are quite similar, yet their rates of Alzheimer's varied considerably. Clearly, environmental or cultural factors must play a role in the disease.

Probable Risk Factors for Alzheimer's Disease

Considerable evidence shows that the following factors increase the risk of Alzheimer's, but experts do not yet consider them well established:

MEAT-BASED, HIGH-FAT DIET

One clear difference between Japanese in Japan and Japanese-Americans is their diet. Native Japanese eat less meat, and follow a lower-fat, higher-fiber diet with more fish. Japanese-Americans, on the other hand, generally adopt the burger-fries-and-shake American diet—meat-based, high-fat, and low-fiber. High-fat, low-fiber diets have been persuasively linked to heart disease and many cancers, and recently they have also been linked to increased risk of Alzheimer's disease.

At Erasmus University in the Netherlands, researchers gave cognitive function tests to a large number of Dutch people and asked 5,300 who were cognitively normal and over age fifty-five to fill out diet questionnaires. Two years later, they retested them. Those with the poorest cognition scores had the diets highest in total fat, saturated (animal) fat, and cholesterol. In contrast, the more fish the participants ate, the higher their cognitive scores. In food folklore, fish has a reputation as a "brain food." There may be something to this. Cold-water fish, for example, salmon and mackerel, are high in omega-3 fatty acids, which help prevent the blood clots in the brain that cause most strokes. As fish consumption increases, high-fat meat consumption and the cognitive impairment linked to it tend to decline.

Corroborating evidence of diet as a risk factor for Alzheimer's comes from a study by Yorktown, Virginia, Alzheimer's researcher William Grant, Ph.D. He compiled statistics from eleven countries around the world (in Africa, Asia, Europe, and North America) and found that the highest rates of Alzheimer's occur in countries with the highest-fat diets. Alzheimer's risk also correlated to total number of calories consumed.

He then zeroed in on the United States, Canada, and five European countries: England, Italy, Spain, Finland, and Sweden. The populations of all these countries consume about the same proportion of total calories as fat, but the Finns and Swedes eat considerably more fish. They also have lower rates of Alzheimer's disease.

Why would a meat-based, high-fat diet raise Alzheimer's risk? Because dietary fat causes "oxidative damage." We humans need oxygen to live, but oxygen also has a major downside. In the body, some oxygen molecules become so highly chemically reactive that they disrupt other body processes. These troublemaker molecules are called "free radicals," and a meat-based, high-fat diet floods the bloodstream with them. The emerging scientific consensus is that the oxidative damage that free radicals inflict plays a significant role in the development of cancer, heart disease and, it now appears, Alzheimer's.

The role of free radicals in Alzheimer's risk was recently confirmed by a team of researchers led by Garret FitzGerald, M.D., chair of the department of pharmacology at the University of Pennsylvania Medical Center in Philadelphia. The autopsy study compared evidence of free-radical activity in the brain tissue of people who died with and without Alzheimer's. Those with Alzheimer's had double the free-radical activity in their frontal and temporal lobes, areas critical to memory and cognitive function.

Smoking also greatly increases the number of free radicals in the blood (see below).

DEFICIENCY OF ANTIOXIDANT NUTRIENTS

Fortunately, certain nutrients called antioxidants can, to a considerable extent, prevent the oxidative damage free radicals cause. Antioxidant nutrients include: vitamin A (and its close chemical relatives, the carotenoids, among them beta-carotene), vitamin C, vitamin E, and the mineral selenium. These nutrients are abundant in plant foods, and many studies show that as fruit and vegetable consumption increases, the risk of diseases linked to oxidative damage—notably cancer and heart disease—decreases. Antioxidants are also available as supplements. Researchers at Harvard and elsewhere have shown that a diet high in vitamin E, or daily consumption of 100 IU of a vitamin E supplement, reduces the risk of heart attack by more than 30 percent.

Recent research has also shown that antioxidants, notably vitamin E and the antioxidant Parkinson's drug selegiline (Eldepryl), slow the rate of cognitive decline in Alzheimer's disease (see chapter 10).

Might antioxidants also reduce the risk of Alzheimer's? To date, no rigorous studies have investigated this issue, but it's a good bet that the answer is yes. Oxidative damage contributes to the brain changes that result in Alzheimer's, and antioxidants help treat the disease. It makes sense that deficiencies of these nutrients would be a risk factor for Alzheimer's.

CARDIOVASCULAR DISEASE: HEART DISEASE, STROKE, HIGH BLOOD PRESSURE (HYPERTENSION), AND DIABETES

These diseases damage the blood vessels, including those in the brain. Given sufficient blood-vessel damage, enough brain cells can die to cause vascular dementia ("vascular" refers to the blood vessels). Stroke is the best-known cause of vascular dementia. In addition, a series of mini-strokes, medically known as transient ischemic attacks (TIAs) can cause a similar type of vascular dementia (multi-infarct dementia, or MID). Recent research shows that chronic high blood pressure, cardiac arrest, and diabetes, which also damage the blood vessels and greatly increase the risk of heart disease, are all risk factors for vascular dementia.

Until recently, researchers believed that vascular dementia and Alzheimer's were two entirely different diseases. A person might have both (mixed dementia), but scientists considered Alzheimer's a neurological condition, and vascular dementia a disease of the circulatory system. Then both vascular dementia and Alzheimer's were linked to oxidative damage, and the line between them began to blur. Recently, Alzheimer's was linked to activation of platelets, the blood cells that play a key role in clotting. The platelets are also involved in cardiovascular disease. The upshot is that Alzheimer's and cardiovascular disease appear to have more and more in common. The underlying cause of cardiovascular disease is atherosclerosis, arterial narrowing by cholesterol-rich plaque deposits. Not surprisingly, the latest studies show that atherosclerosis also raises the risk of Alzheimer's.

At Erasmus University Medical School in Rotterdam, Dutch researchers discovered a correlation between atherosclerosis and Alzheimer's disease. They studied 1,900 people, 207 of whom had Alzheimer's. Using sophisticated ultrasound equipment to measure atherosclerosis in the carotid arteries that carry blood into the brain, they discovered that as carotid atherosclerosis increased, so did the risk of both MID and Alzheimer's.

Stroke also raises the risk of Alzheimer's. In a study of elderly Roman Catholic nuns at the Sanders-Brown Center for Aging at the University of Kentucky, David Snowdon, Ph.D., and colleagues have discovered that even small strokes in certain areas of the brain dramatically increase the risk of Alzheimer's disease. They tested the cognitive function of 102 elderly nuns, aged seventy-six to one hundred, and then performed brain autopsies after they died. Of the sixty-one nuns who showed autopsy evidence of Alzheimer's disease, those who also had strokes were significantly more likely to have developed Alzheimer's before they died. Those with small strokes in certain specific areas of the brain were twenty times more likely to have developed Alzheimer's.

Meanwhile, the APOE gene that plays a role in Alzheimer's risk also appears to relate to dementia risk after a stroke. At Columbia University in New York, researchers analyzed the APOE allele status of 594 stroke survivors, 187 of whom had suffered significant dementia. Stroke survivors who became demented were significantly more likely to have at least one copy of high-risk allele 4. Compared with those who had two copies of allele 3, those with one allele 4 had twice the risk of post-stroke dementia, while those with two allele 4s had seven times the risk.

Diabetes damages the blood vessels, substantially increasing the risk of heart disease. It also raises the risk of Alzheimer's, according to researchers at the Mayo Clinic in Rochester, Minnesota, and the Mayo Foundation in Scottsdale, Arizona. They followed 1,455 type-2 diabetics (people who did not inject insulin) for fourteen years. Various types of dementia developed in 101 of them, of whom seventy-seven were diagnosed with Alzheimer's. Compared with nondiabetic controls, those with diabetes were 66 percent more likely to develop Alzheimer's.

Finally, chronic high blood pressure (hypertension) raises the risk of Alzheimer's disease. Ingmar Skoog, M.D., an assistant professor of medicine at Göteborg University in Sweden, followed a group of elderly Swedes for fifteen years and found that a ten-year history of hypertension significantly increased the risk of both stroke and Alzheimer's.

SEDENTARY LIFESTYLE

Regular, moderate exercise helps prevent cardiovascular disease and many cancers. Add Alzheimer's to the list. At Case Western Reserve University in Cleveland, neurologists Robert Friedland, M.D., and Arthur L. Smith, M.D., asked the family members of 126 Alzheimer's sufferers and 247 other older adults about their exercise habits from age twenty to fifty-nine. Then the researchers calculated an activity index based on both time spent exercising and the strenuousness of their subjects' activities. Compared with those who were the most active, the least active group had 3.5 times the Alzheimer's risk.

SMOKING

Smoking is a disaster for the circulatory system. It boosts blood levels of free radicals, damages the blood vessels, raises blood pressure, contributes to atherosclerosis, and is a major risk factor for heart disease and stroke. It should come as no surprise, therefore, that smoking also increases the risk of Alzheimer's disease.

Back in 1990, the previously mentioned Alzheimer's researchers at Erasmus University in Rotterdam surveyed eight thousand Dutch people over age fifty-five about their smoking habits. Five years later, in 1995, they determined who among them had developed Alzheimer's. The smokers were at significantly greater risk.

A 1998 study by the same group showed that compared with lifelong nonsmokers, women smokers are twice as likely to develop Alzheimer's, and men who smoke have six times the risk.

Ironically, nicotine, the addictive drug in cigarettes, boosts cognitive function in people with Alzheimer's and is under investigation as a possible treatment for the disease (chapter 10).

INFREQUENT USE OF NONSTEROIDAL
ANTI-INFLAMMATORY DRUGS (NSAIDS)

Some years ago, researchers noticed that people with severe arthritis have unexpectedly low rates of Alzheimer's. More recently, Japanese researchers noted a similar unusually low rate of the disease in people being treated for leprosy. The medications used to treat both leprosy and arthritis are nonsteroidal anti-inflammatory drugs (NSAIDs).

Around the same time, researchers discovered that inflammation of brain tissue plays a key role in the development of the neurofibrillary tangles and beta-amyloid plaques of Alzheimer's disease. These observations strongly implied that the anti-inflammatory action of NSAIDs might prevent, or at least delay, Alzheimer's, and possibly help treat it.

Several widely used over-the-counter drugs are NSAIDs: aspirin, ibuprofen (Motrin, Advil), and naproxen (Naprosyn). (Acetaminophen [Tylenol] is not an NSAID. It is only a pain reliever and has no anti-inflammatory action.) In addition, there are dozens of prescription NSAIDs.

Powerful evidence of NSAID protection against Alzheimer's comes from the Baltimore Longitudinal Study of Aging (BLSA). Every two years for almost forty years, BLSA participants have filled out extensive food, drug, and lifestyle questionnaires, and have taken a battery of cognition and memory tests. Recently, researchers from the National Institute on Aging assessed NSAID use in 1,828 people in the study, 110 of whom developed Alzheimer's between 1980 and 1995.

As the frequency and duration of NSAID use increased, the Alzheimer's risk decreased—by up to 60 percent. All NSAIDs (except aspirin) significantly reduced the risk, including ibuprofen, naproxen, indomethacin (Indocin), and meclofenamate (Meclomen). Aspirin's effect did not reach statistical significance, but there was a trend toward lower risk with increased duration of more-than-occasional aspirin use.

NSAIDs also help slow cognitive deterioration in Alzheimer's (chapter 10).

Unfortunately, NSAIDs often cause side effects—abdominal distress and potentially serious, even life-threatening, ulcers and gastrointestinal bleeding.

IN WOMEN, NO USE OR BRIEF USE OF
POSTMENOPAUSAL HORMONE REPLACEMENT THERAPY

Compared with men, women are at somewhat greater risk of Alzheimer's disease. However, several recent studies show that postmenopausal hormone replacement therapy (HRT), which contains the female sex hormone estrogen, helps prevent, or at least delay, Alzheimer's in women. In other words, little or no use of HRT is a risk factor for the disease.

Here's the evidence:

- Animal studies show that estrogen improves blood circulation through the brain and stimulates nerve cell growth in the parts of the brain affected by Alzheimer's.
- Several epidemiological studies show that taking HRT, which is primarily estrogen, reduces women's risk of Alzheimer's disease. New York City researchers followed 1,124 elderly women for many years. Among those who had never used estrogen, 16.3 percent developed Alzheimer's, but among women who had used HRT for at least one year, only 5.8 percent developed the disease.
- As part of the previously mentioned Baltimore Longitudinal Study of Aging (BLSA), Claudia Kawas, M.D., an associate professor of neurology at Johns Hopkins University and clinical director of Alzheimer's research there, assessed sixteen years of medical records for 514 postmenopausal women. Compared with women who had never taken HRT, those who had were 54 percent less likely to develop Alzheimer's disease.
- In another study of BLSA participants, researchers tested the memories of 288 women, none of whom had Alzheimer's. One hundred sixteen of them had used HRT, and they made significantly fewer errors on the memory test.

- HRT use reduced Alzheimer's risk 75 percent in a 1998 report by Marzia Baldereschi, M.D., of the Italian National Research Council in Rome. She analyzed HRT use by 2,816 women enrolled in the Italian Longitudinal Study. Ninety-two eventually developed Alzheimer's, but only three of them had ever taken HRT.

- Tamoxifen, a close chemical relative of estrogen prescribed to treat breast cancer, also helps prevent Alzheimer's disease, according to a 1998 study by New York researchers. Brenda Breuer, Ph.D., associate director of research at the Jewish Home and Hospital in New York, analyzed the medical records of all 93,031 women who resided in nursing homes in New York State in 1993. Among the 1,378 who had taken tamoxifen to treat breast cancer, 8 percent also had Alzheimer's. Then, for each tamoxifen-user, Breuer identified up to four very similar nursing home residents who had not taken the estrogen drug. Among those 5,167, the prevalence of Alzheimer's was 12 percent.

- Finally, in a 1998 analysis, a research team led by psychiatrist Kristine Yaffe, M.D., of the University of California Medical Center in San Francisco, amalgamated the results of ten previous studies of HRT in postmenopausal women. Overall, HRT users were 29 percent less likely to develop Alzheimer's.

Estrogen reduces the risk of Alzheimer's in several ways: It boosts production of acetylcholine, a brain chemical (neurotransmitter) involved in sending nerve impulses across the tiny gaps between nerve cells (synapses). It reduces production of the type of beta-amyloid that forms senile plaques, it improves blood flow through the brain, and it aids the function of the hippocampus, an area of the brain involved in memory. Stanley Birge, M.D., a geriatrician at the Washington University School of Medicine in St. Louis, calls these findings about estrogen's ability to prevent Alzheimer's "among the most promising recent discoveries about the disease."

Beyond Alzheimer's, a great deal of research shows that HRT also helps prevent heart disease, the leading cause of death among women, and osteoporosis, bone-thinning that can lead to serious fractures. Despite these benefits, HRT also increases the risk of breast cancer by about 30 percent.

If you're a postmenopausal woman, should you take HRT? This question has no easy answer. The best advice is to discuss the issue with your doctor, weighing your individual risk of heart disease, osteoporosis, Alzheimer's, and breast cancer, and your own personal level of anxiety about each of these diseases.

HEAD INJURIES

Some evidence suggests that head injuries resulting in loss of consciousness increase the risk of Alzheimer's disease and other cognitive problems that afflict about 20 percent of former boxers.

While the research has been inconsistent and inconclusive, a recent study done at New York Hospital–Cornell Medical Center suggests that the APOE allele 4 gene again plays a role in increased risk for dementia. The researchers studied thirty former boxers, all of whom had sustained countless blows to the head. Eleven showed normal cognitive function. Twelve showed minor deficits. Four were moderately impaired. Three were severely demented. The risk of cognitive impairment increased in relation to the length of the boxer's career, showing that the number of blows to the head is indeed a risk factor for dementia. However, boxers with an APOE allele 4 showed significantly more mental impairment, and every boxer with severe dementia had at least one copy of allele 4.

Scientists cannot explain why the combination of head injuries and allele 4 conspires to cause Alzheimer's-like dementia, but they speculate that the head injuries trigger Alzheimer's-type changes in the brain and that APOE allele 4 prevents the body from repairing them.

Controversial Risk Factors
for Alzheimer's Disease

Some research suggests that the following factors might raise the risk of Alzheimer's, but as this book goes to press, they remain highly controversial.

LOW EDUCATIONAL LEVEL

Several studies show that intellectual pursuits—college education, recreational reading, taking classes for personal enrichment, doing crossword puzzles, etc.—help preserve cognition. Or, to put it another way, lack of education is a risk factor for Alzheimer's, but controversy surrounds this issue.

In fact, the latest research casts substantial doubt on the notion that lack of education is a risk factor for Alzheimer's. The problem, according to many prominent researchers, is not with the minds of those who have little education, but rather *with the tests used to assess them*. According to the researchers, the tests are biased in favor of those with considerable education and make those without it appear demented when they are actually cognitively normal.

A common test used in Alzheimer's assessment is the Mini-Mental State Exam (MMSE). According to F. M. Baker, M.D., a professor of psychiatry at the University of Maryland, several studies have shown that when African-Americans take the MMSE, if they have fewer than eight years of formal education, the test often produces false findings of dementia.

The same is true for Hispanic individuals. According to dementia researchers I. Maribel Taussig, Ph.D., of Naples, Florida, and Marcel Ponton, Ph.D., of the department of psychiatry at UCLA, many studies "have shown convincingly that [on standard tests] less educated individuals tend to score much like brain-injured individuals. Education makes a significant difference in the performance of Spanish-speaking individuals on tests such as the MMSE." Even when cognitive assessment tests are written and given in Spanish, they may produce false indications of impairment. One widely used test, the Wechsler Adult Intelligence Scale–Revised (WAIS–R) was translated in the mid-1960s with the help of Puerto Rican Spanish speakers. Drs. Taussig and Ponton contend that it is of dubious value in testing elderly Spanish speakers from Mexico or Central America almost forty years later, especially if they are fairly recent immigrants. (As this book goes to press, the WAIS is being revised to increase its applicability to Spanish speakers from Mexico or Central America.)

The situation is similar for elderly Asians and probably applies to poorly educated whites as well.

POOR LINGUISTIC AND WRITING ABILITY

In 1996, University of Kentucky researchers suggested that analysis of people's writing ability during their twenties could accurately predict their development of Alzheimer's sixty years later. A team led by David Snowdon, whose work has been mentioned previously in this chapter, studied ninety-three nuns who joined the Sisters of Notre Dame in the 1920s. As part of their preparation, each wrote an autobiography, which the order archived. Sixty years later, by the 1980s, almost one-third of the nuns, by then in their eighties, had been diagnosed with Alzheimer's disease. Fourteen had died, and the researchers performed brain autopsies to look for the characteristic abnormalities of Alzheimer's. Five autopsies showed signs of the disease.

The researchers then went back to the deceased nuns' archived autobiographies to see if they might offer clues to their later development of Alzheimer's. Without knowing who had written which essays, the researchers evaluated them for two aspects of language ability—grammatical complexity and idea richness. The scientists judged nine of the autobiographies to be grammatically complex and intellectually rich. They considered the other five to be idea-poor and grammatically simple. Finally, they linked each of the nuns to her autobiography. None of the nine whose writing was idea-dense and grammatically complex had developed Alzheimer's, but all of those whose work was idea-poor and grammatically simple had succumbed. The researchers suggested that young-adult writing samples might predict later development of Alzheimer's with up to 90 percent accuracy. They wrote: "Our findings indicate that low linguistic ability early in life is a potent marker . . . of Alzheimer's disease risk late in life."

Other researchers have raised serious doubts about this study, questioning the evaluation criteria. While grammar can be assessed objectively using standardized tests of sentence structure, assessment of grammatical simplicity or idea density, which the Snowdon team relied on heavily, is a much more subjective criterion.

In addition, critics have judged the study's sample size—just five nuns out of ninety-three with autopsy-confirmed Alzheimer's disease—too small to determine anything conclusively.

It is possible that language ability during young adulthood may have something to do with developing Alzheimer's later in life, but more conclusive research must be done.

A HISTORY OF SEIZURES

Seizures are caused by electrical problems in the brain. Because Alzheimer's disease also affects the brain, researchers have wondered if the two might somehow be connected.

Researchers at the Mayo Clinic in Rochester, Minnesota, compared 145 people suffering various forms of dementia with 290 similar people, age fifty-five and older, who were cognitively normal for their age. Compared with the controls, the people with Alzheimer's were six times more likely to have suffered seizures as adults, and those with other forms of dementia were eight times more likely to have had at least one seizure.

This is a provocative finding, but it has yet to be replicated, so it must be viewed with caution.

HEAD CIRCUMFERENCE

According to a study by researchers at Columbia University in New York, people with statistically small heads have a greater risk of Alzheimer's. They measured head circumference of 649 residents of Manhattan who were participants in the North Manhattan Aging Project, and then correlated those measurements with their cognitive abilities, while controlling for potentially confounding factors: height, weight, ethnicity, education, and APOE allele status.

For both men and women, those whose head circumference was smallest had the greatest risk of Alzheimer's disease. Compared with women who had the largest heads, women with the smallest heads had 2.9 times the risk. Men with the smallest heads had 2.3 times the risk.

A few other studies have suggested that as head size increases, Alzheimer's risk decreases. Why would head size relate to Alzheimer's risk? Because in general, people with larger heads have larger brains. A larger brain might protect against Alzheimer's in any of several ways. The leading theory is that people with large brains have more brain tissue in reserve, so that the changes of Alzheimer's disease don't manifest as quickly or as severely. It's also possible that a small brain might reflect a genetic predisposition to the disease or result from exposure to environmental factors that increase risk.

At this writing, the role of head size in Alzheimer's risk, if any, remains controversial.

EXPOSURE TO LARGE AMOUNTS OF ZINC

To date, research on the effect of zinc, an essential trace mineral and an antioxidant, has been confusing and inconclusive. In a test-tube study, Australian researchers discovered that an unusually large intake of zinc promotes changes in brain cells similar to the senile plaques of Alzheimer's disease. The study showed that beta-amyloid, which is a protein found in soluble form in the healthy brain, forms plaque-like clumps around zinc at concentrations only slightly higher than those typical of the normal brain.

The authors based their work on earlier trials in which people with Alzheimer's disease were given zinc supplements and appeared to show accelerated cognitive deterioration.

Recently, however, a good deal of research has shown that a diet high in antioxidants, like zinc, helps *prevent* Alzheimer's (see "Deficiency of Antioxidant Nutrients" earlier in this chapter). Indeed, other research has shown that Alzheimer's disease may well be linked to a zinc *deficiency.*

Clearly, additional research is needed to determine what role, if any, zinc plays in the risk—or prevention—of Alzheimer's.

CHLAMYDIA INFECTION

Infection with a common bacteria, *Chlamydia pneumoniae*, may increase the risk of Alzheimer's, according to researchers at Johns Hopkins University. During brain autopsies, they found the bacteria in seventeen of nineteen Alzheimer's sufferers, but in only one of nineteen similar people who had died of other diseases. In those who had Alzheimer's, chlamydia infection was most likely to affect regions of their brains that also showed the characteristic abnormalities of the disease.

Chlamydia pneumoniae causes sinus infection, bronchitis, and other upper respiratory ailments. These infections can be treated with antibiotics. Chlamydia can also enter the brain and might conceivably play a role in triggering the inflammation that contributes to Alzheimer's.

However, research focusing on the possible chlamydia-Alzheimer's connection is in its infancy. It remains unclear whether the purported link is real and, if so, whether the infection is a cause or a result of Alzheimer's.

EXPOSURE TO ALUMINUM

Aluminum is unusually abundant in the neurofibrillary tangles of Alzheimer's disease. During the 1980s, rumors circulated that aluminum cookware contributed to the disease. Most scientists scoffed at this, because aluminum is one of the most abundant elements on earth. Everyone is exposed to a great deal of it, but very little enters the bloodstream through the digestive tract.

In 1989, a study in the British medical journal *The Lancet* showed a significant increase in Alzheimer's risk among people whose drinking water contains more than 11 micrograms of aluminum per liter. Since then, about a dozen studies have explored the aluminum/Alzheimer's question, with results all over the map. Some show an increased risk from drinking water that contains aluminum. But a 1996 study by University of Toronto researchers suggests that water must contain at least 100 micrograms of aluminum—nine times what the earlier British study found—to increase risk significantly. Other studies show no link between Alzheimer's and aluminum in drinking water at any concentration.

Some studies show that aluminum by itself does not increase risk of Alzheimer's, because so little is absorbed in the digestive tract. One study suggests that aluminum in acidic solutions—for example, aluminum that enters soft drinks from the cans—is more readily absorbed, and may increase risk. Meanwhile, some studies show that consumption of other minerals, notably silicon and calcium, protect the brain from any toxicity caused by aluminum.

None of these studies can be considered definitive. There is no scientific consensus on the role of aluminum, if any, in Alzheimer's risk, and the connection remains extremely controversial.

If you're worried about the possibility that aluminum exposure may increase the risk of Alzheimer's, you might limit your consumption of soft drinks from aluminum cans. You might also have your water tested. For about $100, the National Testing Laboratory of Cleveland will conduct a seventy-four-item test of water quality and check for aluminum content. The lab sends you sampling test tubes, which you fill with your water and send to the lab in a Styrofoam-lined box. About a week later, the lab sends you a report on what's in your water, detailing the aluminum content, among other things. For more information, call 1-800-458-3330.

6.

The Diagnostic Dilemma

Is It Really Alzheimer's?

Ideally, there would be a quick, simple, reliable, inexpensive, non-invasive test that could diagnose Alzheimer's disease very early, well before affected individuals suffered significant cognitive decline. Early definitive diagnosis would allow them—and their loved ones—the time to prepare for and adjust to the life changes the disease brings.

Unfortunately, no such test currently exists. Alzheimer's cannot be diagnosed with certainty until a brain autopsy after the person's death reveals the disease's characteristic neurofibrillary tangles and senile plaques. While people are still living, Alzheimer's diagnosis involves a judgment call, and physicians who do not specialize in Alzheimer's make more diagnostic errors than those who specialize in the disease.

Fortunately, the specialists' judgment has become fairly sophisticated. On average, according to neurologist Robert Friedland, M.D., chief of the laboratory of neurogeriatrics at Case Western Reserve University School of Medicine in Cleveland, experienced clinicians diagnose Alzheimer's with about 90 percent accuracy. In a 1996 study, researchers performed brain autopsies on 220 people who, while living, had been diagnosed with Alzheimer's based on clinical assessments. On autopsy, 88 percent had the brain abnormalities of the disease, while 12 percent of those diagnosed with Alzheimer's *did not* have it.

Alzheimer's diagnosis, therefore, is part science, part skill and experience, leaving enough room for uncertainty to make a difficult situation all the more distressing. That's why anyone interested in Alzheimer's disease should understand how it is diagnosed, the limits of current diagnostics, and the emerging new tests that may increase diagnostic accuracy.

Several sets of criteria have been developed to diagnose the disease. The two most widely used are based on neurological and psychological assessments, and on tests that rule out other possible diseases. One comes from the American Psychiatric Association's handbook *The Diagnostic and Statistical Manual of Mental Disorders, 4th edition* (DSM-IV). The other was developed by a joint task force of the National Institute of Neurological and Communicative Disorders and Stroke, and the Alzheimer's Disease and Related Disorders Association (since 1989, the Alzheimer's Association) (NINCDS/AA).

The American Psychiatric Association's DSM-IV Criteria

The American Psychiatric Association adopted its current criteria when its DSM-IV was published in 1994. A panel of distinguished psychiatrists periodically revises *The Diagnostic and Statistical Manual of Mental Disorders.* Future editions may change these criteria. The following material has been adapted from DSM-IV with permission.

Alzheimer's disease involves the progressive decline and ultimately the loss of multiple cognitive functions, including memory, the ability to learn new information or recall previously learned information, and at least one of the following:

- Loss of word comprehension ability, for example, inability to respond appropriately to "Your daughter is on the phone." (Aphasia)

- Loss of ability to perform complex tasks involving muscle coordination, for example, bathing or dressing. (Apraxia)
- Loss of ability to recognize and use familiar objects, for example, clothing. (Agnosia)
- Loss of ability to plan, organize, and carry out normal activities, for example, shopping.

For a diagnosis of Alzheimer's, the person's cognitive impairment must begin slowly and gradually, become more severe, represent substantial deterioration of previous abilities, and cause significant problems in daily functioning.

The person's problems must *not* be due to stroke; depression; Parkinson's disease; hypothyroidism; HIV infection; syphilis; brain tumor; delirium; schizophrenia; Huntington's chorea; deficiencies in niacin, vitamin B_{12}, and folic acid; or some other physical or mental illness.

The National Institute of Neurological and Communicative Disorders and Stroke, and the Alzheimer's Association (NINCDS/AA)

A joint task force of these two organizations developed the following criteria for diagnosis of *probable* Alzheimer's disease in 1984:

Dementia must be established by clinical examination and documented by a standard test of cognitive function (e.g., Mini-Mental State Examination, Blessed Dementia Scale, etc.) and confirmed by neuropsychological tests. In addition, the person must show:

- Significant deficiencies in two or more areas of cognition, for example, word comprehension and task-completion ability.
- Progressive deterioration of memory and other cognitive functions.
- No loss of consciousness.

- Onset from age forty to ninety, typically after sixty-five.
- No other diseases or disorders that could account for the loss of memory and cognition.

The following factors support a diagnosis of probable Alzheimer's:

- Progressive deterioration of specific cognitive functions: language (aphasia), motor skills (apraxia), and perception (agnosia).
- Impaired activities of daily living and altered patterns of behavior.
- A family history of similar problems, particularly if confirmed by neurological testing.
- A normal electroencephalogram (EEG) test of brain activity.
- Evidence of cerebral atrophy in CT scans.
- Normal cerebrospinal fluid, the fluid that surrounds the brain and spinal cord, determined by a lumbar puncture (spinal tap).

These features are also consistent with Alzheimer's disease:

- Plateaus in the course of the progression of the illness.
- CT findings normal for the person's age.
- Associated symptoms, including depression; insomnia; delusions; incontinence; hallucinations; weight loss; sexual problems; and significant verbal, emotional, and physical outbursts.
- Other neurological abnormalities, especially in advanced disease, for example, a shuffling gait.

On the other hand, the following features decrease the likelihood of Alzheimer's disease:

- Sudden onset.
- Such early symptoms as seizures, gait problems, and loss of vision and coordination.

The Quick Screening Test

If a person has memory and behavior problems that raise suspicions of Alzheimer's, it's expensive and time-consuming to administer all the tests that might lead to a diagnosis. In an effort to separate people with normal, age-related memory lapses from those who need to be carefully evaluated for Alzheimer's disease, Paul R. Solomon, Ph.D., codirector of the Memory Clinic at Southwestern Vermont Medical Center in Bennington, recently developed a quick screening test. In just seven minutes, the test allows family physicians to determine if a person should be referred for a full Alzheimer's workup. Recently, Dr. Solomon gave his test to 120 elderly persons, half of whom exhibited some signs of memory problems. It was more than 90 percent accurate in distinguishing those with normal memory problems from those with Alzheimer's. But Solomon insists that the test does not diagnose Alzheimer's. It simply identifies those who should be evaluated more extensively.

The seven-minute screening test has four components:

- Cued recall. The person briefly views four flash cards, each containing a picture of a common object. A minute or two later, the person is asked to recall the cards. Elderly people with normal memory lapses make few mistakes, and, if they do, they recall the objects when given hints. People with early Alzheimer's make more errors, and hints don't help them.
- Orientation to time. The person is asked to state the year, month, day, and time of day. People with normal memory loss may get mixed up about the time or day. People with early Alzheimer's often miss the month or year.
- Clock drawing. The person is given a blank sheet of paper and asked to draw a clock face with the hands showing 3:40. People with normal memory lapses rarely have much trouble with this exercise. Those with early Alzheimer's often have trouble positioning the numbers around the clock face, and they frequently misplace the hands.

- Verbal fluency. The person is given a category, for example, animals, and is asked to list as many items in it as possible in one minute. People with normal memory loss compile considerable lists. People with Alzheimer's come up with only a few.

In addition to the qualitative differences mentioned here, each component of the test can be scored numerically for greater accuracy.

Medical professionals can obtain the test, along with an instruction booklet and training video, by contacting Dr. Solomon's clinic.

Complete Clinical Assessment

If screening suggests that a person needs more extensive testing, a doctor—sometimes the affected individual's family physician, sometimes a psychiatrist or neurologist—begins with a complete clinical assessment. The doctor asks the affected individual and family members or close friends to describe why suspicions of a problem developed and how the person functions compared with past performance.

Next comes a thorough medical history to see if the observed problems might be caused by something else, for example, stroke, depression, exposure to toxic substances that can cause neurological damage, among them, lead or drug side effects.

A surprisingly large number of common medications may cause side effects that suggest Alzheimer's. These medications include antihistamines, decongestants, tranquilizers, antidepressants, anticonvulsives, steroids, narcotics, ulcer drugs, high blood pressure medication, and some antibiotics.

Part of a complete clinical assessment involves standard laboratory tests:

- A complete blood count (CBC) to check for vitamin deficiencies and lead poisoning.
- A blood chemistry panel to check for kidney failure and thyroid problems.
- Tests for syphilis and HIV infection.

- Possibly a lumbar puncture to obtain cerebrospinal fluid, which can diagnose meningitis and encephalitis.
- An electroencephalogram to check for Creutzfeldt-Jakob disease.
- A CT scan or MRI to look for brain tumors, stroke, and other dementing brain conditions.

After other possible diagnoses have been ruled out, the doctor interviews the person's loved ones to assess the degree of cognitive decline. Interviews differ. The following questions come from a recent study that correlated well with other diagnostic evaluations for Alzheimer's:

- What was the first problem you noticed?
- When did you first notice this?
- Once it started, was the problem always present, or was it intermittent?
- Have you ever noticed memory problems? If so, when did you first notice them? And once they started, were the problems always present, or were they intermittent?
- Have you ever noticed performance problems? If so . . .
- Have you ever noticed language problems? If so . . .
- Have you ever noticed trouble knowing the date? If so . . .
- Have you ever noticed personality changes? If so . . .
- Have you ever noticed depression? If so . . .
- Have you ever noticed behavior problems? If so . . .
- Have you ever noticed hallucinations, delusion, or paranoia? If so . . .

Next comes an interview with the affected individual to assess cognitive competence. The doctor might test recent and long-term memory by asking:

- What day is it today?
- Who are the president, and vice president, and who is the governor of your state?
- When was the Vietnam War?

- When was World War II?
- When were you married?

Recall tests are also popular. The doctor lists familiar objects—a pen, a quarter, a shoe, a scarf—and then asks the person to repeat them. The doctor asks for the list again five minutes later.

Other questions might involve calculation: Start at one hundred and subtract seven serially. Or judgment: What would you do if you found a stamped, addressed, sealed letter on the sidewalk by a mailbox? Cognitively normal people typically say, "Someone must have dropped it. I would mail it." People with Alzheimer's might say, "I don't know," or "Open it," or "Throw it away."

Following an informal cognitive-function test, most specialists administer a standardized test, for example, the Mini-Mental State Examination (MMSE). This brief, eleven-question test developed in 1965 asks a variety of questions—the year, season, date, day, month; the person's state, county, and town of residence—and gives a list-repetition exercise; a serial subtraction exercise; and simple writing, copying, and task-completion exercises. The person gets points for correct answers, and on the basis of thousands of scores over thirty years of using this test, relative level of mental competence or dementia can be estimated.

If a complete clinical assessment points to probable Alzheimer's disease, you might want to have some of the tests repeated after a while to confirm whether the disease is spreading as Alzheimer's typically does.

Important Note #1: Depression can be mistaken for Alzheimer's disease or coexist with it. A complete clinical assessment should carefully evaluate the person for depression. (For more on depression and dementia, see chapter 9.)

Important Note #2: If the person being tested is not a high-school graduate or is a member of a racial or ethnic minority group, the MMSE may indicate dementia when in fact the individual is cognitively normal (see the discussion about education in chapter 5). Recently, a group of researchers under the direction of Malcolm Dick, Ph.D., of the Alzheimer's Disease Research Center at the University of California at Irvine, modified the MMSE to eliminate its cultural biases. The result is the Cognitive Abilities Screening Instrument (CASI), a family of tests now available in six languages: English, Spanish, Chinese, Japanese, Vietnamese, and Korean. It does not solve all the problems inherent in cross-cultural cognitive testing, but early results show that it is as good as, or better than, the MMSE for screening Asian-Americans. To obtain the CASI, specify the language you need and send a check or money order for $20 payable to the University of California Regents. Send your order to Malcolm Dick, Ph.D., Alzheimer's Disease Research Center, Institute for Brain Aging and Dementia, Medical Plaza Building, Room 1100, University of California at Irvine, Irvine, CA 92697-4285.

Genetic Testing

Rare family clusters of Alzheimer's share specific genetic mutations. Even without these mutations, people with a twin who has the disease are at high risk, and those with other close relatives who have Alzheimer's are at somewhat increased risk. These observations show that genetic makeup plays a role in the disease (chapter 5).

Recently, researchers have focused tremendous interest on a gene located on chromosome 19 that codes for apolipoprotein E (APOE), a protein involved in cholesterol metabolism. Its six possible natural variations (alleles) correlate intriguingly but imperfectly with Alzheimer's. APOE allele testing is not terribly expensive, but the test is nowhere near predictive enough to justify mass screening. However, several recent studies show that in people with suspected Alzheimer's, this gene's allele pattern correlates fairly well with Alzheimer's risk and can help make a diagnosis.

Allen Roses, M.D., the Jefferson-Pilot Corporation professor of neurology and director of the Joseph and Kathleen Bryan Alzheimer's Disease Research Center at Duke University School of Medicine, says that when people with strongly suspected Alzheimer's have at least one copy of APOE allele 4, subsequent brain autopsies show that 97 percent of them have the disease, a considerable improvement in diagnostic accuracy over clinical assessment alone. (For more on the APOE gene and Alzheimer's risk, see chapter 5.)

AD7C

In late 1996, a small biotechnology company, Nymox Pharmaceutical, of Rockville, Maryland, began marketing a test for Alzheimer's disease with ads in decidedly nonmedical publications, such as *The Wall Street Journal* and *TV Guide*. The ads made a bold claim: "Alzheimer's: Now You Can Rule It Out. Introducing AD7C, the first test proven to help physicians be certain in the diagnosis of Alzheimer's disease."

The test and ad campaign stirred a controversy. Many Alzheimer's experts criticized Nymox for (1) releasing the test before it had been more extensively tested, (2) advertising in consumer publications, a scientific faux pas, and (3) overselling the test in its ads. Meanwhile, mounting evidence suggests that the AD7C test has considerable value.

Back in 1992, Suzanne de la Monte, M.D., and colleagues at the Alzheimer's Disease and Cancer Research Centers at Harvard-affiliated Massachusetts General Hospital discovered that a specific protein (21 kD neural thread protein, or NTP) appears in cerebrospinal fluid (CSF) very early in Alzheimer's disease, and that its level increases as the disease progresses. Nymox turned this discovery into its AD7C test.

In an early clinical trial at the University of Minnesota, the test distinguished with substantial accuracy between those who did and those who did not have early Alzheimer's. Compared with age-matched controls who were cognitively normal, 121 brains with autopsy-confirmed Alzheimer's had AD7C levels up to ten times higher. In 87 percent of the brains with autopsy-confirmed Alzheimer's, 21 kD NTP levels were higher than 3 nanograms per milliliter of CSF, while in the controls, only about 5 percent had levels that high. The Food and Drug Administration liked those results and approved the test. Soon after, Nymox launched its advertising campaign.

Skeptical Alzheimer's experts charged that the test was marketed prematurely, before larger studies had confirmed the early trial. In addition, critics said, even if the test distinguishes between people with Alzheimer's and those who are cognitively normal, it remains unclear if it can distinguish between Alzheimer's and other dementing ill-nesses. The AD7C test needs to be evaluated in large-scale studies, but that has not deterred Nymox from introducing a urine test it claims is as accurate as its AD7C test, only simpler and less expensive.

MRI, PET Scans, SPECT Scans

Three other potential tests for Alzheimer's disease involve brain-imaging technologies: magnetic resonance imaging (MRI), positron emission tomography (PET), and single photon emission computed tomography (SPECT).

MRI provides images of the body's soft tissues, for example, the brain. Over the past few years, Dr. Mony de Leon, a professor of psy-chiatry and director of the Neuroimaging Research Laboratory at New York University Medical Center, has used MRI scans to inves-tigate brain changes caused by Alzheimer's, particularly in its early stages. He has discovered that in 100 percent of those with severe Alzheimer's, the brain's hippocampus region, a memory-learning center, is unusually shrunken. In those with early Alzheimer's, about 80 percent show hippocampal shrinkage. In contrast, only a small mi-nority of normal elderly people show similar shrinkage—and they are at high risk for developing Alzheimer's.

In early 1999, de Leon used MRI scans to discover an even more intriguing anatomical change—significant shrinkage of another key memory center—the entorhinal cortex. The researchers autopsied the brains of people who had died with or without Alzheimer's. The entorhinal cortexes of those with the disease were 45 percent smaller. Then the researchers tested healthy volunteers and people with very early Alzheimer's. The entorhinal cortexes of those with the disease were 27 percent smaller. Moreover, the damage to the entorhinal cor-tex was greater than damage to the hippocampus, and it proved a more reliable disease marker. This work needs to be corroborated, but if confirmed, entorhinal cortex MRI may help diagnose early Alzheimer's—possibly even before any memory loss occurs.

PET scans reveal regional differences around the brain in the metabolism of blood sugar, or glucose, the body's main fuel. People with early-stage Alzheimer's show unusually decreased glucose metabolism in one specific area of the brain (the posterior temporoparietal region). Unfortunately, people with atherosclerosis of the brain, the arterial narrowing that causes most strokes and the mini-strokes known as transient ischemic attacks (TIAs), also show similar impairment of glucose metabolism, so the value of PET scans in the diagnosis of Alzheimer's disease remains unclear.

In addition, PET scans are experimental and very expensive. This technology is not widely available, and where it is, health insurers do not cover it. Nonetheless, PET scan research continues. Several researchers have paired PET scans with APOE genetic evaluations in hopes that the combination might prove more definitive than either test by itself.

SPECT scans help evaluate blood flow through the brain and brain metabolism, both of which decline in Alzheimer's disease. Compared with PET scans, the information provided by SPECT scans is less precise, but these scans are considerably less expensive, so if a complete clinical assessment points to a diagnosis of Alzheimer's, and a SPECT scan shows low brain blood flow and metabolism, some clinicians consider that evidence supportive of a diagnosis of Alzheimer's.

Tau Protein and Beta-Amyloid$_{42}$

Tau and beta-amyloid$_{42}$ are proteins that appear in cerebrospinal fluid. Compared with those who have normal brain function, people with Alzheimer's have unusually high levels of tau protein (more than 420 picograms/ml) and unusually low levels of beta-amyloid$_{42}$ (less than 1,240 picogram/ml; see chapter 3).

These markers have become the basis for a new test for Alzheimer's disease, ADmark Assays, from Athena Neurosciences of South San Francisco, California. The company claims that in people over sixty years of age, the two-protein test can diagnose or rule out Alzheimer's disease with up to 95 percent accuracy.

Experts caution, however, that the test is not definitively diagnostic and that, despite the manufacturer's claims, it has not been used long enough to have a compelling track record. Nonetheless, it is a potentially exciting development in Alzheimer's disease testing.

Free-Radical Activity

In late 1998, researchers at the University of Pennylvania Medical Center announced that it might be possible to diagnose Alzheimer's—or confirm a diagnosis—based on free-radical activity in the person's cerebrospinal fluid (CSF) the fluid surrounding the brain and spinal cord.

Garret A. FitzGerald, M.D., chairman of the department of pharmacology, and colleagues performed autopsies on people who had died with or without Alzheimer's. Those with Alzheimer's showed double the cell-damaging free-radical activity in their memory and cognitive-function centers. This finding confirms free radicals as a risk factor for Alzheimer's (chapter 5). In addition, the researchers also discovered that those with Alzheimer's showed clear evidence of abnormally high free-radical activity in their cerebrospinal fluid. CSF is fairly accessible through a spinal tap (lumbar puncture). Testing it for free-radical activity may one day help diagnose Alzheimer's.

Pupil Dilation

In 1994, during routine eye exams, ophthalmologists noticed that the pupils of people with Alzheimer's disease seemed to open (dilate) unusually quickly in response to a certain compound called tropicamide. In one study, tropicamide had no effect on the pupils of thirty out of thirty-two people who were free of Alzheimer's, but it dilated the pupils of eighteen out of nineteen with the disease. The effect was equally clear in people with mild and severe Alzheimer's disease.

The possibility that a simple, noninvasive eye test might diagnose

Alzheimer's generated considerable excitement among Alzheimer's researchers, but since then, eighteen studies have tested the diagnostic value of tropicamide eyedrops. Not one has shown the drops to have any value, and it appears that the original study was a fluke.

To Tell or Not to Tell?

Fifty years ago, Americans with cancer or other serious diseases were often not informed of their diagnoses because their physicians and family members feared that the news would unduly upset them. That is still the policy today in some families, and in some cultures around the world, like Japan, for example.

In contemporary America, however, the pendulum has largely swung the other way, toward full disclosure. American physicians and most of the public believe that people have a right to know about their medical condition, even if the news is bad. Knowledge allows time to plan for the future, whatever it may bring, and if an illness is terminal, full disclosure allows time to say goodbye.

The culture of full disclosure seems to be here to stay, but friends and family should still be sensitive to the significant minority of people who *don't want to know.* A University of Virginia study suggests that some people would rather not be told of an Alzheimer's diagnosis.

The researchers surveyed 156 healthy residents of a Virginia retirement community, average age seventy-nine. They were given two vignettes to read—one describing a medical workup leading to a diagnosis of cancer, the other describing a workup leading to a diagnosis of Alzheimer's. Then they completed a questionnaire that asked what they knew about cancer and Alzheimer's, if they knew anyone with these diseases, if they would want to be informed of such a diagnosis themselves, and if they would want their spouse informed if the spouse were diagnosed.

Ninety-two percent said they would want to be told they had cancer. But only 80 percent said they would want to be informed about an Alzheimer's diagnosis.

The disparity was even more pronounced with regard to spouses. If the spouse had cancer, 80 percent said they thought the person should be told. But if the spouse developed Alzheimer's, only 65 percent said they would want their spouse to know.

A majority of this survey group wanted to be informed and wanted their spouse informed, but some felt differently. What should a family member do? Alzheimer's expert William Haley, Ph.D., a professor of psychology and director of the Gerontology Center at the University of South Florida in Tampa, advises, "Answer all questions truthfully, but don't hit people over the head and force them to hear things they don't want to know. Most people with Alzheimer's want their questions answered but are not interested in all the details."

Use your judgment. If you have any doubts about what to do, consult the diagnosing physician, a clinical social worker, or a member of the clergy.

7.

Coping with Alzheimer's Disease: The Experts' Ten-Step Program

A diagnosis of Alzheimer's disease brings dramatic life changes for the affected individual and the person's family and friends. The news often leaves everyone in shock and may send some into emotional tailspins that become serious depression. Suddenly there are so many issues to consider, so many changes to anticipate. The implications are staggering, and not surprisingly, most people touched by this illness initially feel overwhelmed, which is perfectly natural—for a while.

But after you've processed the initial shock, it's time to get organized. Dealing with the disease step-by-step cannot eliminate the trauma and heartache, but it can help assert some control over the situation. This is the first step toward successful coping.

Every Alzheimer's sufferer is unique, as is every family's reaction, but the disease raises many common issues that everyone must face. The rest of this book deals with those challenges. The nation's Alzheimer's experts offer many valuable suggestions that we have distilled into a 10-step program:

STEP 1. BE CONFIDENT OF THE DIAGNOSIS

Today, Alzheimer's disease can be diagnosed definitively only on autopsy, after the person's death. In the living, diagnostic accuracy varies considerably. At specialized Alzheimer's centers, experts diagnose the disease accurately in about 90 percent of cases. Nonspecialist physicians are less accurate (chapter 6), which makes evaluation by an Alzheimer's expert imperative.

Still, even the specialists make mistakes. Some people diagnosed with Alzheimer's *don't have it.* Instead they may have one or more other conditions that can be treated, for example, a combination of depression, alcohol abuse, nutrient deficiencies, sleep disturbances, and medication side effects, which can mimic the symptons of Alzheimer's (chapter 9).

A physician should rule out other causes of dementia before making an Alzheimer's diagnosis. The person's family doctor may not be an expert in dementing illnesses. In addition, people with memory loss may not be entirely honest about certain aspects of their lives (alcohol abuse, poor eating and sleeping habits, etc.) and keep them hidden from their loved ones.

When having a family member evaluated for possible Alzheimer's disease, consult a physician experienced in diagnosing it. If you have any doubts, get a second expert opinion. To find doctors who specialize in diagnosing dementing illnesses, ask your family doctor for a referral or obtain one from the Alzheimer's Association affiliate or the federal Alzheimer's disease research center nearest you (appendix I).

STEP 2. BE REALISTIC

Short of a medical miracle, Alzheimer's follows a relentlessly downward course. Current treatments can slow its progression, but they neither halt nor reverse it. Those with the disease slowly lose their memories, their judgment and reasoning faculties, and their ability to take care of themselves (chapter 3). Lost memories and skills do not return. Over time, the person requires more and more care. Behavior problems usually develop. As the disease becomes severe, the person may need to move to residential care.

It's horrible to contemplate a loved one descending into the mysterious abyss of Alzheimer's, but it's even worse to deny the course of the illness. Learn what's in store for the person—and for you, if you're the caregiver. Understand what to expect. The person's journey—and your caregiving experience—will be easier if you face the illness realistically.

STEP 3. ENJOY ANY PLEASANT SURPRISES

Alzheimer's is a terrible affliction, but it's not entirely grim. The disease may bring some pleasant surprises. It makes some people more likeable. Old resentments and irritating personality traits sometimes disappear, replaced by affection, tenderness, acceptance, and good humor. Of course, any personality changes, including improvements, can be disconcerting. Even if you never cared for your mother's sharp, judgmental tongue, or your father's temper, it can be unnerving to see these traits fade away as the person changes. But perhaps those new, more pleasant traits were always there, hidden deep within the person but never revealed until Alzheimer's inexplicably liberated them. Many of the changes Alzheimer's brings are heartrending. Try to appreciate any pleasant surprises along the way.

STEP 4. TREAT EVERYTHING

The more researchers learn about Alzheimer's disease, the more they understand that few people have "pure" Alzheimer's. Most have mixed dementia—Alzheimer's plus other conditions: depression, heart disease, stroke, mini-strokes, diabetes, nutritional deficiencies, sleep disorders, hearing and vision loss, etc. Treating these other problems does not change the course of the person's Alzheimer's, but it can lead to improvements in quality of life for both affected individuals and their caregivers (chapters 9 and 10).

STEP 5. COMBINE MEDICATION WITH PSYCHOLOGICAL AND COMPLEMENTARY THERAPIES

New drugs get most of the publicity, but other therapies also slow the progression of Alzheimer's and improve quality of life. Consider a support group, cognitive-behavioral therapy, behavior modification, antioxidant vitamin therapy, herbal medicine (ginkgo), exercise, massage, pet therapy, music therapy, and aromatherapy. A great deal of research shows that these approaches have real benefits (chapter 10).

STEP 6. ASSEMBLE AN EXTENSIVE SUPPORT NETWORK

You cannot care for a person with Alzheimer's disease by yourself. This bears repeating: *You cannot care for a person with Alzheimer's by yourself.* You need help—and lots of it.

Many people find it difficult to ask for help or to accept it. Needing assistance hurts their pride and undermines valued feelings of self-sufficiency. But some jobs are simply too big to tackle alone, and Alzheimer's care is one of them.

Your support network should include four types of helpers: family and friends, professionals, community agencies, and a support group. Family and friends can help with caregiving or take care of other chores so you can devote more time to caregiving. Neighbors can alert you if the person wanders.

Professionals include the person's attorney, financial consultants (accountant, tax preparer, investment advisor, etc.), health care providers (doctors, dentist, optometrist, etc.), and professionals experienced in dealing with dementing illnesses (geriatric psychiatrists, psychologists, and/or social workers). Seek them out. Make use of their expertise.

Finally, join a support group. The Alzheimer's Association and many community mental health agencies sponsor them, or you can start your own by posting notices in the offices of physicians who deal with Alzheimer's disease. Support groups are invaluable for Alzheimer's caregivers. There is nothing quite as comforting as talking with people who know *exactly* what you're going through (chapter 12).

STEP 7. TAKE GOOD CARE OF YOURSELF

You cannot provide good care for a person with Alzheimer's disease unless you take good care of yourself. This, too, bears repeating: *You must take good care of yourself, or you cannot care for anyone else.* Alzheimer's caregiving is one of life's most challenging occupations. Having an extensive support network is a start, but there's a great deal more to good self-care. You need time off. You deserve to have fun. You have other relationships with family and friends that require nurturing. You have hobbies and interests that help you recharge your personal batteries. It's not selfish to take time for yourself, it's an *absolute necessity* (chapter 12).

STEP 8. TAKE GOOD CARE OF THE PERSON WITH ALZHEIMER'S.

Caregiving involves much more than adult baby-sitting. Good caregiving incorporates the individual's history, personality, likes, and dislikes. It preserves the person's dignity and focuses on remaining abilities, rather than on growing disabilities (chapter 13).

STEP 9. PLAN FOR THE FUTURE EARLY

When a loved one is newly diagnosed with Alzheimer's disease, the first thing that comes to mind is probably not a durable power of attorney that allows you to make financial, housing, and medical decisions when the person becomes incapacitated several years down the road, but the sooner you begin planning for the future the better. Cataloging the person's financial assets early on can save tremendous time and heartache later. Ditto for having dentures replaced with permanent dental implants that are easier to care for, and investigating residential care facilities—the best ones often have long waiting lists, so it pays to sign up well in advance of the time your loved one might need twenty-four-hour care (chapters 13 and 14).

STEP 10. STAY INFORMED

The news media have not kept the public well informed about Alzheimer's disease. Reports of its biology, risk factors, diagnosis, and the issues involved in caregiving have been scant and disjointed. Almost all treatment news focuses on medications. Psychological and complementary therapies have been underreported and in many cases ignored. If you have access to the World Wide Web, you can stay abreast of Alzheimer's news by visiting Alzheimers.com, the world's most comprehensive English language source of information on all aspects of Alzheimer's.

8.

"Poor Tyrone"

Profile of Sandra and Tyrone Worthington

Some marriages are made in heaven. Sandra and Tyrone Worthington's was made in church, the Rock of Salvation Baptist church in Denver. "I noticed him when he first started attending on Sundays," Sandra, now sixty-eight, recalls. "He was jovial and easy to talk to, and he loved the choir, loved gospel music."

Sandra and Tyrone didn't have much to do with each other for several months, but then their congregation's minister began espousing some opinions that alienated much of the congregation. He left in a huff, taking about a third of the members with him. The loss of his leadership and the lost donations of those who followed him threatened the congregation's survival. The remaining members, including Sandra and Tyrone, banded together to deal with the crisis. They found a new minister, recruited new members, and solidified the church's finances. Sandra and Tyrone worked together closely, and it didn't take long for their relationship to become romantic. The year was 1979. At the time, Sandra was forty-eight, Tyrone, sixty.

Tyrone grew up outside of Jasper, a rural town of eight thousand in the hill country of east Texas near the Louisiana border and about seventy miles north of Beaumont. From an early age, he had a flair for mechanical things and loved to fix bicycles, and then cars. For a young African-American man who came of age during the Depression, however, rural Texas did not offer much opportunity, so Tyrone joined the Army Air Force, became an aircraft mechanic, and served in France during World War II. After the war, when the Air Force became its own branch of the military, he opted for the new service, and maintained aircraft at bases in Japan, California, and Ohio.

Despite his globetrotting, Tyrone remained close to his family back in Jasper and visited often. While he was in the service, he married, had two daughters, and got divorced. His daughters wound up in New Orleans.

Tyrone spent his final years in the service at Peterson Air Force Base in Colorado Springs, about fifty miles from Denver. During the 1970s, while stationed there, he bought a house in Denver, which had a larger black community than Colorado Springs. He grew to like the Mile High City, became a Broncos fan, made some good friends, and eventually joined Sandra's church. His house was only a few blocks from hers.

Sandra had grown up in Denver as an only child. She married, had four children, then she, too, divorced. She worked for the phone company until her kids left home, then suffered a back injury and retired on disability. None of her children stayed in Colorado, so she put most of her energy into the church.

After things settled down at church, Sandra and Tyrone spent much of their time together. Within a year, they were planning to marry. "Back when we were courting, Tyrone was a wonderful person," Sandra recalls. "Very jovial, always telling jokes. He was congenial, very easygoing and easy to talk to. He also flirted a great deal with the ladies, but that didn't bother me. It never went beyond flirting, and he was always very attentive to me. He was also generous, always sending money to his family back in Texas. We both liked movies, and gospel music, and taking care of our homes, and he was very handy in the kitchen. Cooking was a hobby of his. After we got married, I made most of the meals, but every so often he'd surprise me with a special dinner or a fancy dessert. I really liked that."

There was just one problem. After he retired, Tyrone yearned to return to Jasper, but Sandra didn't want to go. "I'd lived in Denver my whole life. I was a city person. I had no interest in moving away, especially to Jasper, Texas, a little country town where I didn't know a soul." But love changed her mind.

In 1980, Tyrone sold his house in Denver and bought one north of Jasper near the huge Sam Rayburn Reservoir. Sandra kept her home in Denver but closed it up and moved to Texas with him. They were married outside Jasper, in his sister's apple orchard, and joined the church Tyrone had attended as a child. The congregation included his sister and her family, several cousins, and a half-dozen of his childhood friends.

Tyrone was delighted to be back home in Texas with his new bride, but the transition was difficult for Sandra. Compared with Denver, Jasper seemed like the end of the earth. They lived far out in the country and had to drive to visit their nearest neighbors, who weren't very friendly. There were only a few black families in their immediate vicinity. Sandra had neither friends nor family in the area, just Tyrone, and as they settled into their new home, she began noticing odd quirks in his behavior.

"He began talking to himself," Sandra recalls. "I'd say, 'Who are you talking to? You talking to me?' And he'd say, 'No, I'm just muttering.'" Sandra didn't think much of her husband's muttering. It was harmless, after all, and she was still getting to know him.

But as time passed, Tyrone's muttering evolved into swearing, first under his breath, and then out loud: "Goddamn this. Goddamn that." Sandra felt offended that he was taking the Lord's name in vain, and asked him why he talked that way. He dismissed her concerns. "I'm just talking. It doesn't mean anything."

At the same time, Tyrone's posture and gait slowly changed from the tall, proud, striding military man to someone who began to stoop over and walk with a tentative, shuffling gait. Tyrone also began having trouble with his balance.

"When he sat in a chair, he'd lean to one side and not be able to get himself back upright," Sandra recalls. "Sometimes he'd slip right out of his chair, and I'd find him on the floor looking embarrassed, confused, and helpless. Now and then, while working in the yard, he'd fall down. One time he came inside with a bloody lip from a fall."

Meanwhile, Tyrone's swearing continued, especially when he was in the shower. "Why are you cursing?" Sandra asked.

"I just don't like this goddamned water," Tyrone replied. "I hate water."

The remark struck Sandra as bizarre. She knew Tyrone didn't hate water. On the contrary, he'd always showered at least once a day, and he'd been a regular at the Peterson Air Force Base swimming pool. "Looking back now," Sandra says, "I guess showering was one of the first things he realized he couldn't handle, and it bothered him."

Fortunately, Tyrone's foul-mouthed outbursts were brief. "He'd swear, and then it was over, and he'd go back to being the jovial, easygoing man I knew. I wondered about him, but usually he seemed fine."

Then Tyrone became forgetful, especially about recent events. "He'd reminisce about his childhood in Jasper or about places he'd been in the service, and remember all sorts of detail, but then he'd forget what day it was, or when our truck needed service, or what he was supposed to buy down at the market."

Tyrone's driving also deteriorated. "He'd always been an excellent driver," Sandra recalls, "and he was very proud of that. Soon, though, I began noticing dents and scratches around our pickup truck, nothing major, just lots of little dents and scratches. When I asked Tyrone about them, he'd just say, 'Oh, it's nothing. The world's full of terrible drivers.'"

Then one day, while at the grocery store, Tyrone hit another car in the parking lot. No one got hurt, but the fender-bender upset him. "He blamed the other driver," Sandra recalls.

Sandra thought about her husband's quirks from time to time but wasn't terribly concerned. She'd heard plenty of swearing in her life. Tyrone was in his mid-sixties and diabetic, so his slowing down, his shuffling walk, his balance problems, and his forgetfulness didn't alarm her. She figured he was just getting older. She knew his driving was getting clumsy, but they lived in a rural area with little traffic, and he'd never had a real accident.

But mostly what reassured Sandra was Tyrone's disposition. Except for his brief outbursts, he was the same jovial, congenial, cooperative man he'd always been. He rarely made a fuss about anything. And even at its worst, his forgetfulness didn't disrupt their lives. "His mind seemed okay to me," Sandra explains. "I'd forget things, too. I wrote off his little problems to the fact that he was twelve years older than I was."

A few years passed, and Tyrone's quirks grew worse, but they progressed so slowly that Sandra hardly noticed her husband's increasing impairment. Then, in 1992, the handyman who looked after her house in Denver said the place needed some maintenance work, and Sandra returned to Colorado to supervise. She was gone for several weeks, and when she returned to Jasper, she was struck by the extent of Tyrone's deterioration. In addition to all of his old quirks, he had developed several new ones she found particularly disturbing.

"Tyrone stopped shaving and brushing his teeth. He didn't want to change his clothes, and if he was out back and had to use the bathroom, he wouldn't walk through the house to the bathroom. Instead, he urinated in the kitchen sink."

Sandra felt distressed and very confused. Tyrone had always been so fastidious about his personal cleanliness. Was he just getting old and lazy, she wondered, or was something wrong?

When she mentioned her concerns, Tyrone just smiled in his charming way and told her he was fine, not to worry. Initially, Sandra felt reassured, but that didn't last long. Tyrone just didn't seem to care about himself anymore, or about Sandra's sensibilities around bathroom etiquette. She caught him urinating in the sink several more times, but when she asked him to stop it, he just smiled and made jokes.

Meanwhile, Tyrone's driving continued to deteriorate. Sandra became increasingly uncomfortable as a passenger. She sent him off on errands by himself, but he'd sometimes forget where he'd parked the truck. Fortunately, it was painted a distinctive yellow, and either Tyrone eventually found it or people helped him locate it.

In addition, Tyrone's forgetfulness grew more disconcerting. "It wasn't just the date or errands anymore. He started forgetting people he knew. He remembered the childhood friends he grew up with, but we'd be out shopping and run into someone we knew from church, someone he'd met since returning to Jasper, and right away, Tyrone would say that we were in a hurry and had to go. But it wasn't true. Afterward he'd turn to me and say, 'I know I should know that person, but I don't.' I'd tell him who it was, and he'd nod and look like he was making a mental note of the name, but the next time the same thing would happen all over again. He'd get frustrated, and swear, and say, 'I can't remember who anyone is.'" Sandra became quietly alarmed.

Months passed. In early 1993, Tyrone had an appointment with his doctor. Sandra decided the time had come to confront her husband's problems. "I wrote down everything that had been going on with him," Sandra recalls, "and went to the doctor with him and laid it all out."

As Sandra ran down the list of her husband's increasingly bizarre foibles, Tyrone did not interrupt her or try to stop her. Nor did he get angry. He just sat in his chair impassively. When Sandra was finished, he announced, "I'm fine, woman. Stop bothering about me."

"But I'm worried about how you're changing," Sandra replied.

Tyrone's doctor shared Sandra's concerns. Tyrone was diabetic, which meant he was at considerable risk for heart disease and stroke. Tyrone did not appear to have had a full-blown stroke, but the doctor thought that the falls Sandra had witnessed and Tyrone's other balance difficulties might have been caused by transient ischemic attacks (TIAs), momentary mini-strokes that, over time, can lead to a major stroke or cause vascular dementia (see chapter 9). The doctor recommended tests.

Sandra accompanied Tyrone to a hospital in the Beaumont area, where he spent several days having brain X rays and all sorts of other tests. Tyrone did not complain about the tests. In fact, he didn't take much notice of them. When Sandra or the doctors spoke to him, he replied with his trademark joviality. Most of the time, he just sat in a chair and stared off into the distance. "The only thing that really interested him," Sandra recalls, "was the nurses. Tyrone was always a flirt, and when a pretty nurse came around, he'd say, 'Hi, beautiful,' and try to talk to her."

Finally, Sandra and Tyrone were called into a conference room where a neurologist and a social worker awaited them. They said that Tyrone had three problems. One was his diabetes, which had caused nerve damage that gave him his shuffling gait. Another, as his family doctor had suspected, was TIAs. They seemed to be the cause of his balance problem. In addition, he also had Alzheimer's disease.

Alzheimer's? Sandra and Tyrone looked at each other quizzically. Neither had ever heard of it. The neurologist and social worker described Alzheimer's in considerable detail. The more they talked, the more distressed Sandra became. He's going to get worse and worse, she thought, with mounting dread. The doctors can't do anything to help, and I'm going to have to take care of him as he turns into Lord-knows-what.

Meanwhile, Tyrone sat impassively. Sandra wasn't even sure if he was listening until the social worker said, ". . . and because you have a dementing illness, we've had to report you to the Department of Motor Vehicles. Your driver's licence is being revoked. You can't drive anymore—"

Suddenly, Tyrone was fully alert, not angry, just determined. "You can't stop me from driving," he insisted. "If you take my license, I'll drive anyway."

"If you do," the social worker retorted, "you're risking jail."

Tyrone's jaw dropped. The specter of jail instantly deflated him. He became quiet and distant again. He didn't say another word until they were on their way back to Jasper. Sandra drove. Tyrone never got behind the wheel again.

Sandra bought a few books on Alzheimer's and read them with a growing sense of dread. They said that people with the disease needed all sorts of support services, none of which existed in the hills outside of Jasper. The closest Alzheimer's services were more than an hour's drive away. The books also said that Alzheimer's caregivers need support groups and professional counseling and that they can use all the help they can get. Again, Jasper fell short. Tyrone's family was nearby, but they made it clear that caring for him was Sandra's job, not theirs. Sandra tried to find a support group around Beaumont but couldn't, and the social workers at the hospital where Tyrone was diagnosed did not seem interested in her plight. One woman she talked to said, "Call us when he needs diapers." Nor did Tyrone's doctor offer tacrine (Cognex), the first drug to treat Alzheimer's, which had been approved shortly before his diagnosis.

At least they had a diagnosis. Sandra's reading explained a good deal about her husband's bizarre behavior. "The books helped me forgive him," she explains. "I realized that what Tyrone was doing wasn't his fault." That was especially true about his swearing. "He was usually a very easygoing man, but if he couldn't express himself or finish a sentence, or if his words came out in the wrong order and I didn't understand him, he'd get frustrated and start swearing. Before we had the diagnosis, I felt offended, but afterward, I understood that he felt abandoned by the Lord and that's why he took His name in vain."

At times when Tyrone became frustrated and swore, Sandra tried to comfort him by holding him close and repeating "Poor Tyrone" over and over again as one might to a child who'd fallen and scraped a knee. After a while, Tyrone picked up on the phrase. If he couldn't finish a sentence, he would display a strange expression—frustration and anger mixed with sheepishness and embarrassment. He would swear, and then say, "Poor Tyrone."

Sandra also realized that there was no point in trying to stop her husband's swearing or arguing with him. "I figured it was best to agree with whatever he said. I'd just do what I had to do anyway and he rarely made much of a fuss. I was fortunate that he was basically an easygoing man."

Tyrone was oddly indifferent to his diagnosis. "I'd fret over him, and he'd say, 'Ain't nothing wrong with me,' but clearly, his mind was going." Once Sandra's reading clued her in on what to expect as her husband slid deeper into Alzheimer's, the signs became very clear:

"He became more and more forgetful," Sandra recalls. "He got really bad about paying bills. I'd find them all piled up, with late notices, and threats to put a collection agency on us." Tyrone was aware that he'd become financially irresponsible, and he reacted the way many people with Alzheimer's do: he became obsessed about money. "He asked me over and over again, 'What's our balance? Do we have enough money?' And when I reassured him that we were fine, either he didn't believe me or he forgot what I said and went to the bank every day to check on our money." Sandra realized that she had to assume responsibility for paying the bills and all other financial matters. "Tyrone didn't mind. He hardly noticed. After a while, he stopped asking me about our financial affairs."

As his Alzheimer's progressed, Tyrone had increasing difficulty keeping his balance and walking. "Before the Alzheimer's," Sandra explains, "he used to take a long walk every morning. He loved those walks, but with his balance going and his stride turning into more of a shuffle, he had trouble getting around. It was sad. He started spending most of his days just sitting around the house."

Tyrone's sedentary ways were, to some extent, a blessing in disguise. "He never wandered off like so many people with Alzheimer's do." But after a while, Sandra found his moping unnerving. "I'd say, 'Let's go somewhere,' but often he didn't want to. That kept me at home because I didn't feel all that comfortable leaving him alone there."

The one outing Tyrone still enjoyed was church, but even that caused problems. "He recognized fewer and fewer people there. I'd prompt him with names, but it got awkward and embarrassing. The minister and the congregants knew he had a memory problem. Some of them were very nice about it, but others were not. That was hard for me because I was new in the area and didn't feel right telling people they were being unkind."

Then one Sunday, Tyrone lost control of his bowels in church. "That was awful," Sandra recalls. "It was very embarrassing for both of us. I had to hustle him home and clean him up. He cried and kept saying, 'Poor Tyrone.' When we went back to church the following week, one elderly lady who'd been a member since Tyrone was a boy said he shouldn't come if he couldn't control himself. I got angry and lectured her about Christian charity. That was a real low point."

What bothered Sandra most was the shroud of silence that slowly enveloped her husband. "Tyrone could still talk," she explains. "He'd answer when I asked him questions, or say 'Poor Tyrone' when something went wrong, but we stopped having conversations. That was very hard for me because I'd always enjoyed talking with him, and I didn't have many other people in the area I could talk to. I'd say, 'Tyrone, what are you thinking about?' He'd just smile or ignore me, like his mind was a million miles away. Sometimes I'd get up right in his face and say, 'Are you unhappy?' and he'd say, 'No, I'm just sitting here.'"

Little by little, Sandra became overwhelmed. She was way out in the country a thousand miles from her home, her friends, and her support community, with a husband who was deteriorating more with each passing day. She realized she needed help, and called the hospital social worker who had put her off previously. She figured Tyrone's Alzheimer's was advanced enough by now to warrant some help, but again she was met with indifference. "No one at the hospital offered me any real assistance. At first, his family and old friends and members of our church helped out some, but as Tyrone's illness got worse, all but a few of them pulled away from us."

Sandra felt depressed and isolated, alone with a husband who was not really a husband anymore. She needed support. She needed friends. She needed social services, and she knew where to get them. One day, she announced to Tyrone, "We're moving back to Denver."

Tyrone didn't want to leave Jasper. He's spent much of his adult life dreaming of returning home, and when he finally did, he loved it. Despite Tyrone's protests, Sandra insisted that Denver worked better for both of them and when she finally packed them up, he did not resist the move.

Sandra and Tyrone reoccupied her Denver home in 1994, and not a moment too soon. Shortly after their return, Tyrone began having even more difficulty taking care of himself. "He lost the ability to button shirts," Sandra recalls. "He couldn't shave, or handle socks, or tie his shoes. He stopped caring for his feet."

This was particularly ominous. Tyrone's diabetes had already damaged the nerves in his feet, affecting his ability to walk properly. Nerve damage also affects the ability to feel pain. As a result, diabetics often don't experience pain from minor foot injuries, and they ignore them. Because diabetes also impairs circulation to the feet, those injuries don't heal, and they often turn gangrenous and require amputation. Diabetes accounts for most of the nation's foot amputations. "Tyrone had always been real good about examining his feet and making sure any cuts got treated," Sandra explains, "but then he just stopped, and I had to do it."

Fortunately, true to his easygoing nature, Tyrone didn't put up a fuss when Sandra began dressing and shaving him, and checking his feet. "He appreciated it. I'd say, 'It's time for a shave,' and he'd jump into the chair like an eager little child."

In time Tyrone said less and less, and it drove Sandra crazy. "He could still talk. He still liked to flirt and make conversation at church, but at home with me, he hardly said a word. In Alzheimer's support groups, you hear caregivers complain about loved ones who accuse them of abuse or who can't stop chattering nonsense. That's very hard, but silence is just as hard. It was like I was living with a statue."

Sitting was about all that Tyrone did. He could still walk, albeit shakily, but he preferred to plop down in an easy chair in their family room or in a lawn chair in their yard and just sit there silently for hours on end.

"It didn't feel like we were married anymore," Sandra recalls. "I felt like a maid. I was spending all my time taking care of him, but he returned less and less. When I asked him questions, all he'd say was 'yes' or 'no.' When I tried to start conversations, he'd get frustrated and swear, or say 'Poor Tyrone' and then ignore me. I wasn't living. I was just existing."

Once they'd settled back into Denver, Sandra asked the VA hospital there to reevaluate Tyrone. "I didn't doubt his diagnosis, I just hoped the VA doctors could tell me a little more." The VA doctors confirmed Tyrone's diagnosis of mixed dementia—vascular dementia from TIAs and Alzheimer's disease—but they discovered another problem the Texas doctors had missed: a buildup in Tyrone's brain of cerebrospinal fluid, the fluid that surrounds the brain and spinal cord. They thought that the pressure generated by this fluid might explain some of his balance problems and assured Sandra that the fluid could be drained surgically.

Tyrone had the surgery in late 1994. "The operation helped his balance for a while," Sandra recalls, "but then he got real shaky on his feet again. As time passed, he got worse. The surgery didn't help his mind at all. There was no improvement." Tyrone's postsurgical balance problems along with his shuffling gait and falls led his VA doctor to modify his diagnosis to probable Lewy body variant of Alzheimer's, which is often accompanied by the shuffling walk Tyrone had developed (chapter 9). This change didn't matter to Sandra, and didn't open new treatment avenues or change the course of his illness.

A few months later, Tyrone's dislike for water and showering turned into a phobia. "He compeltely refused to bathe," Sandra recalls. "I tried to get him into the tub, but he was a lot bigger than me. If he wouldn't get in, there was nothing I could do to make him." In the end, Sandra was able to coax him into sitting on the kitchen floor while she gave him sponge baths. "He let me do it, but it was hard for me to bend over him with my bad back."

The sponge baths caused other problems as well: "Once he was down on the floor, it was very hard for him to get back up, and I couldn't lift him." When Tyrone finally got up on his feet, he was standing on a wet, slippery linoleum floor, and with his balance problems Sandra feared he might fall and hurt himself, or bring her down with him. Fortunately, that never happened.

One morning, while sitting on the side of their bed pulling on his pants, Tyrone lost his balance, fell to the floor, and could not get up. Sandra was in the kitchen. He called out to her, but she couldn't lift him. "Between his size and my back, it was impossible."

Sandra knocked on some neighbors' doors looking for help, but no one was home. When she returned to Tyrone, she expected to find him cursing and squirming, but he just sat there, still and silent, waiting for her. A statue, Sandra thought. She considered calling the police but decided to give it one last try. Slowly, inch by inch, Sandra pulled Tyrone up to his knees. From there, he was able to struggle to his feet, but the incident unnerved her. "It was one of the first times I remember asking myself, Can I take care of him? I began wondering how we were going to survive."

Not long after the bedroom incident, while watching the ebb and flow of their neighborhood from a lawn chair in their front yard, Tyrone leaned too far to one side and again lost his balance. He called to Sandra, and again she couldn't lift him. Fortunately, one of their neighbors, a big, brawny man, was doing some yard work a few doors away, and he pulled Tyrone back up to his feet.

Soon after the lawn-chair incident, Sandra dropped Tyrone off at the mall near their house while she ran some errands. He could spend hours sitting on a bench in the central walkway watching the world go by. As frustrated as Sandra felt about Tyrone's slide into seated silence, it had some advantages; she could leave him at the mall while she took care of business and feel confident that he wouldn't wander away or get into trouble. "But one day, when I came back to pick him up, a small crowd had gathered around him. Tyrone had fallen off the bench, and people were helping him up."

With her husband's balance so precarious, Sandra became increasingly apprehensive that Tyrone would crack his skull at the mall. She stopped taking him there and kept him at home, where the floors were mostly carpeted, where pillows could be placed around the sofa, and where the lawn around their patio furniture was soft enough to cushion any falls.

By mid-1995, Tyrone had descended deep into the incomprehensible realm of Alzheimer's. "He used to love sports," Sandra recalls. "He was devoted to the University of Texas football team and watched them whenever they were on TV. He was also a fan of the Denver Broncos, but the time came when he couldn't follow sports on TV. He stared at the set blankly. I'd ask what was happening, and he wouldn't say a word, just looked glassy-eyed, and I knew he had no idea what was going on."

Tyrone couldn't follow movie or sitcom plots either. The only TV programs he still enjoyed were the cooking shows. They somehow touched the part of his mind that still remembered his hobby. "He'd smile at the TV chefs and sort of talk to them, though it wasn't really talking, more like grunting with an occasional word here and there."

Day by day, Tyrone became more immobile. He stopped venturing out into their yard and instead spent his entire day sitting on the sofa in the family room, glassy-eyed and silent. "He got up only to eat and use the toilet," Sandra explains, "but usually he got to the bathroom too late or couldn't aim right. I was always cleaning up."

Sandra realized that she had no marriage anymore, no relationship, no life. All she had was an incredible amount of responsibility and the unending grind of caring for a husband who didn't talk to her and hardly moved. She hated her husband's silence and stillness and felt utterly trapped by his disease. That's when she developed an illness of her own—depression.

"I'd be in the middle of something like peeling carrots, and I'd just start to cry. I cried a whole lot. Taking care of Tyrone was a very heavy burden, the heaviest burden I'd ever faced. Many times, I said to myself, This is going to kill me. My children and Tyrone's children were far away. My friends and the people at church didn't understand Alzheimer's. They tried to help, but didn't do much. I had to do almost everything myself. It got harder and harder to keep him bathed and dressed and take him anywhere. I had no life, no one to talk to. Even though Tyrone was right there all the time, he gave me no companionship, and I got very lonesome. I became a prisoner in my own home, and there was no way to escape."

Fortunately, Sandra remained in contact with the Alzheimer's experts at the Denver VA, who sensed her turmoil and invited her to come in for counseling. She saw a psychologist once a week for an hour on Friday mornings. "I liked her. She sympathized with my situation and made some good suggestions, but mostly I cried. I'd come in saying, 'I'm not going to cry this time,' but then I would. Caring for Tyrone was so hard, the hardest thing I've ever done."

Tyrone's doctor offered Sandra antidepressant medication, but she didn't think she needed it. "The counseling was helping. Having some respite from Tyrone and a sympathetic ear helped a lot."

After three months of individual counseling, Sandra joined a weekly Tuesday-morning support group. "There were five of us— four caregivers and a facilitator from the VA. I liked it. I felt supported and less burdened. I didn't cry much. I even laughed now and then. That felt good." But getting to the group involved forty minutes of driving each way, and Sandra's back bothered her in the car. "The group helped me get through my worst time, but once I felt better, I started feeling like going wasn't worth the effort, and I stopped."

Then the support-group facilitator suggested that both she and Tyrone might benefit if he spent some days in an adult daycare center. Adult daycare? Sandra had never heard of it. "In my family, we always took care of our own." But the idea immediately made sense to her, and a VA staff member suggested a center near their neighborhood. "It appealed to me right away. It was clean and affordable, and had lots of activities."

Sandra told Tyrone they were going to visit a place where he could have fun. He balked. "When I first took him there, he didn't want to enter the building," Sandra recalls, "but I told him he had to go. I told him it would be for just a few hours a day, and that I really needed the break. He still didn't want to go inside, but I kind of pushed him through the door."

Once Tyrone got used to the center, he went with no fuss, but he didn't do much when he got there. "He mostly did what he did at home—sat in a chair and looked around. He did eat the lunches and snacks, and he also flirted with the staff women. He'd say, 'Hi, Miss Beautiful. Are you married?' Otherwise, he kept pretty quiet."

In mid-1997, Sandra decided to return to Jasper to put their home there on the market. But what could she do with Tyrone? That's when she learned about respite care at the Denver VA. The hospital was willing to take care of him for two weeks. It was a godsend.

But after only a week in Jasper, a VA nurse called to say that Tyrone had stopped eating. Sandra cut her trip short and jetted back to Denver. When she first saw Tyrone, she hardly recognized him. He'd lost a good deal of weight, his face was drawn, and he wouldn't talk at all. He just lay in his bed in a daze. "I was very frightened. I thought he might die."

The staff tried to reassure Sandra that Tyrone was in no physical danger, but she had difficulty believing it. She visited every day and begged him to eat, but to little avail. His doctor put him on an antidepressant. A parade of nurses trooped in and out of his room coaxing him to eat, and Sandra is convinced that they turned him around. "Some of them were young and pretty, and I think he noticed." Eventually, over a period of several weeks, Tyrone went from taking sips of juice, to nibbling on crackers, to eating treats that Sandra brought. Finally, he began eating more or less normally again, but Tyrone was in no shape to go home. He remained at the hospital for ten months.

Oddly, Tyrone's deterioration had one unexpected benefit: he stopped cursing. "I have no idea why," Sandra muses. "One day I just noticed he wasn't doing it anymore. He still got riled up now and then, but it passed quickly and quietly."

While Tyrone was hospitalized, his doctor, a social worker, and two nurses sat Sandra down and said he needed round-the-clock nursing care. They suggested three shifts of home health aides or a nursing home. "I'd never really thought about any of that," Sandra reflects. "He was my husband and I figured I would take care of him to the end."

The VA people questioned her ability to provide the level of care Tyrone needed, and Sandra had to agree. She was in her late sixties with a bad back. She wasn't up to a twenty-four-hour-a-day job nursing a man pushing eighty who could hardly communicate and was too big to lift. "I didn't want people in my house. A nursing home sounded better to me. They gave me a list of homes to consider."

Sandra visited several facilities that were acceptable to her, but they refused Tyrone. His condition was too medically complicated: Alzheimer's plus vascular dementia, with diabetes, and the balance problem. Eventually, she found a home that would take him, a fifty-bed Alzheimer's unit that was only a few miles from their home.

Some people from the VA transported Tyrone to the nursing home, and Sandra was there waiting for him. She introduced him to the staff and they introduced him to the other residents. "Tyrone hardly said a word the first hour or so. Then we were sitting in the day room, and he turned to me and said, 'Everyone in here is crazy.' No, I told him, they're ill. They have the same illness you have—Alzheimer's disease." That reassured him, and he settled in quickly.

Today, Tyrone lives in a clean, spare, double room in this home with one roommate, another elderly man. The two men largely ignore each other. Sandra brought Tyrone a radio, and when she visits on Sunday, they listen to gospel music together, which he still enjoys. Otherwise, he spends his days sitting quietly in the day room. He gets up only to eat. At first, the staff encouraged him to participate in the unit's activities, especially walks around the grounds, but he didn't want to, and on a few walks, he fell, once injuring his arm. Now the staff let him sit, though they talk to him and try to include him as best they can.

Sandra visits Tyrone every other day, bringing him little treats from home—usually fruit and diet soda. "When he sees me coming, he smiles and says, 'What did you bring me?' Otherwise, he's pretty quiet, except when he flirts with the nurses. The home has some pretty nurses, who talk to him and tease him, which he enjoys."

Sandra still washes Tyrone's clothes. "I don't have to. They'd do it at the home, but it makes me feel like I'm contributing to Tyrone's care, and he seems to appreciate it." She also tries to take him for brief walks. Tyrone is more open to walking with her than with the staff.

Tyrone recognizes Sandra as the person who brings him treats, but he's usually only dimly aware of who she is. "Sometimes he remembers my name," she says. "Other times, he thinks I'm his sister, and sometimes he has no idea who I am." Sandra felt distressed the first few times she realized that Tyrone didn't recognize her. "That was hard, but over the years, I've done lots of reading about Alzheimer's. Forgetting those closest to you is part of the disease. When Tyrone forgets me completely, it won't be easy, but I have to accept it."

Yet occasionally, Tyrone still has flashes of coherence. "On one visit, I cut his hair," Sandra explains. "The staff would do it, but I like to. A few other residents walked by, and very proudly Tyrone said, 'This is my wife, Sandra.' Another time, out of the blue he turned to me and said, 'Some people here have no visitors.' I knew that was his way of thanking me for coming."

But most of the time, Tyrone is silent or monosyllabic. During visits, Sandra typically sits beside Tyrone. They hold hands and she fusses over him, serving him the treats she brings. He still has a sense of humor and chortles quietly when he sees anything that strikes him as funny. Otherwise, he remains silent.

Tyrone still feeds himself, and he still understands how and when to use the toilet. Unfortunately, since his mobility has become so compromised, he can never get to the bathroom in time, and as a result, he wears diapers.

Because of Tyrone's military career, the VA paid for his first six months in the nursing home. Afterward, Sandra began paying with the proceeds from the sale of their Jasper home, but the money won't cover the $50,000 annual cost of the nursing home for long. In the meantime, Sandra is going through the bureaucratic process necessary to qualify Tyrone for Medicaid. She's not entirely clear how to do it and may have to hire a lawyer to help her. She hopes Tyrone will qualify before the house money runs out. She shudders at the thought of having to take him home but says, "I'll just have to do the best I can."

9.

The Other Dementias

Some Causes of Dementia May Be Treatable

Alzheimer's disease is the nation's leading mind-robber, but it's by no means the only one. Many other conditions can cause symptoms that might be mistaken for Alzheimer's. Some, which we'll discuss in this chapter, are very rare and even less treatable, but most of the other dementias are *more* treatable than Alzheimer's.

Currently, doctors diagnose Alzheimer's disease with about 90 percent accuracy. This means that some people diagnosed with the disease do not have it and, tragically, may not receive appropriate treatment.

Consider the case of painter Willem de Kooning (1904–1997), a towering figure in modern abstract expressionism. In the early 1970s, the then seventy-year-old artist began showing signs of what his doctors called Alzheimer's disease. De Kooning forgot people's names and recent events. He covered up his obvious confusion with lies and wisecracks, sometimes bursting into rages, while at other times lapsing into extended silences. He had increasing difficulty working. His output declined, and eventually he stopped painting altogether. As the news spread, the art world mourned the loss of a great painter to Alzheimer's.

But de Kooning's wife, Elaine, refused to believe that he had Alzheimer's. The couple had been separated for many years, but Elaine reentered de Kooning's life and discovered that it was a mess. Instead of buying into his diagnosis, she shepherded him through a major lifestyle-improvement program.

De Kooning had been drinking so heavily that he suffered blackouts. Elaine insisted that he lay off alcohol. He had been eating very poorly, which is common among heavy drinkers. She improved his diet. He had become almost completely sedentary, so she insisted he take daily walks. In addition, he had been sleeping erratically, so she regularized his sleep schedule and made sure he got enough rest. Slowly, de Kooning's mental acuity returned, and eventually he began painting again. Ironically, de Kooning did develop true Alzheimer's disease ten years later, in the early 1980s. He was declared legally incompetent in 1989 and died in 1997.

Mistakes like de Kooning's original misdiagnosis are less likely today. Since the 1970s, physicians' ability to diagnose Alzheimer's accurately has improved considerably. Because misdiagnosis is still possible, anyone concerned that a loved one might have Alzheimer's should become familiar with the other possible causes of dementia, especially those that can be treated successfully. Frequently, people have mixed dementia—Alzheimer's plus, say, depression. Treating the other dementia can restore some cognitive function and make a major difference in the affected individual's quality of life, even as the Alzheimer's progresses.

Depression

Mention depression, and the symptoms that come to mind are profound sadness, helplessness, hopelessness, weeping, apathy, and lethargy. In the elderly, however, depression often presents with different symptoms, such as confusion, distraction, irritable outbursts, difficulty concentrating, loss of appetite, sleep problems, and unexplained weight loss. These symptoms are sometimes mistaken for Alzheimer's.

In addition, when people are diagnosed as having early Alzheimer's and are still cogent enough to understand what that means, they often—understandably—become quite depressed. Shortly after diagnosis, an estimated 35 percent of people with early Alzheimer's suffer serious ("clinical" or "major") depression. Postdiagnosis depression can cause rapid cognitive deterioration, which is an important tip-off that the person is depressed. The cognitive decline of Alzheimer's disease occurs slowly. Rapid loss of mental function suggests another cause. Treating depression in Alzheimer's sufferers can bring significant, albeit temporary, cognitive improvement.

Depression is *not* a normal part of aging, however, many people over sixty-five suffer serious depression. Although surveys suggest that only about 5 percent of healthy elderly people living independently are clinically depressed at any given moment, an estimated 15 percent experience depression at some point during their elderly years. Some 25 percent experience periods of persistent sadness that last two weeks or longer, and more than 20 percent report persistent thoughts of death and dying.

Quite often, it's not easy to tell where Alzheimer's ends and depression begins. But here are some tips for distinguishing the two:

- In Alzheimer's, recent memories go first, but early-life memories remain much longer. In depression, recent *and* early memories tend to be affected more equally.
- Both Alzheimer's and depression can lead to social withdrawal and feelings of failure or being punished. Alzheimer's alone does not trigger thoughts of death or suicide. Depression often does.

If you notice that a loved one has lost mental acuity and you begin to suspect Alzheimer's, make sure the person gets thoroughly tested for depression, but be careful how you raise the idea of a workup for depression. Many elderly people view depression as a moral weakness and won't hear of the possibility that they might suffer from it. Reassure them that depression is a *physical illness.* It is no reflection on their character. It can be treated in a number of ways, and treatment makes people feel better and restores some of their mental abilities.

Depression treatments include exercise, cognitive therapy (changing self-destructive thought patterns, chapter 12), individual psychotherapy, group therapy or a support group, nutritional support (the B vitamins, especially B_6 and folic acid), acupuncture, massage therapy, music therapy, the medicinal herb St.-John's-wort, SAM-e, and antidepressant medication.

Even without a clear diagnosis of depression, one or more of these treatments may help those with early Alzheimer's cope with the emotional impact of their diagnosis. However, be aware that some antidepressant drugs—notably MAO inhibitors, tricyclics, and the Prozac family of medications (selective serotonin reuptake inhibitors, or SSRIs)—may cause side effects that aggravate Alzheimer's, such as confusion, memory loss, anxiety, difficulty concentrating, or insomnia.

Yet if a person with early Alzheimer's becomes severely depressed and nondrug approaches do not provide sufficient relief, it can be risky *not* to prescribe antidepressant drugs, despite their possible side effects. Suicide is a real possibility in the wake of a diagnosis-induced depression. Compared with all other age groups, the elderly commit suicide twice as frequently. Suicides are especially common among elderly white men. In addition, on top of Alzheimer's-related memory loss and confusion, the added cognitive impairment caused by depression increases the person's risk of accidents and potentially fatal judgment errors, for example, crossing a busy street against the light.

Recently, researchers in Argentina showed that antidepressant medication helps depressed individuals with Alzheimer's. They identified thirty-seven people (average age seventy-two, 78 percent women) who had both probable Alzheimer's and major depression. For six weeks they were given one of two different chemical families of antidepressants, either Prozac (10 mg) or Elavil (25 mg). Those who completed the study showed significant mood elevation on standard psychiatric tests and better day-to-day functioning, even as their Alzheimer's slowly progressed.

If you suspect depression in anyone recently diagnosed with Alzheimer's, don't wait until the person starts discussing suicide before you consult a doctor. Compared with younger people, the elderly talk about killing themselves less but do it more.

If a doctor prescribes antidepressants for your elderly loved one, here are important points to remember:

- Older adults should start on a low dose. Compared with younger people, the elderly are more sensitive to drugs and more likely to suffer side effects.
- Become familiar with all of the medication's possible side effects. Discuss them with your pharmacist.
- Beware of drug interactions. Antidepressants may interact with other drugs the person needs to take for other medical problems. Make sure your loved one's doctor and pharmacist are aware of all the drugs the person takes regularly. This is especially crucial with MAO inhibitors. Make a list and ask about possible drug interactions.

Vascular and Multi-Infarct Dementia (MID)

After Alzheimer's disease, the nation's second leading cause of progressive mental deterioration is vascular dementia. "Vascular" refers to the cardiovascular system, the heart and blood vessels.

Stroke. The best-known type of vascular dementia is caused by stroke. It's highly unlikely that a stroke would be mistaken for Alzheimer's or vice versa. Strokes occur suddenly, and when they cause dementia, it develops quickly. Alzheimer's has very gradual onset and slow progression. However, stroke and Alzheimer's often coexist as mixed dementia.

Americans suffer about 500,000 strokes each year, and 150,000 stroke deaths. Approximately 3 million living Americans have had strokes. Some recover fully, but many suffer permanent disabilities, such as paralysis or speech problems. Almost one-third of stroke survivors suffer some dementia, according to a recent study by University of Helsinki researchers. A team led by Timo Erkinjuntti, M.D., examined 337 elderly men and women who had had ischemic strokes (see below) within the previous three months. Thirty-two percent showed measurable dementia. The risk of dementia increased with age and smoking.

A stroke occurs when an artery in the brain becomes blocked or ruptures and can't deliver oxygen and nutrients to part of the brain. Deprived of nourishment, affected brain cells die. At the same time, the body parts controlled by those cells become impaired, causing stroke-related disabilities.

There are four major types of stroke, two caused by blocked blood flow in the brain (ischemia) and two by ruptured blood vessels that bleed (hemorrhage). The former, cerebral thrombosis and cerebral embolism, together known as ischemic stroke, account for about 80 percent of all strokes. The latter, cerebral hemorrhage and subarachnoid hemorrhage, collectively known as hemorrhagic stroke, occur much less frequently but are more likely to prove fatal. The vast majority of stroke survivors have had ischemic strokes.

About 65 percent of strokes are the result of cerebral thrombosis. Its cause is atherosclerosis, the same narrowing of the arteries that causes heart attacks. Instead of impairing blood flow into the heart, cerebral thrombosis affects blood flow through the brain. Because of its similarity to heart attack, the American Heart Association now calls this type of stroke a "brain attack." A key risk factor for cerebral thrombosis is high blood pressure (hypertension). Other risk factors include a family history, male sex, African-American race, diabetes, smoking, elevated cholesterol, and heart disease.

To prevent cerebral thrombosis, control its risk factors. Don't smoke. Keep your blood pressure in the normal range. Exercise regularly. Eat a low-fat, high-fiber diet to keep your cholesterol low, and if that doesn't do it, consider cholesterol-lowering medication. In addition, low-dose aspirin can help. "Low-dose" means one-half to one standard tablet a day. That's not enough to cure a headache, but it helps prevent the internal blood clots that cause cerebral thrombosis and heart attack.

In the event of a stroke, prompt administration of clot-dissolving drugs can minimize brain damage.

Multi-Infarct Dementia (MID). Just as the chest pain of angina often precedes heart attacks, strokes caused by cerebral thrombosis may be preceded by mini-strokes, called transient ischemic attacks (TIAs). These occur when an internal blood clot temporarily blocks an already narrowed artery in the brain and then dissolves on its own,

restoring blood flow. A TIA causes a brief period of substantially reduced blood flow through the brain. TIAs are the most predictive risk
factor for cerebral-thrombosis stroke. They multiply the risk ten-fold.
About one-third of those who experience a TIA have a stroke within
five years. Half of post-TIA strokes occur within a year.

Like strokes, TIAs strike suddenly and usually don't last more than
five minutes. They typically cause brief, mild symptoms, including
numbness, faintness, dizziness, clumsiness, and/or loss of speech or
vision, particularly in one eye. Some TIAs go unnoticed or get dismissed as fatigue, especially if they cause only momentary dizziness or
faintness. Even though most people appear to recover completely
from TIAs, each one causes some cell death in the brain (infarction).
Those who experience several TIAs (multi-infarcts) may suffer
enough cumulative brain damage to develop multi-infarct dementia
(MID).

MID usually develops more quickly than Alzheimer's disease, and
the person often suffers some stroke-related physical problems, for
example, partial paralysis or slurred speech, which are not features of
Alzheimer's. Nonetheless, MID might be mistaken for Alzheimer's,
especially if the TIAs that cause it go unnoticed and any physical
symptoms are mild. In addition, Alzheimer's disease and multi-infarct
dementia often coexist.

Fortunately, like cerebral thrombosis, MID is both preventable
and, to some extent, treatable with low-dose aspirin. A study at the
Cerebral Blood Flow Laboratory at the Veterans Administration
Medical Center in Houston showed that aspirin not only slows the
progression of MID, but in some cases reverses it. Researchers divided seventy MID sufferers, average age sixty-seven, into two
groups. One received 325 mg of aspirin a day (one standard tablet).
The other took no medication. The participants' cerebral blood flow
and mental faculties were evaluated yearly. Those taking low-dose aspirin stabilized or improved three-to-one over the controls. The researchers concluded that the aspirin group showed "significant
improvement in cerebral blood flow and cognitive performance.
Their quality of life and independence appeared to improve. Daily
aspirin appears to stabilize declines or improve cognition in multi-
infarct dementia."

Today, low-dose aspirin is widely recommended as a stroke preventive for people who have had TIAs. Many neurologists also recommend it to treat MID. In cases where MID and Alzheimer's
coexist, low-dose aspirin can help minimize the MID part of the
overall problem.

Because TIAs can go unnoticed, it's possible that a loved one diagnosed with Alzheimer's actually has mixed dementia with some
MID. Most people can safely take low-dose aspirin. Discuss this possibility with the affected person's physician.

Post–Cardiac Arrest Syndrome. Recent advances in emergency
medicine have improved the odds of surviving cardiac arrest, but the
downside of survival is memory loss. Today's treatments often start
the heart up again, but they cannot compensate for the brain's loss of
oxygen during the arrest.

A recent Scottish study identified thirty-five survivors of cardiac
arrest and compared them with thirty-five matched heart attack survivors who had not suffered cardiac arrest. Both groups had the same
ability to repeat a phone number immediately after hearing it, but the
cardiac arrest survivors had significantly more difficulty with longer-
term memory.

Post–cardiac arrest syndrome differs significantly from Alzheimer's.
It is linked to a medical emergency, and it develops fairly quickly.
However, post–cardiac arrest syndrome might conceivably be mistaken for Alzheimer's, since many people assume that *any* persistent
memory problem in an elderly person is Alzheimer's. They may not
distinguish between recent and long-term memory loss. If post–
cardiac arrest syndrome takes a few months to develop, it might not be
associated with the arrest. Post-arrest syndrome is not that well known,
even among medical professionals, whereas most people are aware of
Alzheimer's. When memory problems develop, family members and
the person's doctor might jump to the wrong conclusion.

Heart Bypass Surgery. Coronary artery (heart) bypass surgery
has become a common treatment for severe heart disease. As is not
the case with cardiac arrest, during the surgery, blood continues to
circulate through the brain. Nonetheless, according to Guy McKhann,
M.D., a professor of neurology and neurosciences at Johns Hopkins,
post-bypass cognitive problems are quite common. Two weeks after

surgery, about half of the people complain of trouble with reading and difficulty concentrating and following instructions. Six months after surgery, about 40 percent continue to complain of mental fuzziness. These post-bypass cognitive problems are unlikely to be mistaken for Alzheimer's disease because they develop suddenly, shortly after bypass surgery, and do not affect learning and memory in the way Alzheimer's does. Still, when any cognitive problem develops in an elderly individual, some people fear that it could be Alzheimer's.

If you become concerned about an elderly loved one's memory loss, pay attention to which memories are affected. In Alzheimer's, the newest memories are the first to go. When discussing memory loss with a doctor, be sure to mention if the person has also had recent cardiovascular problems or surgery.

Post-Surgery Memory Problems

Coronary bypasses are not the only operations that can interfere with cognitive functioning. A recent study coordinated by researchers at the University of Florida College of Medicine in Gainesville shows that 10 percent of elderly individuals develop memory and concentration problems after *any* surgery that involves general anesthesia.

The Florida researchers and colleagues around Europe gave cognitive function tests to twelve hundred people, age sixty or older, who were scheduled for surgery involving general anesthesia. A week after their surgery, they were retested. Twenty-six percent showed confusion, memory loss, difficulty concentrating, and other cognitive problems. Three months after surgery, 10 percent still showed cognitive deficits.

Cognitive impairment after general anesthesia clears up over time, but few people are aware that such problems are possible after general anesthesia and may mistake the lingering effects of anesthesia for Alzheimer's disease.

Drug-Related Dementia

Elderly people often take medication to treat chronic medical conditions. Over time, many widely used drugs can cause subtle cognitive impairment. The more drugs, the worse this impairment is likely to become. Many elderly individuals take several drugs simultaneously (polypharmacy). Side effects of polypharmacy may well mimic Alzheimer's, with memory loss, absentmindedness, confusion, disorientation, and emotional outbursts.

In addition, many prescription drugs can cause depression or have side effects that aggravate depression, for example, the Valium family of tranquilizers (benzodiazepines), Parkinson's medication (levodopa), and some blood pressure drugs (propranolol).

Finally, alcohol aggravates drug-related dementia, which can begin gradually and insidiously and might be mistaken for Alzheimer's, especially in cases of polypharmacy where the various drugs are added slowly over time.

If you suspect a loss of cognitive function, present the affected individual's physician with a list of *all* the medications the person takes—both prescription and over-the-counter. In addition, estimate the person's alcohol consumption. Removal of the offending drug(s) allows recovery of cognitive function. Of course, the person may not be able to discontinue medications that are medically necessary, but dose adjustments and drug substitutions may be possible.

Alcoholic Dementia

The typical person with alcoholic dementia has a long history of alcohol abuse, but it's not always easy to spot someone with a drinking problem. In fact, many alcoholics function reasonably well for many years and drink in secret, so their friends and loved ones may be unaware of the extent of their addiction.

In addition, whether or not an individual is alcoholic, as age increases, a given amount of alcohol causes more cognitive impairment. Over time, even a couple of drinks a day might be enough to cause memory loss, confusion, and disorientation significant enough to raise suspicions of Alzheimer's disease.

The effects of alcohol are also weight-related. The less you weigh, the harder each drink hits you. If an elderly loved one weighs less than he or she did a few decades ago, a given amount of alcohol can be expected to cause them more problems.

Finally, alcohol-related dementia may be just one element of a problem that may also include one or more of the following: multi-infarct dementia, nutritional deficiencies, problems caused by other drugs, and Alzheimer's disease.

If you suspect a loss of cognitive function, encourage the person to drink less or to stop drinking altogether. With abstinence, people with alcohol-related dementia improve dramatically over a few weeks to months but may still experience some permanent cognitive impairment.

Parkinson's Disease

Parkinson's disease was first described by the British physician James Parkinson in 1817. It involves progressive degeneration of the cells in the part of the brain that controls muscle movement. Symptoms include shaking or trembling while at rest (tremor), loss of facial expression, slow movements, a shuffling gait, limb stiffness, balance problems, and speech and eating difficulties. In addition, about 25 percent of people with Parkinson's disease also develop dementia.

It's unlikely that Parkinson's would be mistaken for regular Alzheimer's. The tremor, gait problems, and other muscle-related symptoms typically precede any dementia, but it might be confused with diffuse Lewy body disease, a variant of Alzheimer's that combines Alzheimer's dementia with muscle problems similar to Parkinson's (see below).

The progress of Parkinson's can be slowed with a variety of medications.

Nutritional-Deficiency Dementia

The nutrient deficiencies most closely associated with dementia are the B vitamins: thiamin (B_1), niacin (B_3), folate, and B_{12}. Of these, folate and B_{12} deficiencies are the most common. Blood tests to assess their levels are a standard part of the clinical assessment for Alzheimer's disease. The hallmark of B-vitamin-deficiency dementia is memory loss with possible coordination problems (ataxia).

Some experts have questioned whether B-vitamin deficiencies actually cause dementia, or whether the deficiency is a result of the Alzheimer's, but several studies have shown that demented individuals with B_{12} deficiencies recover when given the vitamin by injection. Other studies have shown mental improvement when people with folate, niacin, and thiamin deficiencies are given vitamin supplements.

If you suspect a loss of cognitive function, encourage the affected person to eat a nutient-rich diet—at least five servings of fruit and vegetables a day—and to take a multivitamin-mineral formula in consultation with a physician or clinical nutritionist.

Brain Tumor–Related Dementia

A complete clinical assessment of the affected individual should include CT scans and other tests to check for brain tumors. These tumors can be mistaken for Alzheimer's disease because early symptoms include memory problems, reasoning difficulties, and personality changes. But most brain tumors also cause persistent headaches, often with nausea and vomiting, symptoms not characteristic of Alzheimer's.

Brain tumors can be benign or cancerous. Many benign tumors can be cured surgically. Some brain cancers are treatable, notably by radiation. Currently, 29 percent of people diagnosed with brain cancer survive five years. Twenty-five percent live ten years.

Infections

Several infections can cause cognitive impairment, including meningitis, encephalitis, syphilis, Lyme disease, and HIV, the virus that causes AIDS. Typically, these infections cause other symptoms that clearly distinguish them from Alzheimer's disease, but at times, in the elderly, they may have unusual presentations and be mistaken for Alzheimer's.

A complete clinical assessment of the affected individual should include tests for all infections that may be dementing.

Exposure to Indoor Air Pollutants

Many physicians overlook indoor air pollution as a possible cause of dementia in the elderly. Consider this case, documented in a medical journal: A seventy-nine-year-old widow suffered progressive cognitive deterioration during the six months after her husband's death. Though she was grieving, her doctor ruled out clinical depression. His diagnosis: Alzheimer's. Her children did not live nearby, and the woman had deteriorated to the point that her family thought it best to place her in a nursing home.

By chance, a family friend was a physician well informed about environmental medicine. The more he heard about the woman's case, the more skeptical he became about her Alzheimer's diagnosis. Despite her grief over losing her husband, she remained mentally sharp for four months after his death. She sold their home and moved into a new condominium. Her symptoms appeared after living in her new place for two months, and progressed more quickly than Alzheimer's usually does.

Further investigation revealed that she had high blood levels of toluene, a toxic chemical used in construction materials, whose release can contaminate the indoor air of new buildings, even those that appear to be adequately ventilated. On the advice of the environmental physician, the woman moved out of her condominium and went to her daughter's home for an extended visit. Her cognitive abilities improved, and within two months she was back to her old self.

This story is by no means unique. The elderly spend about 80 percent of their time indoors, and as a result they suffer greater-than-average exposure to indoor air pollutants, among them carbon monoxide from gas appliances; volatile organic compounds from paints and polishes; and formaldehyde from new carpets, drapes, paneling, and furnishings. In addition, compared with most adults in the prime of life, the elderly are more sensitive to low-level toxic exposures.

If you suspect a loss of cognitive function in a loved one, consider the possibility of toxic exposures. Red flags include a newly constructed residence; new carpeting, drapes, furniture, or paint; newly refinished floors; and poor ventilation. When toxic exposure ends, cognitive function usually returns.

Lead Poisoning

Lead is infamous for its toxic effects on children. Even low doses can cause learning disabilities, and high doses cause mental retardation. Lead poisoning and the cognitive problems it causes are also problems for the elderly, especially elderly women.

Lead was once a common ingredient in paints and gasolines. While lead was banned in these products more than twenty years ago, today's elderly spent most of their lives exposed to it. In addition, lead can still be found in much of the nation's air and water because of its persistence in the environment.

The body accumulates lead in bone tissue. After age fifty, bone begins to break down. The process, osteoporosis, affects both sexes, but it proceeds more quickly in women. Symptoms of osteoporosis include loss of height, stooped posture, and increased risk of fractures. In addition, as bone deteriorates, the lead stored in it gets released into the bloodstream, giving many elderly women surprisingly high blood levels—even if they currently reside in a lead-free environment. Unfortunately, public health efforts to control lead exposure have focused almost entirely on children and on those who are occupationally exposed.

It's unlikely that lead poisoning by itself would be mistaken for Alzheimer's disease, but in conjunction with depression, nutritional deficiencies, alcohol abuse, medication side effects, and exposure to indoor air pollution, it might be. If you suspect a loss of cognitive function, have the person's blood tested for lead. If it's high, the lead can be removed (chelated) with drugs—notably, edetate calcium disodium (EDTA) and succimer (Chemet)—and high doses of vitamin C.

Sundown Syndrome

Strange things sometimes happen to elderly people who are hospitalized or institutionalized. If you visit in the morning, the person seems reasonably alert and mentally competent, but if you visit in the late afternoon or evening, the person may not recognize you or may seem lethargic or become easily agitated, confused, or disoriented.

Doctors have various terms for this phenomenon—organic brain disorder or encephalopathy. Nurses who work with the institutionalized elderly call it sundown syndrome, or sundowning, a loss of cognitive function toward the end of the day. Researchers who have studied sundown syndrome say it usually results from living in institutions that do not offer adequate sensory stimulation to keep people's minds active and alert.

Sundown syndrome is rarely mistaken for Alzheimer's disease because it typically has fairly rapid onset and occurs only toward the end of the day, but it may coexist with depression, nutritional deficiencies, medication side effects, and exposure to indoor air pollution, possibly making it appear more similar to Alzheimer's.

Experts recommend increased physical, mental, and social activity and bright-light therapy, which is used to treat winter depression (seasonal affective disorder).

Obstructive Sleep Apnea

"Apnea" means lack of breathing. Obstructive sleep apnea is a particular type of snoring that can impair cognitive function. Unfortunately, many people—including some physicians—are unaware of sleep apnea's possible effects on mental acuity.

When a spouse snores persistently despite swift kicks in the night, most people try to escape by using earplugs or moving to the guest bed, but before you do anything else, *listen carefully.* The combination of loud snoring punctuated by choking silences is almost always obstructive sleep apnea.

The National Commission on Sleep Disorders Research estimates that apnea afflicts 8 percent of Americans, some 20 million people, the vast majority of whom are undiagnosed. Most are paunchy, middle-aged men, but apnea affects women as well, particularly those who are overweight and postmenopausal.

Obstructive sleep apnea typically begins as ordinary snoring, which occurs when a partial obstruction in the back of the throat restricts air flow during inhalation. Causes include allergies and colds, which swell throat tissue; obesity, which adds excess tissue to the throat; alcohol, tranquilizers, and sedatives, which relax the throat muscles; and anatomical abnormalities—unusually large soft palates or nasal malformations that restrict air flow.

During ordinary snoring, people don't stop breathing, but with apnea, they do. As they struggle to inhale enough air through a narrowed airway, they suck the passage closed and stop breathing. Apnea episodes usually last only a few seconds, though they may last a minute. A sudden choking silence replaces the snoring. When the airway closes, the lack of oxygen sets off an internal alarm, and the brain rouses the person, restoring breathing. With every episode of sleep apnea—and affected individuals may suffer a hundred a night—the blood's oxygen level plummets. The heart must pump extra-hard to compensate, causing blood pressure to rise, and over time the risk of heart attack and stroke increases.

In addition, obstructive apnea destroys sleep, which in turn impairs daytime cognitive function. A recent study by French researchers surveyed 1,389 elderly people about their sleep habits. Half reported snoring, and about half of that group (27 percent of those surveyed) reported symptoms that suggested sleep apnea, such as day-time drowsiness and spousal observations of snoring alternating with choking silences. The researchers gave all 1,389 people a set of cognitive performance tests. The snorers performed significantly worse.

It's unlikely that apnea by itself would be mistaken for Alzheimer's disease, but in conjunction with depression, nutritional deficiencies, alcohol abuse, medication side effects, and exposure to indoor air pollution, it might be.

If you suspect that a loved one is suffering a loss of cognitive ability, try to find out if he or she snores loudly. If so, have the person evaluated by a sleep disorders clinic. Apnea is remarkably easy to treat. All it takes is a $1,200 device that delivers continuous positive airway pressure (C-PAP). A C-PAP device includes a mask that fits over the nose and is attached to a small pump that gently pushes extra oxygen into the lungs with each breath. C-PAPs prevent airway collapse and maintain a healthy blood oxygen supply. They're not much fun to wear at night, but they work. For a referral to a sleep center near you, send a stamped, self-addressed envelope to the American Sleep Disorder Association, 1610 14th St., N.W., Rochester, MN 55901.

Creutzfeldt-Jakob Disease (CJD) and Mad Cow Disease

CJD is a rare degenerative disease of the nervous system that typically strikes people between the ages of fifty and seventy-five. Early symptoms include headache, dizziness, visual disturbances, and problems with gait and motor control, which help distinguish it from Alzheimer's, but it can also be accompanied by progressive loss of memory, reasoning ability, and the ability to care for oneself. Still, it's unlikely that CJD would be misdiagnosed as Alzheimer's or vice versa because CJD progresses much more rapidly. More than half of CJD sufferers die within six months, and only 10 percent survive two years after diagnosis. Alzheimer's sufferers typically deteriorate much more slowly and can survive ten years or more. In addition, researchers at the National Institutes of Health and the California Institute of Technology recently announced the development of a spinal-fluid test that can diagnose CJD. Nonetheless, anyone concerned about Alzheimer's should become familiar with CJD because its close relative, mad cow disease, has become a news item.

The cause of CJD is unknown, but it appears to be an infectious disease caused by a transmissible agent. The first inkling of this was the observation of an unusually high risk among Libyans, who eat sheep's eyeballs. Sheep can develop a degenerative neurological disease similar to CJD called scrapie.

The case for infectious transmission of CJD has grown stronger in recent years because of instances of mad cow disease in Great Britain. Mad cow disease was first identified in 1986 and eventually was traced to cattle feed that contained the remains of sheep with scrapie. The transmission of the disease through feed led Britain to ban sheep and cattle remains in animal feed, and British farm officials destroyed thousands of animals that showed signs of the disease. The scientific name for mad cow disease is bovine spongiform encephalopathy (BSE), because it leaves cow brains riddled with tiny holes.

Contaminated beef cattle have transmitted the disease to humans. Recently, the British medical journal *The Lancet* described ten cases of what initially looked like CJD but on closer investigation appeared to be the human version of BSE. The average age of CJD onset is sixty-five, but in the ten cases *The Lancet* described, the average age at diagnosis was just twenty-seven. In addition, the victims—eight of whom had died by the time of the report—suffered a dementia that progressed somewhat more slowly than CJD usually does.

Scientists have recently discovered that scrapie, BSE, and similar diseases in other animals are caused by poorly understood infectious particles called prions (PREE-ons). Prions are made entirely of protein and are distinct from bacteria and viruses. They are also very stable and can survive freezing and heating to normal cooking temperatures, which allows transmission through contaminated meat.

The risk of CJD is tiny—about one in a million. The risk of human BSE appears to be even smaller. About 50 million British people have eaten beef potentially contaminated with BSE prions, yet only ten cases of the human form of the disease have turned up so far.

As this book goes to press, mad cow disease has not appeared in either U.S. cattle or any people living in America. To make sure things stay that way, the U.S. Department of Agriculture has banned the use of sheep and cattle remains in feed, and for a time banned importation of British and European cattle and sheep.

However, a rare homegrown variant of mad cow disease has been discovered in the Southeast among people who eat squirrel brains, an Appalachian delicacy typically served with white gravy or scrambled eggs. Since 1994, eleven cases of spongiform encephalopathy have been diagnosed in western Kentucky. All the affected individuals had eaten squirrel brain, according to Eric Wiseman, M.D., clinical director of the Neurobehavioral Institute in Hartford, Kentucky, where the eleven people were treated. Without some other cause, the natural incidence of CJD would be one person in the region afflicted every ten years. The current cluster represents eleven times the expected incidence, all in squirrel-brain eaters. The eleven people ranged in age from fifty-six to seventy-eight. They lived in different towns, were not related, and did not know one another. Their only link was a taste for squirrel brains. By the time of Dr. Wiseman's report in 1997, six had died. It's not clear how long it took for those who ate squirrel brains to develop the mad-cow-like disease.

In rare cases, deer, elk, and other Appalachian wild mammals have also been known to develop conditions similar to mad cow disease.

Diffuse Lewy Body Disease

Lewy bodies are microscopic structures that may develop in the brain. In Parkinson's disease, they develop in one particular part of the brain. When they develop all over, they cause diffuse Lewy body disease, a dementing condition also known as Lewy body variant of Alzheimer's.

Lewy body disease is similar to regular Alzheimer's in that it develops in the elderly and causes gradual cognitive decline and eventually dementia, but unlike regular Alzheimer's, it is more common in men than women, often causes a Parkinson's-like shuffling gait and muscle rigidity, and is more likely to involve paranoia, hallucinations, loss of balance, and repeated falls. The gait and balance problems can be treated to some extent with drugs used to treat Parkinson's disease, but this medication has no effect on the progressive dementia. Life expectancy from the time of diagnosis is about six years.

Pick's Disease

Pick's disease is a very rare form of dementia. It was first identified in 1892 by Dr. Arnold Pick, who described progressive mental deterioration in a seventy-one-year-old man. On autopsy, his brain showed unusual shrinkage of the cortex, the region involved in reasoning and other higher mental functions. Cortex shrinkage is different from the anatomical changes in the brain associated with Alzheimer's disease. The brains of people with Pick's also show unusual protein deposits called Pick bodies.

The first person with Pick's disease was unusual; the condition is more common in women than men, and most sufferers develop it between age forty and sixty. It is rare in people over seventy-five. Like Alzheimer's, Pick's disease progresses slowly, but its symptoms differ. Pick's disease sufferers experience less disorientation and memory loss early on, and more pronounced personality changes and loss of social restraints. As it progresses, profound dementia develops until eventually sufferers are mute, immobile, and incontinent.

Pick's disease is diagnosed in a process similar to Alzheimer's. Frequently, an affected individual is diagnosed with probable Alzheimer's, and later the diagnosis is changed to Pick's. Pick's disease is not currently treatable. Affected individuals typically survive about seven years.

10.

The New Alzheimer's Treatments

The Latest Drugs, Medicinal Herbs, and Other Therapies

Until recently, nothing seemed to slow the inexorable cognitive decline of Alzheimer's disease. Fortunately, within the last few years researchers have learned more about the disease, and treatment options have expanded considerably. There is still no cure for Alzheimer's, no treatment that reverses cognitive decline and allows recovery of lost mental abilities. Nor is there any treatment that permanently arrests the cognitive deterioration of Alzheimer's, but the list that follows gives examples of real progress.

- Two drugs have been approved that slow cognitive decline in many people with Alzheimer's, and several drugs currently in development promise to slow the progression of Alzheimer's for more people with the disease.
- Several familiar drugs, approved to treat other conditions, also help slow the progression of Alzheimer's.
- Several psychological therapies help people with Alzheimer's retain cognitive function longer than was previously thought possible.

- Certain nutrients and supplements have been shown to slow cognitive decline.
- One herbal approach has similar benefits.
- Several nondrug therapies help improve quality of life for both Alzheimer's sufferers and their caregivers and minimize the need for behavior-control medication that hastens cognitive decline.

Treatment of Alzheimer's disease is still in its infancy, and researchers are quick to concede that they have a long way to go. But today, for the first time, prominent experts have become cautiously optimistic that in the not-too-distant future, new treatments may be able to delay the onset of the disease and significantly slow the mental deterioration it brings.

One day, some future treatment may restore normal cognition in those with Alzheimer's, but because the disease almost always strikes the elderly, the current treatment goal is not restoration of normal cognitive function but, rather, delay of cognitive decline. If the development of Alzheimer's could be delayed just five years, researchers at the National Institute on Aging estimate that the number of affected individuals could be reduced by as much as 50 percent. These elderly people would die of other causes before they developed Alzheimer's, and live their final years in reasonably normal cognitive health.

Increasingly, experts predict that within the next decade, Alzheimer's disease may become a fairly manageable chronic illness, rather like diabetes or asthma. We're not there yet, but every day, researchers are getting a little closer.

Tacrine (Cognex) and Donepezil (Aricept): The Cholinesterase Inhibitors

Most people think of the nervous system as the body's electrical wiring. This is correct—up to a point. Nerve cells carry neuroelectrical impulses around the body much like wires carry electricity, but unlike wires, which are continuous filaments, nerve cells do not touch one another. Instead, they have microscopic gaps between them called synapses. Nerve impulses must jump these synapses to proceed on their way. They do this with the help of special chemicals known as neurotransmitters. As a nerve impulse passes through a nerve cell, it triggers the release of neurotransmitters into the cell's synapses, allowing the impulse to jump the gap and move along. Once an impulse crosses a synapse, special enzymes sweep the neuro-transmitter away, leaving the cell and synapse ready to react to the next nerve impulse. One important neurotransmitter is acetylcholine (a-see-till-KOH-leen).

During the late 1970s, researchers discovered that people with Alzheimer's disease suffer a loss of acetylcholine from their synapses. This observation fueled theories that Alzheimer's might disrupt the synthesis of this neurotransmitter or that the disease might trigger overproduction of the enzyme that eliminates it, acetylcholinesterase, generally known as cholinesterase (koh-lin-ES-ter-aze). Scientists speculated that drugs that either increased acetylcholine or inhibited cholinesterase might help treat Alzheimer's.

Cholinesterase inhibitors have yielded the best results so far. The two drugs currently approved to treat Alzheimer's—tacrine (Cognex) and donepezil (Aricept)—are both cholinesterase inhibitors. They do not cure Alzheimer's, and they don't work for everyone who takes them, but in those who respond, these drugs slow cognitive decline.

▪ **Tacrine (Cognex, from Parke-Davis).** The FDA approved tacrine in 1993, largely because a thirty-week study showed that high doses improve cognition in many, but not all people with mild to moderate Alzheimer's disease. Tacrine has also shown some limited benefit for those with more advanced Alzheimer's.

Since its approval, clinical experience with tacrine has been disap-pointing. Depending on the study, the drug helps only 20 to 40 per-cent of those who take it, and there's no predicting who will respond, to what extent, or for how long. People taking tacrine typically start with 40 milligrams a day (mg/d), with dosage increasing incremen-tally at six-week intervals to 80, 120, and finally 160 mg/d. However, some clinicians say the dose can be increased more rapidly. Tacrine must be taken four times a day, and people with Alzheimer's may re-sist taking it (or any drug) so frequently.

Tacrine also has significant side effects, including nausea and vomiting, but the one that has caused the most concern is the possibility of liver damage. Tacrine substantially increases levels of the liver enzyme alanine transaminase (ALT)—to three to five times normal levels. The rise in ALT typically begins about six weeks into treatment. The long-term effects of high ALT levels remain unclear, but doctors who prescribe tacrine generally advise blood tests to assess ALT level every two weeks, with a reduction in dose if the level rises beyond about five times the norm. Such frequent blood tests would be a hassle for anyone, but people with Alzheimer's may resist them quite vigorously, causing problems for caregivers and making it impossible for them to continue taking the drug.

Tacrine is cost-effective for the minority of people who respond to it, but because of its limited utility, four-times-a-day regimen, and side effects, it is not prescribed very often.

▪ **Donepezil (Aricept, from Pfizer-Eisai).** The FDA approved this cholinesterase inhibitor in 1996, based on several clinical trials. Among them was a twenty-four-week study by S. L. Rogers of Eisai and colleagues at Mount Sinai Medical Center in New York, Indiana University School of Medicine in Indianapolis, and Baylor College of Medicine in Houston. The researchers gave 473 Alzheimer's sufferers either a placebo or donepezil (5 or 10 mg a day). Compared with the placebo group, those taking the drug showed significant improvement in cognitive skills and daily functioning. Both doses of donepezil produced cognitive improvement, but the higher dose was more likely to cause side effects, including diarrhea, nausea, and vomiting.

Recently, at the University of Pittsburgh in Pennsylvania, Daniel Kaufer, M.D., prescribed donepezil for forty people with mild to moderate Alzheimer's. After several months, most showed cognitive improvement. Their caregivers also reported that the drug seemed to minimize their wandering and emotional outbursts.

Donepezil is better targeted than tacrine. It inhibits cholinesterase only in the brain, while tacrine affects related compounds throughout the body. Better targeting means fewer side effects. Like tacrine, donepezil may cause nausea, vomiting, and diarrhea, but unlike tacrine, donepezil does not cause liver enzyme abnormalities. Users need not have regular liver-function tests. Donepezil is also more convenient than tacrine—one pill a day.

Like tacrine, donepezil does not work for everyone who uses it, but its response rate is better, as shown in one study conducted at Ceighton University in Omaha, Nebraska. David Folks, M.D., chair of the psychiatry department, tested people with mild to moderate Alzheimer's before and after taking donepezil for twenty-four weeks. The drug improved cognitive function in 80 percent of them.

▪ **Metrifonate (Promem, from Bayer).** Metrifonate has not yet been approved by the FDA, but as this book goes to press, it is in the final stages of preapproval testing. Latest studies make it look less promising. In addition to improving the cognition of people with Alzheimer's disease, clinical trials have shown that it also helps minimize the disruptive behavior common among Alzheimer's sufferers.

In a six-month study by researchers at the University of California, at Los Angeles, Alzheimer's Disease Center, 408 people with mild to moderate Alzheimer's were given either a placebo or metrifonate (30 to 60 mg once a day based on their weight). Cognition tests showed that those taking the drug improved significantly. In addition, they also experienced significantly fewer typical Alzheimer's behavior problems, notably less depression, lethargy, and apathy.

Researchers at the Washington University School of Medicine in St. Louis confirmed those results in a six-month study involving 334 Alzheimer's sufferers who took either metrifonate or a placebo. In the placebo group, cognitive function declined significantly, but among those taking metrifonate, it remained stable. In addition, metrifonate users suffered less agitation.

Metrifonate is given once a day. Common side effects include nausea, diarrhea, leg cramps, and muscle weakness.

Bayer petitioned the FDA to approve metrifonate in 1997. As this book goes to press, the application is pending.

▪ **New Cholinesterase Inhibitors on the Horizon.** In one six-month trial, 699 Alzheimer's sufferers took either a placebo or ENA-713 (from Sandoz). The drug group showed significant cognitive improvement. Side effects included nausea, vomiting, diarrhea, and loss of appetite.

Another cholinesterase inhibitor, physostigmine (fie-zo-STIG-meen), has been shown to increase levels of acetylcholine in the brains of people with Alzheimer's. Unfortunately, in early studies the drug had to be injected and worked for only about thirty minutes, which made it impractical. Recently, however, Jacobo Mintzer, M.D., a psychiatrist at the Medical University of South Carolina, tested a novel time-release form of physostigmine (from Forest Laboratories) that allows once-a-day administration. He gave either a placebo or time-released physostigmine to 475 people with mild to moderate Alzheimer's. The placebo group showed no improvement, but those taking the drug experienced significant cognitive benefits.

Other cholinesterase inhibitors currently in development include NXX-066 (from Astra Arcus) and galanthamine (Janssen).

▪ **Acetylcholine Boosters on the Horizon.** Even though cholinesterase inhibitors have been more successful than acetylcholine boosters, several of the latter look promising, notably phosphatidylserine (PS), a compound related to lecithin. At the Memory Assessment Clinic in Bethesda, Maryland, a team led by T. Crook, M.D., gave fifty-one people with suspected or probable Alzheimer's either a placebo or PS (100 mg) three times a day. After twelve weeks, the PS group showed significant cognitive improvement, including memory for names and recall of locations of objects and events from the previous day. PS is available over the counter as a supplement at many health food stores and supplement outlets.

Other promising experimental acetylcholine boosters include xanomeline (from Eli Lilly), milameline (Parke-Davis), SB-202026 (SmithKline Beecham), AF-102B (Snow Brand Products), and ABT-418 (Abbott).

Nonsteroidal Anti-Inflammatory Drugs (NSAIDs)

NSAIDs include such common, over-the-counter medications as aspirin, ibuprofen (Motrin, Advil, Nuprin), and naproxen (Naprosyn), plus many prescription drugs—but *not* acetaminophen (Tylenol), which relieves pain but has no anti-inflammatory action.

People who take NSAIDs to treat arthritis or leprosy are at unusually low risk for Alzheimer's disease (chapter 5). The reason appears to be that inflammation of brain tissue plays a role in the disease, and NSAIDs minimize imflammation.

In addition to reducing Alzheimer's risk, NSAIDs also help treat the disease. In one study, researchers at the Johns Hopkins Alzheimer's Disease Research Center observed 210 Alzheimer's sufferers over time to see how rapidly they lost cognitive ability. Some showed rapid mental deterioration, while others declined more slowly. Then the researchers reviewed the affected individuals' medical records to see who had been taking NSAIDs. They found that as NSAID use increased, the rate of mental deterioration decreased.

In another study, researchers gave forty-four people with mild to moderate Alzheimer's either a placebo or the NSAID indomethacin (Indocin, 100 or 150 mg/d). After six months, the placebo group showed an 8.4 percent decline in cognitive test scores, but the indomethacin group registered a 1.3 percent improvement.

Many different NSAIDs slow the progression of Alzheimer's, among them, ibuprofen, naproxen, indomethacin, and meclofenamate (Meclomen). The jury is still out on aspirin, though many researchers believe it probably helps.

The main problem with NSAIDs is that they carry a significant risk of abdominal distress, gastrointestinal bleeding, and ulcers. However, these side effects can be minimized by taking an enteric-coated NSAID that dissolves in the intestine, not in the stomach, or by taking the newest type of NSAID, Cox-2 inhibitors, which cause fewer gastrointestinal side effects (Celebrex).

Estrogen

Although women have a greater risk of developing Alzheimer's disease than men, women also have a treatment option unavailable to men: hormone replacement therapy (HRT). According to several recent studies, HRT helps prevent, delay, and treat the disease in women. (See chapter 5 for more on HRT.) A key component of HRT is estrogen, the female sex hormone, which many women take to prevent hot flashes and other discomforts associated with menopause.

In an eight-week study, twelve women in Tacoma, Washington, with mild to moderate Alzheimer's received skin patches—half that released estrogen that entered their blood, and half that released a placebo. "Within a week, the women on estrogen showed cognitive improvement," said Sanjay Asthana, M.D., who presented the results at a recent meeting of the Society for Neuroscience. By the end of the study, the estrogen users' cognitive test scores had almost doubled. The more estrogen the women absorbed, the greater their mental improvement.

Estrogen has several effects that help slow the progression of Alzheimer's disease. It boosts production of acetylcholine; it impedes deposition of beta-amyloid, the protein involved in senile plaques; and it improves blood flow through the brain. And in animal studies, it stimulates nerve cell growth in areas of the brain affected by Alzheimer's. Finally, it helps maintain the integrity of the hippocampus, a structure in the brain involved in memory.

In addition to helping prevent and slow the progress of Alzheimer's disease, a great deal of research shows that HRT also helps prevent heart disease, the leading cause of death among women, and osteoporosis, bone-thinning that can lead to life-threatening fractures.

Unfortunately, for all its benefits, estrogen also increases the risk of breast cancer an estimated 20 to 30 percent, and the risk of uterine endometrial cancer if women take it without another sex hormone, progesterone. The taint of breast cancer is the main reason why only about one-quarter of postmenopausal women take HRT. Ironically, compared with women who don't take HRT, those who do and go on to develop breast cancer are less likely to die from it. Scientists are not sure why, but they speculate that the hormone somehow makes breast tumors less aggressive.

If a woman you love has Alzheimer's, ask her physician if she should take estrogen.

New Drugs on the Horizon

Nicotine. Smokers often say that cigarettes help them think more clearly. The reason is nicotine, the addictive compound in tobacco smoke. Several studies have shown that nicotine improves cognitive function by enhancing the release of acetylcholine. Nicotine appears to do the same for people with Alzheimer's disease.

Recently, researchers at the Veterans Affairs Medical Center in Albany, New York, taped nicotine patches to the arms of seven non-smoking men with Alzheimer's. The men wore the patches sixteen hours a day for two weeks. Based on pre- and post-tests of cognitive function, nicotine improved their cognition, though the results did not quite reach statistical significance.

No Alzheimer's experts encourage those with the disease to begin smoking, as smoking increases atherosclerosis and oxidative damage, both of which have been linked to Alzheimer's risk. In the future, however, a nicotine-based drug might be used to treat Alzheimer's.

Ampakines. Ampakines are a new class of memory-booster. According to Gary Lynch of the University of California at Irvine, who has studied them for almost a decade, ampakines increase cortical brain activity.

Lynch and Cortex Pharmaceuticals in Southern California have developed an ampakine drug, Ampalex, that increases levels of a specific neurotransmitter in the brain, AMPA-glutamate. In animal studies, Ampalex substantially improves memory, and it appears to do the same in humans. A German–Swedish study of fifty-four people, ages twenty-one to seventy-three, showed that compared with those taking a placebo, Ampalex users scored twice as high on short-term memory tests, but that study involved people who did not have Alzheimer's.

In 1996, Cortex contracted with the National Institute on Aging to test Ampalex on a small group of people with Alzheimer's disease. At press time, results have not been released.

Taxol. Taxol, a drug derived from the needles or bark of the yew tree, is currently used to treat ovarian and breast cancer. Studies by Mary Michaelis, Ph.D., a professor of pharmacology at the University of Kansas in Lawrence, hint that Taxol may also protect brain cells from damage by amyloid protein, the major component of the senile plaques of Alzheimer's. When animal brain cells are exposed to amyloid protein, they typically die within forty-eight hours, but if the cells are treated with taxol and then exposed, they live more than three times as long. Taxol seems to slow the degeneration of dendrites, the branching ends of nerve cells that deteriorate in Alzheimer's.

Should Your Loved One Enroll in a Clinical Trial of a New Drug?

A clinical trial is a test of a new drug in people. All new drugs must pass through several stages of these trials before the FDA approves them for general use.

If a person with Alzheimer's has not benefited from the approved medications, enrollment in a test of an as-yet-unapproved drug is an option. These tests are reasonably open, though they all have eligibility criteria. Participation has potential advantages and disadvantages. On the plus side, if the new drug works, the person gets to take it for months and possibly years before it is widely available, usually for free. On the minus side, the new drug may not provide any benefit, and it might cause side effects.

Before you make any decisions one way or the other, here's how the drug-approval process works:

When researchers come up with a promising new drug, they first test it in laboratory animals, which usually takes one to six years. The researchers test different doses in animals with a variety of medical conditions, hoping to learn what the drug treats, its best dose, and any side effects. If animal studies lead researchers to believe that the new drug is both therapeutic and not unduly toxic, they petition the FDA for permission to test it on people.

There are three stages of clinical—that is, human—trials: Phase I, II, and III. Phase I trials are small-scale safety tests. About twenty to a hundred healthy volunteers (usually prison inmates) take different doses for several months to a year so researchers can learn how the human body metabolizes the drug, how the various body systems react to it, and what side effects it causes. Researchers can usually predict how new drugs affect people in Phase I clinical trials because human reactions are generally similar to those of laboratory mammals (rats, dogs, etc.). However, sometimes people and animals react differently, which is why the FDA requires these trials.

If the new drug's potential benefits outweigh the side effects that turn up in Phase I trials, the FDA approves it for Phase II studies. Phase II clinical trials are longer, larger-scale effectiveness and dosage tests. Researchers recruit one hundred to three hundred people with the condition they think the new drug treats. They give them varying doses to see if it helps, and if so, they attempt to determine which dose works best.

Phase II trials use a placebo-controlled, double-blind design. Half the volunteers receive the new drug; the other half receive a placebo (placebo-controlled). Neither the researchers nor the participants know who has received what (double-blind). Phase II trials typically last around two years. While they focus on effectiveness and dosage, the researchers also continue to monitor the new medication's side effects.

If the drug appears to be effective at a practical dose without side effects the FDA considers too toxic, it is then approved for Phase III trials. Phase III clinical trials mark the final stage of pre-approval testing. By the time a drug reaches Phase III trials, researchers are fairly confident that a known dose helps treat the target disease without unacceptable side effects.

Phase III trials last two to four years and typically involve several thousand individuals at medical centers around the country. Like Phase II trials, Phase III studies are double-blind and placebo-controlled. In some, the placebo is a true placebo, a medically inert substance. In others, it is a standard medication already in use. In some trials, the experimental group receives just the new drug. In others, participants receive the new drug in addition to standard medication. Trial designs depend on the specific drug being tested and on the condition it appears to treat. The FDA requires at least two Phase III trials per new drug to reduce the possibility of false-positive results appearing by some fluke.

Many Phase III trials also offer an "open label" study; after the double-blind, placebo-controlled portion of the trial is complete, the researchers offer the new drug to all participants, who use it for up to several years before the FDA approves it for general use.

After completion of Phase III trials, the sponsoring drug company submits its clinical trial data to the FDA, whose staff and outside consultants review it and recommend either approval, denial, or further testing. Final approval may take several years.

The Alzheimer's Association maintains a list of all the clinical trials of promising new Alzheimer's drugs that are currently enrolling participants. You can learn:

- What the new drug appears to do.
- The eligibility criteria for participation.
- The size and duration of the trial, with its start and finish dates.
- A list of contact phone numbers of participating researchers around the country who can accept enrollees.

This information is also available on the World Wide Web at www.alz.org/medical/drug/enroll/Top.html.

When considering enrolling a loved one with Alzheimer's in a clinical trial, many caregivers hesitate for fear of turning the person into a guinea pig. This is a valid concern, but a surprising 1997 study by researchers at Harvard, Columbia, and Johns Hopkins showed that compared with Alzheimer's sufferers who do not participate in clinical trials, those who do participate stay out of nursing homes longer—*even if the experimental drug they take doesn't help them*. The researchers studied 215 noninstitutionalized people with Alzheimer's disease, 101 of whom enrolled in clinical trials of new drug treatments. After more than three years, the two groups showed no differences in cognitive deterioration, hospitalizations, and death, but the incidence of nursing home placement differed significantly. In the control group, about one-third of participants were placed during the study period, while among those enrolled in clinical trials, the figure was only 17 percent.

The researchers were unsure why clinical trial participation reduced nursing home placement, but they suggested three possibilities:

Perhaps participation had some placebo effect. Maybe doctors were more emotionally supportive of caregivers whose loved ones were in clinical trials, which helped them continue providing care longer. Or perhaps the outreach necessary for caregivers to arrange enrollment carried over to greater outreach to other community resources that helped them keep the affected individual with them longer.

Whatever the reason, if you are an Alzheimer's caregiver, consider a clinical trial for your loved one.

Psychosocial Therapies

Media reports of Alzheimer's treatment focus almost entirely on drugs, practically ignoring the psychological and social approaches to treatment. Medications are certainly important, but there's more to treating this disease than just drugs. Like current medications, psychosocial therapies do not halt or reverse cognitive decline, but like the latest drugs, they can slow it down, help preserve remaining cognitive abilities, and improve quality of life for both Alzheimer's sufferers and their caregivers.

Support Groups

Support groups have become a coping mainstay for Alzheimer's caregivers (chapter 12). Several studies show that they also help those in the early stages of the disease.

At the University of California's San Francisco Medical Center, Joseph Barbaccia, M.D., and Robin Yale, L.C.S.W., recruited fifteen people newly diagnosed with Alzheimer's disease, all of whom received standard medical care. In addition, eight of the fifteen joined a weekly support group that met for two months. Compared with the seven who did not participate in the group, those who did said the experience allayed their fears, brightened their mood, and helped them accept their illness and plan more constructively for the future.

However, support groups have limits. Their value depends a great deal on the skills of those who lead them, and they do not slow the progession of Alzheimer's.

Cognitive-Behavioral Therapy

Cognitive-behavioral therapy builds on what can be gained from a support group. Cognitive therapy is a treatment for depression that involves correcting distorted thinking and substituting more accurate, less depressing thoughts. When other elements are included, such as increasing pleasant activities or systematic problem-solving, it is called cognitive-behavioral therapy.

At the University of Washington School of Medicine in Seattle, Linda Teri, Ph.D., has enjoyed considerable success using cognitive-behavioral therapy to treat depression in people in the earliest stages of Alzheimer's. Working with small groups, she probes their feelings about their diagnosis. People newly diagnosed with early Alzheimer's disease typically reply, "I'm worthless," or "I can't think," or "I can't do anything anymore."

While these feelings may be understandable, they are often incorrect. Teri applies cognitive therapy in an effort to correct them. "You're not worthless, you're ill. It's not your fault. You have a disease that over time will make it harder and harder for you to remember, and think, and function. That's a major blow. It's sad. But it hasn't happened yet. You still function reasonably well now. You still can think and do things. You're not as sharp as you once were, or as able to juggle as many responsibilities, but don't write yourself off. You still have time before your illness becomes severe."

On the behavioral side, Teri has found that Alzheimer's-related depression is often linked to a lack of stimulation. She asks the people in her groups to keep track of the pleasant experiences they have each day and to try to have more of them, for example, getting a massage, playing with pets, or listening to music. (Massage, pet therapy, and music therapy are discussed in greater detail later in this chapter.)

Cognitive-behavioral therapy is simple, but it often relieves what Teri calls the "excess disability" caused by diagnosis-related depression. In a study of this approach, Teri and colleagues assessed depression in seventy-two people with mild to moderate Alzheimer's, and then enrolled some, plus their caregivers, in a cognitive-behavioral therapy program for an hour a week for nine weeks. Compared with those who did not participate, those who did showed significant mood elevation, despite the progression of their Alzheimer's.

Cognitive-behavioral therapy works best in cases of mild to moderate Alzheimer's, when individuals still retain enough cognitive function to participate. A similar approach is very effective with caregivers (chapter 12).

Behavior Modification

A good deal of research shows that Alzheimer's suffferers retain their abilities longer and become more cooperative and manageable when caregivers reward them consistently for behaving competently. Part of the memory loss of Alzheimer's involves forgetting how to act properly. Consistently rewarding desired behavior helps maintain appropriate behavior.

In separate studies, Louis Burgio, Ph.D., of the Center for Aging at the University of Alabama at Birmingham, School of Medicine, and John Schnelle, Ph.D., of Middle Tennessee State University in Murfreesboro, used behavior modification successfully to treat a major problem of Alzheimer's care—urinary incontinence. In both studies, instead of just fitting incontinent nursing home residents with diapers and cleaning up after their accidents, staff proactively encouraged residents, many of whom were demented, to use the bathroom more frequently, and applauded residents' competent toileting. In both studies, incontinence diminished significantly. In Dr. Schnelle's study of 126 people, it was cut in half with just twenty days of behavior therapy.

Dressing is another activity that lends itself to behavior modification. At the University of Arkansas for Medical Sciences in Little Rock, Cornelia Beck, Ph.D., trained nursing assistants to lavish consistent praise on nursing home residents with Alzheimer's who dressed themselves adequately. In just one week, 75 percent of the residents improved, needing less assistance with dressing.

Frank Vaccaro, Ph.D., of Hofstra University in Hempstead, New York, has used behavior modification to minimize aggressive outbursts in assaultive nursing home residents. For six weeks, every ten minutes staff consistently rewarded nonaggressive, socially desirable behavior with fruit, cookies, or juice, and punished aggressive behavior with reprimands and isolation (time-outs) for ten minutes. During the study, the residents' aggressiveness decreased markedly. Dr. Vaccaro obtained similar results when appropriate behavior was rewarded every twenty minutes.

If you are an Alzheimer's caregiver, behavior modification can work for you, too. Here are some suggestions:

- Reward desired behavior every time.
- Provide multiple rewards, including a kiss, a hug, a smile, a tender touch, and verbal reinforcement, such as "Thank you," "Good," "Terrific."
- As much as possible, ignore undesired behavior. Withdraw eye contact. Try not to show any emotion.
- Reward steps in the right direction. If you want the person to sit at your kitchen table to eat, offer praise for entering the kitchen and moving toward the table.

Intensive Communication Programs

A good deal of research has shown that in residential care facilities, the more intensive, creative, and enriching the activity program, the more sociable, responsive, and coherent people with Alzheimer's and other forms of dementia remain.

Mary Jo Santo Pietro, Ph.D., of Kean University in Union, New Jersey, and Faerella Boczko, M.S., of the Jewish Home and Hospital in the Bronx, New York, combined creative enrichment with behavior modification in a program they called the Breakfast Club. At the Jewish Home, four groups of five residents met for breakfast five days a week for twelve weeks, with staff facilitators who shepherded them through a structured program:

- As the group convened each morning, a facilitator greeted the participants and offered two name tags, one with their name, one with someone else's. By trial and error, participants chose their own tag and pinned it on. The facilitator then greeted them by name and coached the participants to greet one another by name.
- Next, the facilitator introduced a breakfast item, for example, juice. The participants examined the item, read its label, and the facilitator asked questions that elicited participants' experiences with the item.
- The facilitator did the same with other breakfast items—coffee, cereal, toast, eggs, pancakes, French toast, etc.—encouraging the participants to name, discuss, and reflect on each item.
- Then, with the facilitator's help, the participants made themselves breakfast. The facilitator prompted and encouraged them to keep naming the foods as they prepared them.
- When breakfast was ready to serve, the group set a table and ate together, family style. The facilitator prompted participants to ask one another by name for the various dishes. The facilitator also served coffee, prompting participants to specify how they liked it. During breakfast, the group discusses the food, how they had prepared it, and any thoughts the experience may have triggered.
- After breakfast, the participants cleared the table, and the facilitator introduced a topic of conversation (chosen in advance) that elicited both short- and long-term memories from the participants.
- After ten minutes of conversation, the Breakfast Club adjourned. The facilitator collects the name tags, thanked everyone by name for coming, and encouraged them to say goodbye to one another by name.

All the club sessions were videotaped and reviewed by two different speech pathologists who did not participate in the program. Analysis of the tapes showed that over the twelve weeks, most participants became more communicative with improved language skills. They also became more sociable, more interested and involved in the club, and better able to accomplish the tasks involved in making, serving, and cleaning up after breakfast. In addition, by week five, all the participants who had previously wandered off stopped wandering and stayed seated with the group. By week twelve in one group, one member was able to pass out all the name tags without error, without prompting. In several groups, members made empathic statements to one another, made up spontaneous jokes, laughed frequently with one another, and broke into spontaneous singing.

Complementary Therapies

Treatments outside the medical mainstream used to be called "unorthodox" or "alternative." Today, they are increasingly called "complementary" because, when used sensibly, they usually don't *replace* mainstream medicine, but rather *complement* it.

Many complementary therapies—from acupuncture to yoga—are being incorporated into mainstream medicine. The approaches that have won the most mainstream acceptance are those that are inherently health-promoting: good nutrition, regular exercise, psychological support, and stress management. These approaches have shown tremendous value in the treatment of heart disease, and they show considerable promise in cancer therapy. They also appear helpful for Alzheimer's disease, particularly nutritional therapy.

Recent research shows that antioxidant nutrients, one amino-acid supplement (carnitine), and a medicinal herb (ginkgo) all slow cognitive decline. Also, exercise, massage, pet therapy, music therapy, and aromatherapy all help calm agitated Alzheimer's sufferers, which improves quality of life for both them and their caregivers, and reduces the need for anti-anxiety and antipsychotic medication, which can cause unpleasant side effects and hasten cognitive deterioration.

Antioxidants

Oxidative damage caused by highly reactive oxygen molecules (free radicals) appears to contribute to the development of Alzheimer's disease (chapter 5). Smoking and a high-fat diet, both of which greatly increase the number of free radicals in the blood, are risk factors for Alzheimer's. They also cause cardiovascular disease, another Alzheimer's risk factor.

Antioxidant nutrients—vitamin C, vitamin E, selenium, and the vitamin A family of nutrients, the carotenoids, including beta-carotene—help prevent oxidative damage and reduce the risk of Alzheimer's (chapter 5). According to several studies, antioxidants can help treat Alzheimer's disease.

- Dutch researchers gave thirty people with mild Alzheimer's either a placebo or nutritional supplementation including large doses of the essential trace mineral selenium, a potent antioxidant. After five months, those in the supplementation group showed improved cognitive function.
- Czech researchers gave the antioxidant Parkinson's medication selegiline (Eldepryl) to 173 people with mild to moderate Alzheimer's. After six months, their memory improved significantly. In another study, selegiline enhanced the benefits of tacrine.
- The largest investigation of antioxidants to date was a 1997 study by Mary Sano, Ph.D., an associate professor of neuropsychology at Columbia University. She showed that selegiline and high doses of vitamin E slow the cognitive decline of Alzheimer's by about 25 percent. This study involved 341 noninstitutionalized Alzheimer's sufferers. They received one of four treatments: 2,000 International Units (IU) of vitamin E (sixty times the recommended daily allowance), 10 mg of selegiline, both vitamin E and selegiline, or a placebo. The researchers measured how quickly each group progressed to severe dementia or had to be placed in residential care.

  Those taking the placebo became severely demented or were institutionalized after an average of 440 days. The same level of decline was delayed by 215 days for those taking selegiline and 230 days for those on vitamin E—about seven months.

  Oddly, people taking both drugs fared worse than those taking one or the other. Their deterioration was delayed only 145 days. The researchers could not explain this.

Selegiline is a prescription drug, but vitamin E is available over the counter at pharmacies, supermarkets, and health food stores. The dose that slowed cognitive decline was 2,000 IU a day.

Carnitine (Acetyl-L-Carnitine)

Alzheimer's disease is associated with decreased brain levels of the neurotransmitter acetylcholine. A key ingredient of acetylcholine is the amino acid choline, but for reasons that remain unclear, supplementation with choline has little effect on acetylcholine levels in the brain, or on the progression of Alzheimer's.

However, a chemical combination of two other amino acids, lysine and methionine, called acetyl-L-carnitine, appears to help. Three recent studies show that this compound, generally called carnitine, slows Alzheimer's-related cognitive deterioration:

- At the Mario Negri Institute for Pharmacological Research in Milan, Italian researchers gave 130 people with mild to moderate Alzheimer's either a placebo or carnitine (2,000 mg a day). After one year, both groups showed cognitive deterioration, but those taking carnitine showed significantly less decline in thirteen of fourteen cognitive functions, including memory, logic, verbal skills, and attention to tasks.
- At the Neurological Institute in New York City, Mary Sano gave 30 people with mild to moderate Alzheimer's either a placebo or carnitine (2,500 mg a day for three months, and then 3,000 mg a day for another three months). After six months, compared with the placebo-takers, the carnitine group showed significantly less cognitive decline.
- Finally, at the University of Pittsburgh, a team of psychiatric researchers led by Jay Pettegrew, M.D., gave twelve people with mild to moderate Alzheimer's either a placebo or carnitine (3,000 mg) daily for one year. Based on standard cognition tests, the carnitine group showed significantly less mental deterioration.

Carnitine is available over the counter at health-food stores and supplement outlets. The dose that helps Alzheimer's sufferers is 2,000 to 3,000 mg a day.

Ginkgo

Ginkgo (*Ginkgo biloba*), a living relic of the Dinosaur Age, is the oldest surviving species of tree on Earth. Poetically, an extract of ginkgo leaves benefits the oldest surviving people, notably those with Alzheimer's disease.

Medical interest in ginkgo stems from this herb's ability to interfere with the action of a substance the body produces called platelet activation factor (PAF). Discovered in 1972, PAF is involved in an enormous number of biological processes. By inhibiting PAF, ginkgo has been shown to improve blood flow throughout the body, notably, through the brain.

Even if people do not develop Alzheimer's disease, blood circulation through the brain declines with age. If this becomes significant (cerebral insufficiency), it causes memory lapses, problem-solving difficulties, and other cognitive deficits but does not progress to dementia. In the early 1990s, several European studies demonstrated that ginkgo extract helps restore blood flow through the brain, mitigating cerebral insufficiency.

In one twelve-week trial by researchers at Humbloldt University of Berlin, Germany, ninety people with cerebral insufficiency, average age sixty-three, were given either a placebo or a standardized extract of ginkgo (50 mg three times a day). After three months, the placebo group showed only minor cognitive improvement, but those taking ginkgo showed significantly improved memory, concentration, and reaction time. The ginkgo extract caused no side effects. Ten other studies have shown that ginkgo is an effective treatment for cerebral insufficiency.

In addition, a pilot study in Britain shows that ginkgo can improve memory in young people with normal brain function. University of Leeds researchers administered memory tests to eight women, average

age thirty-two, and then gave them either a placebo or ginkgo (120 mg, 240 mg, or 600 mg). The placebo produced no memory improvement, but the ginkgo did, with increasing doses showing increasing benefits. The women's memory improved "very significantly" after taking the 600-mg dose.

With findings like these, it was only a matter of time before researchers tested ginkgo for treatment of Alzheimer's disease:

- In a twenty-four-week 1996 study, German researchers gave 156 people with Alzheimer's disease or multi-infarct dementia a placebo or ginkgo (120 mg twice a day). Compared with the placebo group, those taking ginkgo showed significant improvement in cognitive function. Side effects were mild and infrequent, with about 6 percent of the ginkgo users reporting headache, stomach upset, or allergic skin reactions.

- In another German trial, researchers in Frankfurt gave twenty people with mild to moderate Alzheimer's either a placebo or ginkgo (80 mg three times a day). After three months, standard tests of cognition showed that the placebo group had deteriorated. Meanwhile, most of the ginkgo group improved, and the rest of those taking ginkgo showed no change. It took four weeks of ginkgo treatment for those taking it to show any improvement. Ginkgo caused no side effects.

- The first U.S. test of ginkgo as an Alzheimer's treatment was published in the *Journal of the American Medical Association* in 1997. A team led by Pierre LeBars, M.D., of the New York Institute for Medical Research (NYIMR) gave 202 people with mild to severe Alzheimer's either a placebo or ginkgo (120 mg a day). After a year, 14 percent of the placebo group showed improved memory, but in the ginkgo group, the figure was 27 percent. "Ginkgo," they concluded, "appears safe and in a substantial number of cases, capable of improving the cognitive performance and social functioning" of people with Alzheimer's.

Another study at NYIMR used sophisticated neurological tests to assess the effects of both ginkgo and tacrine on the brain. The herb and the drug had very similar effects.

In Germany, ginkgo has been approved by that nation's counterpart of the Food and Drug Administration as a treatment for Alzheimer's disease. In addition to treating Alzheimer's and cerebral insufficiency, European physicians also prescribe ginkgo for many other conditions associated with aging, conditions that may coexist with Alzheimer's disease:

- Stroke recovery. French and German research shows that ginkgo improves blood flow through the brain.
- Atherosclerosis. German studies indicate that gingko helps prevent narrowing of the arteries, the underlying cause of coronary heart disease, and intermittent claudication, which causes pain in the legs.
- Vascular impotence. One cause of erection impairment is diminished blood flow into the penis. American researchers have shown that ginkgo treatment results in "significant improvement" of this condition.
- Macular degeneration. This condition involves deterioration of the macula, the part of the retina involved in color vision and fine detail. A six-month French study of thirty-six people with macular degeneration showed that compared with a placebo, ginkgo produced "significant improvement."
- Cochlear deafness. This form of hearing loss results from decreased blood flow to the nerves involved in hearing. A French study comparing ginkgo to standard therapy showed "significant recovery in both groups, but distinctly greater improvement in the ginkgo group."
- Chronic ringing in the ears (tinnitus). A thirteen-month French study of 103 chronic tinnitus sufferers showed ginkgo "conclusively effective." Ginkgo "improved all the patients" who took it.
- Chronic dizziness (vertigo). French researchers gave a placebo or ginkgo to seventy people with chronic vertigo. Eighteen percent of the placebo-takers noted improvement, but among those who took ginkgo, the figure was 47 percent.

Europeans spend more than $500 million a year on ginkgo. The herb is not as popular in the United States, but as word of its benefits to the elderly spreads on this side of the Atlantic, its popularity has increased considerably.

Ginkgo is available over the counter at health-food stores and supplement outlets. The medicinal chemicals in ginkgo leaves appear in concentrations too low to have any effects in a tea, so standardized extracts concentrate them by processing fifty pounds of leaves into one pound of extract—a 50:1 extract. The studies indicate cognitive improvement in Alzheimer's sufferers at doses of 40 to 240 mg a day. Improvement may take several months to become noticeable. Ginkgo side effects, if any, are typically minor, including stomach upset, headache, and allergic skin reactions. If any develop, reduce the dose or stop using ginkgo.

Recently, researchers at Georgetown University in Washington, D.C., and the Weizmann Institute in Israel identified another herbal medicine that shows promise as a treatment for Alzheimer's. The herb, *Huperzia serrata,* is a moss that traditional Chinese physicians call *qian seng ta* and use to treat fever and inflammation. This plant contains a compound, huperzine A (HupA), which is a potent cholinesterase inhibitor, with effects similar to tacrine and donepezil. Preliminary studies in China suggest that it is as safe as these two drugs. As this book goes to press, its effectiveness is being investigated.

Exercise

People with Alzheimer's disease often suffer sleep disturbances and become anxious, unruly, and disruptive. When this happens, adult daycare centers and residential care centers often ask the family to grant permission to give the person sedatives, tranquilizers, or antipsychotic medication. These drugs help Alzheimer's sufferers sleep and control the behavior problems the disease causes, but they also exacerbate the cognitive deterioration of Alzheimer's.

In healthy people, regular moderate exercise improves sleep, elevates mood, and calms anxiety. A 1998 pilot study shows that walking, the exercise most widely recommended for the elderly, has similar benefits in people with Alzheimer's.

Researchers at the Veterans Affairs Medical Center in Bedford,

Massachusetts, focused on seven largely sedentary men with severe Alzheimer's who were disruptive during the day and sleepless at night. The men were fitted with wraparound walkers specially designed not to tip over and with seats that allowed them to rest when tired. Staff coaxed the men to use their walkers to move around the Alzheimer's unit for two hours a day, five days a week for two weeks. By the end of the study, the men slept more soundly, seemed less depressed, and spent more time nondisruptively in group activities. "One family member was so impressed," commented Scott Trudeau, an occupational therapist involved in the study, "that she offered funds to purchase several walkers for the unit."

People with Alzheimer's don't even have to stand up to gain benefit from exercise. At the University of Rochester, Nancy Watson, Ph.D., and colleagues studied twenty-five residents of a dementia unit, some of whom preferred to sit in regular chairs, while others preferred to rock in rocking chairs. Over time, the rockers also exhibited less anxiety and depression.

If you're an Alzheimer's caregiver, take your loved one for regular walks, and encourage the person to use a rocking chair.

Massage

Anyone who has ever had a good massage knows how relaxing this hands-on complementary therapy can be, and according to studies by Florida psychologist Tiffany Field, Ph.D., a professor of psychology, pediatrics, and psychiatry at the University of Miami Medical School and director of The Touch Research Institute there, massage does a great deal more. It triggers the release of neurotransmitters in the brain that enhance feelings of well-being. As a result, it helps treat headaches and enhances athletic performance. It encourages premature infants to thrive. It decreases anxiety and depression among workers suffering job stress and teens with psychiatric problems. It also helps relieve labor and cancer pain, and reduces the muscle rigidity of Parkinson's disease.

Massage can benefit people with Alzheimer's by relieving their anxiety and agitation, which often lead to unruly, disruptive, and aggressive behavior typically treated with medication.

At Vrije University in Amsterdam, Erik Scherder, Ph.D., and colleagues had nurses in the Alzheimer's unit of a nursing home assess sixteen residents' temperament, anxiety, depression, alertness, social involvement, and ability to perform activities of daily living. Then they gave half the group thirty-minute back-rub massages five days a week for six weeks. Subsequently the nurses, who did not know who had been massaged, reevaluated all the participants. The group receiving massage was less depressed and anxious, more alert, more willing to participate in social activities, and more able to manage activities of daily living independently. Then, after six weeks without massage, those who had been massaged slipped back toward their baseline behavior, suggesting that massage must be given regularly to maintain its benefits.

In one study, fifty-seven people living in three Alzheimer's units in British Columbia received either no massage or two six-minute massages a day for three days. Despite the brevity of the massages and the short duration of the study, compared with the controls, the massaged individuals became less agitated, less disruptive, and less likely to wander.

If you are an Alzheimer's caregiver, try giving your loved one regular massages.

Pet Therapy

More than a hundred years ago, pioneering nurse Florence Nightingale said, "A small pet is often an excellent companion for the sick." Unfortunately, her words were largely forgotten until 1980, when Erika Friedmann, Ph.D., of the University of Pennsylvania, stumbled on an unexpected correlation. Independent of all other medical and lifestyle factors, men who'd had heart attacks were more likely to survive if they had pets.

Since then, many studies have shown that human-pet interactions, such as playing with a dog, having a cat purr in your lap, or gazing at a fish tank, can speed the recovery of people with a broad range of medical problems. More than two thousand animal-assisted therapy programs now operate in pediatric hospitals, psychiatric units, re-habilitation centers, and nursing homes around the United States.

Patty Beyersdorfer, R.N., and Donna Birkenhauer, R.N., decided to test pet therapy in the Alzheimer's unit of Maple Knoll Village nursing home in Cincinnati. For thirty minutes a week for five weeks, they brought two golden retrievers into the unit. The dogs were an instant hit with the eighteen residents, aged sixty-five to ninety-five. Residents who were chronically agitated became noticeably calmer around the dogs. Those who were withdrawn climbed out of their shells and fed, brushed, and petted the dogs. Residents who'd lapsed into silence began talking, either to the dogs or about them, and two of the Alzheimer's sufferers delighted in walking the dogs up and down the hall. As an added bonus, the staff reported increased job satisfaction on days when the dogs visited.

If you care for an Alzheimer's sufferer, encourage the person to play with a pet regularly. If you don't have one, perhaps a friend or neighbor does.

Music Therapy

Apollo, the Greek god of medicine, was also the god of music. Down through the ages, music has been used extensively in healing, mostly to calm people made tense and agitated by illness. Edison invented the phonograph in 1877. The first scientific study of music as medicine was published in 1899. Since then, an entire field has developed called music therapy.

Starting in the 1940s, music therapy programs were established at several university psychology departments. The National Association for Music Therapy was formed in 1950, and today more than five thousand music therapists work around the country. Often their services are covered by Medicare.

Music works its healing magic in several ways. It reduces levels of stress hormones in the blood and has a tranquilizing effect on the limbic system of the brain, which plays a role in emotions. It also triggers the release of endorphins, powerful compounds produced in the brain that relieve pain, elevate mood, and encourage feelings of well-being.

Music calms people with Alzheimer's disease. At two residential care centers in central Massachusetts, researchers led by Patricia Tabloski, Ph.D., associate director of the Travelers Center on Aging at the University of Connecticut in Storrs, used standard psychological tests to measure agitation in twenty disruptive Alzheimer's sufferers. Then, for several fifteen-minute sessions, they played calming music (Pachelbel's "Canon in D"). Post-music tests showed that the Alzheimer's sufferers were significantly less agitated.

In addition, for reasons that remain a mystery, many Alzheimer's sufferers who lose the ability to speak or read retain the ability to sing or read and play music, or drum a steady rhythm. Considerable anecdotal evidence suggests that Alzheimer's sufferers who are encouraged to sing, play music, or dance to music are better able to manage activities of daily living.

Music therapists generally say that for a calming effect, soothing, slow-tempo pieces work best. To complement exercise, more rhythmic pieces work best. If possible, affected individuals should choose their own music, but if your loved one can no longer do that, try pieces they enjoyed during adolescence and young adulthood, the time when musical taste generally solidifies.

Or try these calming selections recommended by music therapists:

CLASSICAL

Bach:	"Air for G-String"
	"Jesu, Joy of Man's Desiring"
Beethoven:	*Pastoral* (Symphony No. 6)
	"Moonlight Sonata" (Piano Sonata No. 14 in C Sharp Minor)
	"Pathétique" (Piano Sonata No. 8 in C Minor)
Brahms:	"Lullaby"
Chopin:	Nocturne in G
Debussy:	"Clair de Lune"
Handel:	*Water Music*

Liszt:	*Liebesträume*
Mozart:	"Laude Dominum" from the *Vespers*
Pachelbel:	Canon in D
Saint-Saëns:	"The Swan" from *Carnival of the Animals*
Schubert:	"Ave Maria"
Vivaldi:	*The Four Seasons*

SOUNDTRACKS

Born Free
Chariots of Fire
The Sound of Music

COUNTRY-WESTERN

| Willie Nelson: | "Stardust" |
| | "Sweet Memories" |

GUITAR

Will Ackerman:	"Childhood and Memories"
	"Passages"
Alex de Grassi:	"Southern Exposure"
	"Slow Circle"

PIANO

George Winston:	"Autumn"
	"December"
	"Winter into Spring"
Roger Williams:	"Nadia's Theme"

SYMPHONIC

| Kitaro: | *Silk Road Suite* |

Aromatherapy

Aromatherapy is a complementary healing art that uses fragrant plant oils (essential oils) to benefit the body and mind. Aromatherapy dates back to the ancient Egyptians, pioneers in the creation of perfumes. Today it's used by real estate agents, who advise sellers to bake cookies on days the house will be shown to fill the house with an inviting aroma that prospective buyers associate with "home."

Scientific studies have shown that subtle fragrances can have major effects on behavior. At the Smell and Taste Research Foundation in Chicago, neurologist Alan Hirsch, M.D., ushered volunteers into one of two rooms containing an identical pair of Nike athletic shoes, and asked them to fill out a questionnaire about them. One room was unscented, while the other was infused with a pleasant floral fragrance. Compared with those who considered the shoes in the unscented room, those in the perfumed room liked the shoes more and said they would be willing to pay an average of $10.33 more for them.

In another series of studies, when Dr. Hirsch infused various concentrations of a pleasant aroma into the air of a Las Vegas casino, gamblers happily plunked down 45 to 53 percent more money. The more intense the fragrance, the more the gamblers wagered.

The effects of fragrance go beyond spending. People in a pleasant-smelling environment are also more relaxed. At Memorial Sloan-Kettering Cancer Center in New York, physicians became concerned about the anxiety attacks many people experience during magnetic resonance imaging (MRI), a high-tech diagnostic procedure that involves full-body enclosure in a noisy, claustrophobic machine. In preparation for MRIs, some people were exposed to heliotropin, a fragrance similar to vanilla, whose scent aromatherapists recommend for relaxation. Compared with those who received no pre-MRI aromatherapy, the heliotropin group reported significantly less anxiety associated with the exam.

Scientists are not sure exactly why fragrant scents have a calming effect, but the evidence points to the chemical structures of essential oils. Fragrance molecules are very small and quickly reach the brain either by inhalation or through skin penetration in massage lotions. They appear to work directly on the brain.

Relaxing fragrances—either by themselves or in combination with massage—also calm anxious, agitated Alzheimer's sufferers. Back in 1988, Megan Carnarius, R.N., worked in the Alzheimer's unit of a Colorado nursing home, where agitated residents who became unruly or violent were often given powerful antipsychotic medications that aggravated their dementia. Carnarius wondered if there might be a nondrug treatment for disruptive behavior. She focused on six severely demented Alzheimer's sufferers who had been placed on antipsychotic medication. She gave them two forty-minute massages a week, using lotions containing calming essential oils. After five weeks of aromatherapy massages, none of them needed antipsychotics any longer.

The following year, Carnarius joined the staff of the Alzheimer's unit of Manor Care Nursing Home in Boulder, Colorado, and began using diffusers—special devices that broadcast fragrances—to spread a lemon scent around the Alzheimer's unit each morning. Aromatherapists consider lemon a refreshing, wake-up fragrance. In the afternoon, she diffused any of several calming aromas around the unit— chamomile, geranium, lavender, marjoram, or rosemary. She also recruited students from the nearby Boulder School of Massage Therapy to give people on the Alzheimer's unit aromatherapy massages using the calming essential oils.

The aromatherapy-massage program has not been evaluated in a rigorous scientific study, but Manor Care staff agree that it has had a significant positive impact on the residents. Behavior problems have decreased, and positive social interactions have increased. Recently, the program has been expanded to the Alzheimer's units of several other Manor Care facilities. Some use diffusers and essential oils. Others bake bread and cookies.

Aromatherapy has a calming influence not only in residential care centers, but in any caregiving situation. If you'd like to incorporate aromatherapy into your caregiving, Carnarius and Laraine Kyle, R.N., have developed an Alzheimer's-oriented aromatherapy kit containing fifteen oils and instructions for their use. For more information, contact Aromatic Arts, 1750 30th St. #333, Boulder, CO 80301; (303) 545-2002; fax: (303) 444-0533; e-mail: laraink9@idt.net.

11.

"It's Nothing to Be Ashamed Of,
It's a Disease"

Profile of Faith Hung and Her Family

In 1983, a year after her grandmother was diagnosed with Alzheimer's disease, Huai-Shang (Faith) Hung of Fullerton, California, received a call from a social worker involved in programs for the elderly in Orange County. A new organization, the Alzheimer's Association, had formed in Chicago just three years earlier, and its officers were interested in launching an affiliate in Southern California. They asked if Faith would like to attend the first meeting.

"Right away, I said I'd be there," Faith recalls, "although I had no idea how I'd find the time. With my job, my husband, two young children, and Grandmother's Alzheimer's, I didn't have a minute free, but somehow, instinctively, I knew I should go."

About twenty people attended that first meeting of what would later become a large and active chapter of the Alzheimer's Association, despite its inauspicious founding. The meeting convened in a dreary conference room in an Anaheim hospital. The decor did not matter to Faith. "The moment I walked in, I felt comforted. I remember thinking, My God, I'm not the only one. All these people are doing what I'm doing—caring for a relative with Alzheimer's."

Most of the participants were white, but several were Hispanic, African-American, or Asian-American. One by one, they recounted their stories: the shock of the diagnosis, the growing forgetfulness, the increasingly bizarre behavior, and hardships and isolation of caregiving. As each person spoke, Faith thanked her lucky stars she'd been invited. Until that moment, she had not met a single caregiver outside her immediate family. Each person told a different story, but every saga sounded a great deal like hers.

After a while, it was a young Chinese-American woman's turn to speak. She looked around the circle and burst into tears. Composing herself, she told her story. Her father had Alzheimer's, but in traditional Chinese culture, mental health problems were a source of shame. Her mother had locked him in a room and let him out only to use the bathroom. She rarely let the children visit him, and never spoke of him with anyone outside the family. During this period, the young woman got married, but her father did not attend her wedding. A few months after the ceremony, the woman's new mother-in-law, who had a very traditional worldview, somehow learned of her father's Alzheimer's. The mother-in-law confronted her, saying, "Your father is crazy. That means you're going to become crazy, and that all your children will be crazy. I don't want crazy grandchildren, so"—she turned to her son—"I want you to divorce her immediately." The son did as his mother demanded, leaving the young woman abandoned, thunderstruck.

The woman wept softly as she finished her story. For a long, awkward moment, no one spoke. Faith scanned the room, making eye contact with another Chinese-American woman. They recognized the mother-in-law's attitude. Finally, Faith said, "Alzheimer's is nothing to be ashamed of, it's a disease."

Everyone in the room nodded and tried to comfort the young woman. Faith decided that, on top of everything else, she would take on an additional mission—educating the Asian-American community about the true nature of Alzheimer's.

Faith Hung was born in 1953 in Taipei, Taiwan, the eldest child of affluent parents who had fled China in 1949 when the Communists took over. Her father, Ting (Jimmy), had been a police detective in Amoy, a city in Fuken province, near Canton. He used his police connections to help his family and all of his in-laws escape the mainland, including his widowed mother-in-law, who moved in with him and his wife, Cheng (Chris), and their four children.

Faith's father was successful in several business ventures in both the United States and Taiwan, including a decorative Christmas lighting business and, later, hotels. Her mother worked long hours at her husband's side, and like many affluent Chinese in Taiwan, she left her mother, Faith's grandmother, in charge of the household. "It was really Grandmother who raised us," Faith recalls. "She was the one who got us up each morning, packed us off to school, greeted us when we returned, cooked our dinner, supervised our homework, gave us big birthday parties, and nursed us when we were ill. She was also very beautiful. I never understood why she didn't remarry, but she never did. Instead she threw herself completely into raising me and my brother and sisters. The only time she reserved for herself was her weekly mah-jongg game with some lady friends. Otherwise, she was totally devoted to our family."

Grandmother was born in 1910. She married at sixteen, had Chris at eighteen, adopted a son at twenty, and lost her husband to tuberculosis when she was twenty-four. Grandmother was very strict with her daughter, Faith's mother, who considered her insufferably mean, but with her grandchildren, Grandmother was permissive to a fault, and they worshiped her. "I loved Grandmother more than I loved my parents," Faith says, "more than my husband, as much as my children. She was always there for me, always very loving and generous. Later in life, when I learned that my mother resented Grandmother for being so strict with her, I couldn't believe it. She never acted that way toward me or my siblings."

Faith, like her father, tried her hand at several careers after college, moving from medicine to computer programming. While attending California State University in Long Beach, she fell in love and married her American-born husband, Bradley Chin. Finally, after their first son was born, Faith became a real estate broker, which allowed her the freedom of self-employment but kept her very busy.

Meanwhile, her father's business interests had become increasingly centered in Orange County. By the time Faith graduated from Long Beach State, her whole family, including Grandmother, had settled in Fullerton, just a short distance away from her and her new husband. One thing Faith liked about real estate was that while running around Orange County dealing with property, she could usually manage to visit Grandmother several times a week.

During the years Faith was a programmer, her father traveled back and forth between Taiwan and California, but her mother spent most of her time in Fullerton, managing a hotel the family had acquired there. Her three siblings attended Fullerton schools under the watchful eye of Grandmother, who continued to do what she'd done in Taiwan—hold the family together and raise the children.

By the time Faith entered real estate, things had changed. Her siblings were out of the family home, all married and living in their own homes, and her mother spent most of her time back in Taiwan. Grandmother was now all alone in a big house with nothing to do except watch the Chinese television station that broadcast in Mandarin. Faith worried about her. She had few friends in America and spoke no English. Suppose there was an emergency. She couldn't even alert 911.

Faith spoke with her siblings. Chinese families honor their elders, and the Hung children revered Grandmother. "We decided that we would all stop by the house more regularly," Faith recalls, "and take her places with us, incorporate her into our lives."

Faith, in particular, took Grandmother under her wing, to the point that her husband began to grumble about feeling neglected, but Faith dismissed Bradley's complaints. "I really loved Grandmother, and cherished the time I spent with her."

In 1979, when she was sixty-nine, Grandmother began acting odd. "She asked the same questions over and over again," Faith recalls, "silly things like: 'Where's my purse?' 'Do we need gas?' 'When did your mother call?' It was strange. She'd never been absentminded before."

At first, Faith and her siblings thought Grandmother was feeling insecure about being on her own in America. They spent as much time as they could with her. Grandmother appreciated the attention but kept asking the same questions over and over again.

Then one day, Faith's brother stopped by and found Grandmother strangely disoriented. When he asked her what was wrong, she didn't answer. He thought she wanted to speak but couldn't. He called Faith, who called their family doctor. The doctor said Grandmother might have had a stroke, and told Faith to call an ambulance.

The doctor's instincts were correct: Grandmother had had a mild stroke. She spent four days in the hospital and seemed to recover completely. "It was a miracle," Faith recalls. "Four days after her stroke, she was fine, completely normal again."

But very gradually over the next year, Grandmother became forgetful again. "One afternoon I stopped by," Faith recalls, "and found one of her stove burners on. She'd forgotten to turn it off. Another time, I found her front door wide open, and she hadn't noticed it. Once, when my sister picked her up, Grandmother had her blouse buttoned all wrong. She had no idea."

These lapses alarmed Faith and her siblings, but they wrote off most of her absentmindedness to aging—she was almost seventy, which seemed ancient to the grandchildren, who were still in their twenties. When Grandmother had trouble cooking, they cooked for her. When she forgot how to work the washing machine, they did her laundry. "It never occurred to me that she had a disease," Faith says. "I thought that was what happened when you got old. That's why we were taking care of her—because she was an elder and needed help."

Now Faith knows differently. "The latest research shows that even minor brain damage from a mild stroke can often accelerate the progression of Alzheimer's. Grandmother's stroke seemed to trigger everything that followed it."

Faith's first inkling that something beyond aging might be wrong came one afternoon in 1980 when she picked up Grandmother at her weekly mah-jongg game with Faith's aunt and several elderly ladies.

One of the women took Faith aside and recounted a disturbing tale. "She told me the game was going along nicely, when Grandmother excused herself to use the bathroom. When she returned, she asked, 'What are you all doing in my house?' Everyone was taken aback. They were not in Grandmother's house, and it was obvious what they were doing—playing mah-jongg—but Grandmother did not understand. She said, 'Thank you all for coming. Since you're here, let's play mah-jongg.' And with that, she sat down and finished the game."

Faith listened with mounting dread. "Grandmother hasn't been feeling well lately," she fibbed. "Sometimes she gets a little confused."

The friend looked at her intently and replied, "If she's not well, perhaps she should see a doctor. She's not herself."

Soon after the mah-jongg incident, Grandmother's personality began to change. "She had always been gentle, loving, and generous," Faith explains, "but she became moody, suspicious, and short-tempered. It was very strange. I'd never seen her act that way before."

In late 1981, Grandmother visited her son and his wife, who lived about an hour away, in Santa Monica. After the visit, Faith's aunt called and announced that Grandmother had given her a magnificent gift—a beautiful diamond ring. It was not the aunt's birthday. There was no reason for such a gift, except love. The aunt felt very moved by Grandmother's generosity, but Grandmother told Faith a very different story: "Your aunt stole my diamond ring. I demanded it back, but she refused to return it. She's a wicked woman, a thief."

Faith could not believe her ears. Her aunt? A thief? It was unthinkable. She'd called the ring a gift. Could Grandmother be lying? That seemed equally impossible.

Faith called her aunt and reported what Grandmother had said. Her aunt was incredulous. The ring was a gift, she insisted. She would never steal anything from her mother-in-law. How could Grandmother accuse her of such a horrible thing?

But Grandmother stood firm: "She stole it. I confronted her. She wouldn't give it back."

Faith's aunt was mortified. She drove to Fullerton and returned the ring. Crying, she implored Grandmother to remember that she had freely given it. Grandmother snatched the ring up and, without saying a word, turned and silently padded off to her room.

———————

Faith and her siblings were mystified by Grandmother's slow transformation. She'd always been so capable. Now she was increasingly incompetent. She'd always been so loving and generous. Now she was suspicious and sullen. The grandchildren did not want to leave her alone, but they had their own lives to live. They couldn't provide the care she increasingly needed, so they decided to find her a live-in companion. "I made some inquiries at the organizations that help new Chinese immigrants," Faith recalls, "and found a middle-aged woman who spoke Mandarin and was willing to move in with Grandmother."

At first, the arrangement worked out well. Grandmother appreciated the companionship and help, and Faith and her siblings continued to visit and help the caregiver. Despite this initial improvement, Grandmother continued to deteriorate, and her demands on the caregiver increased dramatically. Grandmother needed help dressing. She needed someone to check that her clothes were selected and arranged properly. She lost the ability to prepare food for herself, and meals had to be cut up for her. Once, Faith found her making a sandwich by putting a bar of soap between two pieces of bread. "She thought it was tofu." Grandmother also needed help bathing and, after a while, using the toilet. Then she became restless and started to wander. The caregiver had to chase after her. "It would have been hard for anyone to handle," Faith says, "but it was especially exhausting for a middle-aged woman who felt disoriented herself in a new country and didn't speak English."

There were major advantages to having a caregiver from China. She could cook the food Grandmother knew and speak her language, but there was also a big disadvantage. Without English, the family worried that in an emergency she wouldn't be able to call 911. The caregiver also held a very traditional attitude about mental health problems. "Over time," Faith explains, "she became convinced that Grandmother was crazy and became scared of her—so scared that she quit."

Faith hired several other caregivers, one after another, but caring for Grandmother burned them out, and their fear of her "craziness" drove them out. Meanwhile, Grandmother became progressively more

disoriented, agitated, and restless. She wandered more frequently. Usually, she confined her roaming to the immediate neighborhood around
her home. If she escaped the caregiver, the neighbors knew her and
were good about bringing her home. Once, on an outing, Faith's husband pulled into a car wash, and before anyone noticed, Grandmother
disappeared. Faith panicked and called the police. "We were right by a
huge boulevard. I feared she might wander into traffic and get hit by a
car."

A half hour later, the police found Grandmother. She'd crossed
eight lanes of traffic and had wandered into a department store. After
that, the family exhorted the caregivers never to let her out of their
sight, but the caregivers were willing to do only so much. As they
came and went, Faith became increasingly critical of their quality of
care. She decided to play a more active role in Grandmother's caregiving, neglecting her own family in the process. Her husband grum-
bled. Her children whined.

In addition, Faith became dubious of her siblings' caregiving. "I
didn't think they took good enough care of Grandmother. I felt I had
to check up on them, and they didn't like it."

With their sister constantly criticizing them, Faith's siblings resented her. Over time, their resentment evolved into anger and, finally,
estrangement. "My biggest regret," Faith concedes, "is that I felt no
one but me was good enough to care for Grandmother. My siblings
actually did a fine job, but I couldn't see it. I was so worried about
Grandmother that my concern for her blinded me to a lot of things—
my siblings' devotion to her, their anger at me, the problems in my
marriage, and the fact that I was neglecting my children. At the time
I thought, I have a lifetime to spend with everyone else. Who knew
how much longer I had with Grandmother?"

Meanwhile, Grandmother's restlessness, agitation, and wandering
grew steadily worse. Faith was at her wits' end, so she took Grandmother to their family doctor. "This was 1981," she recalls, "when no
one, not even doctors, knew much about Alzheimer's disease. Our
doctor never even suspected Alzheimer's."

Hearing that Grandmother was restless and agitated and had
trouble sleeping, the doctor prescribed a powerful tranquilizer. Im-

mediately, she calmed down, but she also deteriorated rapidly. "Grandmother was in a daze," Faith recalls. "She could hardly walk, and barely recognized us."

Faith stopped giving her the pills, and Grandmother perked up again, regained her ability to walk, and recognized her family again. Still, things were clearly going from bad to worse. Faith found herself juggling her business, her family, and caring for Grandmother, whose memory loss and general helplessness were becoming increasingly severe. The least little excitement unnerved her, made her flee into her bedroom or out of the house only to wander off unless she was stopped.

Grandmother could still speak, and ask and answer simple questions in a few words, but it was clear that her language skills were fading. She could not follow conversations, which frustrated her tremendously. She alternated between brooding silences and inappropriate outbursts. Eventually Faith realized she needed professional help.

In 1982, between real estate appointments, Faith visited the Orange County Department of Social Services, hoping to get referred to an agency that could supply a trained nurse who spoke both English and Mandarin to assist the live-in caregiver with managing Grandmother. She met with a social worker who asked her to describe Grandmother's situation. When Faith mentioned memory loss, personality changes, agitation, and wandering, the social worker grew pensive.

"Read this," she said, handing Faith a brochure on the warning signs of Alzheimer's disease from the Alzheimer's Association, then only two years old. "The brochure described Grandmother almost perfectly," Faith recalls. "I thought, Oh my God, she has this disease."

Faith had never heard of Alzheimer's. The social worker gave her what little printed information she had—a few more pamphlets from the Alzheimer's Association—and outlined what the future held. From Faith's description, Grandmother was already beyond early Alzheimer's and into more severe dementia. She urged Faith to place her in a nursing home.

As the social worker spoke, Faith reeled. She'd come for a simple referral and had received horrible news. Loss of all memory. More behavior problems. Total dependence. No recognition of relatives. Silence. It couldn't be true, but Faith feared it was. The pamphlet had described Grandmother to a T.

"How long will she live?" Faith asked through tears.

"I honestly don't know," the social worker replied, "but for as long as she survives, she's going to need a lot of help. *You're* going to need a lot of help."

Faith glanced at her watch. She had to meet a client. She called and begged off, then drove home crying a river of tears and called her siblings and her mother, who happened to be in California.

Everyone met at Faith's house, where Faith asked Grandmother to play with her great-grandchildren. While she was occupied, Faith, her husband, her mother, and her siblings and their spouses met in the study, and Faith explained what the social worker had told her. Tears flowed around the room.

Soon after, everyone got down to business. Did Grandmother really have this disease? She needed a medical evaluation, which Faith volunteered to arrange. Grandmother also needed better-trained caregivers, and down the road she might have to move into a nursing home. Faith's brother said he'd look into homes around Orange County. In the meantime, everyone agreed to be even more devoted to Grandmother, to shower her with love and attention and make her as comfortable as humanly possible.

As the family discussed how to proceed, Faith thanked her lucky stars that her American-born husband and her family viewed Alzheimer's as an illness, and not as craziness and a source of shame. Unfortunately, she soon learned that her parents had not superseded the traditional view entirely. As the meeting ended, Faith's mother said, "One more thing. I don't want your father to know the details of Grandmother's illness. We'll tell him she has a memory problem, but that's all." Then she went on to list several other relatives in Taiwan who should not be told the entire truth. Faith felt chagrined, but she honored her mother's requests. She didn't realize how enlightened her family was until the following year when she heard the story of the young woman who had been divorced because her father had Alzheimer's.

Faith and her sister, Joann, took Grandmother to a neurologist at the University of Southern California in Los Angeles. It didn't take long for him to diagnose Alzheimer's.

"Is there any treatment?" Faith inquired.

The doctor shook his head. "I'm sorry."

"How long will she live?" Faith asked.

"I can't say," the doctor replied. At the time, 1982, little was known about the course of Alzheimer's. Nonetheless, the doctor ventured an uninformed guess. "Not long. Maybe a year." (In fact, Grandmother lived another nine years.)

A year to live, an anguished Faith thought, just one year. She took the neurologist's wild guess as unquestionable truth: "I have only one more year to be with Grandmother. If that's all she has left, I'm going to give her the best care I possibly can, and cherish every moment with her as if it's our last together."

Once Grandmother was diagnosed, it became increasingly difficult to find Mandarin-speaking caregivers who would move in with her. "They didn't want to be left alone with a 'crazy' woman." Faith and her siblings stopped by as often as they could, but they had their own lives to live, and their visits did not satisfy several of the paid caregivers, who quit one after the other. "We ran through a lot of people," Faith sighs.

Faith deplored the fact that the paid caregivers seemed unable to distinguish between Alzheimer's disease and insanity, but there was no getting around the fact that Grandmother was a handful. To assist the caregivers, Faith decided to stay at Grandmother's every weekend. From the moment she arrived on Friday evening until she left on Sunday, Faith was run ragged. She fed Grandmother, cleaned up after her, dressed and bathed her, cut her hair, cleaned the house, did her laundry, took her out for walks, and chased after her when she wandered.

As if that weren't enough, Faith often had one or both of her children with her. "My kids were still very young at that time. I remember many occasions when I had a baby in one arm while I helped Grandmother dress or bathe with the other. Looking back, I have no idea how I did it."

As the months passed, Grandmother became increasingly resistant to bathing. Faith cajoled her, and when that stopped working, she made up an elaborate story. "I told her that she was a young bride, and that I was her maid, getting her ready for her big wedding. She liked that, but she wouldn't sit in the tub and couldn't shower by herself, so I had to get into the shower with her, hold her up, and wash her."

Then Grandmother developed difficulty falling asleep. "We'd get her ready for bed, but she wouldn't settle down to sleep," Faith recalls. "She kept asking about dead relatives. Where were they? When were they coming to visit? Why hadn't they written? At first I told her they were long dead, but that just got her upset, and then she really wouldn't sleep. So after a while, I just played along with her: 'They're in Fuken. They're coming to visit tomorrow. Get some rest so you'll be refreshed when they arrive.'"

Eating became a bigger problem for Grandmother. "It seemed that she forgot how to chew," Faith explains. Cutting her food into ever-smaller pieces stopped working. Eventually, all Grandmother could eat were pureed fruits and vegetables fed to her through a big syringe. "It was like feeding a baby," Faith recalls, "only a lot more trouble because she resisted the syringe. It took about an hour per meal."

Around 1985, Grandmother lost bladder control. This was before today's convenient adult diapers were widely available. Grandmother resisted cloth diapers and became quite adept at pulling them off. "For an old lady, she was very strong." Desperate, Faith consulted several social workers and doctors. They agreed that there was only one other alternative to following her around with a mop—a catheter. "At first, it helped," Faith explains. "She couldn't figure out what it was, or where it was, or how to pull it out, so we got a few months out of it, but over time, Grandmother discovered how to pull it out. As if that weren't bad enough, it took a visiting nurse to reinsert it. We were calling the Visiting Nurses Association at all hours several times a week." Meanwhile, as the catheter got pulled out and then went back in, the possibility of bladder infection increased. "That was the last thing we needed, something else to worry about."

Grandmother also developed fecal incontinence. Faith's worst moment as a caregiver came when she found Grandmother playing with some of her own stool. "She thought it was a toy." Faith took it from her and cleaned her up. "A day or two later, I spoke to my mother in Taiwan and told her what had happened. Her only comment was: 'Don't tell your father.'"

By 1987, it had become impossible to find Mandarin-speaking caregivers who would move in with Grandmother, even if they were amply assisted by Faith and her family. "The caregivers wanted a family member there all the time."

That was impossible, so Faith proposed what she considered to be the next best option: Grandmother and the caregiver could move into *her* home. She would be there much of the time, and her parents and siblings could help out whenever possible, but Bradley wouldn't hear of this arrangement.

"We don't have the room," he insisted, "and we have two young children. It's not safe for the kids to be around Grandmother. She leaves her stove on, and makes soap sandwiches. She has no judgment anymore. Even with a caregiver watching her, something very bad could happen." Faith accused him of selfishness and cruelty. Bradley retorted that she was threatening their marriage.

Faith's parents also opposed the idea. They felt that if any family members took Grandmother in, they should be the ones, but because of how much time they spent in Taiwan, that was impossible. They considered it unseemly for Faith to assume a responsibility that was theirs, and feared it would reflect badly on them with their friends and relatives.

Faith's siblings were also united in their opposition. They were convinced that if Grandmother moved in with Faith, their sister would become even more domineering and insufferable. Except for Faith, the entire family believed that the best way to deal with Grandmother was to place her in a nursing home.

Faith's brother had taken the lead in investigating homes around Orange County, but unfortunately, the family's top choice—the cleanest, brightest, best-staffed facility—was about a forty-minute drive away. Faith pleaded against moving Grandmother there. "It's too far," she argued. "We'll hardly be able to see her. There are no other

Chinese people there. She'll feel isolated and lonely. They don't serve Chinese food, and she'll refuse to eat and starve to death. The staff can't possibly care for her as well as we do."

Faith's brother acknowledged that the home was rather distant, but pointed out that Grandmother hardly recognized the family anymore. She wouldn't notice if they visited her a little less frequently. As for Faith's ethnic objections, they were ridiculous. Grandmother no longer felt any particular affinity for Chinese people. For months she'd been fed pureed food through a syringe. The lack of Chinese cuisine wouldn't matter at all. Grandmother needed round-the-clock professional supervision, and there was only one way to get it. Still Faith pleaded against placement.

Finally things got personal. "You think you're the only one who loves her," Joann said bitterly. "Guess what, Faith, we all love her."

Finally, Faith reluctantly relented. Looking back years later, she concedes that she dismissed her family's devotion too lightly and lost perspective about Grandmother's needs. "I feel bad about it, but I can't change what happened. Part of my reaction came from my love for Grandmother. Part stemmed from the fact that as caregivers, we were on our own with very little support from the community. Another part had to do with my fear of Grandmother's death. The thought of her dying made me crazy."

In early 1988, the siblings arranged the move.

Grandmother gave no sign of any discomfort with her new surroundings, but Faith could not adjust to having her in a nursing home. She complained bitterly that the nursing home attendants were not sufficiently attentive to Grandmother's needs. "Sometimes they leave her sitting all by herself," Faith reported to the family.

Of course they do, her siblings replied. Grandmother is not the only resident there. The staff can't focus exclusively on her. But, they insisted, the home was the best in their area. It provided excellent care, and Grandmother was doing fine there. Faith couldn't hear it: "My attitude was that Grandmother had to have the absolute best, and nothing the people at the home did was good enough to satisfy me."

Faith fretted and complained to the home's management. She demanded that a staff person be assigned exclusively to Grandmother. Of course, the management took a dim view of that idea. Faith kept pestering, and the replies she received became progressively less polite. Finally, exasperated, she told the director, "All right. I'll bring a caregiver for Grandmother out here myself!" That's fine, the director replied, but you must agree to three conditions: You pay this caregiver. She obeys our rules, and she doesn't sleep here. She goes home at night. Faith agreed.

Faith's family thought she'd lost her mind, but she was determined to give Grandmother the very best. Luckily, through family friends, Faith found a woman who seemed perfect. She was sixty but very energetic. She'd worked as a nurse and could adapt to the rules at the home, and she spoke both Mandarin and Cantonese. Her name was Ho-shu Yuan, but everyone called her Grandma Ho.

Grandma Ho took such excellent care of Grandmother that Faith and the rest of her family quickly adopted her as an honorary relative. Faith's parents arranged jobs for several of Grandma Ho's family in their growing network of businesses in Southern California.

The problem was that Grandma Ho didn't drive. To get her to the nursing home and back required *two* round-trips a day—more than three hours of driving. Faith's siblings loved Grandma Ho, but her placement at the nursing home had been entirely Faith's idea, and they refused to provide much of her transportation, so most of the driving fell to Faith. "I had no life. My business suffered. My children suffered. My husband got very angry, and all that driving drove me crazy."

After three months, Faith couldn't take it anymore. One day, she ran into an old friend who made the mistake of asking how she was. Faith broke down sobbing. The friend listened to her story and then said, "Wait a minute. Doesn't your family own a hotel? Couldn't your grandmother live there?"

Faith loved the idea, and so did the rest of her family. Why hadn't they thought of it themselves? The hotel's two-bedroom manager's apartment was vacant, and it was perfect for Grandmother and Grandma Ho. In emergencies, or when Grandma Ho needed help, the hotel was staffed twenty-four hours a day by people who spoke both Mandarin and English. Two of Faith's siblings and Grandma

Ho's grandson worked there, so they could check on Grandmother and Grandma Ho several times a day. Faith lived only about fifteen minutes away, and the two women could live at the hotel for free.

The move to the hotel worked out wonderfully. Grandmother could no longer walk, so Faith bought her a large stuffed chair and positioned it near a window overlooking the hotel grounds. Freed from her daily trek to and from the nursing home, Grandma Ho was also ecstatic about the move. Faith's siblings doted on Grandmother, and Faith visited every day, quite frequently with her children, who enjoyed playing with their great-grandmother, even though she had no idea who they were.

At the hotel, Grandmother continued to deteriorate, but it was a gradual and fairly peaceful decline. Two and a half years later, in 1991, Grandmother developed pneumonia. She was hospitalized and slipped into a coma. Four days later, she died. She was eighty-one and had survived with Alzheimer's for more than a decade.

Shortly after Grandmother's death, Faith and Joann found themselves in her apartment making funeral arrangements. Faith wanted her to have a magnificent coffin.

"Why?" Joann asked. "She's going to be cremated. Why not have a modest coffin and donate the money saved to Alzheimer's research?"

"We'll do both," Faith decreed, "have the best coffin *and* make a donation."

"There you go again," Joann shouted bitterly, "assuming you know what's best, making all the decisions yourself."

"What?" Faith was taken aback by her sister's vehemence.

"You think you're the only one who loved her." Joann was crying now. "We all loved her!"

Suddenly a decade of repressed frustration and anger erupted inside Joann and she snapped. She slapped Faith hard across the face, grabbed her hair, and pulled her to the floor, hitting and kicking her. Faith was flabbergasted. The altercation lasted only moments before Joann let Faith go and rolled off her. Both sisters lay on the floor sobbing. Then, without saying a word, Joann got up and left.

Faith was well aware of the sibling tensions over Grandmother's

care, but she had no idea that Joann had been so furious with her. In
her eulogy at Grandmother's funeral, Faith tried to mend fences by
lavishing praise on her siblings for their devotion. The gesture helped,
and it started an extended healing process that eventually reconciled
Faith and her family. Today, she is close to all of her siblings.

Faith's marriage did not fare as well. Shortly after Grandmother's
funeral, Bradley left her, and eventually the couple divorced. "The
energy I put into caring for Grandmother was not the only reason we
broke up," she explains, "but it was a big reason. Bradley always complained, 'I'm not number one with you. Grandmother is.' It was true.
I thought I had my whole life to spend with Bradley but so little time
left with Grandmother. As things turned out, I had a lot more time
with Grandmother than the doctor predicted, and a lot less with
Bradley."

Faith moved the chair in which Grandmother spent most of her
final years from the hotel to the study in her home. When she sits in
it, she feels Grandmother's presence: "When I was a caregiver, I made
mistakes. I was too dominant, too dictatorial. I didn't realize how
deeply my family resented me. I should have seen it, but I didn't, and
I feel badly about it. That was a very stressful time, and none of us
handled Grandmother's illness all that well. I feel lucky that my siblings and I are close again and that Bradley and I are still friends and
cooperative as divorced parents."

For the last several years, Faith has been active in the Alzheimer's
Association, trying to help caregivers manage better than she did. "It's
my way of honoring Grandmother's memory, turning my grief into
action."

She still feels haunted by the young woman whose mother-in-law
forced her divorce. "I do a lot of outreach to Asian-Americans, but
they're not the only ones with mistaken ideas about Alzheimer's. All
sorts of people are in the dark. I keep delivering one simple message:
Alzheimer's is nothing to feel ashamed of. It's a disease."

12.

Before You Do Anything Else, Take Care of Yourself

A Lesson for Caregivers

It's a familiar litany to frequent flyers. Shortly after takeoff, a flight attendant explains how to use the oxygen masks: "If you are traveling with small children or anyone who needs assistance, put *your* oxygen mask on first, and then help those traveling with you." Why should you don your own mask first? Because in an emergency, you can't help anyone else if you're struggling to breathe yourself. You have to take care of yourself before you can help others.

Alzheimer's is also an emergency, but unfortunately, many caregivers live in denial of this simple but profound truth. In the interest of helping loved ones with the disease make the most of what remains of their lives, many caregivers *withdraw from their own lives.* The results have been documented in many studies: Alzheimer's caregivers are at high risk for burnout, depression, other illnesses, elder abuse, loss of friends, and strained relationships with spouses and other family members.

Many books on Alzheimer's caregiving subtly encourage this martyrdom by discussing at great length how to care for the Alzheimer's sufferer and failing to deal adequately with caregivers' needs. With Alzheimer's disease, there are *two* affected individuals—the person with dementia and the primary caregiver. Both people have needs that must be met for the caregiving relationship to work. It's *not* selfish for caregivers to have a life apart from caregiving—time off for fun, friends, hobbies, vacations, and relaxation. In fact, it's an *absolute necessity.* "The research is quite clear," notes Colorado Springs, Colorado, psychologist Raye Lynn Dippel, Ph.D., coeditor (with J. Thomas Hutton, M.D.) of *Caring for the Alzheimer Patient* (third edition). "Caregivers who do not obtain sufficient time away from the responsibilities of caregiving feel a much greater sense of burden, and have less success managing their own physical and emotional health." In other words, if you don't take good care of yourself, you can't take good care of anyone else.

Good self-care also postpones placement in residential care, which keeps your loved one at home longer and can save you tens of thousands of dollars. In a landmark study at New York University Medical Center's Aging and Dementia Research Center (NYU-ADRC), Mary Mittelman, Ph.D., and colleagues recruited 120 New York–area caregivers whose husbands or wives had been recently diagnosed with Alzheimer's. About half were assigned to a control group, who received standard NYU-ADRC advice on managing home care. The other half were assigned to a group that received intensive support. In addition to standard NYU-ADRC advice, the second group participated in a weekly support group and received both individual and family counseling to coach their caregiving, connect them with community support services, and help maintain their mental health. Finally, they were given the phone numbers of on-call counselors who were available to provide support and caregiving advice twenty-four hours a day, seven days a week.

Three and a half years later, after all the spouses with Alzheimer's had been placed in residential care, the researchers calculated how long the caregivers had been able to keep their spouses at home. Members of the control group provided care for an average of 874 days (about two years and five months). Those who received intensive support lasted 1,203 days (about three years and three months), a ten-month difference.

Meeting the caregivers' needs not only extended the period of time they could manage their spouses well at home; it also saved them $30,000 to $50,000 per family on residential care. (The support program cost only a small fraction of that.)

One of the coauthors of this book, Dolores Gallagher-Thompson, Ph.D., specializes in caregiver support, which includes individual counseling, support groups, and innovative classes that train caregivers to cope more calmly, creatively, and effectively with the many challenges of Alzheimer's caregiving. She and a growing number of Alzheimer's experts are convinced that caring for caregivers is as important as caring for those with the disease. The National Institute on Aging and the National Institute for Nursing Research agree. They recently funded a new program, Resources for Enhancing Alzheimer's Caregiver Health (REACH), a five-year effort to support caregivers across the ethnic and cultural spectrum using many of the approaches used in this chapter.

Who Are the Caregivers? How Does Caregiving Affect Them? What Advice Do They Offer?

During the last decade, many researchers have surveyed Alzheimer's caregivers. More recently, three organizations have independently compiled overviews. The Family Caregiver Alliance, based in San Francisco, analyzed thirty reports on caregivers published in social science journals. *Caregiving* newsletter, based in Park Ridge, Illinois, surveyed its readers, and the Alzheimer's Association national office in Chicago commissioned a nationwide survey of five hundred caregivers. What emerges from these efforts is a portrait of who caregivers are and how caregiving affects their lives. It is a cautionary tale.

- About 55 percent of caregivers are spouses, 35 percent are adult children (overwhelmingly daughters and daughters-in-law), 5 percent are siblings, and 5 percent are other relatives, friends, or paid companions.

- Women account for about 75 percent of primary caregivers. Wives are much more likely to provide care for husbands with Alzheimer's than husbands are to care for affected wives. When children provide care, about 80 percent are daughters or daughters-in-law.
- Caregivers range in age from teens to people in their nineties, but the most typical caregiver is fifty to seventy years old.
- About one-third of caregivers provide care entirely unassisted.
- About half of caregivers under age sixty-five work at least part-time.
- Caregivers spend an average of *seventy hours a week* in caregiving. Caregivers who work typically devote about forty hours a week to caregiving, while nonworking caregivers spend up to a hundred hours a week.
- Half of caregivers live with the Alzheimer's sufferer.
- About two-thirds of caregivers say that their loved one cannot bathe, dress, or toilet without assistance.
- Seventy percent of caregivers are reluctant to leave their loved one alone even for brief periods.

Why do caregivers do it? Almost all (96 percent) call caregiving a "labor of love," and say that caregiving can provide emotional fulfillment. Some 75 percent of caregivers say it makes them feel "useful." Unfortunately, it often takes a major toll:

- More than two-thirds of caregivers call it "frustrating," "draining," and "painful."
- Two-thirds report symptoms of depression.
- Half say caregiving causes considerable stress within their immediate families.
- Half complain that they do not have enough time for themselves.
- Almost half say they do not get enough sleep.
- Almost half say their health has deteriorated since they became caregivers.
- One-third say they are near burnout.

Caregiving costs caregivers not only time and energy, but also money:

- Sixty percent largely support the affected person financially.
- About half say that caregiving has forced them to make financial sacrifices.
- One-third say caregiving has forced them to work less, reducing their own income.
- One-third say that preoccupations with caregiving have reduced their productivity at work.
- One-fifth of caregivers stopped working because of the demands of caregiving.
- Ten percent complained of being turned down for a promotion because of the time and energy they devoted to caregiving.
- Working caregivers take an average of seventeen days a year off work because of the demands of caregiving.

What are the most challenging aspects of caregiving?

- Getting time off.
- Finding affordable help.
- Managing day-to-day stress.
- Managing the person's behavior problems.
- Mourning the loss of the relationship with the person.
- Finding the energy to continue providing care.

What advice do caregivers have for those considering caregiving?

- Do whatever is necessary to take at least one night a week for yourself and, ideally, more time off.
- Learn as much as possible about Alzheimer's disease.
- Get help—as much as you can afford.

Help may be obtained from several sources, such as the Alzheimer's Association and adult daycare centers. Services vary depending on their cost, accessibility, and outreach. Here are a few options to consider:

▪ **Household assistance.** Getting help with non-caregiving chores—shopping, cooking, laundry, etc.—lets you devote your time and energy to Alzheimer's care. In general, it's easier to arrange for non-caregiving help because it's less demanding physically and emotionally.

If you love to cook, or garden, or do laundry, or clean house, by all means keep doing them, but most people would gladly give up at least some household chores if they could, especially when they're preoccupied with Alzheimer's caregiving.

Consider hiring a neighborhood teen to do chores for you. Teenagers are often happy to work for the minimum wage, and incorporating them into your care plan also helps your neighbors adjust to the idea of having a person with Alzheimer's in the neighborhood.

Consider hiring neighbors—homemakers, retirees, disabled people, or other adults with time on their hands—to help you provide care. A network of nearby helpers can work wonders for your peace of mind when minor emergencies arise.

Consider delivery services. Most cities have grocery-delivery services for the elderly, disabled, or for people who simply would rather not shop. An increasing number of restaurants deliver, and many areas have Waiters on Wheels services—special services that publish books of menus from selected restaurants and pick up meals you order and deliver them to you. A few takeout or delivered meals a week can be a tremendous help. Many areas also have low-cost Meals on Wheels programs for the elderly and disabled.

▪ **Caregiving help from family members.** If at all possible, before you begin caregiving, sit down with relatives who say they want to help and get them to commit to specific times on specific days, or specific chores. Ideally, get these commitments in writing. Asking for specific written commitments does not mean that you mistrust your relatives. You are about to embark on one of the most challenging tasks people ever undertake. You need to know exactly what kind of help you can expect. When commitments are left vague, misunderstandings are much more likely. Get it in writing. And don't be surprised if relatives follow through for a while and then withdraw.

▪ **Share-care.** Who knows as much as you do about Alzheimer's caregiving? Other people who are doing the same thing. If you belong to an Alzheimer's support group, perhaps you and another member can arrange to take turns giving each other time off by caring for both of your loved ones.

▪ **Caregiving help from friends.** The best course of action is to have heart-to-heart talks with close friends *before* you become a caregiver. Tell them you're seriously considering it. Talk about your feelings and the changes the move will bring to your life and your friendships. If friends offer to help, ask for specific commitments, but don't be surprised if friends help for a while and then withdraw.

▪ **Video respite.** Several videos of relaxing scenes have been produced specifically to keep people with Alzheimer's calm and occupied, so caregivers can have time to themselves. (See appendix I.)

▪ **Help from religious or social organizations.** Church or social organizations (Lions, Kiwanis, Junior League, etc.) may be willing to help out from time to time, especially with specific projects, for example, spending one day moving the person from independent living into your home. Assess your extended social support network and consider how to use it most strategically. Church groups and other clubs may not be willing or able to commit to ongoing help, but every now and then they might prove very helpful.

▪ **Home aides.** Many different types of people can provide in-home care. The most skilled—and expensive—are registered nurses. They can be invaluable if the person has a physical illness or disability that requires nursing care. If so, Medicare may help pay for home nursing care.

Most people with mild to moderate Alzheimer's don't need skilled nursing care, but other types of aides function as companions. Their training varies, and some may have had no formal training at all. Get referrals from your Alzheimer's support group, the Alzheimer's Association, social workers, or senior citizens or religious organizations.

▪ **Adult daycare.** Adult daycare not only gives you time off, but quite frequently it provides clear benefits to people with Alzheimer's disease. Just as you need time away from your loved one, the person you care for may want some time away from you. People with Alzheimer's often enjoy being around others their own age in a facility that caters to their needs and interests in ways you may not be able to, for example, by playing the music they grew up with. You may find that once the person gets used to going to adult daycare, he or she begins to look forward to it and returns home more relaxed.

Adult daycare centers offer a variety of group activities, including music, games, stories, and exercise, along with lunch, snacks, and sometimes pick-up and drop-off services. Different facilities offer different programs. Visit the one(s) in your area and see which one you like best. Evaluate adult daycare centers as you would a nursing home (chapter 14). Typically centers admit participants with a variety of health problems, but the one(s) in your area may or may not welcome people with Alzheimer's. Some centers, though, specialize in people with dementia.

Daycare can also help pave the way for eventual residential placement. Some daycare centers are affiliated with residential care facilities. The combination often eases the transition into residential care because by the time the person needs to be placed, the facility and staff are familiar.

▪ **Short-stay residential care.** Some residential facilities permit short stays that will allow you to take a short vacation. Check with facilities near you.

Preparing to Be a Caregiver

Those who cope most successfully with caregiving don't jump into it impulsively. Instead they take time to adjust to the idea and to allow the rest of their household and extended family to adjust as well. Consider:

▪ **Division of responsibilities.** Who is going to take care of what? Are you prepared to shoulder the entire burden? Or are your spouse, siblings, children, other relatives, and friends willing to help? If so, what exactly are they willing to do?

▪ **Your marriage.** What does your spouse think of housing someone with Alzheimer's? Even if your spouse is supportive and helpful, the responsibilities and stresses of caregiving are bound to strain your marriage. Can you handle it? Listen closely to how your spouse feels. Consider discussing your plans with a marriage counselor, clergyman, social worker, or some other professional who can help you sort out how caregiving might affect your marriage.

▪ **Your children.** Kids will be kids, and a lot of what kids do can be very upsetting to people with Alzheimer's. Likewise, the behavior of someone with Alzheimer's can upset kids. How do your children feel about sharing their home with a mentally impaired relative? How will their friends react? How will the person's presence affect your relationship with your children? You probably won't be able to give them as much of your undivided attention. Can they handle that? Can you?

▪ **Your siblings and other relatives.** You take in a loved one with Alzheimer's, and your siblings say, "We'll help. We'll be there for you." But suppose they don't come through the way you thought they would. You confront them. They insist that they're doing everything they can. Meanwhile, you're stuck doing a great deal more than you thought you would. How would you feel?

Or, conversely, your relatives spend more time at your home than you'd planned on. Perhaps they don't trust your caregiving. How would you feel about that? Or maybe their constant presence puts a burden on you and your immediate family. How would you deal with this?

▪ **Your job.** It's not easy to provide quality care and work at the same time. Do you have the energy to do both? Do you have the kind of relationship with your boss and coworkers that would allow you the flexibility caregivers need? Could you work part-time?

▪ **Your home.** Do you have room for the affected individual? Do you have furnishings? Bathroom facilities? Are you sacrificing a den, family room, study, or guest room to house the person? If so, how do you plan to cope with the loss of that space? The long-term presence of any new person changes household dynamics, often in unexpected ways. Try to anticipate as much as possible.

▪ **Your finances.** Alzheimer's caregiving is expensive, and as the person deteriorates, costs escalate. Do you have the resources to cope? Are other family members willing to contribute? Does the affected person have financial resources you can draw on? Meanwhile, you may have to cut back on work or stop working. Can you afford to do that?

- **Your leisure time and social life.** You'll have less of both. As the disease progresses, you may have to severely curtail your hobbies, dates with friends, outings to cultural events, etc. Can you cope with that? How deprived do you think you'll feel?

- **Your sleep.** People with Alzheimer's often do not sleep through the night. That means that you may not, either. Sleep deprivation causes irritability and depression, reduces energy, threatens sense of humor, and makes daily stresses feel even more challenging. How do you plan to cope?

- **Your things.** People with Alzheimer's don't mean to make messes. They can't help themselves. You can understand that intellectually, but what happens when you find your jewelry strewn about the house? Or when your spouse finds a crafts project destroyed? Or when your daughter finds her closet a shambles?

- **Your neighbors.** Having an Alzheimer's sufferer in the neighborhood affects them, too, and their concerns are legitimate. The affected individual might wander into their homes, or step in front of their cars, ruin their gardens, or intimidate their children. How do you plan to keep the peace?

- **Your own physical and mental health.** In the face of responsibilities that can feel overwhelming, how do you plan to take care of yourself? Remember, if you don't take good care of yourself, you cannot provide good care.

Caregiver Distress: Its Signs and Impact

Caring for a loved one with Alzheimer's takes the wisdom of Solomon, the patience of Job, and the selflessness of a saint. Very few people possess this combination of qualities even some of the time. If you do, it's highly unlikely that you'll exhibit them during every moment of your caregiving career, an enterprise that might well extend many years. Inevitably, things slip out of control, leading to physical and psychological distress.

In a recent Consensus Statement published in the *Journal of the American Medical Association,* experts with the Alzheimer's Association, the American Geriatrics Society, and the American Association for

General Psychiatry determined that *half* of primary caregivers develop significant distress. Here are the signs:

- **Activity withdrawal.** Have you given up your favorite pastimes? The demands of caregiving always mean less time for gardening, movies, hobbies, and other activities you enjoyed before you became a caregiver. But if you've cut out your activities entirely, you're in distress.

- **Social withdrawal.** Have you withdrawn from close friends? Fewer visits? Shorter phone calls? Routine refusals of invitations? The responsibilities of caregiving always involve seeing less of acquaintances, but if you've withdrawn from close friends, you're in distress.

- **Depression.** Do you feel persistently sad, irritable, helpless, or hopeless? Do minor upsets make you cry? These are classic symptoms of depression. Of course, it's sad to watch a loved one descend into Alzheimer's, but if you start to feel overwhelmed by sadness or weep over minor upsets, you're in distress.

- **Frustration and anger.** Do minor hassles make you furious? Are you yelling more lately? Having trouble controlling your temper? It's natural to yell if the Alzheimer's sufferer breaks a family heirloom, but if your blood begins to boil when the person ahead of you in the supermarket express checkout line has eleven items instead of the limit of ten, you're in distress.

- **Weight changes.** Have you gained or lost more than five pounds in the last few months? Weight changes are another sign of depression and distress.

- **Sleep problems.** Do you have trouble sleeping? Caring for a loved one with Alzheimer's can cause periodic anxiety dreams, nightmares, and sudden wake-ups in the wee hours, but frequent sleep disturbances signal distress.

- **Exhaustion.** Do you feel tired all the time? If you frequently wake up feeling you're too tired to get out of bed despite a good night's sleep, you're in distress.

- **Illness.** Do you seem to be getting sick more often than you used to? If you seem to be getting one illness after another, and if they linger longer than you think they should, you're in distress.

- **Chronic health complaints.** Anyone can experience occasional headaches, diarrhea, constipation, stomach distress, back or neck pain, heart palpitations, or other complaints. But if they become severe and persistent, chances are you're in distress.

▪ **Escape fantasies.** It's natural to react to the demands of caregiving by occasionally wishing you were elsewhere, but if you have frequent escape fantasies, you're in distress.

Some people react to caregiver distress by lashing out at the affected individual. Various studies show that 67 percent of caregivers admit getting angry at the person "frequently." About 40 percent admit occasionally "losing control" by shouting at the person or throwing things. In one survey of 340 Alzheimer's caregivers, 12 percent admitted shoving, pinching, biting, hitting, or kicking the person at least once. (Chances are, the real figures are higher because even in surveys that guarantee anonymity, people tend to be reluctant to admit abusive behavior.)

Typically, caregivers take their frustration and anger out on themselves, which causes both physical distress, notably immune impairment, and psychological distress, in the form of depression.

▪ **Immune impairment.** At Ohio State University College of Dentistry, John Sheridan, Ph.D., a professor of oral biology, tracked the effectiveness of flu vaccination in sixty-four elderly men and women, half of whom were caring for spouses with Alzheimer's. Vaccines stimulate the immune system to produce a specific defense (antibodies) against specific germs. However, if your immune system is impaired, you don't produce as many antibodies and so have less protection against the illness. In the non-caregivers, the flu shot stimulated the desired response, but among the Alzheimer's caregivers, only 37 percent produced an adequate antibody response.

Next door, at Ohio State's College of Medicine, the husband-wife team of Ronald Glaser, Ph.D., a professor of microbiology and immunology, and Janice Kiecolt-Glaser, Ph.D., a professor of psychiatry and psychology, studied the rate of healing of surgical incision wounds, another indication of immune function, in twenty-six elderly people, half of whom were Alzheimer's caregivers. In the non-caregivers, complete healing took thirty-nine days. In the caregivers, it took forty-nine days, 26 percent longer, clearly indicating immune impairment.

The immune impairment that results from chronic emotional distress has been linked to many illnesses, from the common cold to heart disease. No wonder that compared with non-caregivers, Alzheimer's caregivers report more health problems than the general population and take longer to recover from them.

- **Depression.** An estimated 5 percent of Americans suffer serious ("clinical" or "major") depression at any given moment. Another 5 percent experience mild depression. By comparison, some 20 to 80 percent of Alzheimer's caregivers become depressed. The most accepted estimate is that during several years of caregiving, *half* of caregivers become clinically depressed.

If you experience five or more of the following over a two-week period, chances are you're depressed enough to need professional help:

- Severe anxiety or worry.
- Significant weight gain or loss.
- Difficulty thinking, concentrating, remembering, or making decisions.
- Headaches, abdominal distress, or other significant aches or pains.
- Feelings of worthlessness or guilt.
- Loss of interest in usual activities.
- Sadness.
- Hopelessness.
- Helplessness.
- Loss of interest in sex.
- Sexual problems.
- Sluggishness or restlessness.
- Insomnia or excessive sleeping.
- Thoughts of death or suicide.

Of course, during the typical "caregiving career," the demands and pressures of the job change a great deal as the person progresses from mild to moderate to severe Alzheimer's, but caregivers can develop depression at any time. According to a study by Dolores Gallagher-Thompson and colleagues at VA Palo Alto and Stanford, caregiver depression is not related to care recipients' loss of abilities, but rather to caregivers' perceptions of their ability to cope successfully with the situation. Those who are confident of their coping abilities are much less likely to become depressed than those who doubt themselves and feel overwhelmed.

In addition, some caregivers are more susceptible to depression than others. Researchers at the University of Wisconsin School of Social Work in Madison studied 252 caregivers—103 wives of affected husbands and 149 daughters caring for a parent with Alzheimer's. The daughters were significantly more likely to become clinically depressed. It's not difficult to understand why. When spouses marry, they commit to caring for each other "in sickness and in health." Caring for a demented spouse is, to be sure, a major challenge, but the caregiving spouse, in effect, "signed up" for the task years earlier. That's not the case for daughter-caregivers. Caring for the parent who raised you turns the long-established parent-child relationship upside down, hence the greater likelihood of depression in daughters (or daughters-in-law).

If you're an Alzheimer's caregiver, distress is not inevitable, but it is likely. Fortunately, there are may ways to relieve it.

Psychotherapy

Even if you've thought long and hard about becoming a caregiver and have planned the transition carefully, the adjustment can still be emotionally wrenching. Short-term traditional talk therapy, even for as little as ten to twenty weeks, can be extremely helpful.

Bob Knight, Ph.D., of the University of Southern California, and colleagues reviewed twenty studies comparing the benefits for Alzheimer's caregivers of individual psychotherapy with support groups. Individual therapy was more beneficial in relieving caregiver distress, especially for those new to caregiving. At the Older Adult and Family Center of the Veterans Affairs Medical Center in Palo Alto, Dolores Gallagher-Thompson and Ann Steffen, Ph.D., assigned sixty-six clinically depressed Alzheimer's caregivers to receive either twenty sessions of individual psychotherapy focused on resolving issues of loss of the relationship with the Alzheimer's sufferer, or twenty sessions of training in cognitive-behavioral therapy (see below) focused on problem-solving. Overall, the two therapies were equally effective, and depression lifted substantially in 70 percent of the caregivers, but caregivers' reactions to the two therapies varied significantly depending on how long they'd been providing care. Among participants assigned to psychotherapy, those who had been caregivers for less than 3.5 years showed the most benefit, while in the cognitive-behavioral group, those who'd been caregivers for more than 3.5 years improved the most.

It appears that loss-focused psychotherapy is particularly beneficial early in caregiving careers because talk therapy helps people process the grief they feel over the loss of the person they knew and their grief over the life changes caregiving has imposed on them. Cognitive-behavioral therapy, on the other hand, becomes particularly beneficial later because it teaches quick, practical ways to deal with the person's increasing impairment, and inspires hope that even in the later stages of the disease, actions can still be taken to improve the quality of life of both the affected individual and the caregiver.

To find a psychotherapist near you, ask friends, your doctor, a social worker, your local psychological association, or the nearest Alzheimer's Association affiliate.

Cognitive Therapy

You're at the mall with your father who has mild to moderate Alzheimer's. One moment, he's standing next to you. The next, he's gone. Immediately, you start berating yourself: You're a failure as a caregiver. This realization sends you into an emotional tailspin. You decide you're a worthless person. What's wrong with you anyway? You never keep close enough watch on Dad. Now he's sure to wander out into the street and get hit by a car. Then the whole family will hate you. Now you feel really awful—depressed, stressed out, and self-loathing. How did you ever think that a dolt like you could care for anyone with Alzheimer's?

If any of this sounds familiar, then a pair of pioneering psychiatrists, Aaron Beck, M.D., and David Burns, M.D., have two words for you: cognitive therapy.

Dr. Beck developed cognitive therapy in the late 1960s, when he discovered that simple exercises designed to correct distorted thinking had powerful benefits for those suffering from depression and anxiety.

"Cognitive" refers to your thought processes, the very reasoning abilities people with Alzheimer's lose. Cognitive therapy is a powerful, deceptively simple self-help technique for coping with emotional challenges by consciously changing the way you think. It's especially valuable for relieving the anxiety, depression, and helplessness that are rife among Alzheimer's caregivers. Cognitive therapy is easy to learn, either from a psychotherapist-coach or from Dr. Burns's two books on the subject: *Feeling Good: The New Mood Therapy* (1980) and *The Feeling Good Handbook* (1989), both available at most bookstores.

Recent research shows that cognitive therapy has a great deal to offer people who must contend with the stress, anxiety, and frustrations of Alzheimer's caregiving.

What Causes Negative Feelings? The cause of negative emotions—anxiety, anger, impatience, depression, frustration, guilt, irritability—is a matter of opinion. To Freudian psychoanalysts, these feelings result from emotions repressed since childhood. To biological psychiatrists, they stem from chemical imbalances in the brain. To cognitive therapists, negative emotions are caused by *distorted thinking*. This view is comparatively new to the modern mental health profession, but it was first espoused more than two thousand years ago by the Greek philosopher Epictetus, who said, "People are not disturbed by events themselves, but rather by the views they take of them." Shakespeare echoed him in *Hamlet:* "There is nothing either good or bad, but thinking makes it so."

The Ten Forms of Twisted Thinking. In his books, Dr. Burns describes the ten types of twisted thinking that often lead to depression, anxiety, or anger. How many of these emotional traps have you fallen into?

- **All-or-Nothing Thinking.** You see things as black or white. If your father wanders away from you at the mall, you're not the perfect caregiver; therefore, you're a total failure.
- **Labeling.** An extension of all-or-nothing thinking. You take your eyes off your father for one moment, but instead of realizing you made a mistake, you label yourself an idiot, a worthless person.
- **Overgeneralization.** The tip-offs are the words "always" or "never." Your father wanders off and you think, I never keep close enough watch on him. I always mess up.
- **Mental Filtering.** In situations that involve both positive and negative elements, you dwell on the latter. For example, your father had a good time at the birthday party you threw for him, but he didn't eat any cake. You filter out everything positive but the leftover cake and whip yourself for being a lousy baker.
- **Discounting the Positive.** The tip-offs here are: "That doesn't count," "That wasn't good enough," or "Anyone could have done that." You manage to get your father to your cousin's wedding bathed, well dressed, and happy. A relative praises your caregiving, and you reply, "It's nothing. Anyone could have done it."
- **Jumping to Conclusions.** You assume the worst. Your father wanders away at the mall, and you assume he'll be hit by a car.
- **Magnification.** You turn minor problems into major disasters. Your father drops a plum into the toilet, and you worry that you need your entire plumbing system replaced.
- **Emotional Reasoning.** You mistake your emotions for reality. You feel nervous about sending your father to adult daycare; therefore, it must be wrong for him.
- **"Should" and "Shouldn't" Statements.** I shouldn't have allowed Dad to wander away. I should have kept an eye on him. Other tip-off words include "must," "ought to," and "have to."
- **Personalizing the Blame.** You hold yourself personally responsible for things beyond your control. Your dad can't handle a neighbor's barbecue, and you think, I'm a lousy caregiver.

Six Ways to Untwist Your Thinking. When you feel badly, your thinking turns negative. This is what Dr. Burns and psychologist Albert Ellis, Ph.D., another pioneer in cognitive therapy, call the ABC of emotion: A stands for the Actual event, B for your Beliefs about it, and C for the emotional Consequences you experience because of your beliefs.

Let's return to the mall example. The actual event was your father's disappearance. Your beliefs are that you're a failure as a caregiver, a worthless person who never watches him well enough. He'll get hit by a car, and all your relatives will hate you. The consequences of those beliefs are anxiety and depression. Cognitive therapy tries to change the B's so you don't experience the C's.

You can adjust this negativity by subjecting your thoughts to the following tests:

▪ **What would you say to a friend?** People are generally much harder on themselves than they are on others. Suppose a caregiver-friend's father wandered away at the mall. Would you call that person a failure? Never. You'd probably say, "I know how horrible you feel, but it wasn't your fault. People with Alzheimer's develop an uncanny knack for slipping away. My mom did the same thing. She could slip away from me in the blink of an eye. It's impossible to keep them under constant surveillance."

▪ **Examine the evidence.** You berate yourself for never watching your father well enough, but is that really true? You've installed gates and safety hardware around your home to deter his wandering. You've alerted the neighbors, nearby shopkeepers, the mailman, and the police to his tendency to wander. You've gotten him a medical ID bracelet that says "Alzheimer's" and has your phone number. You've done everything Alzheimer's experts advise doing, but in spite of your best efforts, your father still slipped away. That's unfortunate, of course, but overall, you watch your dad quite well.

You also jump to the conclusion that he'll get hit by a car, but what are the chances of that? It's possible, of course, but lately your dad has been quite leery of crossing streets. Chances are he won't wander into traffic.

▪ **Experiment.** If anything bad happens to your father, you think your relatives will hate you. Is this really likely? That time he tripped over your nephew's tricycle at your sister's house and sprained his ankle, no one criticized your sister. She'd done everything she could to Dad-proof her home, but your nephew wanted to impress his grand-father with how well he rode. Everyone understood that his accident was not your sister's fault. If something bad happens because your father wandered away at the mall, chances are they'll understand.

▪ **Look for partial successes.** Instead of condemning yourself as a caregiving "failure," consider your successes. You've managed your father quite well when several relatives insisted that only a nursing home could handle him. Your caregiving has strained things with your spouse and kids, but less than you'd feared, and by keeping your father out of residential care for the past year, you've saved the family about $45,000.

▪ **Define your terms.** Your father's wandering made you feel worthless. Define "worthless." The dictionary says "completely with-out value." That's not you. You've given your father remarkably pa-tient and loving care. Your friends have called you a saint. Okay, you're not perfect. He wandered away. That doesn't make you worthless.

▪ **Solve the problem.** A mall security guard calls. He found your father in the candy store. Of course, you think, he's always loved candy. You realize it's impossible to keep him under constant surveil-lance while you're shopping, so you decide to shop only when he's at daycare. If you have to take him shopping with you, you decide to buy children's mitten-keepers, and clip one end to your sleeve and the other to his.

Seven Steps to Feeling Better. Seven steps is not many, but simplic-ity is one of the major strengths of cognitive therapy. It's quick and easy, and once you understand the basic concepts, it becomes second nature. Sometimes, however, the very simplicity puts people off. They say, "It's so simple, it can't possibly work." Of course, that's jumping to a conclusion. Experiment. Try the seven steps cognitive therapists recommend and see if the process helps you. Chances are, it will.

▪ **Step 1. Get pen and paper.** Write everything down. Getting things down on paper automatically puts some distance between you and your negative thoughts. It provides perspective.

- **Step 2. Identify the upsetting event.** What's *really* bothering you? The fact that your father wandered off? Or that dealing with it made you late for your daughter's soccer game? Or that you feel the incident reflects badly on your caregiving?
- **Step 3. Identify your negative emotions.** You might feel *annoyed* and *worried* about his wandering, *frustrated* and *guilty* about being late for the game, and *depressed* about your abilities as a caregiver.
- **Step 4. Identify the negative thoughts that accompany these emotions.** About the wandering: I'm not vigilant. About the game: I'm a bad parent. About your caregiving: I'm a lousy caregiver.
- **Step 5. Identify distortions and substitute rationality.** About the wandering: I usually watch Dad like a hawk, especially when we're out together. I slipped up for a moment at the mall, but all things considered, it's a relatively safe place to wander. Security is bound to pick him up before he gets into any real trouble. About the game: My daughter knows I love her. If I'm late, she knows that whatever detained me was beyond my control. She won't think the worst of me. About your caregiving: Everyone says I'm a good caregiver. I am, but I'm not perfect. This was just a moment of imperfection.
- **Step 6. Reconsider your upset.** Are you still depressed? Probably not, or at least not as much, but you still feel annoyed that you allowed your dad to wander away. That's okay.
- **Step 7. Plan corrective action.** You decide to shop only when he's at daycare or to connect the two of you with mitten-keepers.

Count Your Blessings. Cognitive therapy is simply an organized way to implement age-old psychological self-care advice. It boils down to counting your blessings. Most stressful, depressing, or anxiety-producing events are not inherently awful. What makes them feel that way is how we react to them. Counting your blessings forces you to step back, get some perspective, and see your problems in a larger context. Cognitive therapy provides a step-by-step program, and when negative thoughts are spinning out of control, an organized program helps.

There is also some research to show that cognitive therapy can help people newly diagnosed with early Alzhiemer's disease adjust to some of the feelings of hopelessness that often accompany diagnosis.

Antidepressant Medication

If nondrug approaches don't relieve your distress, your physician might offer antidepressant medication. Antidepressants help about three-quarters of those with serious ("major" or "clinical") depression who take them as directed. However, they provide considerably less benefit for those with mild depression.

Compared with older classes of antidepressants (MOA inhibitors, tricyclic and tetracyclic drugs), the newer medications (Prozac, Paxil, Zoloft, Wellbutrin, Effexor, and Serzone) are equally effective but cause fewer side effects. However, side effects are still likely, among them: dry mouth, nausea, diarrhea, drowsiness, dizziness, insomnia, and sexual problems.

You usually have to take antidepressant medication for several weeks before you notice any mood elevation.

Antidepressants are no substitute for the other self-care strategies discussed in this chapter. Mix and match the approaches that work best for you.

Support Groups

For anyone involved in Alzheimer's caregiving, a support group can be a godsend. Support groups take caregiving—an experience that leaves most people feeling terribly isolated—and turn it into the sole criterion for membership. Studies of Alzheimer's support groups show that the vast majority of participants call them "helpful" or "very helpful."

In support groups, participants come together with dignity, compassion, and cooperation to share their frustrations, gain perspective, and share advice. When you ask, "Has anyone ever felt . . . ?" or "Has this ever happened to you?" the answer is almost invariably yes. You realize that you're not alone, that you can still laugh, that you can offer advice as well as receive it. And then something magical happens; you feel the profound camaraderie and comfort of being around people who know *exactly* what you're going through.

"Doctors, social workers, and psychologists can't be all things to all people all the time," says Edward Madara, M.S., director of The American Self-Help Clearinghouse in Denville, New Jersey, which helps people around the country find and organize support groups. "When you sit down with others who share your experience, you feel a connection no professional relationship can match."

We humans are fundamentally social animals. A tremendous amount of research shows that close social ties increase resilience, reduce depression, and improve overall health. In previous generations, social support came largely from family and the communities where most people spent their entire lives, but in modern, mobile America, family and close friends may be thousands of miles away. Hundreds of thousands of support groups have, to some extent, taken their place. Support groups are empowering and comforting. They teach practical coping skills, and they're free. The Alzheimer's Association formed in 1980 from a coalition of seven caregiver support groups. Today the association sponsors groups from coast to coast.

While support groups can be a godsend, they rarely meet all of the typical Alzheimer's caregiver's needs for assistance. In the study of Alzheimer's support groups, only one-third of participants said their group helped them resolve feelings of guilt or anger. Individual psychotherapy works better for that. Only one-quarter said their group taught them all they needed to know about caregiving. Classes on caregiving work better for that (see below).

Nonetheless, the vast majority of Alzheimer's caregivers who join support groups value the experience and recommend participation to other caregivers. To find a group near you, contact your nearest Alzheimer's Association affiliate, or a physician or social worker who deals with the disease. Or locate an on-line support group through Alzheimers.com, at www.alzheimers.com.

Classes for Caregivers

Some people shy away from psychotherapy, believing that their problems aren't severe enough to require a "head shrinker." Others avoid support groups because they don't consider themselves "group people." Many people are more comfortable with the idea of taking a class, in which you won't be expected to reveal things you'd rather keep private.

At the VA Palo Alto/Stanford Older Adult and Family Center, staff who specialize in assisting caregivers have enjoyed tremendous success with two eight-week classes for groups of up to ten caregivers: "Coping with the Blues" for caregivers who get depressed and "Coping with Frustration and Anger" for caregivers who lose their tempers. Both classes are based on cognitive-behavioral psychology, described earlier in this chapter.

"Coping with the Blues" begins with the two instructors validating participants' distress and explaining the commonsense widsom of the cognitive-behavioral approach of the class. Their message is: *You're not helpless; you have the the power to change your situation for the better.* One sign of caregiver depression is a seemingly uncontrollable cascade of negative thoughts and feelings. Class participants use cognitive therapy to correct this pattern. Another sign is withdrawal from pleasurable activities. Participants keep a weekly tally of experiences that are fun, and work to have more of them. If it sounds simple, it is. It also works. Participants' evaluations consistently report significant mood elevation, more fun, and increased emotional resilience.

The class called "Coping with Frustration and Anger" is similar. The instructors begin by affirming that it's perfectly normal to feel frustrated and angry as an Alzheimer's caregiver, and that losing your temper (or worse) doesn't make you a bad person. The key to quality caregiving is to learn how to deal with inevitable frustrations and anger in a constructive, nonabusive way. Participants discuss the sources of their frustration and anger and how they respond. Like the class on the blues, participants learn cognitive therapy. In addition, they also learn a relaxation regimen—deep, meditative breathing and guided imagery, imagining serene scenes where they feel calm. They also keep weekly logs of situations they find frustrating, and in class the group discusses how best to handle them. Finally, participants learn to become more assertive without backing down or blowing up. One particularly popular assertiveness lesson is a role-playing exercise in which participants learn to insist, gently but firmly, that other family members follow through on their promises to supervise the Alzheimer's sufferer for a brief period, allowing the primary caregiver some time off. In their evaluations, participants report a significant decrease in hostility and an improved sense of support from their families.

A variation on these two classes is a ten-week session that combines highlights from both. Other classes for caregivers include one on dealing with bereavement and one on staying healthy while caring for a person with Alzheimer's. Similar classes have been developed for Spanish-speaking caregivers and Asian-Americans.

Exercise

No doubt you know that exercise is good for you. While no studies have specifically addressed the effects of exercise on Alzheimer's caregivers, there's every reason to believe that exercise is as beneficial for caregivers as it is for anyone else, if not more so.

Exercise has beneficial effects on your mood, stamina, reaction time, and memory. It also helps relieve pain, improves your sleep, and reduces the risk of common colds as well as many serious diseases. Because the demands on a caregiver are so strenuous, perhaps no one needs exercise more.

Finding time for exercise is a challenge, especially for busy caregivers, but we can't stress enough the importance of the major physical and emotional benefits you'll reap from just a little activity every few days. The latest findings from the nation's leading exercise researchers now show that *any* short-duration exercise that adds up to thirty minutes a day works just as well as longer, more strenuous work-outs. This means that many of the physical activities you may already enjoy—such as walking, gardening, folk dancing—can be great exercise. You might try engaging in some of these activities with the person you care for, and you'll both enjoy the added activity.

Keep in mind that you're never too old to start modest exercise. No matter how long you've been inactive, you can get back into shape. If you're in good health, you probably don't have to consult your doctor before starting a modest exercise program. But if you're over fifty or if you smoke or have a personal or family history of heart disease, high blood pressure, diabetes, asthma, varicose veins, or any other chronic medical condition, it's prudent to consult a physician first.

Respite Care: The Precious Gift of Time Off

When asked what advice they have for new Alzheimer's caregivers, veteran caregivers agree: Do whatever it takes to get at least one night off each week. Remember, taking time off is not selfish. On the contrary, if you hope to provide quality care, time off or respite is an absolute necessity. Here's why:

- Time off allows you to recharge your physical and emotional batteries. You deserve to have some fun.
- Time off allows you to attend a support group.
- Time off allows you to invest some energy in your other relationships—spouse, children, other relatives, and friends—all of which require nurturing. When caring for someone with Alzheimer's, it's natural to let go of relationships with some acquaintances. But don't do that with people who are important to you. You need them, and they need you.
- Time off allows you to make arrangements for the person. If the affected individual is with you, you may not be able to concentrate on matters that deserve your undivided attention: financial

and legal issues, adult daycare centers, residential care facilities, and so forth.

Of course, taking time off from caregiving requires getting organized. Decide what kind of help works best for the person and for you. Then look at your week and arrange to have some blocks of time to yourself.

13.

A Practical Introduction to Loving Caregiving*

How to Care for Someone with Alzheimer's

Despite the many challenges of caring for a person with Alzheimer's disease, the vast majority of caregivers can provide good care until the day—if that day comes—when the affected individual requires residential care.

Be a Best Friend

Some people view caregiving as essentially adult baby-sitting, but this attitude is unfair to both the caregiver and the Alzheimer's sufferer. You will burn out faster, and the person you care for will deteriorate faster and become harder to care for. Most important, you sacrifice what makes caregiving fulfilling—the enduring connection between

---

*This chapter focuses on direct caregiving. If you are involved in long-distance caregiving, contact the American Association for Retired Persons. The AARP sponsors a special program that helps long-distance caregivers.

you and the little joys that emerge when you're emotionally open to receiving them.

In their outstanding book *The Best Friends Approach to Alzheimer's Care,* Virginia Bell, M.S.W., and David Troxel, M.P.H., have articulated a subtly revolutionary approach to caregiving, based on being the person's best friend and showing deep respect for the individual. Here are some of its key elements:

▪ **Treat the person as an adult, not as a child.** Until recently, experts considered the descent into Alzheimer's as child development in reverse, with the person regressing from adulthood to adolescence to toddlerhood to infancy. This conception is incorrect. Alzheimer's sufferers do not devolve from adulthood to infancy. Even when severely demented, they continue to be adults and retain vestiges of their pre-Alzheimer's adult worldliness, knowledge, and personality. Address the person as an adult. Avoid childishness. Modify adult activities to suit the person's remaining abilities.

▪ **Take the person's feelings seriously.** People with Alzheimer's may not be able to express their feelings, but they still *have* them. Sometimes behavior that seems irrational or disruptive is in fact an attempt to communicate a need or desire. Look for meaning in the person's actions. Even when severely demented, most people with Alzheimer's have moments of relative lucidity. Give them the benefit of the doubt.

▪ **Take the person's interests, history, and heritage seriously.** Recent memories tend to fade first with Alzheimer's. Older, deeper memories generally last longer, and some remain despite severe dementia. You know your loved one best. Acknowledge the person's unique individuality, and respect his or her taste in food, recreation, and entertainment. Play the music he or she enjoys and celebrate the holidays that have meaning to the person.

▪ **Be a Best Friend.** Talk to the person as an equal. Respect the person's dignity. Show affection frequently. Have empathy. Try to imagine what it must be like to lose your cognitive abilities. Tell jokes and funny stories. Look for ways to laugh together.

▪ **Be flexible.** In Alzheimer's caregiving, your best-laid plans frequently don't work out as you'd hoped. Learn to let go and live in the moment, taking cues from the affected individual as much as possible.

▪ **Be nonjudgmental.** People with Alzheimer's disease are not being malicious or diabolical, even though it sometimes seems that way. They do what they do because of the disease.

Don't judge yourself harshly either. You're certain to become frustrated, exhausted, and infuriated by the demands of caregiving. You're certain to say and do things you regret. Work to forgive your own imperfections.

To help cultivate the empathy necessary for a Best-Friends approach to caregiving, we present excerpts throughout this chapter from a remarkable book, *My Journey into Alzheimer's Disease,* by the Reverend Robert Davis, written with his wife, Betty (Tyndale House, Wheaton, Illinois, 1989). Davis developed Alzheimer's in 1987 at the unusually young age of fifty-three, when he was a minister at the Old Cutler Presbyterian Church in Miami, Florida. Forced into retirement, he decided to chronicle his experience of Alzheimer's to give caregivers and others insight into the disease. When he began the book, he was still able to write, though some words escaped him, and Betty filled them in. As the months passed, he lost the ability to write and switched to a Dictaphone. Eventually, that skill faded, and Betty finished the book by coaxing the final material out of her husband.

> *While I am still able to communicate, I want to share this incredible journey into Alzheimer's disease. [Families,] be gentle with your loved ones. Listen to them. Hear their whispered pain. Touch them. Include them in your activities in meaningful ways. Let them draw from your strength. [Remind yourself that] the illness will bring changes to your lives and your family. The illness steals your loved one. It brings sleepless nights and fear-filled days. But your loved one is the victim, not the perpetrator, of this crime.*

Helping the Person
Let Go of Independent Living

People who develop Alzheimer's begin their journey into dementia as competent, independent adults, possessing the skills we all take for granted—until Alzheimer's develops. Imagine how you would feel if you developed nagging doubts about your competence in the world. Worse, imagine your reactions if your spouse or your children questioned your ability to manage your affairs. Now imagine how you'd feel if a doctor told you, "You have Alzheimer's disease." The news is shattering, infuriating, depressing, and humiliating. It rarely brings out the best in anyone.

Sometimes affected individuals are the first to become concerned about their cognitive lapses, but many are not, and when a spouse or child raises the issues, they typically dismiss any concerns as ridiculous and insulting.

The key at this stage is to communicate your love as you urge the person to undergo medical evaluation. Remember, although Alzheimer's disease is the most prevalent dementing illness, it's by no means the only one (chapter 9), and many of the others are treatable. Suggest a routine checkup and offer to make the appointment with the doctor, but don't expect the person to take it lightly or go quietly. "Of course you're fine, Mom. But you've said yourself that your absentmindedness is bothering you. It's probably some minor thing your doctor can treat, and then you'll be back to your old self again."

When the diagnosis is Alzheimer's, life suddenly changes for the affected person and the entire family. A journey into Alzheimer's disease brings many losses, but frequently the early ones are the hardest because affected individuals still have enough cognitive function to understand and feel horrified by what's befallen them. Early losses are also very hard on caregivers because they're still adjusting to the wrenching reality of a future increasingly consumed by the enormous demands and expense of caregiving.

Early losses include withdrawal from productive activities, giving up driving, turning over financial affairs, and finally, saying goodbye to independent living.

It's impossible to generalize when these changes should take place, but as long as the person can handle the daily demands of independent living adequately, safely, and calmly, there's no rush to make major changes. As soon as the person can no longer function well independently, it's time for a caregiver to step in.

Withdrawal from Productive Activities

I was totally exhausted. My pulpit robe lay on the communion table. I leaned against the table and wept uncontrollably. Tears cascaded down my face. I had just preached my farewell sermon to the congregation I loved so dearly. I had shut the book on [my] ministry. Why had this happened to me at the very apex of my career? [Now] I can no longer speak in public. I shatter psychologically in any pressure situation. Mental and emotional fatigue leave me exhausted and confused. Mental alertness comes now only in waves at random hours of day or night.

Some people still hold jobs when diagnosed with Alzheimer's disease. Most are retired and continue to make contributions doing volunteer work. When the diagnosis is Alzheimer's, the best course of action is to inform the person's employer or supervisor immediately. Over time, lapses are bound to affect the person's performance, and the boss has a right to know. However, people also have a right to medical confidentiality, so ask the supervisor to inform only those who truly need to know. Affected individuals are, of course, free to discuss their situation with anyone they choose.

Depending on their specific activities, affected individuals may be able to continue for a while or might switch to less demanding tasks. Eventually, supervisors will insist that people with Alzheimer's can no longer function competently enough to continue. This news is often very difficult to hear, particularly for those with paying jobs. Most people have a great deal of identity tied up in feeling productive. It's devastating to be told you can no longer pull your weight.

Many people resist withdrawing from their activities. They insist that they are still fine, that their supervisors and loved ones are persecuting them for no reason. Even if errors can be monitored and recorded, don't expect a tally of inadequacies to persuade stubborn Alzheimer's sufferers to call it quits. It might come down to a dismissal notice from the employer, at which point most people simply retire to avoid embarrassment.

Urge the person to obtain counseling from an employee assistance program, a member of the clergy, or a social worker or psychotherapist familiar with dementia. You might call a meeting in which a group of close friends and relatives affirm their love and respect for the affected individual, while insisting that it's time to retire.

As Alzheimer's disease progresses, affected individuals refer less and less to their working years, and attachments to work fade. Eventually, the whole subject is forgotten.

If Alzheimer's forces retirement from paying work, the disease may have profound financial implications. Urge newly diagnosed individuals to allow you to help them assess their financial condition, and assist them in obtaining Social Security benefits or pensions, or tapping personal retirement assets (IRAs, 401-Ks, annuities, private pension plans, etc.).

In addition, Alzheimer's is a disabling condition, and the Social Security Disability Act specifies financial aid for those who can no longer work because of a disability. To qualify, the person must have worked for twenty of the past forty calendar quarters (five of the last ten years), and have been disabled for at least twelve months. You may need medical records to document the duration of the disability. The Alzheimer's Association can help you document disability, so contact your local chapter. Be prepared to have a petition for disability benefits denied initially. You may need to retain an attorney. If you are persistent, benefits may be granted on appeal.

Giving Up Driving

I was driving the three miles from our house to the church when the unimaginable happened. I was lost. I pulled over to the side of the road, having forgotten my way to the church. I sat there thinking. At last I remembered that to get to the church all I had to do was keep driving down the road I was on. I [finally] got there.

Like a job, a driver's license is a symbol of competent adulthood and independence, but driving ability is often one of the first skills lost to Alzheimer's. Even mild Alzheimer's disease more than doubles the risk of auto accidents, according to the National Institute on Aging. A recent Swedish study shows that auto accidents may even serve as an early warning sign of the disease because driving demands skills often lost very early in Alzheimer's—continual processing of newly learned information and split-second decision-making based on that information (chapter 2).

When should a person diagnosed with the disease stop driving? This is a major unresolved issue in early-stage Alzheimer's care. It's also a crucial issue because 95 percent of Alzheimer's sufferers whose licenses are not revoked continue to drive alone after their diagnoses (though one-third confine their driving to their own neighborhood for fear of getting lost).

Laws governing driving for people with Alzheimer's vary from state to state. Some states immediately revoke the license of anyone diagnosed with Alzheimer's. Others require frequent driving tests and revoke the license when the person fails. Several researchers are working to develop objective standards that might be applied nationally. In the future, driving simulators may allow objective assessment of drivers with Alzheimer's, but until such a test becomes widely accepted, caregivers must decide for themselves, in consultation with the person's physician, when the affected individual should stop driving. The stakes are high. If the person can still drive competently, forbidding it is a wrenching life disruption that turns the caregiver into a chauffeur. However, if the person can no longer drive competently yet continues to drive, the caregiver might be held legally liable for accidents in which the person is at fault. Consider your decision carefully.

When you suggest that the affected person stop driving, expect resistance. Expect to be reminded of all the times *you* have gotten lost, missed stop signs, run red lights, gotten tickets, and had accidents. At some point, however, you must demand that the person stop driving. Try to be tactful. People with early Alzheimer's know their diagnosis and are aware of its implications. Do what you can to allow the person to save face and preserve personal dignity. Suggest that *you* drive, which allows your loved one to enjoy the scenery or nap. Suggest that the person take cabs or walk to close destinations.

If the person adamantly refuses to stop driving, you have several options:

- Ask the person's doctor to lower the boom. That way the physician is the bad guy, not you.
- Disable the car. Talk with your mechanic.
- Quietly take away the person's car keys.
- Sell the car.

Once people with Alzheimer's stop driving, obtain a nondriver state ID card for check cashing and identification needs.

The end of driving can prevent potential tragedy, but it also marks the beginning of another thorny problem for caregivers—becoming a chauffeur. Don't feel as though all the responsibility must fall on you. Try to recruit other family members and friends to help. Look into transportation programs for the handicapped and adult daycare programs that offer outings. For as long as the affected individual can handle cabs, use them. Cabs cost money, but if you compute the cost of car ownership, cabs once or twice a day may be comparable—or even cheaper.

As Alzheimer's progresses, affected individuals care less about driving and eventually forget that it was ever important to them.

Relinquishing Finances

How frightening it is to go into a large, familiar shopping center with crowds and blinking lights, and become totally lost. How humiliating it is to be unable to make the right change and ask the cashier to pick the correct coins from my hand.

Like other aspects of independent life, for most people, money management is closely linked to adult competence. Even after they've lost some ability to balance a checkbook, deal with investments, file tax returns, or make change, many people with early Alzheimer's cannot conceive of turning over their financial affairs to anyone else. As you assume more responsibility for the person's finances, be prepared for accusations of theft. Try not to take such accusations personally, and remember that Alzheimer's experts generally interpret such outbursts as anger against the illness that has stolen their former lives from them.

Begin the process of financial transition by offering to "check" the person's checkbook, tax returns, etc. Then, over time, quietly assume more financial responsibilities. Gather bills and pay them yourself. With trusted local merchants, establish tabs so that the affected individual can still shop but without regard to what they pay. The merchant simply accepts whatever the person offers, and you settle up periodically. Once you have established legal guardianship, you can take over all of a person's financial affairs (chapter 14).

In an effort to keep people with early Alzheimer's from squandering money—paying $20 for a pound of coffee and then refusing to take change—some caregivers try to keep money away from them. This often leads to nasty accusations. Instead, provide small bills and change, so they can feel the security and self-esteem of having money, without being able to lose very much.

As Alzheimer's progresses, affected individuals lose interest in money and their finances.

Saying Goodbye to Independent Living

I tried doing the mental math I sometimes entertained myself with, [but that skill] was gone. I began to panic, and got a sheet of paper and put down some problems. I could no longer do them. Panic filled me. My career was gone and my life was ruined.

It can be wrenching to leave one's own home and move in with a loved one or enter an assisted-living facility. Reactions to this transition vary tremendously. Some people go meekly, relieved to be rid of the increasingly confounding burdens of independent living, while others flatly refuse to leave their homes and accuse caregivers of kidnapping them.

A good way to ease this passage is with a slow transition process: first a combination of frequent visits from one or more caregivers who help with cooking, housework, and daily activities; next, a Meals on Wheels program, a maid, and a daytime aide or adult day-care visit a few days a week; then, finally, full-time at-home help or moving in with a caregiver.

When are people no longer able to live on their own? That depends on the individual, but here are some signs to look for:

▪ **Persistent confusion.** Increasing loss or misplacement of everyday objects, for example, finding the person's toothbrush in the refrigerator.

▪ **Changes in personal care.** Wearing dirty or ripped clothing, wearing shirts backward, going outside barefoot.

▪ **Changes in eating habits.** Food left out to rot, meals uneaten, the stove left on, evidence of burned food, evidence of eating raw food that should have been cooked.

▪ **A large number of reminder notes.** Most of us write a few reminder notes, but someone who can no longer live independently might leave twenty notes around the house—and then still not accomplish the task.

▪ **Changes in home management.** Running the air-conditioning in winter or the heat in summer, leaving windows open in the rain or the water running.

▪ **Persistent problems with the telephone.** Conversations become increasingly vague as memory for detail fades. The person calls at inappropriate hours, or an excessive number of times, or not at all.

▪ **Handwriting deterioration.** As Alzheimer's progresses, writing ability fades.

▪ **Wandering.** You find your loved one walking up and down the street, unable to recognize home, or neighbors or the police call you about the person's wandering.

Once you make the decision that your loved one can no longer live independently, together you must decide where the person will live. If you decide to become a caregiver, expect the transition to be difficult for both of you. If the person moves into your home and has significant adjustment problems, don't face the situation by yourself. Get help from a support group, the Alzheimer's Association, or other resources in your community.

To the extent that you can, involve the person in planning the move. If the person refuses to move, it doesn't help to negotiate. Simply proceed, with gentle reminders that there is no other alternative. It's normal for caregivers to feel guilty, anxious, and depressed about moving a loved one with Alzheimer's, especially if the person is uncooperative. Remember: You are not abusing or abandoning the person. You are doing the best you can to cope with a horrible disease.

Over time, as the illness progresses, attachments to former surroundings fade.

Household Modifications to Consider

With toddlers, the term is "childproofing," household modifications that keep little ones out of harm's way. Of course, people with Alzheimer's are adults and should be treated as adults, so to reinforce this point, we use the term "safety hardware." Furthermore, while some childproofing devices may prove useful to Alzheimer's caregivers—for example, latches for drawers and cabinet doors—other hardware can be hazardous, notably doorway gates that people with Alzheimer's might trip over. Several catalogs offer safety hardware for the protection of demented adults. See the list at the end of this chapter.

Even with the best safety hardware, it's impossible to make any home absolutely safe, but with a little forethought, you can modify your home to reduce the risk of injury and the problems loved ones can cause you when they get into things they shouldn't. You probably won't feel compelled to make all of the modifications that follow, but consider them. As the disease progresses, you may let go of some as you implement others.

OUTSIDE YOUR HOME

I can still work in the yard. The most important thing is knowing where I become lost and confused, and staying away from those places.

Walkways and steps should be clear of debris and accessories, for example, flowerpots. They should be well lighted, and all stairs should have secure railings. Stair edges can be marked with grip tape or painted to make them more visible.

Porches and decks should have railings at least waist high. Lower railings are tripping hazards. Consider having a carpenter make gates (ideally chest high) for the tops and bottoms of stairs.

Yard hazards include uneven ground, holes in the ground, thorny bushes, swing sets, low fencing, barbed-wire fencing, rickety lawn furniture, children's toys, and lawn borders, such as decorative brick, that present a tripping hazard.

Keep all yard and garden tools put away and locked up. If you have a compost pile, cover it securely.

Keep your garage locked securely.

Secure your garbage cans and recycling containers.

Remove clotheslines the person might walk into. Remove other hanging decorations, like wind chimes that might bang the person's head, or raise hanging ornaments out of the way.

When grilling on an outdoor barbecue, never leave it unattended. Afterward, while it's still hot, make sure the person cannot get near it. If you have a gas grill, make sure the person cannot turn it on. Disconnect the gas supply, or remove, lock, or disable the gas flow valve.

Swimming pools and hot tubs are particular hazards. They should be secured. Draining them does not eliminate the hazard, since the person with Alzheimer's can still fall in and get injured.

AROUND YOUR HOUSE

Waking up from sleep is a real experience. I have no idea where I am at times. I am totally lost. I have run into more objects in our bedroom and have more bruises from getting up and wandering around in the middle of the night than I care to state. I forget the pattern of my own bedroom, even though it has been my bedroom for the last 10 years.

Spare is better than cluttered. The less there is to trip over or break, the better. In addition, clutter can confuse or agitate Alzheimer's sufferers. Move knickknacks out of harm's way or eliminate them.

Accidental scaldings are quite common among people with Alzheimer's. Lower the temperature of your water heater.

Keep your basement door locked.

In the basement, clearly label paints, insecticides, cleaning solvents, and other poisonous items. Keep them locked. Also keep the phone number of your local Poison Control Center by each phone. Find it in the first-aid section of most phone books, or in the white pages under "Poison."

Install safety latches on the drawers of basement cabinets.

Install gates at the top and bottom of basement staircases.

Make sure all stairs have secure railings anchored in wall studs, not held in place by screw anchors in Sheetrock.

Eliminate area rugs, which present a tripping hazard even if secured.

Move all fragile valuables to secure locations.

Check for sharp edges on furniture and counters. Consider covering them with foam sheeting secured with duct tape.

Glass-topped coffee tables of any sort are not a good idea. Glass doors on china cabinets can also be a problem. Many china cabinets have removable glass panels. Consider removing them and substituting curtains.

People with Alzheimer's spill things. Consider slipcovers or stain-resistant fabric coatings. If you buy new furniture, vinyl and leather are more spill- and stain-resistant than cloth.

All your upholstery, curtains, drapes, and linens should be flame resistant.

Install safety locks on all windows the person might fall out of. Safety locks allow windows to be opened about three inches for ventilation, but no more.

Radiators can get very hot in winter. Use furniture or fencing as a barrier.

Keep sewing supplies out of reach. People with Alzheimer's may swallow buttons and stick themselves with pins.

Alzheimer's sufferers may eat houseplants. Make a list of all your houseplants, and consult a nursery or your Poison Control Center to see if any are poisonous. Many common houseplants are, for example, Diefenbachias. Eliminate potentially poisonous plants.

Consider installing locks or safety latches on your closet doors.

Increase the brightness of lighting during the day, and decrease it during the evening to provide Alzheimer's sufferers with a better sense of day and night.

Monitor television programs. Try not to expose Alzheimer's sufferers to violent images and sounds that might cause anxiety.

Remove mirrors. They often confuse and agitate people with Alzheimer's.

Remove recliner chairs or disable the reclining mechanism. Alzheimer's sufferers can become terrified when they sit in what appears to be a chair and suddenly find themselves on their backs.

IN YOUR KITCHEN

Stoves and ovens are a particular hazard. If you use gas, remove the knobs so the person cannot turn anything on. If you have an electric kitchen, have an electrician install a hidden switch that allows you to shut the appliance off.

Keep matches well hidden.

Fit drawers with safety latches to keep the person away from knives and other potentially hazardous implements.

Consider switching from ceramic dishes to unbreakable plastic.

People with Alzheimer's may open the refrigerator or freezer and then not close the door. Consider safety hardware that prevents this.

Toasters, food processors, and other countertop appliances may cause injury. Consider storing them out of reach.

Lock your liquor cabinet or secure its contents some other way.

IN YOUR BATHROOM

People with Alzheimer's may lock themselves in the bathroom and not be able to get out. Consider removing bathroom locks or installing a keyed lock you can control.

Install safety hardware on medicine cabinets.

If the person throws things into the toilet, install safety hardware that prevents lifting the lid.

Install handrails in the bath/shower. Also consider a grab bar by the toilet.

Place slip-preventing mats or decals on the floor of the tub/shower.

Consider raising the height of the toilet seat. Medical supply houses sell raised-seat devices. They also sell adult-size Porta Potties that can be placed in the person's bedroom or elsewhere.

AROUND YOUR CAR

Think twice before leaving anyone with Alzheimer's alone in a car. The person may release the emergency break, or turn the lights on, or cause other potentially hazardous mischief.

Power windows are hazards for people with dementia. They may get their fingers, arms, hair, or heads caught in them. Assign your loved one a regular seat in the car, and have your mechanic disable the power window next to it.

People with Alzheimer's may unlock car doors and open them while the car is moving. If your car does not have safety latches, ask your mechanic to install them. These hidden latches prevent passengers in certain seats from unlocking the adjacent door.

SMOKING

Smoking can be a disaster for people with Alzheimer's, so work to eliminate the habit completely. To help with the process, you might permit the person to have cigarettes, but get rid of all matches and lighters. That way the person can "smoke" unlit cigarettes.

If anyone in the house smokes, all matches and lighters should be carefully secured out of reach.

The Alzheimer's Association can also provide home-safety suggestions and referrals to helpful resources. Some communities have experts on home safety willing to inspect your home and make specific suggestions. These people may also be willing to install hardware to make your home safe.

Managing Activities of Daily Living

In my rational moments, I am still me. At other times, I cannot follow what is going on around me. The conversation whips from person to person too fast, and before I have processed one comment, the thread has moved to another person or another topic, and I am left isolated from the action, alone in a crowd. If I press myself with greatest concentration to try to keep up, I feel as though something short-circuits in my brain. I become disoriented. If I am standing, I have difficulty with my balance. My speech slows and I cannot find the right words to express myself.

It can be very upsetting to face the fact that a parent or spouse can no longer function independently. It can be even more distressing to provide care as you watch the person descend into the mysterious abyss of Alzheimer's, but as ghastly as the disease can be, daily caregiving also has rewards. To reap them, it helps to adopt the best-friends approach to caregiving, mentioned at the beginning of this chapter, and to get well organized.

DRESSING

People with Alzheimer's often become distressed by having too many clothing choices. Limit the person's wardrobe to a small number of possibilities.

Limit colors so that everything matches. Buy ten identical pairs of socks, so any two make a matching pair.

Eliminate accessories like belts, scarves, ties, jewelry, and eventually even sweaters. Keep outfits as simple as possible. Look for pants and skirts with elastic waistbands. Athletic sweatsuits work well.

Loose-fitting clothing is most manageable. This is particularly true of underwear. If it's loose, it works even if donned backward.

Look for clothes that do not need ironing or special care. You already have enough to do.

Lay out clean clothes every morning for the affected person.

Buttons and zippers often frustrate Alzheimer's sufferers. Replace them with Velcro wherever possible. Velcro tape is available at fabric stores. The same goes for shoelaces. Look for slip-ons or shoes with Velcro closure.

Look for reversible shirts and jackets. That way, there's no inside out.

Forget slips and panty hose. To get a bra on a woman with the disease, have her lean forward to settle her breasts in the cups. Perhaps you can eliminate the bra and have her wear a loose pullover undershirt.

Several catalogs offer clothing specially designed for impaired adults. See the list at the end of this chapter.

BATHING

I see the great value in establishing routines within my limits. [Routines] reduce confusion. [During a family trip to Disney World,] leaving the routine of being around my familiar home, having more people and excitement than I am accustomed to, varying my ritual for taking care of my grooming and bathing, all brought me to a place of being unable to make even the most basic decisions for myself. If I want to function at the top of my limited capacity, I must establish a routine and keep to it.

Try to preserve the person's former routines. People who spent decades showering in the morning usually prefer to continuing doing that instead of taking baths in the evening.

As Alzheimer's progresses, the complexities of bathing often become quite daunting and upsetting to the person. Break the task down into simple components. Don't say, "Time for your shower." Instead say, "Take off your shirt. Good. Now your pants. Great. Now . . ."

People with Alzheimer's often resist bathing. If this becomes a problem, they don't have to bathe every day, but try not to get drawn into negotiations about whether a bath is necessary. When it's time to bathe, simply shepherd the person through the process. If you encounter resistance, wait a while and try again.

Don't use bubble bath products, bath oils, or anything that can make a tub or shower slippery.

Getting in and out of a tub can be difficult for Alzheimer's sufferers. Bath rails and other aids are available. One approach many caregivers endorse involves a plastic stool and a hand-held shower-massage device. Buy a stool whose seat is at about the same level as the top of the side of the tub. Place the stool in the tub. Have the person sit on the stool with feet out of the tub, then swing the person's feet into the tub. Use the shower massage for wetting and rinsing. Reverse the process to get the person out of the tub.

If you fill a tub, use only a few inches of water.

Don't leave anyone with Alzheimer's alone in a tub or shower. If the phone rings, let the machine answer.

It can be awkward to insist that loved ones with Alzheimer's wash their genitals, or that women wash under their breasts, but you have to insist or do it yourself. Otherwise, rashes can develop.

Sponge baths can work as a last resort.

Towel-drying can present problems. Instead, buy a fluffy terrycloth robe, help the person into it while wet, and let the robe act as a towel. However, if your loved one is heavy, skin folds that remain damp can lead to irritation and rashes. Dry those areas or apply cornstarch.

People with Alzheimer's tend to sit or lie down a lot, which increases the risk of bedsores and other skin ulcers. Bath time is a good time to inspect for red areas, rashes, etc. If you see any, consult a physician.

GROOMING

Have the person's hair cut short in a style that's attractive and easy to care for.

Women who went to beauty parlors regularly before they developed Alzheimer's disease may enjoy continuing to do so for quite a while, but eventually such outings may become upsetting or impossible. When that happens, stop going. The same goes for using makeup.

If the person showers or bathes using the stool-and-hose approach described above, hair can be easily washed while bathing. Another option is to wash hair over the kitchen sink using the spray gun.

Keep the person's nails trimmed short. Short nails are easier to keep clean and less likely to get injured or to cause injury.

Grooming, bathing, and dressing people with Alzheimer's disease takes tremendous energy and patience. Caregivers often feel as if they're living life in slow motion. You may be tempted to let your loved one wear pajamas all day, but try to keep the person dressed and presentable. It helps maintain the person's dignity and often improves cooperation. Compliment the person's appearance.

TOOTHBRUSHING AND DENTURES

It's important to maintain oral hygiene. People with Alzheimer's who retain their teeth should keep flossing as long as they can. At some point you may need to let flossing go but continue brushing their teeth. Some dentists recommend foam applicators instead of brushes.

Dentures are troublesome for people with Alzheimer's; as soon as possible, ask the person's dentist about the possibility of switching to permanent dental implants. If the person continues to wear dentures, have them checked frequently to make sure they fit well. The person may not be able to tell you about problems. In addition to being annoying, ill-fitting dentures increase the risk of mouth sores and discourage people from eating, which threatens their health and may aggravate their dementia.

Dentures should be cleaned daily. Affected individuals should do it as long as they can. Eventually you will have to assume the responsibility.

INCONTINENCE (URINARY AND FECAL)

[After a long, tiring drive] we carried our things into the motel room, and I [Betty] collapsed on the bed. Bob just stood by the dresser. As I looked at him, my heart was gripped by an icy terror. How can I describe the look on his face? Empty, confused, blank, perplexed, unmoving. I said, "Honey, what's wrong?" He replied in the most

pitiful, pleading tone, "I can't find the bathroom." "It's right here," I directed.

The ability to deal with one's own toilet functions is fundamental to personal dignity. Anyone who needs help managing urination and defecation is bound to feel ashamed and distressed. In addition, it can be emotionally challenging for caregivers to intervene in what is usually regarded as a private activity, not to mention, one that might elicit feelings of revulsion. But you *can* adjust to assisting your Alzheimer's sufferer in the bathroom. Take a few deep breaths and read on.

Both urinary incontinence (wetting) and fecal incontinence (soiling) may be caused by medical problems that can be treated. If you notice either one, pay close attention: What exactly is the problem? When does it happen? Is it occasional or persistent? Does it seem to be linked to anything else going on in the person's life? Then take your observations to a physician and insist on a thorough medical evaluation.

One common response to urinary incontinence is to have the person drink less. This is a big mistake. Adequate hydration is critical to well-being, and even minor dehydration can cause confusion, particularly in the elderly. Additional confusion is the last thing your loved one needs.

If incontinence is related to a mobility problem—not getting to the toilet in time—consider placing Porta Potties strategically around your house, especially in the person's bedroom if nighttime accidents are a problem.

If the problem is difficulty undoing clothing, substitute Velcro for buttons or zippers, and elastic waistbands for belts, buckles, and snaps.

If the problem results from an inability to find the bathroom, decorate the door so it stands out.

Sometimes, people with Alzheimer's mistake wastebaskets for toilets. Put lids on wastebaskets or put them out of sight.

If problems persist, take the person to the bathroom every ninety minutes or so.

As language ability fades, the person may develop idiosyncratic names for bathroom functions. Listen closely. "I have me" may mean "I have to pee." Nonverbal forms of communication may also mean "I have to go," for example, dropping one's pants.

Adult diapers can be a godsend, and today's brands are easy to use. Some come with plastic over-covers and elastic bands that help prevent leakage, but they may chafe. Experiment to see what works best.

Incontinence might damage your furniture. Place washable covers on furniture. Encase mattresses in plastic covers.

Urinary incontinence produces a persistent odor in clothing. One way to minimize this is to encourage the person to drink cranberry juice, which helps deodorize urine.

It's important to clean up quickly after the person defecates because skin irritations and painful rashes can develop.

When necessary, use alcohol-soaked wipes in addition to regular toilet paper. Just be sure to dry the skin in the anal area afterward to avoid irritation and rashes. Powder or cornstarch can help.

MEAL PREPARATION

Don't feel compelled to cook three meals a day in addition to all your other caregiving chores. There are alternatives. The key to happy, nutritious meals is organization. Plan how you want to handle meals, when you want to cook, when you'll go out or rely on prepared foods, take-out, restaurant delivery, or a Meals on Wheels program. Plan a few weeks at a time to help you feel you have the situation under control.

When you cook, make large amounts and freeze as much as possible for reheating another time.

Eating involves complicated cognitive processes and, often, social interactions that might upset people with Alzheimer's disease. To minimize hassle and behavior problems, adopt mealtime routines. Serve simple fare. Don't subject the affected individual to big dinner parties. If you have guests, stick to one or two.

EATING

Retire ceramic dishes and use unbreakable plastic. If the person knocks dishes off the table frequently, plates and cups with suction cups can be obtained at baby stores. Retire sharp-pointed steak knives and go with less hazardous butter knives.

Many people with Alzheimer's have trouble *seeing* their food. The dining area should be brightly lighted. Use contrasting colors to keep food visible, for example, a blue tablecloth makes a white plate more visible. A white bowl makes red tomato soup more visible.

People with Alzheimer's may become confused or upset sitting down to a plate with three items on it: a salad, sandwich, and piece of fruit. Try serving one item at a time, and cut everything into bite-size pieces.

Utensils demand considerable dexterity. Many Alzheimer's sufferers feel more comfortable eating with their fingers. That's fine.

Messiness is inevitable as the disease progresses. Don't berate the person. It's nobody's fault. Use easy-cleaning plastic tablecloths, and consider fitting the person with a bib or smock.

Some affected individuals leave food around the house or hide it, which may attract mice or insects. The person may be anxious that snacks will be unavailable when they want them. Leave a fruit bowl or cookie jar out and remind the person about it.

Sometimes your loved one may refuse to eat. Don't make a big deal out of it. Offer food again later. Instead of three large meals a day, consider six or seven snacks.

Sometimes Alzheimer's sufferers want to eat again immediately after eating. Offer little nibbles: a cracker, a few grapes, a cube of cheese.

Always check that hot foods and beverages are not too hot.

If you spoon-feed a person with Alzheimer's, don't overfill the spoon. Alternatively, consider smoothie-type blender drinks that can be consumed with a straw.

CHOKING

Sometimes people with Alzheimer's forget to chew their food or can't manage normal swallowing, so choking is a real risk. True choking is different from gagging or coughing. In the latter, some food enters the windpipe, and the person gags or coughs it back out, with no interruption of breathing. In choking, food becomes tightly lodged in the vocal cords and the person cannot gag, cough, or even breathe. Unless the food is removed, the person quickly suffocates. Because choking blocks the vocal cords, chokers cannot talk, so they can't ask for help, not to mention that people with Alzheimer's may be too confused to realize what has happened. They might clutch their throats or look frightened.

The object blocking the airway is like a cork in a plastic bottle. If you squeeze the bottle forcefully enough, the air in it pops the cork. That's the theory behind the Heimlich maneuver rescue technique. If you suspect choking:

- Ask, "Can you breathe?" If the person does not appear to be able to breathe and cannot talk or cough, don't panic. If you panic, the person with Alzheimer's may get very upset. As calmly as possible, say, "I'll help you."
- Step behind the person and clasp your hands around his or her abdomen below the rib cage. Take a moment to be sure your hands are in the soft abdomen below the rib cage. If your hands are not positioned correctly, performing the Heimlich maneuver might injure a rib.
- Make a fist with one hand and hold the thumb side against the person's abdomen.
- Grasp the fist with your other hand and thrust it forcefully in and up.
- If one forceful thrust does not pop out the piece of food and restore free breathing, repeat the procedure.

If the person is bigger than you and you can't reach all the way around, use the grasped-fist technique but apply the upward thrusts higher on the chest.

If a choking person loses consciousness despite your best efforts, lay the person down gently faceup and apply upper abdominal thrusts with the heel of your hand. Then turn the person's head sideways and check the mouth for dislodged food.

If the person is unconscious by the time the trapped food has been expelled, call 911 and begin cardiopulmonary resuscitation (CPR). If you don't know CPR, a 911 operator can talk you through it.

Don't slap the back of a person who is choking. Back-slapping used to be recommended until studies showed that it may lodge objects more permanently in the throat.

The best way to deal with choking is to prevent it. If the person has shown any problems chewing or swallowing, do not serve foods likely to trigger choking, such as nuts, raisins, popcorn, and hard candies. Stick to softer foods. In addition, the risk of choking increases later in the day as the person gets tired, so be especially vigilant at dinner and afterward.

EXERCISE

Vigorous exercise to the point of exhaustion gets my mind out of the black hole. At first it meant riding furiously on an exercise cycle until I was panting and exhausted and my mind was clear. Now I try to schedule my daily routine with physically demanding activity. When I have had a particularly difficult night and awaken foggy and disoriented, I find that vigorous exercise helps me clear my head.

Exercise has many well-documented health benefits. Here are the ones that can particularly help Alzheimer's patients: Exercise is calming. It contributes to longer, better sleep. It helps preserve balance and coordination. It helps relieve constipation, and it boosts feelings of self-esteem.

Consult with a physician about exercise appropriate for the person's medical situation. Just about everyone who is ambulatory can take walks. Walking provides excellent exercise, especially for the elderly.

Don't make a big deal out of exercise. Just tell the person that it's time to go for a walk, or set a modest goal: "Let's get a cookie at the bakery." It works best if exercise is part of a daily routine, for example, a walk before lunch.

Don't push beyond the person's (or your) comfort limit. A walk around the block is an excellent start. After a week or so, move up to two blocks, etc. Increase the duration and strenuousness of exercise very slowly.

People with balance or frailty problems can exercise sitting down, doing gentle arm movements. Local senior centers or the Alzheimer's Association can provide more information about seated exercise.

Have fun, and encourage the person to have fun, too.

RECREATION AND ENTERTAINMENT

I reached for a book I had been looking forward to reading, and started to read. Suddenly, on page 10, I realized a stunning fact. I had forgotten what I had read earlier and could not even bring to mind what the book was about. I was thunderstruck. The next day, the same thing happened. I found that I could not even follow the plot of a television movie.

People with Alzheimer's can still enjoy themselves. As the disease progresses, options become more limited, but the ability to enjoy life remains. Think of creative ways your loved one can have fun. For example, he or she might enjoy pushing a child on a swing, playing with a pet, singing or listening to familiar songs, browsing through magazines, taking walks, or going to concerts. Frequently, musical abilities—singing and playing instruments—linger longer than speech.

As Alzheimer's progresses, television plots become too complicated to follow, and the noise and rapid scene shifting may become upsetting. Look for nature programs or special-interest videos, for example, a log burning in a fireplace or fish swimming in an aquarium.

Limit visits with friends to one or two people at a time. Tell visitors not to reminisce. The person may not recall shared experiences. Instead, suggest that visitors focus on the present moment—having some cake or taking a walk.

Much of my life has been spent in the midst of large crowds of people. I still need social contact, but it must be limited to a few people at a time, and with little stimulation. Extraneous noise, such as a television, a barking dog, or children's interruptions produce overload so that I can no longer participate in the conversation.

LOVING CONTACT

Alzheimer's caregiving is so demanding that it's easy to forget the importance of loving touch. A pat on the back, back rubs, foot massages, hand massages, hugging, or holding hands are calming, and they communicate love and safety in a way even severely demented people can understand. Studies in Alzheimer's residential care facilities show that massage exerts a calming influence and minimizes behavior problems (chapter 10).

Managing Behavior Problems

Never begin speaking to Alzheimer's patients before you are absolutely certain you have their attention. If they catch the last few words of your sentence, they do not have the ability to fill in the part they did not hear, and this creates great confusion and irritation.

Loss of cognitive abilities is bad enough, but what drives most caregivers crazy is the irritability, anger, willfulness, and stubbornness that people with Alzheimer's may exhibit. Always remember: Behavior problems are part of the disease. The person is not being mean or malicious. Your loved one is not responsible for misbehavior.

That said, caregivers must still control affected individuals' behavior. It's not easy, but it is possible. In their classic guide to caregiving, *The 36-Hour Day,* Nancy Mace, M.A., and Peter Rabins, M.D., M.P.H., of the department of psychiatry at Johns Hopkins, conceive of effective behavior management in terms of the "6 R's": restrict, reassess, reconsider, rechannel, reassure, and review.

▪ **Restrict.** First, try to get the person to stop the problematic behavior. Coax, persuade, insist—whatever. The more hazardous the behavior, the more forceful you have to be. Restriction often works, but it may make some people more agitated.

▪ **Reassess.** Ask yourself, Is there a reason for this behavior? Could it indicate discomfort with the situation? Frustration about an inability to do something? Irritability over your efforts to orchestrate some task? A drug reaction? People with Alzheimer's may engage in irrational outbursts, but quite often real complaints underlie the misbehavior. Look for them.

• **Reconsider.** Try to see the situation from your loved one's point of view. The world is increasingly scary and inexplicable. Everyone seems like a stranger. Needs cannot be expressed. No wonder Alzheimer's sufferers become anxious, irritable, and agitated. They're increasingly confused, living in a world that has become incomprehensible.

• **Rechannel.** Try to redirect the problematic behavior in a safer, more socially acceptable direction. If the affected individual habitually throws your newspaper away, hide today's and leave yesterday's out for throwing away.

• **Reassure.** People with Alzheimer's need constant reassurance. They live in a world they don't understand, among people they may not recognize, who do all sorts of odd things to them. Be generous with soothing words and loving touch—a hug, a pat on the back, a hand on an arm. Make physical contact often, ideally every time you speak with them.

• **Review.** After incidents involving problematic behavior, think about what happened and how you handled it. Consider how you might prevent the problem in the future or cope with it more effectively. If you feel you handled the incident badly, don't berate yourself. Forgive yourself and move on. Learn from your mistakes and try to handle things better the next time.

Some problems that at first glance appear to be behavior problems may in fact be communication problems. When speaking to a person with Alzheimer's:

- Approach the person slowly and calmly, ideally with a big smile.
- Speak slowly, clearly, calmly, and loud enough for the person to hear you—but not so loud that the person gets upset. Eliminate distractions and excess noise.
- Stand directly in front of the person. Make eye contact to be sure you have his or her attention. Maintain eye contact.
- Begin by using the person's name. Use it frequently.

- Work to keep the pitch of your voice low. A high-pitched voice suggests that you are upset, which can be distressing.
- Keep requests simple and direct.
- Ask yes/no questions.
- Use hand gestures to help communicate your message.
- Offer praise for correct actions.
- Be patient. Allow plenty of time for the person to process your message and respond to it.
- Use humor whenever possible.

CONCEALING AND DENYING MEMORY LOSS

Some people who develop Alzheimer's disease express concern about their forgetfulness early on, while others vigorously deny their memory loss. It's surprisingly easy to conceal or deny memory problems in the early stages of the disease:

- Affected individuals don't look ill, so it often takes a while to suspect that something is wrong with their memory.
- It can be difficult to distinguish between true memory loss and plain cantankerousness, often a hallmark of aging.
- Most people begin to show Alzheimer's symptoms while living on their own, so cognitive problems remain hidden until minor crises occur—an auto accident or leaving the oven on. Even these signs of the disease are within the range of possible normal memory lapses, and lots of cognitively normal people get into fender benders or forget to turn the oven off every now and then.
- Frequently, personality and social skills remain intact longer than memory. The person appears to be as charming as ever, perhaps just a little absentminded.
- Finally, no one wants to believe that a loved one is developing problems. The tendency toward denial extends to the family. It may take a while for a consensus to develop that something is truly wrong. Be observant. Periodic absentmindedness is normal. Persistent, worsening absentmindedness suggests a problem.

Work at being understanding. It's natural to feel impatient, upset, or angry with someone whose memory lapses disrupt your plans. If your mother forgets the address of her new doctor, it's natural to feel exasperated. If your mother forgets that you invited her to dinner, it's natural to feel annoyed. Experience your irritation—then get over it. Your loved one has a brain-injuring disease and is not responsible for mental lapses. Older loved ones are not long for this world. Alzheimer's care may seem endless, but in fact your time with the person is limited. Try to maintain some perspective.

STUBBORNNESS

When you feel patronized or ordered around like a child, it's only human to dig in your heels. Add to this a fading memory, faltering skills, and terror of what lies ahead, and many people become even more stubborn.

The anxiety the disease engenders makes many Alzheimer's sufferers almost automatically say no even to completely reasonably requests, and in the early stages of the disease there's usually room for doubt: Is it the disease? Or maliciousness? You may never know for sure. This is exasperating, of course, but it's part of the disease.

If saying "Time for your bath" elicits a refusal, the person simply may not understand the statement. Try gently ushering the person into the bathroom, turn on the shower, and say, "Take off your shirt."

Compromise, or offer bribes: "Take a walk and you'll get a cookie." Bribery often makes people feel cheapened and vulnerable to future extortion, but with Alzheimer's, there's no risk of raising expectations of future rewards. Over time, affected individuals forget you ever bribed them. If all else fails, drop your request for a while and raise it again later.

SUNDOWN SYNDROME

Alzheimer's disease often has a daily rhythm—reasonable competence and cooperation in the morning, then a downhill course until, by evening, the person is confused and irascible. Increasing behavior problems as the day wears on are known as sundown syndrome. It's not clear why sundown syndrome occurs, but common sense suggests that fatigue plays a major role.

Take the time of day into account as you plan the person's activities. Do things that absolutely must get accomplished early in the day, and by the afternoon be willing to let go of the rest of your agenda.

WANDERING

Many people have tried to guess why Alzheimer's patients are so restless and want to walk around at all hours of the day and night. I believe I may have a clue. When the darkness and emptiness fill my mind, it is totally terrifying. I cannot think my way out of it. It stays there and sometimes images stay stuck in my mind. Thoughts increasingly haunt me. The only way I can break this cycle is to move.

Wandering is a hallmark of Alzheimer's disease. For the affected individual, it's potentially quite dangerous. For caregivers, it's unnerving, and often a cause of panic and guilt.

New environments increase the risk of wandering because they are unfamiliar. Some people wander during the day, others at night. Most wander for no discernible reason.

Some Alzheimer's sufferers wander because they feel physically restless. It may help to take them on long, tiring walks. Then lead them back home, reassuring them about their safety and comfort there.

Many people with Alzheimer's wander away from adult daycare. You can minimize this by allowing the person sufficient time to get used to the facility:

- Visit the center together before you enroll the person.
- Start sending the person to the center early in the illness.
- Initially, take the person to the center only for brief periods, and over time gradually extend stays.

- Remain with the person at the center initially, and then, after a while, withdraw.

Use a similar approach with all changes in the person's life, and expect wandering to increase during periods of change and stress.

Keep your doors locked, and install safety gates where necessary on porches and decks. Lock interior doors if you don't want the person wandering into your basement or garage, etc. Unfortunately, locks can inconvenience other family members and may prevent escape in case of fire. Another approach is to install a piece of safety hardware called an over-knob on doorknobs. Like modern drug bottlecaps, these devices do not prevent mentally competent people from operating the door, but they usually deter those with Alzheimer's.

Don't forget to secure your windows. Determined wanderers can slip out that way. Use ventilation locks.

Experiment with footwear. Some affected individuals wander only when wearing shoes. Keep them in slippers and they may stop.

As an added precaution, get the person an ID bracelet that says "Alzheimer's disease" and gives your phone number. Otherwise people might think your loved one is drunk, drug-impaired, or crazy.

You might also pin an ID card to the back of the person's clothing to decrease the likelihood that the person will notice it and destroy it.

Alert your neighbors to the possibility of wandering. Make sure they know who the person is and that they can contact you if need be. Also alert the police and local shopkeepers.

Medication is another option, but tranquilizers and other medication aggravate dementia.

OBSESSIVE BEHAVIOR

I find that I am now a victim of obsessive behavior. Whatever I start, I want to get finished as soon as possible with no interruptions. An unfinished task preys on my mind until it is completely finished. I used to have a dozen projects going at the same time. Now I can only concentrate on one thing at a time, and much to everyone's distress, this thing obsesses me until it's completed.

Obsessiveness is the opposite of wandering. Instead of being distractible, the person becomes fixated on one thing and won't stop doing it until it's finished, or keeps doing it over and over again, folding towels, washing hands, pacing, turning lights on and off, for example.

The deteriorating brain sometimes "gets stuck," and the result is obsessive or repetitive actions. If the action is not hazardous, there's nothing wrong with letting it continue for as long as you can stand it. When you must intervene, a "stop" command may work, but it might not. Many caregivers find that gentle touch is a better way to go—leading the person by the arm away from the activity while pointing out something distracting: "Thank you for folding the napkins. Now let's walk the dog."

INSULTS AND ACCUSATIONS

Gradually, because of not hearing, not remembering, and not comprehending, fear swept over me as I lost more and more control over my circumstances. I was gripped by paranoia. The saddest part is that I became distrustful of those who loved me and had my best interests at heart. I saw what was happening in me, and I could name it at the time as paranoia. But I could do nothing to stop the feelings. I worried particularly about money. I had such great fear.

"You're stealing from me." "You're hurting me." "You're poisoning me." "You're trying to kill me." People with Alzheimer's may make accusations that are not only completely mistaken but also cruel—sometimes vicious. Such accusations would hurt under any circumstances, but when you've made major sacrifices to care for the person, insults and accusations can be infuriating.

It's fine to feel angry and hurt, but remember, it's not the person talking. It's the disease. The confusion, disorientation, and fear the disease engenders often combine into paranoia and lashing out at those closest to them. If you're the person's caregiver, that's you.

Try to look beyond insults to their underlying meaning. "You're stealing from me" might mean "This illness has stolen my life from me." "Why don't you feed me?" might mean "I'm hungry." "My daughter locks me up" might mean "I can't find my way around."

Try not to argue when the person insults you. Instead of saying, "No one's trying to poison you," try, "I know you feel frightened." Instead of saying, "I'm not being cruel to you. You're a major pain," try, "I know. This disease has been cruel to you." Arguing only gets the person more agitated and upset. Soothing words are the best option, even if you feel insulted. You might gently change the subject or redirect the person's attention.

Dealing with insults becomes doubly difficult when you find yourself being berated in public. Take a deep breath and simply announce to those around you, "My father has Alzheimer's. Insults are part of it."

HIDING, LOSING, AND HOARDING THINGS

Having experienced [the paranoia of Alzheimer's], I wonder if this is the reason why people with dementia hoard strange items. The loss of self, the helplessness to control this insidious thief who was, little by little, taking away my most valued possession, my mind, made me especially wary of the rest of my possessions in an unreasonable way.

Just when you need something—the vegetable peeler, your keys, or your glasses—you can't find it.

Hiding, losing, and hoarding things are quite common in people with Alzheimer's disease, and you can't ask them to retrieve anything because they may have no idea where the item is. To deal with this, get organized. Work to eliminate your own absentmindedness. Keep necessary items in secure places. Keep duplicates of things you really need handy, like keys, glasses, etc.

Straighten up. Keep your house neat and spare. It's harder for the person to make off with things if your home is not cluttered.

Make a habit of looking through wastebaskets and garbage cans before emptying them. You never know what you might find.

SEXUAL MISCONDUCT

Alzheimer's caregivers often fear the person might expose genitals, grope people, masturbate in public, etc. This is possible, but not that common.

If you notice sexual misbehavior, analyze it carefully. Actions you might see as sexual may in fact mean something else. Finding your loved one naked on the front porch may simply mean that the person forgot to get dressed or perhaps felt too warm. Genital exposure may signal a need to urinate.

If public disrobing is the problem, look for clothes that are difficult to take off, like blouses that button up the back or pants without flies that buckle at the waist.

Public masturbation can be upsetting; however, it's simply another manifestation of the disease. Masturbation feels good. The person has simply forgotten that it's inappropriate to feel good that way in public.

Another upsetting possibility involves parents with Alzheimer's who make sexual advances to their children. This is not incest. It's the disease. Adult daughters and sons often look like their parents looked when they were younger, and remind those with the disease how their spouses looked years earlier. Such advances are almost always cases of mistaken identity.

If you notice any behavior that might be construed as sexual misconduct, try not to get upset. Emotional reactions simply upset the person. Instead, gently lead your loved one to a private place and, once there, deal with the situation as calmly as possible.

FOLLOWING YOU AROUND

Some people with Alzheimer's follow their caregivers from room to room. At first, this may be reassuring—at least they're staying within sight and not wandering off. Over time, it usually becomes exasperating.

Try to be patient. The person lives in a scary world, one becoming less comprehensible with each passing day. You are a source of security, so it's natural that the person would want to follow you.

Of course, when you go to the bathroom or take a shower or want to have a few moments to yourself, it's hard to remember that you're the living embodiment of the person's security. Do what you need to do. You have a right to some privacy, and there's no need to sacrifice it entirely. Set the affected person up with an enjoyable activity for a while and feel free to lock the bathroom door.

TELEPHONE PROBLEMS

Two years ago [when I was still working], I was able to handle sudden surprising situations on a routine basis. Now I am completely paralyzed mentally if I am thrown a question that demands an immediate decision on my part. My wife answers the phone. If she is gone, I turn on the answering machine. This gives me a moment to assess who is calling and prepare myself to speak with them.

The phone may be your main link to people with early Alzheimer's who are still living on their own. Sadly, over time the phone is bound to become a problem. Many Alzheimer's sufferers harass family, friends, doctors, and tradespeople with repeated calls, forgetting that their appointments are weeks away or that their business has already been concluded. This is a sign that the person's days of independent living are numbered.

Another problem develops when you send the person away from the phone to check something. Once the person puts the receiver down, you're left hanging and may face a long wait—if the person returns at all. You might give the person a portable phone, but these often get misplaced.

If the person with Alzheimer's lives with you, the phone can still cause problems, since affected individuals often continue to answer the phone long after they've lost all ability to react appropriately to callers.

To deal with phone issues, consider turning off all ringers and letting a phone machine answer your calls. That way you get accurate messages and can return calls when you're able. You might consider carrying a cell phone and asking people to call you at that number.

SLEEP PROBLEMS

The hardest time for me is at night. Going to sleep requires multiple functions of the brain. We make bodily adjustments so that we will be relaxed and comfortable. After that, we turn our mind off so that we can go into that before-sleep feeling of warmth and comfort. In this before-sleep state, I used to bring beautiful pictures into my mind. Now they were all gone—totally gone. What was in my mind? Blackness and darkness and misery of the worst kind, misery so terrible that I could not drop off to sleep. As soon as I let go of my concentration to try to fall asleep, there was nothing there [except] terrifying blackness. Sometimes Betty would hear me crying. She would hold me, speak soft words of reassurance to gently bring me back to reality. How precious was her touch at those agonizing times.

As people age, they sleep more fitfully whether or not they have Alzheimer's. With advancing years, people spend less and less time in the deepest, most restful stages of sleep. Sleep becomes lighter, and nighttime wake-ups are more common.

Some people with Alzheimer's awaken at night to go to the bathroom, and get lost. Place a night-light and Porta Potti in their room and point the potty out to them every night before bed.

Exercise improves sleep quality and extends its duration. Encourage problem sleepers to get more exercise, but affected individuals should not exercise in the evening, as it can be too stimulating.

Many people develop a pattern of nighttime insomnia and daytime naps. While it's tempting to encourage a nap because it gives you some time off during the day, you wind up paying for it at night, so discourage daytime naps.

The person's bedroom should support sound sleep. Keep it dark (except for a night-light). Make sure the mattress and bedding are comfortable. Quilts are generally less tangle-prone than blankets. Bedrails help some people stay in bed but agitate others. Experiment.

The combination of sleep problems and wandering can be deadly if the person falls down a flight of stairs. Install safety gates and window locks and check to see that they are securely in place before you retire.

End-of-Life Issues

The final stage of Alzheimer's marks a descent into complete silence and immobility, a world the rest of us cannot imagine. End-stage care is perhaps the most difficult time for caregivers because the person is totally dependent and the days take on the macabre, emotionally numbing quality of a deathwatch.

Until recently, there was little help available to caregivers dealing with this troubling stage, but in recent years the hospice movement has brought needed support and comfort to families. In-home hospice care typically involves visits by hospice professionals who keep the person comfortable and ease the transition into death, while simultaneously providing counseling and support to the caregivers.

Medicare does pay for hospice care, but patients must be certified to have a prognosis of six months or less to live. This can be very difficult to certify. The National Hospice Organization developed a guide for a six-month prognosis—which Medicare uses—but it is still a complex process which, at this writing, means that many Alzheimer's patients' hospice care is not covered. The Alzheimer's Association and many experts are lobbying Congress and are cautiously optimistic that in the not-too-distant future, hospice services will become a Medicare benefit.

It's important to prepare for end-stage Alzheimer's well in advance. See chapter 14 for information on durable powers of attorney, conservatorships, advanced medical directives, and other legal issues that allow you to make end-of-life medical decisions for the person.

I am still human. I laugh at the ridiculous disease that steals the most obvious things from my thoughts and leaves me spouting obscure, irrelevant information. I want to participate in life to my utmost. Reduced capacity, however, leaves me barely able to take care of my most basic needs, and there is nothing left over for being a productive member of society. This leaves me in a terrible dilemma. When I go out into society, I look whole. There is no wheelchair, no bandage, or missing part to remind people of my loss. It is difficult to answer the question, "What do you do?" I answer, "I am a retired minister." The next statement hurts. "You look awfully young to be retired." When I answer, "I have Alzheimer's disease," there is a strange look and uncomfortable silence.

Betty Davis, Reverend Robert Davis's wife, cared for him from his diagnosis in 1987 until he developed end-stage Alzheimer's in 1992. He died later that year in a Miami nursing home.

For products that can make caregiving easier, contact:

AdaptAbility: Products for Rehabilitation Therapy
P.O. Box 515
Colchester, CT 06415
(800) 266-8856

Adapted Clothing Unlimited
9437 Chad Burn Pl.
Gaithersburg, MD 20879
(301) 963-3690

Functional Solutions for Independent Living
North Coast Medical Consumer Product Division
P.O. Box 6070
San Jose, CA 95150
(800) 235-7054

Home Health and Easy Dressing
J.C. Penney
P.O. Box 2021
Milwaukee, WI 53201
(800) 222-6161

Home Health Enhancements
2407 East Oakton St.
Arlington Heights, IL 60005
(847) 437-4392

Maxi Aids and Appliances for Independent Living
42 Executive Blvd.
P.O. Box 3209
Farmingdale, NY 11735
(800) 522-6294

Sears Home Health Care
9804 Chartwell Dr.
Dallas, TX 75243
(800) 326-1750

These guides to caregiving offer invaluable support and excellent suggestions:

Alzheimer's: The Answers You Need
Helen Davies and Michael Jensen
Elder Books, Forest Knolls, CA, 1998

Alzheimer's: A Caregiver's Guide and Sourcebook
Howard Gruetzner, M.Ed.
John Wiley & Sons, New York, 1992

Alzheimer's: Finding the Words, A Communication Guide for Those Who Care
Harriet Hodgson, M.A.
Chronimed Publishing, Minneapolis, 1995

The Alzheimer's Caregiver: Dealing with the Realities of Dementia
Harriet Hodgson, M.A.
Chronimed Publishing, Minneapolis, 1998

Alzheimer's Disease: Caregivers Speak Out
Pam Haisman, R.N., M.S.
Chippendale House Publishers, Fort Myers, FL, 1998

Alzheimer's Disease: A Handbook for Caregivers
Ronald Hamdy, M.D., James Turnbull, M.D., Joellen Edwards,
    Ph.D., and Mary Lancaster, R.N.C.
Mosby Publishers, St. Louis, MO, 1997

*The Alzheimer's Sourcebook for Caregivers: A Practical Guide for
    Getting Through the Day*
Frena Gray-Davidson
Lowell House, Los Angeles, 1996

The Best Friends Approach to Alzheimer's Care
Virginia Bell, M.S.W., and David Troxel, M.P.H.
Health Professions Press, Baltimore, 1997

Care of Alzheimer's Patients: A Manual for Nursing Home Staff
Lisa Gwyther, M.S.W.
The Alzheimer's Association, 1985

Caregiving newsletter (monthly)
Denise Brown, Editor
$29.95 per year (12 issues) from
Tad Publishing Co.
P.O. Box 224
Park Ridge, IL 60068
(847) 823-0639

Caregiving Across Cultures
Taylor and Francis, Washington, DC, 1998

Caring for the Alzheimer Patient: A Practical Guide (3rd ed.)
Raye Lynne Dippel, Ph.D., and
    J. Thomas Hutton, M.D., Ph.D. (eds.)
Prometheus Books, Amherst, NY, 1996

Home Is Where I Remember Things
Lisa Gwyther, M.S.W.
Duke University Alzheimer's Family Support Center, 1997

Keeping Busy: A Handbook of Activities for Persons with Dementia
J. R. Dowling
Johns Hopkins University Press, Baltimore, 1995

The 36-Hour Day: A Family Guide for Caring for Persons with
  Alzheimer's Disease, Related Dementing Illness and Memory Loss in
  Later Life
Nancy Mace, M.A., and Peter Rabins, M.D., M.P.H.
Warner Books, New York, 1991

When Memory Fails: Helping the Alzheimer's and Dementia Patient
Allen Jack Edwards, Ph.D.
Plenum Press, New York, 1994

14.

When You Can No Longer Cope with Day-to-Day Caregiving

How to Evaluate, Select, and Pay for Residential Care

For many Alzheimer's caregivers, there comes a time when they no longer feel able to provide adequate care. They realize that they don't have the skill, energy, and support to orchestrate round-the-clock supervision and daily activities tailored to the person's increasing needs and few remaining abilities. That's the time to take the final step in Alzheimer's care—placing the person in residential care, an assisted-living facility, a regular nursing home or one with an Alzheimer's special-care unit.

Some people feel that placing a loved one in residential care signifies some failure. On the contrary, residential placement is often necessary for the person's safety. Many caregivers agonize over placement and then, once the person is in residential care, regret that they did not make the move sooner.

An estimated 13 percent of U.S. nursing homes now include Alzheimer's or dementia special-care units, and the number is growing rapidly. Special-care units often cost more than regular nursing home care, but the staff may be better trained, and families may prefer them for their loved ones. However, placement in a special-care unit, per se, does not slow the progressive decline of Alzheimer's disease. That's what researchers from the Myers Research Institute at the Park Center for the Aging in Beachwood, Ohio, and from the University of North Carolina at Chapel Hill discovered in a recent study of 77,337 nursing home residents in eight hundred facilities throughout the Midwest, including 1,228 residents of forty-eight facilities with special-care units. Compared with residents of regular nursing homes, those in special-care units showed a similar rate of decline in dressing, walking, toileting, self-feeding, and other activities of daily living. However, this study did not address psychological factors, including depression, anxiety, agitation, wandering, and social involvement. You may prefer the program in a special care-unit for your loved one, or you may decide that the program at a regular residential care facility meets the person's needs.

The decision to place a loved one in residential care is difficult, and it's natural to feel that no one can take care of the affected individual as well as you can because no one knows and loves the person like you do. Nonetheless, a good residential care facility, particularly one that specializes in dementia care, can often provide better care because it is set up and staffed to do so.

It's also natural to feel guilty about "abandoning" your loved one, but residential care is not abandonment. Chances are you've sacrificed a great deal caring for the person and simply can't continue to do so.

Start Planning at Diagnosis

Alzheimer's disease follows a steady, downward course, and it's very possible that placement in a residential care facility may become a necessity. Don't deny this possibility. Face it squarely and get used to the idea of talking about placement early on after the diagnosis of the disease. Talk about your feelings. Talk with other family members, your clergy, and people who have already placed loved ones. If the person is amenable, visit some facilities together.

There are probably quite a few residential facilities near you. No doubt some are better than others. Top-rated homes usually have waiting lists. In addition, there is a shortage of homes that specialize in people with Alzheimer's disease. The earlier you begin looking around and signing up on waiting lists, the more likely your loved one is to be able to move into a good facility later on.

Planning early for residential care also saves you the trauma of having to make a hasty decision in a crisis situation. The transition is never easy, but the more reconciled you are to it, the better it is for you and the person.

Finally, planning early is the wisest course financially. It allows the various family members to discuss their budgets and come to a consensus about supporting the person. It also allows time to arrange the affected person's financial affairs to maximize eligibility for government assistance.

How to Find a Good Residential Facility

Many people use the term "nursing home" to describe any type of residential care for people with medical problems. But nursing homes are only one of several residential care possibilities. Traditionally, nursing homes cared for only those who could no longer care for themselves and whose families could no longer provide adequate care for them. Today the trend is toward "life care," or "stepped care," facilities. These complexes typically offer three levels of care: independent apartments for people who can still take good care of themselves; assisted-living facilities for those who need some help with meals, laundry, dressing, medications, etc.; and a nursing home for those who need round-the-clock supervision and care. Once people move into the facility, they transition to increasing levels of care as their needs evolve.

To learn what types of residential facilities are available in your area, talk with friends, social workers, clergy, senior citizens organizations, and your local chapter of the Alzheimer's Association.

If the person is an armed forces veteran, contact the Veterans Administration. A VA hospital might be available to your loved one.

The following organizations and their publications may prove helpful:

▪ **The Alzheimer's Association.** The premiere Alzheimer's organization has a number of resources dealing with residential care, including the valuable booklet "Selecting a Nursing Home with a Dedicated Dementia Unit." Contact your local affiliate or visit the organization's Web site at www.alz.org.

▪ **The American Association of Homes and Services for the Aging (AAHSA).** This organization provides information about—and lobbies for—the nation's nonprofit residential care facilities and nursing homes. 901 E St., N.W., Suite 500, Washington, D.C. 20004-2037; (202) 783-2242; www.aahsa.org.

▪ **The American Health Care Association.** Similar to the AAHSA, this organization's members include both for-profit and nonprofit nursing homes. 1201 L St., N.W., Washington, D.C. 20005; (202) 842-4444.

▪ **The National Citizens Coalition for Nursing Home Reform.** A coalition of organizations working to improve nursing home care. 1424 16th St., N.W., Suite 202, Washington, D.C. 20036-2211; (202) 332-2275.

When discussing residential care with helping professionals in your community, be aware that some physicians and social service agencies own or invest in these facilities. Such ties can bias recommendations. Ask those you consult if they have any financial ties to specific homes. Talk with as many people as you can.

Once you have a list of recommended facilities, call and ask general questions over the phone: Are there openings? Is there a waiting list? Can you get a brochure or information packet by mail? What does the facility cost? What types of financial arrangements do they accept?

Telephone research and what you learn by mail may winnow your list. The next step is to evaluate potential homes yourself.

How to Evaluate a Residential Care Facility

Here are some questions to ask and issues to consider:

- **Is it conveniently located?** Your loved one may live in a nursing home for several years. If it's too far away, visiting may be a problem. A good facility ten miles away might be better in the long run than a great facility a hundred miles away.

- **Is it licensed and accredited?** Check the facility's record with local and state regulatory agencies. A stellar record is great, of course, but a facility that has had a few black marks may still be quite good. Ask if the administration has taken corrective action since any problems were reported. Look for evidence of these actions.

- **Forget the lobby decor.** A nice lobby with artwork, potted plants, and cut flowers is reassuring. So are wood-paneled administrative offices, but residents don't live in the lobby or the administrative wing. Focus your attention on the rooms, bathrooms, kitchen, and day rooms.

- **Use your nose.** In facilities where many residents are likely to be incontinent, bathroom odors are inevitable. However, they should not be overpowering. How does the staff deal with incontinence?

- **Check the menu.** You know the person's tastes. Will your loved one enjoy what the facility serves? If the person has special dietary needs, can they be accommodated? Is food available only during mealtimes, or is snacking possible?

- **Check the bathrooms.** Are they clean? Are they equipped with grab bars and other aids your loved one needs?

- **What proportion of residents have Alzheimer's?** You don't have to place your loved one in a facility devoted exclusively to Alzheimer's disease, but you want a facility whose staff know how to deal with it.

- **How do staff members deal with your loved one's specific problems?** Alzheimer's causes dozens of problems. Talk with some nurses and ask how they deal with them.

- **Note the resident-to-staff ratio.** The lower the ratio, the better the care (usually). Of course, more staff also mean higher costs. Look for value for your money.

▪ **Pay attention to how staff interact with residents.** Number of staff is not the whole story. Are they aloof from the residents? Or do they work closely with the residents? Do they seem to be enjoying themselves, or are they watching the clock, eager to go home?

▪ **Do staff members have questions about your loved one?** No two people experience Alzheimer's the same way. Staff who inquire about the person's likes and dislikes, abilities and problems generally provide better, more individualized care than staff who treat everyone the same way.

▪ **Pay attention to how staff interact with each other.** Happy staff are a good sign of a well-run facility.

▪ **Who develops the care plan?** Federal law requires that residential care facilities have individual care plans for each resident. Who develops the plan? Can you participate? As your loved one's Alzheimer's progresses, how will the care plan change?

▪ **Look for a mental health professional.** A good residential care facility should have a geriatric social worker, geropsychologist, or geropsychiatrist on staff or on call. Many of the problems Alzheimer's sufferers develop in residential care are behavioral. A mental health professional can be invaluable in figuring out what's going on and suggesting corrective strategies that ideally do not involve drugs or restraints.

▪ **Observe the activities.** Do residents watch TV all day, or does the facility have organized activities? People with Alzheimer's disease tend to be less agitated—and require less medication and restraint—in facilities with rich programs that include music, exercise, bingo, dancing, games, etc.

In one study, eighty-nine nursing home residents with dementia were divided into two groups. One received usual nursing and medical care, including antipsychotic medications and physical restraints, while the other participated in an enriched program with exercise, music, crafts, games, relaxation training, and very limited use of antipsychotics and restraints. After six months, half the people in the usual-care group exhibited serious behavior problems, but in the enriched-program group, the figure was only 29 percent. Those in the usual-care group were also 2.5 times more likely to have received antipsychotic drugs and three times more likely to have been physically restrained.

Ideally, a residential facility should have three types of activity specialists on staff or visiting regularly: an occupational therapist, who deals with arts and crafts; a recreational therapist, who organizes music and dance activities and outings; and a physical therapist, who promotes exercise, even for those in wheelchairs.

▪ **Look at the hallways.** People with Alzheimer's often become confused and agitated when they have to contend with long corridors to get to their rooms. When it comes to hallways, the shorter the better.

▪ **Look at the room doors.** If all the doors look the same, it can be difficult for people with Alzheimer's to find their room. Look for individualized doors with distinctive colors and personal touches.

▪ **Is there a secure wandering area?** Many people with Alzheimer's need to wander. Look for a facility with a securely fenced yard where the person can wander safely.

▪ **Look for community involvement.** Do clergy, students, and outside volunteers visit the facility? People with Alzheimer's disease don't do well in crowds, but some variety keeps them interested and helps prevent behavior problems.

▪ **Ask about visiting policies.** When can you visit? Can you have privacy with the resident? Can you take the resident off the grounds? The more open the facility is to visitation, the better. In facilities that severely restrict visitation, you wonder what goes on when no visiting is allowed.

▪ **Ask how staff handle behavior problems.** Are there written guidelines? If so, do they seem reasonable? Are they followed? See how many residents are restrained. Sometimes it's necessary, but only a small proportion of residents should be restrained. Ask what proportion of residents get medicated. What are the medication guidelines? Under what conditions might a particularly unruly resident be expelled?

▪ **Ask about medical and dental care.** How are routine medical and dental care handled? Do health professionals visit the facility, or are residents taken to physicians and dentists? Can they be taken to their own providers?

▪ **Ask about medical emergencies.** Is there a physician on call? Which hospital(s) does the facility use?

• **Ask about end-of-life decisions.** If your loved one has a living will and does not wish to be kept alive with heroic, technological measures, will those wishes be respected?

• **Ask about smoke detectors, fire alarms, and the evacuation plan.** Facilities should have all three, along with periodic fire drills.

• **Ask about disaster planning.** In areas where tornadoes, hurricanes, floods, or earthquakes might strike, facilities should have contingency plans. If there have been natural disasters recently, investigate how the facility and its residents fared.

• **Get fee information in writing.** What is included in the base fee? Are there extra charges? Under what circumstances might fees increase? How far in advance would you be notified? How does the facility work with Medicare, Medicaid, long-term-care insurers?

• **Review the contract with a lawyer.** Even the most wonderful facility administrator is an advocate for the home. You need an advocate for you and your loved one.

• **Keep asking questions.** Even after your loved one has moved in, continue to be observant and raise any issues that come up for you.

• **Befriend the staff.** If you've been an Alzheimer's caregiver, you know how difficult it is. Residential facility staff have many people to care for. They deserve your respect and support. If you help and praise them, they are likely to take more personal interest in your loved one.

Moving the Person In

The actual move is often more traumatic for caregivers than it is for those with Alzheimer's. You're painfully aware of what's happening. You may feel ambivalent, guilty, depressed, anxious, and stressed. Your loved one may not have much idea what's going on.

Should you tell the person about the move? That's a matter of opinion. Some caregivers insist on discussing the move. To them, anything short of full disclosure amounts to deception and kidnapping. Others see no reason to risk upsetting the person. Alzheimer's sufferers who took an interest in residential care early on, or who still have enough cognitive function to understand what's happening, may feel better about being informed. Those with more advanced disease may be incapable of understanding the transition and are better left uninformed. Use your judgment. In general, either tell the truth or say nothing. Don't consciously mislead by saying you're just "taking a drive" or "visiting."

Some people with Alzheimer's resist placement and accuse their caregivers of cruelty. The more ambivalent you are about placement, the more likely this is to hurt, so be firm. Just remember, you're not being cruel. You've made tremendous sacrifices to care for the person and may, in fact, have put off the nursing home transition longer than you should have. All you're doing is what must be done.

Make sure you have the legal authority to move the person. Laws differ from state to state, but all states allow legal guardians of demented individuals to place them in residential care. You may need to consult an attorney.

During the move, take items the person is still fond of—photographs, a radio, a favorite pillow, etc.—but understand that personal mementos upset some people with Alzheimer's because they can't remember what they mean. If you bring mementos, limit yourself to a few items that won't add clutter.

Visiting and Adjusting

Try to visit often during the first few weeks. Allow time for the person to adjust. People have different adjustment periods depending on who they are and the severity of their Alzheimer's. Be patient.

Your loved one may claim that the facility is abusive and beg to return home with you. First, satisfy yourself that no abuse has taken place, then offer understanding and reassurance. Respond by saying, "You're too sick to be at home now."

As time passes, continue to visit. When your loved one no longer recognizes you, visiting may become painful and seem pointless, but Alzheimer's experts agree that visiting is still valuable. Even people with severe dementia seem reassured by the presence of family members.

During visits, it's often difficult to figure out what to do. The person may not be able to do much, as over time, remaining abilities fade. Consult with staff about what the person still enjoys and do those things. Take a walk together. Share a meal. Listen to music. Give a back rub. Or simply sit holding hands. As the disease progresses, the person may think you are someone else. Don't correct or argue. That may cause agitation. Just play along. Stay in the moment.

Visiting also helps you adjust to placement. Initially, most caregivers feel a combination of relief and disorientation. Alzheimer's caregiving is so consuming that despite efforts to maintain friendships and other activities, you're quite likely to feel lost for a while, disconnected from the world beyond Alzheimer's care. Visits can reassure you that you're still connected to the person and still providing some care, even though you've withdrawn from day-to-day caregiving.

Paying for Residential Care

Assisted living facilities cost from $25,000 to $50,000 a year. Nursing homes may cost up to $70,000. Paying for residential care requires careful planning, ingenuity, and often considerable sacrifice. It may precipitate conflict and resentments among family members. That's why you should start planning for it early, ideally, shortly after the person's diagnosis.

Payment options include:

▪ **Self-financing.** You or your loved one may have enough financial assets to pay for residential care. Of course, the person's assets may be tied up in a home and in various investments and insurance policies. You may have to do some detective work to locate them all and liquidate them so they can be used for residential care.

▪ **Loans from life-insurance policies.** You may be able to use the person's life insurance policy(ies) to raise cash. If your loved one has a whole life or universal life policy, it is usually possible to borrow against its cash value. (Cash value is different from the death benefit; check the paperwork or call the insurer to find out the cash value.) You will have to repay the loan with interest. If you repay it in full by

the time the person dies, the beneficiary receives the full death benefit. If not, the insurer reduces the death benefit by the amount of the
unpaid loan balance.

▪ **Viatical settlements.** In recent years, special brokerage firms,
viatical settlement companies, have made a business of buying life insurance policies for cash—but for less than the policy's death benefit.
Viatical settlements are basically a gamble on how long the policyholder lives.

Here's how these settlements work: Say the policy death benefit is
$100,000, and after the viatical company's physician examines the
policyholder, the company decides that the person is likely to live for
four years. The firm might offer $45,000 in cash for the policy. The
family can then use this money immediately to pay for residential
care. The brokerage collects the $100,000 when the person dies. If
the person dies sooner, the brokerage comes out ahead, while the
family loses. The family might have done better holding on to the
policy and collecting the full death benefit. However, if the person
survives longer than expected, the family comes out ahead, and the
firm loses. Viatical settlements typically range from less than 60 percent of the death benefit if the person appears to have more than two
years to live, to around 90 percent if the person appears likely to die
within a few months.

Pre-death sale of life insurance policies initially developed to
cover the cost of AIDS care, but the concept has been expanded to
include Alzheimer's disease and other conditions that require extended residential care. For more information about viatical broker-
ages, contact an insurance broker, the Alzheimer's Association, or
senior citizens organizations.

▪ **A reverse mortgage.** Reverse mortgages allow people age
sixty-two or older to convert their home equity into monthly income
that can be used to cover caregiving costs. Instead of making payments to the bank, the bank pays you. Unlike a regular mortgage, in
which homeowners increase their equity over time, with a reverse
mortgage, the bank buys equity, and when it comes time to sell the
home, the bank owns some—or possibly all—of it.

A reverse mortgage is a good alternative for people with early
Alzheimer's disease who have considerable equity in their homes and

want to continue living in them. They're also worth considering if a caregiver moves into the person's home.

Reverse mortgages are available through many banks, the Federal Housing Administration (FHA), and the Federal National Mortgage Administration (Fannie Mae). In general FHA reverse mortgages work best for those with less than $150,000 of home equity. Fannie Mae reverse mortgages tend to be most attractive for those with home equity of $150,000 to $225,000. Private bank reverse mortgages usually work best for those with home equity of more than $225,000.

For more information, contact your bank or consult the U.S. government listings in your phone book for the FHA or Fannie Mae.

▪ **VA benefits.** If the person is an armed forces veteran, placement might be possible in a Veterans Administration facility. For information, contact the VA medical center or outpatient clinic nearest you.

▪ **Family.** Family members might decide to pool their resources and pay for residential care. In some states, relatives are required to provide a certain amount of support for a certain time. Check your state regulations.

▪ **Medicare.** Medicare pays for up to 150 days of nursing home care if the person needs intensive rehabilitation. Alzheimer's disease does not qualify because currently there is no possibility of rehabilitation. However, if a person with Alzheimer's also has some other condition, for example, a stroke, Medicare financing may be possible for a time. For more information, contact a Medicare office, social worker, the person's physician, or the Alzheimer's Association.

▪ **Medicaid.** Medicaid is a federal safety-net program administered by individual states. It pays for health care, including long-term residential care, for those who have no other financial resources. In most states, it is known as Medicaid, but some state programs have different names. California's is Medi-Cal.

Some people recoil from Medicaid because it feels like welfare. However, there is no shame in receiving benefits. It's more like Social Security. People with Alzheimer's disease paid taxes before they were incapacitated, and some of that money went to Medicaid benefits for other people. Now that they need Medicaid, it's there for them. Medicaid currently pays the bills for about two-thirds of the nation's nursing home residents.

Eligibility criteria differ from state to state, but in most states people in residential facilities receiving Medicaid cannot have more than a few thousand dollars in total personal assets (which can be used for gifts and personal items). Individuals must "spend down" their own funds until they qualify for Medicaid, and then the program assumes the cost of their care for the rest of their lives.

In cases where one spouse has Alzheimer's and the other needs money to live on, asset transfers can be arranged. This strategy enumerates the couple's assets and divides them in two. (The couple's home is exempt as long as the unaffected spouse lives in it.) The half belonging to the affected individual can be spent on residential care until the person has spent down to become eligible for Medicaid. The half belonging to the unaffected spouse can be used by that person with no restrictions, and those assets do not disqualify the spouse with Alzheimer's for Medicaid.

However, asset transfers can be tricky. They must be arranged a considerable period of time before the affected individual applies for Medicaid. In addition, you must keep detailed records and present them for inspection when you apply. The Alzheimer's Association can help you arrange things. You might also need an accountant and an attorney. If you need a lawyer, find one experienced in handling Medicaid applications. For a referral, contact the Alzheimer's Association, your local Bar Association, or senior citizens organizations.

It may be a struggle to obtain Medicaid benefits—even if you're confident that the person qualifies. The reason is that states generally interpret eligibility criteria conservatively in order to save money. Be persistent. File appeals if necessary. For more information, contact the Alzheimer's Association or the National Citizen's Coalition for Nursing Home Reform, 1424 16th St., N.W., Suite 202, Washington, D.C. 20036-2211; (202) 332-2275. You may have to hire an attorney.

For general information on Medicaid, contact the residential care facility you're considering, or your local or state departments of Health, Social Services, or Welfare.

▪ **Long-term-care insurance.** With residential care costing tens of thousands of dollars a year, and the government periodically threatening to cut Medicaid payments for long-term care, many people have turned to long-term-care insurance as a way to guarantee payment for residential care, if they ever need it. But consumer groups complain that long-term-care policies rarely pay out as purchasers hope. Shop very carefully.

Long-term-care policies must be purchased before the policyholder needs long-term care. Many long-term-care insurers do not sell policies to people with preexisting conditions, such as Alzheimer's disease. Therefore, the best time to buy is as soon as you suspect that a loved one might have the disease. Once the person has been diagnosed with Alzheimer's, your options shrink, but you still may be able to buy a policy. Just be sure to examine excluded conditions before you buy.

Long-term-care insurance rarely covers the entire cost of care for the remainder of the person's life. Most policies offer benefits that range from $50 to $200 a day, with a maximum number of days stipulated in the policy.

Cost varies tremendously depending on:

- The age and health of the policyholder. The older and sicker the policyholder is, the more expensive and limited the coverage.
- The daily payout. The more money, the more expensive the coverage.
- The payout duration. The longer, the more expensive.

Some policies cover just nursing home care. Others cover assisted-living facilities and home care. Some cover them all. Check before you buy.

Most policies have deductibles and elimination periods. You must pay a certain amount before the policy pays anything, and you must pay for a certain period of time before coverage begins.

Some policies have fixed premiums. In others, the premiums increase annually to keep up with inflation.

Some policies require continued payment of premiums while the policyholder is in long-term care collecting benefits. Others have a premium waiver that allows policyholders to stop paying when they receive benefits.

Read the fine print and talk with several brokers before you buy.

Financial and Legal Issues

Before you take responsibility for an Alzheimer's sufferer's financial and legal affairs, talk with an attorney. Control of these affairs is a basic legal right of all competent adults. All fifty states and the District of Columbia have laws protecting individuals from the seizure of financial and legal rights by others, even those who are well-meaning caregivers.

Fortunately, all fifty states and the District of Columbia also recognize that in certain situations—Alzheimer's and other dementias and brain injuries—people may become unable to exercise competent control over their financial and legal affairs, and they allow that control to pass to another person.

With Alzheimer's disease, this transition is never easy for either the affected individual or the person who assumes these responsibilities. Here's a brief guide to what people recently diagnosed with Alzheimer's and their caregivers should know.

▪ **When to plan the transition.** The best time is as soon as possible after the diagnosis, when affected individuals can still make legally competent decisions for themselves and know where their assets are located.

Of course, in the immediate aftermath of an Alzheimer's diagnosis, planning for the person's eventual financial and legal dependence may not seem a high priority, but it is. The sooner you and the person tackle the financial and legal aspects of the disease, the better. You can wait until the affected individual is legally incompetent, but if you do, finding the person's assets may be difficult or impossible, and assuming legal and financial control becomes much more problematic, not to mention expensive.

▪ **Durable powers of attorney.** If you want to give another person the right to make some legal or financial decisions for you, for example, signing a contract while you're out of the country, you execute a legal document called a power of attorney. Power-of-attorney arrangements are typically short-lived and very specific, empowering the person you designate to act on your behalf only briefly in a limited capacity.

However, if there is reason to believe that a person might become mentally incapacitated in the foreseeable future, all fifty states and the District of Columbia allow competent adults to execute legal documents called durable powers of attorney, which give the designated decision maker, known as the agent or attorney-in-fact, broad power over the person's life, for example, the power to place the person in residential care and use the person's assets to pay for it.

Durable powers of attorney have advantages and disadvantages:

On the plus side, compared with other ways to assume legal and financial authority, they are relatively inexpensive to arrange and do not require court action or court supervision. In addition, because they bypass the courts, the affected individual's financial affairs remain private and do not become a matter of public record.

On the minus side, durable powers of attorney are not court supervised, so there is more potential for abuse by the attorney-in-fact, which may be an issue in families where members disagree about what's best for the affected individual.

Durable power-of-attorney documents may also include specific instructions about how the person wants to be cared for and a living will outlining advanced directives about end-of-life medical treatment. Doctors sometimes do not honor the wishes expressed in a living will unless it's backed up by a durable power-of-attorney document dealing with end-of-life care.

Most experts in the legal aspects of Alzheimer's recommend durable powers of attorney as the easiest, most efficient, and cheapest approach to caregiver assumption of control of the affected individual's affairs. However, the person granting the durable power of attorney must be competent at the time the documents are signed, so they must be drafted fairly soon after a diagnosis of early Alzheimer's.

Laws governing durable power-of-attorney agreements vary from state to state. Software programs abound for creating them, but they may not meet the specific requirements of your state. Your best bet is to have an attorney experienced in elder law draft your loved one's durable power of attorney, or review any durable power of attorney you draft.

▪ **Conservatorships.** If your loved one becomes legally incompetent and has not executed a durable power of attorney, in order to assume control over the person's affairs, you need a court's permission in the form of a conservatorship. You become the conservator and your loved one becomes the conservatee.

Anyone—a spouse, a relative, or a friend—may petition the court to appoint a conservator for an individual who appears to be incompetent. Once a conservatorship petition is filed, the court assigns an investigator to assess the proposed conservatee's competence and interview any individuals who may have an interest in the conservatorship—the proposed conservator and other family members—to assess the situation.

The next step is a hearing, in which a judge quizzes the investigator and decides whether or not to grant the conservatorship. If the court grants it, the judge appoints the conservator and specifies the conservator's powers and reporting responsibilities to the court.

Conservatorships have advantages and disadvantages:

On the plus side, they are court supervised, so compared with an unsupervised durable power of attorney, there is less potential for abuse by the conservator. A conservatorship might be a good approach in a situation where family members are in conflict and cannot agree how best to care for the affected individual or deal with the person's assets.

On the minus side, conservatorships can be very expensive to establish because the process requires considerable court and investigator time, and family members may feel compelled to hire attorneys to represent their views.

Laws governing conservatorships vary from state to state. Software programs may help you petition for a conservatorship, but they may not meet the specific requirements of your state. Your best bet is to have an attorney experienced in elder law work with you to establish a conservatorship over your loved one with Alzheimer's disease.

▪ **How to find a good attorney.** Only a small proportion of attorneys are familiar with the range of issues now increasingly called elder law.

These issues include:

▪ Executing durable powers of attorney.
▪ Managing the process to obtain conservatorships.

- Dealing with Social Security, Medicare, Medicaid, and long-term-care insurance.
- Handling tax and estate issues.
- Dealing with any legal issues that may arise while the person is in residential care.

The best way to find an attorney familiar with elder law is by word of mouth or through contacts in the Alzheimer's community. Try your local Alzheimer's Association affiliate or your Alzheimer's support group. In addition, other senior citizens organizations in your area may be good resources. Finally, you may be able to obtain useful information from the National Academy of Elder Law Attorneys, 1604 North Country Club Rd., Tucson, AZ 85716; (520) 881-4005; www.primenet.com/elderlaw.

• How to find the person's assets. The sooner you assemble the person's assets, the better. In the early stages of Alzheimer's, the person may still recall where financial documents and other assets are located. But as the disease progresses, people often forget these details or cannot articulate them, and you may have considerable difficulty assembling the person's resources.

Financial items include:

- Cash
- Jewelry
- Collectibles: art, coins, stamps, antiques, etc.
- Other valuables: cameras, furnishings, items in storage, etc.
- Bank records
- Pension and Social Security documents
- Insurance policies
- Safe-deposit-box keys
- Stock, bond, partnership, and mutual fund documents
- Real estate deeds
- A will
- Inheritance documents
- Cemetery plot documents
- Any other business or financial assets

If the person does not recall where financial records are located, you must find them. The rule of thumb is: Debts find you, but you must locate assets.

To find most financial assets, look for paperwork or notices that arrive through the mail, including bank statements, brokerage statements, investment reports, interest and dividend checks, tax information, notices that rent is due on safe-deposit boxes or storage units, and notices that taxes are due on real estate.

Banks usually do not release information about customers, but if your loved one has banked at the same institution for many years and the staff there know the person and you, they may bend the rules and inform you about the person's accounts, investments, and safe-deposit box.

To find cash, collectibles, jewelry, and other real goods, check desks, closets, under beds, in garages, etc. Most people do not hide valuables all that securely, but if you have reason to suspect that your loved one has valuables well hidden, do a more thorough search by looking through books for hidden compartments and in the pockets of old clothing in closets. Check for cuts in furniture linings that might lead to caches. Finally, when packing up the person's home do it slowly and examine every item. Then examine the empty home for loose floorboards, loose bricks, and other places where valuables might be hidden.

15.

"Oh, the Joy of Me!"

Profile of Debbie and Doris Hoffmann

Two women sat in a restaurant, one in her eighties, the other in her mid-forties. The older woman's short, gray hair was turning white, and her wrinkled but still handsome face was dotted with age spots. The younger woman's face was the same shape but less lined. Her smile was also similar. So was her haircut, only the younger woman's hair was brown.

"My father was never talkative," the older woman said, "so I never really knew him as a person. My mother . . . she would talk, but it never seemed to sink in with me."

"Who were you closer to?" the younger woman asked. "Your mother or your father?"

"I was closer to my mother," the elderly woman replied. "Were you closer to one of your parents?"

"I was closer to my mother, also. Do you know who my mother was?"

"No. . . ."

"You!" Debbie Hoffmann exclaimed.

"Me?" Doris Hoffmann was incredulous. "*I* was your mother?"

"You *are* my mother."

"How could I be your mother?" she mused, groping to understand this incomprehensible revelation. "Something must have gone wrong. . . ."

"No, I think something went *right.*"

Doris Hoffmann (née Goodday) was born in San Francisco in 1908, graduated from the University of California at Berkeley, then studied social work at Columbia, in New York, where she met a young physicist/mathematician, Banish Hoffmann, a colleague of Albert Einstein. They married and bought a home on 169th Street in Flushing, Queens, near Queens College, where Banish taught. They lived there for forty years and raised two children, a son and a daughter, Deborah. Debbie remembers her mother as "very together, methodical, and meticulous to a fault."

Debbie attended the University of Rochester but dropped out—"It was the sixties," she explains. She traveled, pursued photography, taught it for a time, and eventually finished her education at Mills College in Oakland, California, where she settled and became a film editor and documentary filmmaker. She spoke with her parents—usually her mother—frequently by phone, and they remained close.

Doris had always been articulate and skilled at the art of conversation. But in the early 1980s, about five years before her husband's death, she began repeating herself oddly. "I'd call," Debbie explains, "and she would say, 'So, how was your week?' And I would answer her, and the conversation would move on, and a few minutes later she'd say, 'So, how was your week?' again." Debbie didn't know what to think. At the time, her mother was in her seventies, and she chalked up Doris's lapses to aging. "It was a little weird," Debbie recalls, "but I sometimes repeat myself. Who doesn't? I figured her repetitiveness was part of being in her seventies. I didn't make much of it."

Then, an old California friend of Doris's called Debbie. Doris was planning a trip to the West Coast and called her friend about getting together. They made a date. Then a funny thing happened, the friend said. Ten minutes after hanging up, Doris called back, again saying she was planning a trip to California and could the two of them get together? The old friend was amused.

So was Debbie . . . until she thought about it. She called her mother's friend back. "Do you think anything is wrong with her?" Debbie asked.

No, she reassured Debbie. Your mother is fine. Debbie believed her.

Soon after that incident, Debbie noticed subtle changes in her phone calls to Queens. Whenever she spoke with her mother, her father was also on the line. She and her father had a warm relationship, but for years he'd generally been content to leave the phone communication to Doris and hear about his daughter's life secondhand from his wife. Now, suddenly, her father was always on the phone. They had three-way conversations, and Doris talked less and less; Debbie's more taciturn father increasingly became the parental spokesman. Eventually, he did most of the talking. If Debbie called when her father was out, her mother asked her to call back when he was home. Still, Debbie didn't suspect that anything was amiss. Her parents were getting older, and if her mother preferred three-way conversations, that was fine with her.

"Later, of course, I realized that my parents had entered into a little conspiracy," Debbie explains. "My father knew my mother's memory was going. He knew she was repeating herself. He consciously covered for her. He was her buffer."

Debbie's father died of heart failure at age eighty in 1986. He and Doris had been married for forty-nine years. Debbie flew back to New York. "That trip was my first indication that my mother had a problem beyond just being a little repetitive. When I arrived, she had no idea that my father had died. She kept asking, 'Where is he?' And I kept answering, 'Uh, Mom, he died yesterday.' She'd say, 'Oh . . .' and then a little later she'd ask the same question. It was very disconcerting."

Friends chalked up Doris's befuddlement to grief, and Debbie bought that explanation at first, but after Doris recovered from the initial shock of her husband's death, she kept repeating herself. Debbie didn't know what to think.

During a visit to Queens several months before her father passed away, Debbie had had a heart-to-heart talk with her mother about her father's condition. Debbie was no doctor, but anyone could see that he had become quite frail. Clearly, his days were numbered. Doris agreed. Then Debbie asked her mother if she'd thought about what she would do after Banish died. "She turned to me, very clear, very focused. 'Of course I've thought about it,' she said. 'I'm going to sell the house and move back to California.'"

In the aftermath of her husband's death, Doris became a jumble of contradictions. Despite her grief, she dealt competently with the financial details of widowhood. She had no trouble driving, and she remained committed to returning to California. However, she also had periods of profound confusion. She could not decide what to take to California and what to sell. Debbie had to do that for her. As her departure date approached, Debbie found her packing the contents of the kitchen garbage pail into a suitcase.

Four months after her husband's death, Debbie and her brother sold the family home and moved Doris to a one-bedroom apartment in San Francisco's Cow Hollow near the Golden Gate Bridge, about an hour's drive from Debbie, who lived across the Bay. "She settled in well," Debbie recalls, "but it was clear that she needed help. Her arrival in San Francisco marked the beginning of my stepping in as her caregiver."

Doris had lived in New York for fifty years, but oddly, as she settled into San Francisco, she did not seem to miss it. "It was strange," Debbie recalls. "She had almost nothing to say about the place where she'd spent two-thirds of her life, the place linked so closely to her late husband and her life as a wife and mother."

Doris was clearly happy to be back in San Francisco. A surprisingly large number of her high school and college friends still lived in the Bay Area, and she eagerly renewed several old friendships, but later, Debbie realized that there was more to her mother's reaction than simply excitement about returning to her old haunts. "By the time she moved back out West, her memories of New York and her life there were already fading fast. She had much clearer memories of her high school and college years, so living in San Francisco and getting together with her old friends fit well with her remaining mental acuity."

Debbie visited her mother often and phoned her at least once a day, often several times. Doris functioned reasonably well on her own, but it was clear that her memory was not what it had once been. "I'm in a muddled period," she told Debbie. "Time seems to run differently." To help out, Debbie encouraged Doris to jot down notes to remind her of things she needed to remember, but in a manner recalling the Sorcerer's Apprentice, the notes got out of hand.

Doris needed some dental work and was afraid she would forget her appointment, so she wrote a note to remind herself of the date and time. Then another note, and another, until there were hundreds of notes littered all over her apartment. "She became obsessed with the dentist," Debbie recalls. "As if all the notes weren't bad enough, while her tooth was on her mind, it was the only thing she talked about for weeks on end."

Debbie called it the Dentist Period. Eventually, Doris had her dental work, and Debbie heaved a sigh of relief. "The Dentist Period was finally over. Only it wasn't. She kept writing notes about the dentist, and obsessing about her dental work, and *showing up* at the dentist. I'd call her in the morning and say, 'Your dental work is *all finished* now. You don't have to see the dentist anymore. You don't have to go *anywhere* today.' And she would say, 'That's right. I'm done with the dentist.' Then an hour later, the dentist's receptionist would call to tell me my mother was there."

There were other "periods" as well. The Hearing Aid Period resembled the Dentist Period, except that Doris wrote hundreds of notes and obsessed about having her hearing aid repaired.

The Lorna Doone Period was a stretch of several weeks when Doris became fixated on Lorna Doone cookies. Debbie would arrive at her mother's apartment and find dozens of boxes scattered everywhere.

The Ticket Period began when Doris saw a play she liked and used her ticket stub to try to see it over and over again.

During the Social Security Period, Doris became convinced (mistakenly) that she was not getting her checks and harassed the local Social Security office mercilessly.

As the months passed, Debbie regretted encouraging her mother to write notes, and came to view Doris's notes as an enemy. They did not help her remember anything. Quite the contrary, they seemed to agitate her all the more because every time she saw one, she realized there was something she was supposed to remember, but she had less and less idea what it was. Eventually, Debbie took to quietly pocketing any notes she found at her mother's apartment. If Doris was obsessed with jotting down notes, Debbie became almost as obsessed with throwing them away. "I even used Wite-Out on her datebook," Debbie recalls. "It got to the point where I began wondering, Who's crazier here? My mother, or me?"

Debbie's other enemy was the telephone. When her mother first moved to San Francisco, the telephone was their connecting link. Before her move, Doris had had problems talking on the phone, and as she became increasingly confused, her telephone problems increased. Debbie would ask her to check on something in the apartment. Doris would put the receiver down and never return. Or Doris would forget to hang up, and all Debbie would get for hours on end would be a busy signal. Sometimes Doris would forget where she kept her phone, and even its incessant ringing could not lead her to it. "My mother's problems dealing with the phone made me frantic," Debbie recalls. "When I'd get busy signals for eight hours or endless rings when I knew she was there, or when she'd disappear and leave me hanging on the phone, it was impossible not to fear the worst."

Doris clearly had problems; she was increasingly confused and repetitive, but Debbie never gave a thought to the possibility that her mother might have Alzheimer's disease. "All I knew about Alzheimer's were the grimmest stereotypes. I thought people went from competent to completely incompetent very quickly. That wasn't my mother. She lived on her own for *four years* before her diagnosis. I had no idea how slowly and insidiously the disease progresses. I thought people with Alzheimer's lost their memory, language facility, and ability to take care of themselves more or less at the same time, but that wasn't the way it worked with my mother. Even though she could be profoundly confused, she retained her ability to speak articulately. She dealt with her own finances. She got around the city on her own. She basically took care of herself. Her problems simply didn't fit my image of Alzheimer's."

Debbie and her lover, Frances, both assumed that Doris's problems were caused by mini-strokes—medically, transient ischemic attacks, or TIAs. Where major strokes can cause sudden, permanent paralysis or loss of ability to speak, TIAs involve only a few seconds to several minutes of dizziness, weakness, or disorientation caused by momentary blockages in blood flow through the brain. Those who suffer TIAs seem to recover completely, but in addition to being a major risk factor for future strokes, TIAs temporarily deprive parts of the brain of oxygen. After several of them, people suffer a loss of cognitive ability called vascular or multi-infarct dementia, which is the second leading cause of dementia after Alzheimer's and often goes hand in hand with it (see chapter 7).

Whatever Doris's problem, there was no denying that her mental abilities were slowly, progressively failing. Debbie knew it, and Doris knew it. One day Debbie returned home to a phone message: "Debbie, darling, I am your stupid mother. I got everything mixed up. I didn't do anything that I wanted to do, and I can't remember from one minute to the next what I do and don't do."

Debbie spent more and more of her time ministering to her mother, helping her shop, cook, clean, and take care of herself, and rushing to San Francisco in a panic because she couldn't reach her mother by phone. "It got to the point," she recalls, "where her life was out of control, and my life was out of control. I stopped *having* a life because all I could do was try to manage hers from across the Bay. I became so wrapped up in the details of my mother's daily crises that I missed the big picture—the fact that something was really wrong with her."

In 1990, four years after Doris moved west, Debbie realized that she had to have her mother medically evaluated. She took her to the geriatrics department at Mount Zion Medical Center in San Francisco. Doris didn't want to go, and her resistance to medical care of any kind became a hallmark of her illness. "Doctor visits were our most stressful times," Debbie recalls. "She became very willful and resistant. My mother never made scenes, but if I mentioned where we were going, she became furious. She screamed at me like she'd never yelled her entire life. Then she would yell at the doctors, call them idiots. Trips to the doctor reduced me to tears."

That first trip to her mother's neurological evaluation did more than make Debbie cry, it brought her face-to-face with the ghastly stereotypes of Alzheimer's. "When the doctor said, 'Your mother has Alzheimer's,' I had a vision of her curled up in a fetal position unable to do anything. Of course, that wasn't my mother. There were still lots of things she could do, but her diagnosis forced me to acknowledge the direction we were heading in."

The staff at Mount Zion—the neurologists, geriatric nurses, and social workers—were amazed that Debbie had managed to maintain Doris's independence for so long. "You mother is beyond early Alzheimer's," they told her. "She's already moderately impaired. We suggest you start looking for a residential care facility. And until you place her, we'd recommend hiring a home health aide immediately."

Debbie was in no shape to consider practicalities like home help for her mother. It was all she could do to shepherd Doris back to her apartment. Debbie considered discussing her mother's diagnosis with her, but realized it would be a mistake. "That kind of conversation was no longer possible with her." That realization forced Debbie to acknowledge that the diagnosis was correct. Her mother had Alzheimer's disease.

Debbie didn't read much about Alzheimer's beyond the basics. She received some helpful advice and referrals from a family service agency, but by and large she was on her own. She tried a support group, but couldn't find one for Alzheimer's caregivers that was convenient. She wound up in a group for children of aging parents. "I had the only parent with Alzheimer's disease. My situation was by far the worst of anyone there, and I had no patience for the other people's issues. They all seemed so trivial. But if I had it to do over again, I'd drive a good distance to attend a group for Alzheimer's caregivers, or start one."

Reflecting on the changes she'd seen in her mother since the period five years earlier when her father had taken over the phone conversations, Debbie realized that even then, her father must have suspected that Doris might have Alzheimer's. "He had her take all sorts of vitamins," Debbie recalls, "and even after he died and she became increasingly confused, she clung to her supplements and took them religiously." She took choline, a B-complex vitamin and a key component of acetylcholine, a neurotransmitter that becomes depleted in Alzheimer's disease. (Choline supplements do not increase brain levels of acetylcholine, but other supplements help treat Alzheimer's, notably vitamin E, the medicinal herb ginkgo, and the amino-acid drug carnitine—see chapter 10.)

Debbie also realized the depth of her mother's suffering. Doris's generally cheerful chatter couldn't hide the fact that she felt stupid, incompetent, and deeply ashamed of her worsening impairment. Sometimes, Doris's shame made her stubborn. "My mother was always a math whiz," Debbie recalls, "and very proud of it. Even after her diagnosis, when the neurologist said she was pretty far gone, she continued to pay her own bills and balance her checkbook with very little help from me." But as the months passed, Doris's treasured number sense failed her. She tried to hide it, but one day Debbie stole a look at her checkbook. "The public television station was making out like a bandit. She was renewing her membership every week. At that point, I had to take the checkbook away from her."

At other times, Doris's shame made her furious—usually at Debbie. "I was the one who was there," Debbie explains, "the one trying to keep order, the one who took care of the things she could no longer manage. My mother had always been very independent. Becoming so dependent frustrated her terribly. And who made her realize that she could no longer manage on her own? Me. Sometimes she turned on me with rages I'd never seen in her before. It was scary. Her angry outbursts were horrible. Although they were understandable, they were very hard to deal with and incredibly painful for me."

Doris's confusion deepened and her memory faded. She began forgetting who Debbie was. Yet her language ability remained remarkably sharp, even though she often had no idea what she or anyone else was talking about.

Then Debbie's brother and sister-in-law came to San Francisco to visit Doris. They spent a good deal of time with her, but also wanted to spend some time doing things as a couple. "They ran into my mother miles from her apartment. She had no idea where she was."

The incident demonstrated that Doris was wandering. It terrified Debbie, and led her to hire a home health aide to keep an eye on her mother.

Through a family services agency, Debbie found a home health aide who seemed competent and personable. She made a date to meet the aide near her mother's apartment so she could introduce her to Doris. Debbie told her mother that she wanted her to meet a friend, and asked Doris to be home on a certain day at a specific time. "But when we got there, my mother wasn't home. She showed up an hour later, confused and disheveled. She'd been wandering. I introduced her to the aide, thinking, Not a moment too soon."

Home care was expensive—$10 to $17 an hour, depending on the provider's level of skill—and Doris wasn't physically sick, so Medicare wouldn't pay for it. "There was no way I could afford it on what I make," Debbie explains. Fortunately, Doris had sizable savings, and Debbie tapped her assets to engage an aide for four hours a day. "It was a godsend. I couldn't believe I waited so long to get someone to help her." Very quickly, the four hours turned into eight. "I didn't realize how tense I'd been about my mother's safety until she had someone with her, and for eight hours a day I didn't have to worry about her. I thought, This is what we both need. This works."

Home care worked well for Doris most of the time. Aides came and went, and Doris liked most of them; however, she took an immediate dislike to a few. She kicked one aide out of her apartment. The aide stood across the street in an effort to keep an eye on her. It was a good thing, too. A short time later, Doris appeared at the front door. She began walking, and wandered around San Francisco for several hours with the aide shadowing her. When Debbie learned of this, she got her mother an ID bracelet that said she was memory-impaired and gave Debbie's phone number.

Some months later, another new aide showed up whom Doris despised. By this time, she had real problems communicating her feelings about things that upset her, so she expressed her misery physically—by slugging the aide in the head with her pocketbook. "My mother was eighty-four at the time," Debbie explains, "but she could still do some damage with a loaded pocketbook. Hitting was something very new for her. She'd always had a temper, but she'd never resorted to violence." The aide soon departed, replaced by someone Doris liked and never hit.

The aides cooked and cleaned for Doris and generally kept an eye on her. They distracted her if she became obsessive about the dentist or Lorna Doones, but did not help her dress, bathe, or use the bathroom. Despite her increasing impairment, she could still do those things for herself, although when Debbie or an aide took over tasks Doris was used to doing for herself, she didn't fight them. "The only thing she ever really resisted was going to the doctor."

With Doris supervised by home aides, Debbie was able to step back from the relentless demands of caregiving and contemplate her mother's decline. Doris's memory was clearly fading fast. "I'd call at the end of the day and say, 'So how was your day with Patricia?' And she'd say, 'No one's been here all day!'"

For the longest time, when things like this happened, Debbie corrected her mother: "No, Patricia's been with you all day. She just left." But as Doris declined, correcting her only agitated and frustrated her. Instead of trying to keep her mother connected to reality, Debbie decided to stop arguing and simply play along with whatever Doris believed was happening. "It finally dawned on me that it didn't matter if she said it was April when it was really May. Why correct her? If she was convinced that we were college sorority sisters, or elementary school friends, why not? It was a very liberating realization. Suddenly, we were in the moment. The truth, the facts didn't matter anymore. I just went along with whatever she was into. It was hard to let go of reality at first, but I got used to it. If I thought of our time together as a game, it was fun."

Sometimes the fun was bittersweet. Doris lost her memory by retreating backward in time, which was hard for Debbie. "By the time the home aides arrived, all memory of the fifty years she'd spent in New York had vanished. She didn't remember my father, or raising my brother and me. Everything that I thought of as 'her life,' the part connected to our family, disappeared. She had no idea that I was her daughter. She knew me only as Debbie, the person who often visited her and did things with her, but her sense of who I was slipped further and further into her past. I became her college friend, then her high school friend, then an elementary school friend. I tried to play along, but connecting with her got harder and harder. It was like interpreting dreams."

On the other hand, some things got easier. As Doris descended into Alzheimer's, she became less critical, less demanding, and more appreciative. "She was easier to get along with than she'd ever been," Debbie says. "The stereotype is that people with Alzheimer's become irascible. That happens, and my mother certainly had her moments. I've also heard a lot of caregivers say just the opposite, that Alzheimer's softened the person."

Doris also became more comfortable with Debbie's lesbianism. While Doris always considered herself socially liberal, she still had real problems adjusting to her daughter's homosexuality. "To her credit," Debbie explains, "she worked on her feelings and eventually became reconciled to who I was, yet she was never comfortable with my relationship with Frances. As her Alzheimer's progressed, she was down to basics. I was good to her and made her happy. I had a friend, Frances, who was also good to her and made her happy. She was happy to be with us. When the three of us got together, things were comfortable."

Doris even became a little goofy. "Before her Alzheimer's, my mother was an intellectual married to an academic, and she often came across as a snob. When she visited me, the *San Francisco Chronicle* was never good enough for her, even though she'd grown up in San Francisco. She had to have the *The New York Times*. She also disdained television as beneath her. But I'll never forget, one day I entered her apartment and heard her laughing uproariously. I found her watching some daytime TV show and loving it. At first I was aghast. *This isn't my mother.* But she was enjoying herself, and there were fewer and fewer things she could enjoy, so I figured, what the hell."

Debbie's father had had chronic allergies and spent much of his life on a restricted diet. That was hard for Doris, who loved fine food. After her husband's death, though, her diet was liberated, and in San Francisco she, Debbie, and Frances often went out to eat. Even as Doris slipped deeper into dementia, Debbie continued to take her to restaurants, though some aspects of their outings became problematic: "My mother enjoyed a good martini, but as she became more demented, I didn't want her drinking. So we'd sit down and order three martinis—one for her, one for Frances, and one for me. Frances and I would drink ours down quickly until only a little remained, and then try to switch glasses with my mother so she wouldn't get much alcohol, but she almost always caught us, even when she was pretty deep into Alzheimer's. It was amazing. It would usually take us several tries to switch drinks on her."

Remarkably, Doris continued to hang on to a good deal of her language ability, often speaking in fairly complicated, complete, rational sentences. Sometimes, this was entertaining, but other times it was mortifying. "Before her illness, my mother was always very proper and straitlaced," Debbie explains. "She *never* made scenes and *never* did anything in public to embarrass herself or anyone she was with. Suddenly the Alzheimer's stripped away her sense of propriety. She would laugh uproariously in restaurants and not care who heard her, which was fun, but she would also comment on other diners. In a pretty loud voice, she would say things like, 'Look at that fat person over there!' I'm my mother's daughter in many ways, and outbursts like that were pretty hard to handle."

About a year after her diagnosis (more than five years into her Alzheimer's), Doris's rate of decline accelerated. She began wandering at night, and some of her apartment neighbors began complaining about her behavior. Debbie saw the writing on the wall. Home aides could no longer provide enough care for her. She needed round-the-clock care, and home health aides twenty-four hours a day cost even more than full-time residential care. Despite the costs, Debbie was in no hurry to visit residential care facilities. She'd heard only horror stories about them and couldn't stand the thought of consigning her mother to a warehouse for the living dead.

Then, oddly, Doris spurred Debbie to begin the search. "She became uncomfortable in her apartment. We'd be sitting at her kitchen table and she'd say, 'I want to go home now.'"

Around that time, Doris entered her Suitcase Period. She pulled out all her suitcases and packed them with anything at hand: clothes, food, small appliances, coat hangers, you name it. Debbie or the aide unpacked the suitcases, but Doris repacked them, over and over again. In some ways the Suitcase Period was similar to her many other periods—strange, quirky, and obsessive—but Debbie had the distinct impression that her mother was trying to tell her something, that she wanted to go somewhere. "I think she was saying that it was time to move, and that she was ready."

So Debbie began visiting residential care centers, technically assisted living facilities, which provide more activities and less care than nursing homes, but care for residents round the clock. The first few centers Debbie visited varied from bad to vile. "Some were filthy. Others were clean but had no programs. The people with Alzheimer's were often drugged, tied into wheelchairs, and ignored." (Debbie visited homes in 1991. Drugs and restraints are less widely used these days.)

Then by chance she stumbled on a small home that was different: "I walked in and immediately felt that the residents were really living, not just waiting to die. It was clean and bright, with a lively, engaging staff who treated all the residents as individuals and let them live their dementia the way they each wanted to live it. I knew it was the place for my mother."

Unfortunately, good assisted living facilities are expensive. This one cost $110 a day, $40,000 a year. Fortunately, Doris had the assets to cover the cost. Debbie met with the director, signed all the papers, and agreed on a move-in date two weeks away.

As she rose to leave, Debbie asked the director, "How should I tell her?"

The director replied, "Don't."

"Excuse me?" Debbie said, horrified. "I have to tell her. If I don't, I'll feel like I'm kidnapping her, taking her to a strange place, and leaving her. I can't do that."

"Trust me," the director reassured her. "Don't say anything. If you try to explain it to her, she'll only get agitated. Just bring her. Everything will be fine."

Debbie was dubious but decided to take the director's advice, and said nothing.

The night before Doris's move, Debbie took her out to dinner at a restaurant down the street from her apartment. Doris ate with gusto and chattered away, coherent speech alternating with nonsense. Debbie found it difficult to eat or speak. After dinner, as they walked back to Doris's apartment, a little miracle occurred. "We were across the street from her building," Debbie recalls, "and my mother pointed to it and said, 'You know, when I was in college, I used to have a room there. But I don't think I'll sleep there anymore after tonight.' As deep into Alzheimer's as she was, she *knew*. And I believe she was telling me, 'It's okay. You're doing the right thing.'"

Nonetheless, moving day was an ordeal for Debbie. "I picked her up, and it was as though we were going for a drive in the country. When we got to the home, my mother was a little cautious walking in, but she got comfortable right away. One staff person took her arm and led her into the day room. Another took mine and led me in the opposite direction. Walking away from her was the hardest thing I've ever done."

Debbie drove home in tears. She felt like she'd done one of the worst things a child could ever do to a parent, but over the phone, the staff assured her that Doris was adjusting beautifully. Two days later, Debbie visited. "When I arrived, she was sitting in the day room, dozing. As I approached her, she woke up, gave me a big smile, and with outstretched hands said, 'Oh, the joy of me!'"

Doris adjusted to the residential care facility considerably faster and more easily than Debbie adjusted to her mother being there.

Debbie brought family photographs, some of Doris's cherished old knickknacks, and some books by her father to decorate her mother's room. Doris accepted the photos but wanted no part of anything else from her past.

The same thing happened with her clothes. Debbie brought several outfits Doris had always liked, but the staff pointed out that sweatshirts and sweatpants were easier to deal with and wash. "Seeing my mother in sweats was tough, but she didn't care what she wore, and I adjusted."

Doris hung on to only one item from her former life—her pocketbook. There was nothing in it and no reason to carry it, but having it made her happy.

Debbie visits her mother often. They take walks, have tea, and play the games and sing the songs the staff organize in the day room. "There's absolutely nothing uplifting about Alzheimer's disease," Debbie says. "It's very hard to deal with all the losses it imposes. Still, if you accept the losses, you can experience moments of joy despite the ravages of the illness."

These days, Doris is happy to see Debbie but has no idea they're related. She neither anticipates her visits nor laments her absences. "She's down to the very basics," Debbie explains. "She's well cared for, so she's happy. And I'm happy for her. Her sense of humor is still there. We tickle each other and laugh a lot."

Although she is severely impaired, Doris still has a huge vocabulary but can no longer speak coherent sentences. Most days she still feeds herself but needs help dressing. She washes her own hands but can't bathe herself. She has lost control of her toilet functions and wears diapers. She is also constipated, which has a major impact on her moods. After about a year in residential care, she stopped carrying her pocketbook.

"My mother no longer has any attachment to anything material," Debbie muses. "She lives totally in the moment. We see it as severe mental impairment, but some religions would view it as a kind of enlightenment."

Looking back on her caregiving experience, Debbie wishes she'd accepted her mother's illness more easily. "Most of the problems we had were problems I created, for example, correcting her mistakes, which upset her, or putting off getting home health aides or placing her in the home. Everything I did, I should have done six months earlier."

The only things Debbie no longer accepts about Alzheimer's disease are the stereotypes about it. "Recently, I heard some news person say Alzheimer's 'robs people of their humanity.' That's so wrong, so demeaning. It robs you of your *memories,* but *not* your humanity. We tend to equate the two because we define ourselves by our experiences and our memories of them. Strip away all of someone's memories, and the person still remains, their humanity remains. In her own way, my mother is still a beautiful human being."

During the years she cared for her mother, Deborah Hoffmann also filmed her, partly to document Doris's life and partly as therapy to deal with the stress of caregiving. After her mother moved to the assisted living facility, Debbie produced Complaints of a Dutiful Daughter. *Sad, humorous, loving, heartrending, poignant, and moving, the film chronicles Doris's decline and Debbie's process of coming to terms with it.* Complaints of a Dutiful Daughter *was nominated for an Academy Award in 1995. (44 minutes, color. $67.00 from Women Make Movies, 462 Broadway, New York, NY 10013; 212-925-0606.)*

16.

The New Science of Staying Mentally Sharp—for Life

The Latest Discoveries About Memory Preservation

You misplace your keys. You forget people's names and phone numbers. You can't recall what you had for lunch or which movie you saw last week. Sometimes, you forget what you're about to say, and occasionally at home, you stride purposefully into a room—and suddenly have no idea why you went in there. When memory lapses strike, you wonder, Is this normal? Or is this the beginning of Alzheimer's disease?

Barry Gordon, M.D., Ph.D., director of the Johns Hopkins Cognitive Neurology, Neuropsychology, and Memory Disorders Clinic, offers some reassuring perspective. Most memory lapses are completely normal. It's also normal to forget more as you age, but this wisdom is lost on most American adults, 67 percent of whom complain of memory loss.

Why do so many people worry about something that's normal? Fear of Alzheimer's is a big reason. The disease can strike surprisingly young people. Fortunately the odds are excellent that your mind is fine. Recall from chapter 3 that among those under sixty-four, Alzheimer's is rare. From age sixty-four to seventy-four, only about 3 percent of the population has the disease. From seventy-five to eighty-four, the proportion rises to about 15 percent, and among those eighty-five and older, Alzheimer's afflicts some 30 to 40 percent. In other words, even if you're over eighty-five, the odds are still *against* your having Alzheimer's.

In addition, the memory losses caused by Alzheimer's are qualitatively different from normal memory lapses. It's perfectly normal to forget a friend's phone number. The time to get worried about Alzheimer's is when you find it and have *no idea what to do with it.*

Another reason we worry about memory loss is the oft-quoted statistic that the typical adult loses some ten thousand brain cells a day. The implication is that by the time we qualify for Social Security, there's not much left between our ears. Dr. Gordon insists that ten-thousand-cells-a-day figure is a myth. Normal adults lose very few brains cells, and even if we did lose ten thousand brain cells a day, the brain is estimated to contain some *ten billion* neurons. If you lost ten thousand a day for seventy years, from age eighteen to eighty-eight, you'd lose just *2.5 percent* of your ten billion neurons.

While it's true that the brain loses some mass with age, by and large what's left compensates. In the words of psychologist and *New York Times* writer Daniel Goleman, Ph.D., the aging brain is rather like a veteran baseball pitcher. His fast ball isn't quite the bullet it was during his rookie season, but he's become wily enough to strike out batters using other pitches.

The good news about memory is that there are many ways to protect and enhance it. Recent research has also identified several strategies that help prevent Alzheimer's.

Memory Quiz: How Sharp Are You NOW?

Before you can improve your memory, you need some assessment of how sharp it is. Take these memory screening tests, based on recent studies in several journals, among them *Archives of Clinical Neuropsychology*, the *Journal of Gerontology*, and the *British Journal of Psychology*.

THE SHOPPING LIST, I

Read the following list carefully just once. Then look away and write down all the items you remember.

onions	shrimp	mangoes
plums	tonic water	pasta
eggs	mayonnaise	ham
blackberries	basil	brownies
hazelnuts	zucchini	oatmeal

Scoring:

The average 18- to 39-year-old recalls ten of the fifteen items.
The average 40- to 49-year-old recalls nine.
The average 50- to 59-year-old also recalls nine.
The average 60- to 69-year-old recalls eight.
The average person 70 or older recalls seven.

THE SHOPPING LIST, II

Read the list once every five minutes. After your fifth reading, put it away and wait thirty minutes. Then try to recall the list.

Scoring:

The average 18- to 39-year-old recalls thirteen of the fifteen items.
The average 40- to 49-year-old recalls twelve.
The average 50- to 59-year-old also recalls twelve.
The average 60- to 69-year-old recalls eleven.
The average person 70 or older recalls ten.

PHONE FUN

Read a ten-digit phone number aloud (the area code plus the number). Then dial it from memory. When it rings (or if it's busy), hang up and redial it from memory. How many digits can you recall?

Scoring:
> The average 18- to 39-year-old recalls six of the ten digits correctly.
> The average 40- to 59-year-old recalls five or six.
> The average 50- to 59-year-old recalls five.
> The average 60- to 69-year-old recalls four or five.
> The average person 70 or older recalls three.

THE NAME GAME

A tester reads you six names, both first and last. Then the tester scrambles the list and reads you just the last names. Your job is to remember the first names. The tester rescrambles the list four more times, for a total of thirty tries. Each time the tester gives you the last name, and you try to come up with the first.

Scoring:
> The average 18- to 39-year-old identifies the correct name twenty-one of the thirty times.
> The average 40- to 59-year-old identifies seventeen.
> The average 50- to 59-year-old identifies sixteen.
> The average 60- to 69-year-old identifies fifteen.
> The average person 70 or older identifies twelve.

NAME THAT FACE

At one-second intervals, a tester shows you six photographs, each of a face, with the person's first name attached. Then the tester removes the names, shuffles the photos, and presents them at one-second intervals. You try to name each face.

Scoring:
> The average 18- to 39-year-old recalls four of the six names correctly.
> The average 40- to 59-year-old recalls three.
> The average 50- to 59-year-old recalls three.
> The average 60- to 69-year-old recalls two.
> The average person 70 or older recalls two.

How to Prevent Normal Memory Lapses

PAY ATTENTION

We often forget this fundamental memory aid. "Focus, focus, focus," says Douglas Herrmann, Ph.D., a memory researcher at the National Center for Health Statistics in Washington, D.C., and author of *Super Memory*. "If information doesn't register in your brain in the first place, you have no chance of remembering it."

MINIMIZE DISTRACTIONS

This is a corollary to paying attention. When receiving information you want to recall, drop whatever else you're doing. Turn off your TV and radio. Stop doing the crossword puzzle.

GET ORGANIZED

Life is too complicated to recall everything we want to remember: appointments, birthdays, errands, financial details, etc. Write things down on calendars and/or datebooks. Keep these items handy. Consult them frequently.

REPEAT NAMES OUT LOUD

More than 80 percent of Americans say they have trouble recalling names. Forgetting names is annoying and embarrassing. It's also the leading reason why so many people are convinced that they suffer memory loss.

Try this old sales trick: When you first meet someone, repeat the person's name *out loud* several times. Repetition and vocalization help cement it in your mind. Greet the person by name: "Hello, Ms. Smith." You might also ask the spelling of the name: "Is that S-m-i-t-h or S-m-y-t-h-e?" and then spell it back: "Ah yes, S-m-i-t-h." Repeat the name in conversation: "Enjoying the party, Ms. Smith?" Repeat the name as you take your leave: "Nice meeting you, Ms. Smith." Afterward, repeat the name aloud a few more times or write it down.

Repeat instructions and directions out loud as well.

WRITE IT DOWN

The act of writing helps cement names, dates, and other facts in memory. If you need to, write things down a few times.

USE MEMORY AIDS

Carry a little notebook so you can jot things down the moment you realize you need to remember them. Buy a watch with an alarm. Tape reminder notes on your bathroom mirror or car steering wheel. Use your memory aids regularly.

HAVE A "KEY SPOT"

If you lose things, especially your keys, find a convenient spot to keep them, perhaps a little basket by your door. Keep them there all the time.

MAKE UP A MNEMONIC

A mnemonic (neh–MAH–nik) is a trick that helps you remember. Here's a classic from music: *Every Good Boy Does Fine*, a mnemonic for recalling the lines of musical notation: E, G, B, D, and F. Another way to use mnemonics is to develop associations. If you meet a woman named Rose from Dallas, you might fix her name in your memory by humming "The Yellow Rose of Texas." Mnemonics come in handy for all sorts of things, for example, words that are difficult to spell, and the order of streets in a city.

PACE YOURSELF

The mind can absorb only so much at a time. Focus on recalling one or two small, discrete bits of information at a time.

BREAK THINGS DOWN

As a ten-digit string, the phone number 4152823575 is hard to remember. Break it down and it gets easier: (415) 282-3575.

RELAX

In school, did you ever know a subject cold, but when under pressure during a test you forgot key points? The reason is that stress impairs memory. Researchers at the Center for the Neurobiology of Learning and Memory at the University of California at Irvine have shown that the stress hormone cortisol interferes with the brain processes involved in initiating and cementing memory. The higher your cortisol level, the more memory problems you have. Researchers have also injected laboratory animals with a drug that blocks the production of cortisol, and the animals had no memory problems at all, even when under considerable stress. When you're under stress, use more memory aids.

CULTIVATE A MEMORY PARTNER

Different people remember different things. Spouses recall more together than separately. Memory is a kind of dialogue. Conversational prompting helps.

HAVE YOUR HEARING CHECKED

If you don't remember what people tell you, the problem might not be in your mind but in your ears. Researchers at the Memory Disorders Clinic at the University of South Florida at Tampa examined fifty-two elderly people, of whom half had been diagnosed with probable Alzheimer's disease and half had other memory problems. Just about all of them (forty-nine of the fifty-two, or 94 percent) also had significant hearing loss. Only about one-third of the healthy elderly have serious hearing problems. Undiagnosed hearing loss interferes with learning and makes people seem distracted, confused, disoriented, and unresponsive, traits that might be mistaken for Alzheimer's disease.

LEAD AN INTELLECTUALLY ACTIVE LIFE

Even though education does not appear to protect specifically against Alzheimer's disease (chapter 5), several studies have linked it to the preservation of general mental acuity throughout life. The theory is that education exercises the brain, increasing its number of neural pathways. If any get damaged as the years pass, others are available to compensate.

In addition to formal education, people who lead mentally active lives—traveling, reading books, taking courses, doing puzzles, and pursuing hobbies and new experiences—maintain their intellectual edge better than those who spend their lives vegetating in front of the TV.

DON'T SMOKE

Smoking is not only stupid, it *makes you stupid*. Smoking constricts the blood vessels, including those in your brain. That means less blood flow to your brain cells—less oxygen and fewer nutrients getting upstairs. Smoking also pumps a great deal of carbon monoxide into your blood. Carbon monoxide displaces oxygen, impairing brain cells even more.

Smoking increases the risk of Alzheimer's disease (chapter 5).

Marijuana also impairs mental acuity. Harvard researchers gave a battery of mental-function tests to two groups of college students. One said they smoked marijuana daily. The other indulged no more than once a month. Both groups lived at the research center for a day before the testing and did not use marijuana during that time. Even after the period of abstinence, the heavy smokers performed significantly worse on the tests.

WATCH THE ALCOHOL

Alcohol is a major cause of memory lapses. More than half of alcoholics show evidence of cerebral atrophy, and even social drinkers who rarely get drunk can suffer cognitive impairment. The memory-scrambling effects of alcohol increase with age. As people grow older, they become more sensitive to alcohol-related memory lapses, meaning that it takes less beer, wine, or liquor to ravage your recall.

However, this is not to say that everyone should quit drinking. Alcoholics should, of course, but for most other people moderate alcohol consumption (up to one drink a day for women, two a day for men) helps prevent heart attack, the nation's leading cause of death, by increasing levels of HDL (so-called good cholesterol).

Additionally, a recent study shows that light alcohol consumption may actually *improve* intellectual abilities in the elderly. Researchers at the Indiana University School of Medicine surveyed 2,040 African-Americans, average age seventy-four, about their lifestyle, including their drinking habits, and then gave them cognitive-function tests. Those who had ten or more drinks a week scored the lowest. Those who had four to ten drinks a week scored higher. Abstainers scored even higher. But those who scored the highest were the light drinkers, who had one to four drinks a week but no more.

It's not entirely clear why light drinking would improve cognition over abstinence. One possibility is that people in the best health feel free to drink a little, while those who have medical problems—including problems that subtly affect cognition—might feel compelled to abstain. Another is that by raising HDL levels, alcohol reduces the buildup of the cholesterol-rich deposits (plaques) that narrow arteries (atherosclerosis) and cause heart attacks, most strokes, and a good deal of cognitive impairment. Atherosclerosis limits blood flow into the brain, so minimizing it with a few drinks a week might explain why light drinkers scored the highest.

But remember, any more than a drink or two a day and over the long term you're risking your memory, and your health.

CONSIDER TAKING A MULTIVITAMIN

Several studies have shown that vitamin supplements improve memory and mental functioning:

- Back in 1971, Swiss researchers tested blood levels of vitamins C and E, and beta-carotene in 6,400 adults enrolled in the Basel Longitudinal Study on Aging. Twenty-two years later, in 1993, they repeated the vitamin blood analysis and gave the participants several memory tests: visual memory, vocabulary memory, and task recall. The higher their blood levels of vitamin C and beta-carotene, the better their memories. (Vitamin E did not improve memory in this study, which is odd because it helps slow the progression of Alzheimer's—chapter 10.)
- Another study showed that vitamin B_6 (pyroxidine) helps elderly memory. Dutch researchers at the University of Amsterdam fo-

cused on B_6 because it is key to the synthesis of several neuro-transmitters involved in memory. They gave seventy-six healthy elderly men, aged seventy to seventy-nine, either a placebo or pyroxidine (20 mg a day) for three months. Pre- and post-tests showed that "vitamin B_6 supplementation improved storage of information modestly but significantly."

- Vitamin B_{12} also appears to play a role in memory. At the University of Oklahoma and the Oklahoma VA Medical Center, researchers gave standard cognitive-function tests to 303 elderly veterans, aged sixty-five to eighty-nine, and then measured their blood levels of B_{12}. The lower their B_{12}, the poorer their memories.

- Finally, David Benton, Ph.D., a professor of psychology at the University College of Swansea in Wales, United Kingdom, asked 127 college students to take either a placebo or a multi-vitamin twice a day for a year. The supplement, an off-the-shelf multivitamin, contained vitamins A, C, E, B_{12}, thiamin, ribo-flavin, pyroxidine, folic acid, biotin, and niacin. In tests of reaction time, both the men and women in the vitamin group initially outperformed the placebo takers. The women continued to do so for the whole year, though the men who took the placebo eventually caught up with those taking the vitamins.

BE CAREFUL WITH MEDICINES

Some commonly used drugs may cause memory loss and cognitive impairment, among them antihistamines, tranquilizers, sedatives, narcotics, antacids, some antidepressants, and certain blood pressure medications (beta-blockers and calcium channel blockers). Whenever you get a prescription, always ask about side effects.

Even if a drug does not blunt mental sharpness by itself, it may do so when taken simultaneously with other medications. As people grow older, they often take several drugs at the same time, which raises the risk of cognitive impairment. Drug-related mental dulling may mimic the symptoms of early Alzheimer's disease, including memory loss, absentmindedness, confusion, disorientation, and emotional outbursts. Alcohol use aggravates drug-related cognitive problems.

In addition, as people grow older, they tend to become more sensitive to drug effects. An appropriate dose for a forty-five-year-old may be too much for a person who is seventy-five. Doctors should adjust drug dosage downward as people age, but some neglect to do this, inadvertently prescribing overdoses that may cause cognitive impairment.

If you develop any persistent memory or reasoning problem and suspect a drug-related cause, do not stop taking your medication. Instead, make a list of *all* the drugs you take—both prescription and over the counter, including your alcohol consumption. Then ask your physician and pharmacist if your combination of medications might impair cognition. Mental acuity returns with removal of the offending drug(s) under medical supervision. Of course, you may not be able to discontinue some medications, but dose adjustments and drug substitutions may help.

GET ENOUGH SLEEP

Sleep needs vary, but according to William Dement, M.D., director of the Stanford University Sleep Disorders Clinic and chair of the National Commission on Sleep Disorders Research, most people need at least seven hours a night to function well. Many need eight or nine. Any less, and they develop a "sleep debt" that interferes with memory, judgment, and reaction time, increasing absentmindedness and the risk of accidents. If you ever find yourself dozing off after lunch or at movies, plays, or concerts, Dement says you need more sleep. Try getting eight hours a night for a week. You'll probably feel better and have a sharper memory.

Benign prostate enlargement forces many men in their forties, fifties, and sixties to get up at night to urinate, often several times. These wake-ups can impair sleep quality. If you suspect a prostate problem, consult your physician.

For information on sleep apnea, a severe sleeping disorder, see page 140.

MANAGE YOUR STRESS

Emotional stress has been linked to all sorts of ills, from heart attack to sexual problems. Recently, a Stanford researcher added memory loss to the list. Robert M. Sapolsky, Ph.D., a professor of biological sciences, says that prolonged stress produces hormones—among them adrenaline and glucocorticoid hormone—that can damage the hippocampus, part of the brain involved in memory and learning. Studies of Vietnam veterans suffering from post-traumatic stress syndrome have shown that many have unusually small hippocampi. Stress management is important not only for mental sharpness but also for general well-being and quality of life. Effective stress management programs include meditation, biofeedback, exercise, volunteering, hot baths, and close social ties.

If you're stressed because you fear that your memory is going, you might enroll in a memory-enhancement class. Such classes are popping up around the country in reaction to our aging population and growing fear of Alzheimer's disease. They advocate many of the approaches discussed in this chapter, such as paying attention, repeating names, limiting alcohol intake, getting enough sleep, etc.

Do memory classes work? Researchers at Mount Sinai Hospital in New York City, Columbia University, Harvard, Johns Hopkins, and the University of Pennsylvania recruited 142 people, aged sixty to ninety, who complained of memory loss but were otherwise healthy. Half watched a public television series on the mind. The other half took a memory-enhancement class. After the class, the researchers tested the participants' memories and also inquired about their confidence in their memory. Initially those in the class scored better on the memory tests and expressed greater confidence in their recall ability.

Over time, however, participants grew lazy, and six months later their memories had slipped back to about where the control group scored. Nonetheless, the class participants retained greater confidence in their memories, largely because the class taught them that most memory lapses are nothing to worry about. In other words, they no longer felt stressed by their memory loss, and when they had to remember something, they could use the techniques they'd learned to do so.

CONSIDER TAKING GINSENG

For centuries, Asians, particularly the Chinese and Koreans, have revered the medicinal root of ginseng for its ability to improve physical stamina and mental acuity. Western scientists remain skeptical, but a recent Danish study suggests that ginseng may improve some aspects of cognitive function. At Gentofte University Hospital in Hellerup, Denmark, researchers tested the cognitive function of 112 healthy middle-aged adults—their memory, concentration, learning ability, attention span, reaction time, and abstract reasoning ability. Then they took either a placebo or ginseng (400 mg/day of *Panax ginseng*) for nine weeks. Those who took the herb showed improved reaction time and abstract reasoning ability, but no improvement in memory. None of the participants reported any side effects from ginseng.

ENJOY COMPLEX MUSIC

Music nourishes the soul. It may do the same for the brain. A 1993 experiment by Frances H. Rauscher, Ph.D., a research fellow at the Center for the Neurobiology of Learning and Memory at the University of California at Irvine, showed that a ten-minute dose of Mozart temporarily boosts intelligence. Dr. Rauscher had thirty-six college students take a standard intelligence test before and after listening to either silence, a tape of relaxing Muzak, or Mozart's Sonata for Two Pianos in D Major (K. 448). After the period of silence, the students' average score was 110. After the Muzak, it was 111, but after listening to Mozart, it jumped to 119. Even students who said they didn't like Mozart's music experienced an intellectual boost. "Listening to complex music like Mozart may stimulate neural pathways that are important in thinking," Dr. Rauscher says. If that's so, other complex musical forms, for example, jazz, should have a similar effect.

BEWARE OF INDOOR AIR POLLUTANTS

Many physicians overlook indoor air pollution as a cause of cognitive problems. This is a mistake. The elderly spend about 80 percent of their time indoors and, as a result, suffer greater-than-average exposure to indoor air pollutants that can cause cognitive impairment, among them carbon monoxide from gas appliances; volatile organic compounds from paints and polishes; and formaldehyde from new carpets, drapes, paneling, and furnishings. In addition, compared with most adults in the prime of life, the elderly are more sensitive to low-level toxic exposures.

If you're concerned about memory loss, be sure to assess possible toxic exposures. Red flags include a newly constructed residence, new carpeting, new drapes, new furniture, new paint, and newly refinished floors (chapter 9).

BEWARE OF LEAD

Mention lead poisoning and most people think of the toxic metal's effects on children, in whom it causes learning disabilities and, in severe cases, mental retardation. But lead poisoning—and the cognitive problems it causes—are also problems for the elderly, especially for elderly women.

Lead was once a common ingredient in paints and gasoline. Lead was banned in these products more than twenty years ago, but today's elderly and middle-aged populations spent decades exposed to it. In addition, lead can still be found in much of the nation's air and water because of its persistence in the environment, and also in some types of calcium supplements many older women take to prevent bone-thinning osteoporosis, notably bone meal and dolomite.

The body accumulates lead in bone tissue. After age fifty, bone begins to break down. Osteoporosis affects both sexes, but it proceeds more quickly in women. Its best-known symptoms include loss of height, stooped posture, and increased risk of fractures. But in addition, as bone deteriorates, the lead stored in it gets released into the bloodstream, giving some elderly women surprisingly high blood levels—even if they live in a lead-free environment (chapter 9).

If you're a postmenopausal woman, ask your doctor to test your blood for lead periodically. Also consider taking hormone replacement therapy (HRT). The estrogen in HRT helps prevent osteoporosis, so it helps keep lead stored in bone out of the bloodstream. In addition, HRT also helps prevent Alzheimer's (see below).

How to Reduce Your Risk of Alzheimer's Disease

PREVENT CARDIOVASCULAR (CVD) DISEASE: HEART DISEASE, STROKE, HIGH BLOOD PRESSURE (HYPERTENSION), AND DIABETES

These diseases all damage the body's blood vessels, including those in the brain. The latest research shows that cardiovascular disease raises the risk of Alzheimer's. For the details, see chapters 5 and 9, but briefly:

- High blood pressure in midlife raises the risk of dementia in later life. Hypertension is a key risk factor for heart disease and the leading risk factor for stroke.
- Smoking increases the risk of Alzheimer's. Smoking is also a major risk factor for CVD.
- Stroke and mini-strokes (transient ischemic attacks, TIAs) often lead to vascular dementia and also increase the risk of Alzheimer's.
- Diabetes boosts the risk of Alzheimer's. Diabetes is also strongly linked to CVD.
- Survivors of cardiac arrest, a condition similar to heart attack, are at unusually high risk for dementia.

Recent studies have shown that several strategies widely recommended to prevent cardiovascular disease also help prevent Alzheimer's:

- Don't smoke (see below).
- Keep your blood pressure in the normal range.
- Keep your total cholesterol below 200 mg/dl (milligrams per deciliter of blood), and ideally below 180.
- Eat a low-fat, low-cholesterol diet. That means little or no meat, and lots of fruits, vegetables, beans, and whole grains (see below).
- Get regular moderate exercise (see below).
- Maintain recommended weight.
- Maintain close social ties to family, friends, and organizations.
- Take vitamin E, 100 to 400 I.U. (international units) a day in consultation with your doctor (see below).
- Take low-dose aspirin, one-half to one tablet a day in consultation with your physician (see below).
- If you're a woman, don't have more than one alcoholic drink a day. If you're a man, two drinks. (A drink is one 12-ounce beer, one cocktail with 1.25 ounces of 80-proof liquor, or 4 ounces of wine, a standard wineglass about half full.)

DON'T SMOKE

In addition to the general cognitive impairment caused by smoking (see above), at Erasmus University Medical School in the Netherlands, Dutch researchers have shown that smoking increases the risk of Alzheimer's disease. Compared with lifelong nonsmokers, longtime women smokers have twice the Alzheimer's risk, and male smokers have six times the risk (chapter 5).

EAT MORE FRUITS AND VEGETABLES

The arterial injuries at the root of cardiovascular disease (oxidative damage) are caused by highly reactive oxygen molecules (free radicals). But certain nutrients—antioxidants—minimize this damage, notably vitamin C, vitamin E, the mineral selenium, and vitamin A and its close chemical relatives, the carotenoids, among them beta-carotene. These antioxidant nutrients are abundant in plant foods.

Many studies show that as fruit, vegetable, and whole grain consumption increases, CVD risk decreases considerably. Antioxidant nutrients also reduce the risk of Alzheimer's (chapter 5) and help slow its progression (chapter 10).

TAKE VITAMIN E

Several studies also show that antioxidants, notably vitamin E, slow the progression of Alzheimer's disease (chapter 10).

DRINK TEA

A recent Dutch study shows that drinking black tea helps prevent stroke. Tea is high in antioxidants and other compounds (flavonoids) that help prevent the formation of stroke-triggering blood clots in the brain. To the extent that antioxidants help prevent Alzheimer's disease, drinking black tea may add benefits to a plant-based diet.

IF YOU'RE A WOMAN, CONSIDER POSTMENOPAUSAL HORMONE REPLACEMENT THERAPY

The bad news for women is that compared with men, they are more susceptible to Alzheimer's disease (chapter 5). However, the good news is that women can do more to prevent it. They can take postmenopausal hormone replacement therapy (HRT). A large body of research shows that the estrogen in HRT helps treat and prevent Alzheimer's disease (chapter 10).

In the most recent—and most persuasive—report (1998), a research team led by psychiatrist Kristine Yaffe, M.D., of the University of California Medical Center in San Francisco, analyzed the results of ten studies of HRT in postmenopausal women. Overall, participants were 29 percent less likely to develop Alzheimer's disease.

Other studies showing that HRT helps prevent Alzheimer's are discussed in chapter 5.

Even if you're not trying to prevent Alzheimer's, estrogen enhances cognition. New York City researchers tested the vocabulary, recall, and reasoning of 727 women. Thirty months later, they tested the women again. Those who had taken HRT scored significantly higher on the tests. In addition, thirty-two of the thirty-three participants who eventually developed Alzheimer's disease had never taken HRT.

Estrogen helps improve cognitive function and prevent Alzheimer's in several ways: It boosts the production of acetylcholine, a key neurotransmitter involved in cognition. The sex hormone also prevents the deposition of beta-amyloid, the protein involved in the characteristic senile plaques of Alzheimer's disease. Estrogen improves blood flow through the brain. Finally, it helps maintain the integrity of the hippocampus, an area of the brain involved in memory.

Estrogen also helps prevent osteoporosis, which reduces the amount of mind-dulling lead in women's bloodstreams (see above).

But the decision to take HRT is complicated. For all its benefits, estrogen also increases the risk of breast cancer an estimated 20 to 30 percent, and the risk of uterine endometrial cancer if women take it without another sex hormone, progesterone. The taint of breast cancer is the main reason why only about one-quarter of postmenopausal women take HRT. Ironically, compared with women who don't take HRT, those who do and go on to develop breast cancer are less likely to die from it. Scientists are not sure why, but they speculate that the hormone somehow makes breast tumors less aggressive.

If you're interested in taking HRT, weigh your individual risk of heart disease, breast cancer, osteoporosis, and Alzheimer's in consultation with your doctor.

FOR PAIN, TAKE NONSTEROIDAL ANTI-INFLAMMATORY DRUGS (NSAIDS)

Many studies show that NSAIDs reduce the risk of Alzheimer's disease (chapter 5) and slow its progression (chapter 10). Beneficial NSAIDs include ibuprofen (Motrin, Advil, Nuprin) and naproxen (Naprosyn). Aspirin is also an NSAID, and many researchers believe that it helps prevent Alzheimer's. But studies to date show that ibuprofen is more effective for Alzheimer's prevention. On the other hand, low-dose aspirin (one-half to one tablet a day) helps prevent heart attack and stroke, and one study shows that aspirin improves cognitive function in people with vascular dementia.

The main problem with NSAIDs is that with regular use, they often cause stomach distress and gastrointestinal bleeding, which can become serious. If you're interested in taking NSAIDs for Alzheimer's prevention, discuss the issue with your doctor.

CONSIDER TAKING GINKGO

There has been no research on the herbal medicine ginkgo specifically for Alzheimer's prevention, but studies to date suggest that it probably has preventive value:

- Studies show that ginkgo helps slow the progression of Alzheimer's (chapter 10).
- Dutch scientists recently reviewed forty studies of the effects of ginkgo on elderly people whose cognitive functions were impaired by poor blood flow through the brain (cerebral insufficiency). Their conclusion: The herb improves memory and concentration and reduces absentmindedness. In Europe, it is widely prescribed for people recovering from stroke.
- Ginkgo helps prevent cardiovascular disease, a risk factor for Alzheimer's.
- You don't have to be elderly to benefit from ginkgo. At the University of Leeds, British researchers tested the memories of eight women, average age thirty-two, and then gave them either a placebo or ginkgo (120 mg, 240 mg, or 600 mg). The placebo produced no memory improvement, but the ginkgo did, with increasing doses showing increasing benefits. The women's memory improved "very significantly" after taking the 600 mg dose.

The dose usually recommended is 120 mg a day of a ginkgo standardized extract. Standardized extracts are available at most health-food stores. The recommended dose rarely produces any side effects. But at very high doses, abdominal distress and restlessness have been reported.

CONSIDER TAKING CARNITINE

Carnitine is a nutrient composed of two amino acids, lysine and methionine. No studies have specifically investigated it for Alzhiemer's prevention, but there's reason to believe it might help:

- Studies by researchers at Columbia University, the University of Pittsburgh School of Medicine in Pennsylvania, and European scientists show that a dose of 2,000 to 3,000 mg a day slows the progression of Alzheimer's by preserving acetylcholine in the brain (chapter 10).
- Carnitine is an antioxidant. Antioxidants help prevent Alzheimer's.

Carnitine, technically acetyl-L-carnitine, is sold over the counter at health-food stores. Doses of 2 to 3 grams a day are considered nontoxic. At doses of 5 to 6 grams, abdominal distress is possible.

WATCH THE ALUMINUM (POSSIBLY)

A few studies suggest that Alzheimer's may be linked to exposure to aluminum, especially in drinking water (at a concentration greater than 100 micrograms/liter) or in soft drinks packaged in aluminum cans. Other studies show no connection between aluminum exposure and Alzheimer's. There is no scientific consensus on the role of aluminum, if any, in Alzheimer's risk, and the question remains extremely controversial (chapter 5).

If you're worried about the possibility that aluminum exposure may increase your risk of Alzheimer's, you might limit your consumption of soft drinks from aluminum cans. You might also have your water tested. For about $100, the National Testing Laboratory of Cleveland will conduct a seventy-four-item test of water quality and check for aluminum content. The lab sends you sampling test tubes, which you fill with your water and then send to the lab in a Styrofoam-lined box. After about a week, the lab sends you a report detailing what's in your water, and how much aluminum. For more information, call 1-800-458-3330.

Epilogue

Only a few years ago, researchers knew very little about Alzheimer's disease, and the public, even less informed, considered it terrifying and hopeless. There is still no way to halt the progression of Alzheimer's, let alone reverse and cure it. But recently, insight into the disease has exploded. Most of the information in this book is less than three years old, and a good deal is less than a year old. The old hopelessness has become outdated.

Alzheimer's is still a terrible disease, but researchers are cautiously optimistic that emerging insights into its biology, risk factors, and prevention will, in the not-too-distant future, allow physicians to significantly delay its development. Experts estimate that if the cognitive deterioration of Alzheimer's could be delayed for just five years, the nation's need for nursing home care would plummet 50 percent, saving billions of dollars a year and incalculable pain for affected individuals and their families. Researchers are also increasingly confident that within the next decade, combinations of currently available medications, new drugs in development, and the broad array of non-drug therapies and caregiver support will turn the disease into a reasonably manageable chronic condition, similar to diabetes or asthma.

People over eighty are at highest risk of Alzheimer's, and with that population increasing rapidly, the need to control the disease has never been more urgent. Researchers have risen to the challenge, discovering more about the disease in the last few years than they'd learned since Alois Alzheimer first described it in 1907. Unfortunately, Americans remain largely in the dark about this progress, unaware of how to reduce their risk and uninformed about treatment options.

It's time to move beyond the old reactions—horror and hopelessness. An Alzheimer's diagnosis still means a grim prognosis, but the disease has begun to yield its secrets. That is reason for hope.

Appendix I. Resources

Alzheimer's Association
919 North Michigan Ave., Suite 1000
Chicago, IL 60611-1676
(800) 272-3900, or (312) 335-8700
www.alz.org

The leading organization in the field. Supports families and caregivers of people with Alzheimer's. Chapters nationwide. Informative quarterly newsletter. To reach a twenty-four-hour hotline for referrals, information, problem solving, and counseling support, call (800) 621-0379, or in Illinois (800) 572-6037.

Alzheimer's Disease Education and Referral Center (ADEAR)
ADEAR Center
Box 8250
Silver Spring, MD 20907-8250
(800) 438-4380, or (301) 495-3311
www.cais.net/adear

Sponsored by the National Institute on Aging, ADEAR is a national clearinghouse for information on Alzheimer's. Offers information and publications on diagnosis, treatment, caregiving, long-term care, and research.

Alzheimer Society of Canada
20 Eglinton Ave. West, Suite 1200
Toronto, Ontario M4R 1K8
(416) 488-8772, or from Canada (800) 616-8816
www.alzheimer.ca

The leading Canadian Alzheimer's organization. Information about affiliates in every province.

American Association of Homes and Services for the Aging
901 E St., N.W., Suite 500
Washington, D.C. 20004-2037
(202) 783-2242
www.aahsa.org.

Provides information about—and lobbies for—the nation's nonprofit residential care facilities and nursing homes.

American Association of Retired Persons
601 E St., N.W.
Washington, D.C. 20049
(800) 424-3410

Information, services, and advocacy for the elderly. One noteworthy service is a discount pharmacy that takes telephone orders twenty-four hours a day. Call (800) 456-2226.

American Bar Assocation Commission on Legal Problems of the Elderly
740 15th St., N.W.
Washington, D.C. 20005
(202) 662-8690

Information and referral for everything from Medicare claims to conservatorships.

The American Health Care Association
1201 L St., N.W.
Washington, D.C. 20005
(202) 842-4444

Provides information about for-profit and nonprofit nursing homes.

American Society on Aging
833 Market St., Suite 511
San Francisco, CA 94103
(415) 974-9600
www.housecall.com/sponsors/asa/asa/

A national nonprofit organization whose mission is to promote the dignity and well-being of the elderly. It does not deal directly with Alzheimer's disease, but its conferences and publications emphasize issues relating to caregiving and home care.

Assisted Living Facilities Association of America
9411 Lee Hwy.
Plaza Suite J
Fairfax, VA 22031
(703) 691-8100

Provides information about what to look for in an assisted living facility.

Children of Aging Parents
1609 Woodbourne Rd.
Levittown, PA 19057-1511
(215) 945-6900

Provides information about all aspects of caring for the elderly. Publishes a bimonthly newsletter.

Eldercare Locator
1112 16th St., N.W., Suite 100
Washington, D.C. 20036
(800) 677-1116

This service of the National Association of Area Agencies on Aging provides information about and referrals to respite care and community care agencies around the country.

Family Caregiver Alliance
425 Bush St., Suite 500
San Francisco, CA 94108
(415) 434-3388, in CA (800) 445-8106
www.caregiver.org

A national nonprofit organization that helps caregivers dealing with adults suffering from memory loss due to Alzheimer's disease and other dementing conditions. It publishes many helpful resources.

National Association for Continence
P.O. Box 8310
Spartanburg, SC 29305
(800) BLADDER

Treatment advice and support for people dealing with incontinence.

National Association of Home Care
228 7th St., S.E.
Washington, D.C. 20003
(202) 547-7424
www.nahc.org

A trade association representing more than six thousand hospices, home care agencies, and home health aide organizations. Its members are primarily other organizations, but members include many individuals involved in hospice or home care. NAHC publishes more than fifty detailed guides, including:

- *How to Choose a Home Care Provider,* an informative booklet aimed at consumers and their families ($5).
- *National Home Care Directory,* which lists 18,500 home care providers ($50 for members, $135 for nonmembers).
- *How to Exchange Hospital Coverage for Hospice and Home Care,* a guide to negotiating with health insurers ($30/$60).

National Center for Home Equity Conversion
7373 147th St., Suite 115
Apple Valley, MN 55124
(800) 247-6553

Send a stamped, self-addressed envelope and $1.00 to receive a list of institutions that offer reverse mortgages in your area.

National Citizens Coalition for Nursing Home Reform
1424 16th St., N.W., Suite 202
Washington, D.C. 20002
(202) 332-2275

A coalition of elder-advocacy organizations working to improve nursing home care.

National Family Caregiver Association
9621 East Bexhill Dr.
Kensington, MD 20895-3104
(800) 896-3650

Provides information about caregiving and support for family caregivers.

National Institute on Adult Day Care
409 3rd St., S.W., 2nd Flr.
Washington, D.C. 20024
(202) 479-6682

This project of the National Council on Aging promotes adult daycare, develops standards for adult daycare centers, and provides information about adult daycare and training and technical assistance to adult daycare programs around the country.

National Institute of Neurological Disorders and Stroke
Building 31, Room 8A16
31 Center Dr., MSC-2540
Bethesda, MD 20892
(800) 352-9424

A branch of the National Institutes of Health. Sponsors research and publishes information about Alzheimer's disease, stroke, Parkinson's, and other neurological conditions.

National Stroke Association
96 Inverness Dr., East, Suite 1
Englewood, CO 80112
(800) STROKES

Information, services, and support for stroke survivors and their families.

Safe Return
Box A-3956
Chicago, IL 60690
(800) 572-1122 to report a lost Alzheimer's sufferer.

A joint program of the Alzheimer's Association and the National Center for Missing Persons. Caregivers fit the Alzheimer's sufferer with a bracelet containing the person's name and Safe Return's 800 number. If anyone calls to report having found the person, Safe Return calls the registered caregiver.

Veterans Affairs Medical Centers

Contact you local VA to learn about specific programs in your area for veterans suffering dementia.

Visiting Nurse Associations of America
3801 East Florida Ave., Suite 900
Denver, CO 80210
(800) 426-2547

Represents and makes referrals to five hundred visiting nurse organizations around the country.

VIDEOS

Lost in the Mind
58 minutes, color, VHS
$49.95
Don Lennox Productions
1627 Connecticut Ave., N.W., Suite 300
Washington, D.C. 20008
(202) 265-4800
www.washingtonvideo.com

An excellent video introduction to the biology and progression of Alzheimer's and the experience of caregiving. Inspired by the producer's mother, who suffered the disease.

Alzheimer's: A Practical Guide for Caregivers
32 minutes, color, VHS
Call for price
Medcom
P.O. Box 6003
Cypress, CA 90603
(800) 320-1444

Insightful vignettes illustrating what it feels like to have mild to moderate Alzheimer's, with many helpful suggestions for caregivers.

The ALZHEIMER List and Alzheimer Digest
www.biostat.wustl.edu/alzheimer/

The List is an e-mail discussion group for anyone interested in Alzheimer's disease. Subscriptions are free. If you subscribe, expect to receive lots of e-mail. If you can't handle it all, consider subscribing to the Digest, which sends you one message every other day containing postings from the previous two days.

Alzheimer Web
werple.mira.net.au/~dhs/ad.html

Information, links, and other resources for researchers studying Alzheimer's disease. There's a Q&A section that answers basic questions about Alzheimer's. But most of the information is aimed at scientists.

Alzheimer's Books and Videos
www.hicom.net/~lakesolitude/index.html

This is the Web site of Lake Solitude Media, which offers a large selection of books and videos about Alzheimer's disease. The videos are produced specifically to appeal to people with Alzheimer's and to offer video respite to caregivers. They focus on calming scenes from nature: Yellowstone National Park, tropical fish on a coral reef in the Bahamas, Saguaro National Monument, and the Blue Ridge Mountains. The site includes ordering information.

Alzheimer's Disease Cooperative Study (ADCS)
www-alz.ucsd.edu

Based at the University of California at San Diego, the ADCS helps coordinate clinical trials of promising new Alzheimer's treatments around the country. This site includes an on-line newsletter that reports on the progress of clinical trials, and a fairly extensive list of links to other Alzheimer's sites.

The Alzheimer's Research Forum
www.alzforum.org

The Alzheimer's Research Forum is a nonprofit organization that promotes collaboration among Alzheimer's researchers worldwide. All the material on this site is prepared by and for Alzheimer's researchers. Nonscientists may find it challenging. But for those who want to keep up with Alzheimer's research, it contains excellent information.

Caregiving Newsletter
www.caregiving.com

"Caring for an aging relative is hard. We know. We're here to help." Those are the reassuring words that greet visitors to this site, operated by the excellent *Caregiving Newsletter,* based in Park Ridge, Illinois.

Elder Books: The Alzheimer's Bookshelf
www.nbn.com/people/elder/alzheimer.html

Elder Books is a small press "dedicated to publishing practical, hands-on guidebooks for family and professional caregivers of persons with Alzheimer's disease." The site contains the table of contents and excerpts from all the books the press publishes, plus ordering information.

Homecare on the Internet
www.homecare.org

This site contains a database of ten thousand home care provider agencies around the United States with contact information, specialties, and types of insurance accepted. There are also dozens of links to home care–related resources on the Internet. And if you need supplies for caregiving, the site contains lists of companies that provide everything from mobility assistance devices to incontinence aids.

Institute for Brain Aging and Dementia
www.alz.uci.edu/dement.html

Contains a wealth of information on age-related cognitive decline from all causes, including Alzheimer's disease. The Institute for Brain Aging and Dementia is part of the University of California at Irvine.

Internet Gerontology References
vanbc.wimsey.com/~bgraham/gerontology.html

This site is a gateway to many Internet resources on the elderly. Its scope is wider than Alzheimer's disease, but it includes many links to Alzheimer's resources.

National Academy of Elder Law Attorneys (NAELA)
www.primenet.com/elderlaw

The NAELA is a nonprofit group based in Tucson, Arizona, that helps lawyers deal with older clients and the legal issues that relate to them. This site contains information about the NAELA, plus fact sheets that can be downloaded on the legal aspects of Alzheimer's: durable powers of attorney, long-term-care insurance, guardianship and conservatorship, Medicare, and Medicaid.

Safe-T-Net
www.safetnet.com

Provides information about insurance, including a great deal of useful information about long-term-care insurance and viatical settlements.

Viatical Association of America
www.cais.com/viatical

Viatical settlements allow people to sell their life insurance policies for a portion of the death benefit while still living to pay for long-term care. This site by the trade association of viatical companies contains a good introduction to the promise—and possible pitfalls—of viatical settlements.

Video Respite
www.europa.com/~adlink/Video_Respite/

Developed by researchers at the University of Utah, Video Respite produces calming videos for people with Alzheimer's that give respite time to caregivers. The major strength of these tapes is their cultural specificity that may resonate with certain Alzheimer's sufferers. There are tapes aimed at Jews, Christians, African-Americans, Canadians, and Hispanics. The site includes ordering information.

NATIONAL ALZHEIMER'S DISEASE CENTERS

The National Institute on Aging currently funds twenty-eight Alzheimer's Disease Centers at medical schools around the country. Activities vary from center to center, from the molecular biology of Alzheimer's to programs that support caregivers.

ALABAMA

Lindy E. Harrell, M.D., Ph.D., Professor
Department of Neurology
University of Alabama at Birmingham
1720 7th Ave. South
Sparks Center 454

Birmingham, AL 35294-0017
(205) 934-9775
fax: (205) 975-7365

CALIFORNIA

William J. Jagust, M.D., Director
Alzheimer's Disease Center
University of California at Davis
Alta Bates Medical Center
2001 Dwight Way
Berkeley, CA 94704
(510) 204-4530
fax: (510) 204-4524

Jeffrey L. Cummings, M.D., Professor
Department of Neurology and Psychiatry
University of California, at Los Angeles, School of Medicine
710 Westwood Plaza
Los Angeles, CA 90095-1769
(310) 206-5238
fax: (310) 206-5287

Leon Thal, M.D., Chairman
Department of Neuroscience (0624)
University of California, at San Diego, School of Medicine
9500 Gilman Dr.
La Jolla, CA 92093-0624
(619) 534-4606
fax: (619) 534-1437

Caleb E. Finch, Ph.D.
Division of Neurogerontology
Ethel Percy Andrus Gerontology Center
University of Southern California
University Park, MC-0191
3715 McClintock Ave.
Los Angeles, CA 90089-0191
(213) 740-1758
fax: (213) 740-0853

GEORGIA

Suzanne Mirra, M.D., Professor
Department of Pathology and Laboratory Medicine
Emory University School of Medicine
VA Medical Center (151)
1670 Clairmont Rd.
Decatur, GA 30033
(404) 728-7714
fax: (404) 728-7771

ILLINOIS

Denis A. Evans, M.D., Professor of Medicine
Rush Alzheimer's Disease Center
Rush-Presbyterian-St. Luke's Medical Center
1645 West Jackson, Suite 675
Chicago, IL 60612
(312) 942-3350
fax: (312) 942-2861

Robert E. Becker, M.D.
Center for Alzheimer's Disease and Related Disorders
Southern Illinois University School of Medicine
751 North Rutledge
P.O. Box 19230
Springfield, IL 62794-1412
(217) 785-4468
fax: (217) 524-2275

INDIANA

Bernardino Ghetti, M.D., Professor of Pathology, Psychiatry, and Medical
and Molecular Genetics
Indiana Alzheimer's Disease Center
Department of Pathology, MS-A142
Indiana University School of Medicine
635 Barnhill Dr.
Indianapolis, IN 46202-5120
(317) 274-1590
fax: (317) 274-4882

KANSAS

William C. Koller, M.D., Ph.D., Professor and Chairman
Department of Neurology
University of Kansas Medical Center
3901 Rainbow Blvd.
Kansas City, KS 66160-7117
(913) 588-6952
fax: (913) 588-6965

KENTUCKY

William Markesbery, M.D., Director
Sanders-Brown Research Center on Aging
University of Kentucky
101 Sanders-Brown Bldg.
800 South Lime
Lexington, KY 40536-0230
(606) 323-6040
fax: (606) 323-2866

MARYLAND

Donald L. Price, M.D., Professor of Pathology, Neurology, and
Neuroscience
Johns Hopkins University School of Medicine
558 Ross Research Bldg.
720 Rutland Ave.
Baltimore, MD 21205
(410) 955-5632
fax: (410) 955-9777

MASSACHUSETTS

John H. Growdon, M.D., Department of Neurology
Massachusetts Alzheimer's Disease Research Center
Massachusetts General Hospital
WAC 830
15 Parkman St.
Boston, MA 02114
(617) 726-1728
fax: (617) 726-4101

MICHIGAN

Sid Gilman, M.D., Professor and Chair
Department of Neurology
Michigan Alzheimer's Disease Research Center
University of Michigan
1914 Taubman Center
Ann Arbor, MI 48109-0316
(313) 936-9070
fax: (313) 936-8763

MINNESOTA

Ronald Petersen, M.D., Ph.D., Associate Professor
Department of Neurology
Mayo Clinic
200 First St. S.W.
Rochester, MN 55905
(507) 284-2203
fax: (507) 284-2203

MISSOURI

Leonard Berg, M.D.
Alzheimer's Disease Research Center
Washington University Medical Center
The Health Key Bldg.
4488 Forest Park Blvd.
St. Louis, MO 63108-2293
(314) 286-2881
fax: (314) 286-2763

NEW YORK

Michael Shelanski, M.D., Ph.D., Director
Alzheimer's Disease Research Center
Department of Pathology
Columbia University
630 West 168th St.
New York, NY 10032
(212) 305-3300
fax: (212) 305-5498

Kenneth Davis, M.D., Professor and Chair
Department of Psychiatry
Mount Sinai School of Medicine
Mount Sinai Medical Center
1 Gustave L. Levy Place, Box #1230
New York, NY 10029-6574
(212) 241-6623
fax: (212) 996-0987

Steven Ferris, Ph.D.
Aging and Dementia Research Center
Department of Psychiatry (THN314)
New York University Medical Center
550 First Ave.
New York, NY 10016
(212) 263-5703
fax: (212) 263-6991

Paul Coleman, Ph.D., Professor
Department of Neurobiology and Anatomy, Box 603
University of Rochester Medical Center
601 Elmwood Ave.
Rochester, NY 14642
(716) 275-2581
fax: (716) 273-1132

NORTH CAROLINA

Allen Roses, M.D., Director and Principal Investigator
Joseph & Kathleen Bryan Alzheimer's Disease Research Center
2200 Main St., Suite A-230
Durham, NC 27705
(919) 286-3406
fax: (919) 286-3228

OHIO

Peter Whitehouse, M.D., Ph.D., Director
Alzheimer's Disease Center
University Hospitals of Cleveland
11100 Euclid Ave.

Cleveland, OH 44106
(216) 844-7360
fax: (216) 844-7239

OREGON

Earl Zimmerman, M.D., Chair
Department of Neurology (L-226)
Oregon Health Sciences University
3181 S.W. Sam Jackson Park Road
Portland, OR 97201-3098
(503) 494-7321
fax: (503) 494-7242

PENNSYLVANIA

John Trojanowski, M.D., Ph.D., Professor
Department of Pathology and Laboratory Medicine
University of Pennsylvania School of Medicine
Room A-009, Basement, Maloney/HUP
36th and Spruce Sts.
Philadelphia, PA 19104-4283
(215) 662-6921
fax: (215) 349-5909

Steven DeKosky, M.D., Director
Alzheimer's Disease Research Center
University of Pittsburgh Medical Center
Montefiore University Hospital, 4 West
200 Lothrop St.
Pittsburgh, PA 15213
(412) 624-6889
fax: (412) 624-7814

TEXAS

Stanley Appel, M.D., Director
Alzheimer's Disease Research Center
Department of Neurology
Baylor College of Medicine
6501 Fanning, NB302

Houston, TX 77030-3498
(713) 798-6660
fax: (713) 798-7434

Roger Rosenberg, M.D., Director
Alzheimer's Disease Research Center,
Zale Distinguished Chair, and Professor of Neurology and Physiology
University of Texas Southwest Medical Center at Dallas
5323 Harry Hines Blvd.
Dallas, TX 75235-9036
(214) 648-3239
fax: (214) 648-6824

WASHINGTON

George Martin, M.D., Professor
Alzheimer's Disease Research Center
Department of Pathology
Box 357470, HSB K-543
University of Washington
1959 N.E. Pacific Ave.
Seattle, WA 98195-7470
(206) 543-5088
fax: (206) 685-8356

Appendix II. Alzheimers.com

If you have access to the World Wide Web and would like to stay informed about the latest developments in Alzheimer's research, the largest, most timely, and comprehensive English-language Alzheimer's resource is Alzheimers.com (at www.alzheimers.com). Published by Planet Rx, the online pharmacy of South San Francisco (www.planetrx.com). Alzheimers.com issues news stories weekly on every aspect of Alzheimer's disease and caregiving.

References and Bibliography

CHAPTER 2. WORRIED ABOUT SOMEONE?

Alzheimer's Association. "Early Warning Signs of Alzheimer's."

Johansson, K., et al. "Alzheimer's Disease and Apolipoprotein E-4 Allele in Older Drivers Who Died in Automobile Accidents." *Lancet* 349 (9095) (1997):1143.

CHAPTER 3. DR. ALZHEIMER'S STRANGE DISCOVERY

Anderson, R. N., et al. "Report of Final Mortality Statistics, 1995." *Monthly Vital Statistics Report* 45 (1997): suppl. 2.

Dickson, D. W. "Discovery of New Lesions in Neurodegenerative Diseases with Monoclonal Antibody Techniques: Is There a Non-Amyloid Precursor of Senile Plaques?" *American Journal of Pathology* 151 (1997): 7.

Ernst, R. L., et al. "Cognitive Funtion and the Costs of Alzheimer's Disease." *Archives of Neurology* 54 (1997): 687.

Evans, D. A., et al. "Prevalence of Alzheimer's Disease in a Community Population of Older Persons: Higher Than Previously Reported." *Journal of the American Medical Association* 262 (1989): 2551.

Evans, D. A., et al. "Estimated Prevalence of Alzheimer's Disease in the U.S." *Millbank Quarterly* 68 (1990): 267.

Fisher, L. "Vaccine in Mice Fights Brain Changes Tied to Alzheimer's." *The New York Times* (July 8, 1999).

General Accounting Office. "Alzheimer's Disease: Estimates of Prevalence in the United States." GAO/HEHS-98-16 (Jan. 1998).

Geula, C., et al. "Aging Renders the Brain Vulnerable to Amyloid Beta Protein Neurotoxicity." *Nature Medicine* 4 (1998): 827.

Goate, A. M. "Molecular Genetics of Alzheimer's Disease." *Geriatrics* (Sept. 1997): S9–S12.

Hendrie, H. C. "Epidemiology of Alzheimer's Disease." *Geriatrics* (Sept. 1997): S4–S8.

Hendrie, H. C. "Epidemiology of Dementia and Alzheimer's Disease." *American Journal of Geriatric Psychiatry* 6 (1998): S3.

Holzman, D. "Platelet Activity Observed in Alzheimer's Patients." *Medical Tribune* (June 18, 1998).

Lendon, C. L., et al. "Exploring the Etiology of Alzheimer's Disease Using Molecular Genetics." *Journal of the American Medical Association* 277 (1997): 825.

Maher, L. "Unlocking the Mysteries of Alzheimer's Disease." *Patient Care* (Nov. 15, 1996): 44–61.

Milius, S. "Dogs and Cats in Their Dotage," *Science News,* Oct. 17, 1998.

Morrison-Bogorad, M., et al. "Alzheimer's Disease Research Comes of Age." *Journal of the American Medical Association* 277 (1997): 837.

Motter, R., et al. "Reduction of Beta-Amyloid-42 Peptide in Cerebrospinal Fluid of Patients with Alzheimer's Disease." *Annals of Neurology* 38 (1995): 643.

Reisberg, B. "Function Assessment of Aging." *Psychopharmacology Bulletin* 24 (1988): 653.

Reisberg, B., et al. "The Global Deterioration Scale for Assessment of Primary Degenerative Dementia." *American Journal of Psychiatry* 139 (1982): 1136.

Schmidt, M. L., et al. "Monoclonal Antibodies to a 100-kd Protein Reveal Abundant A-Beta-Negative Plaques Throughout Gray Matter of Alzheimer's Disease Brains." *American Journal of Pathology* 151 (1997): 69.

Small, G., et al. "Diagnosis and Treatment of Alzheimer's Disease and Related Disorders: Consensus Statement of the American Association for Geriatric Psychology, the Alzheimer's Association, and the American Geriatrics Society." *Journal of the American Medical Association* 278 (1997): 1363.

Tavis, J. "A Vaccine for Alzheimer's Disease?" *Science News* (July 10, 1999).

Weldon, D. T., et al. "New Insights into the Neuropathology and Cell Biology of Alzheimer's Disease." *Geriatrics* (Sept. 1997): S13–S16.

CHAPTER 5. WHO'S AT RISK?

Baker, F. M. "Issues in Assessing Dementia in African-American Elders," in *Ethnicity and the Dementias,* Gwen Yeo, Ph.D., and Dolores Gallagher-Thompson, Ph.D., eds., Bristol, PA: Taylor and Francis, 1996.

Belles, M., et al. "Silicon Reduces Aluminum Accumulation in Rats: Relevance to the Aluminum Hypothesis of Alzheimer Disease." *Alzheimer's Disease and Associated Disorders* 12 (1998): 83.

Bilkei-Gorzo, A. "Neurotoxic Effect of Enteral Aluminum." *Food and Chemical Toxicology* 31 (1993): 357.

Blacker, D., et al. "APOE-4 and Age at Onset of Alzheimer's Disease: The NIMH Genetics Initiative." *Neurology* 48 (1997): 139.

Bush, A. I., et al. "Rapid Induction of Alzheimer's Beta-Amyloid Formation by Zinc." *Science* 265 (1994): 1464.

Domingo, J. L., et al. "Effect of Various Dietary Constituents on Gastrointestinal Absorption of Aluminum from Drinking Water and Diet." *Research on Community Chemistry, Pathology, and Pharmacology* 79 (1993): 377.

Duara, R. "Unlocking the Mysteries of Alzheimer's Disease." *Patient Care* (Nov. 15, 1996): 44–61.

Duggan, J. M., et al. "Aluminum Beverage Cans as a Dietary Source of Aluminum." *Medical Journal of Australia* 156 (1992): 604.

Evans, D. A., et al. "Apolipoprotein E e-4 and Incidence of Alzheimer's Disease in a Community of Older Persons." *Journal of the American Medical Association* 277 (1997): 822.

Farrer, L., et al. "Effects of Age, Sex, and Ethnicity on the Association Between Apolipoprotein E Genotype and Alzheimer's Disease." *Journal of the American Medical Association* 278 (1997): 1349.

Forbes, W. F., and N. Agwani. "A Suggested Mechanism for Aluminum Biotoxicity." *Journal of Theoretical Biology* 171 (1994): 207.

Forster, D. P., et al. "Risk Factors in Clinically Diagnosed Presenile Dementia of the Alzheimer Type: A Case-Control Study in Northern England." *Journal of Epidemiology and Community Health* 49 (1995): 253.

Grant, W. "Dietary Links to Alzheimer's Disease." *Alzheimer's Disease Review* 2 (1997): 42.

Gray, G. E. "Nutrition and Dementia." *Journal of the American Dietetic Association* 89 (1989): 1795.

Hesdorffer, D. C., et al. "Dementia and Adult-Onset Unprovoked Seizures." *Neurology* 46 (1996): 727.

Hoffman, A., et al. "Atherosclerosis, Apolipoprotein E, and Prevalance of Dementia and Alzheimer's Disease in the Rotterdam Study." *Lancet* 349 (1997): 151.

Jacqmin, H., et al. "Components of Drinking Water and Risk of Cognitive Impairment in the Elderly." *American Journal of Epidemiology* 139 (1994): 48.

Jordan, B. D., et al. "Apolipoprotein E e4 Associated with Chronic Traumatic Brain Injury in Boxing." *Journal of the American Medical Association* 278 (1997): 136.

Kalmijn, S., et al. "Dietary Fat Intake and the Risk of Incident Dementia in the Rotterdam Study." *Annals of Neurology* 42 (1997): 776.

Kawas, C., et al. "A Prospective Study of Estrogen Replacement Therapy and the Risk of Developing Alzheimer's Disease: The Baltimore Longitudinal Study of Aging." *Neurology* 48 (1997): 1517.

Kawas, C., et al. "Treating Alzheimer's Disease: Today and Tomorrow." *Patient Care* (Nov. 15, 1996): 62–83.

Launer, L. J., et al. "Association Between Midlife Blood Pressure and Late-Life Cognitive Function." *Journal of the American Medical Association* 274 (1995): 1846.

Lautenschlager, N. T., et al. "Risk of Dementia Among Relatives of Alzheimer's Disease Patients in the MIRAGE Study." *Neurology* 46 (1996): 641.

Law, A., and G. Grossberg. "Several Questions About Zinc: The Role of Zinc in Alzheimer's Disease," in *Research and Practice in Alzheimer's Disease, 1998,* B. Vellas, et al., eds., New York: Springer Publishing, 1998.

Leibson C. L., et al. "Risk of Dementia Among Persons with Diabetes Mellitus: A Population-Based Cohort Study." *American Journal of Epidemiology* 145 (1997): 301.

Lopera, F., et al. "Clinical Features of Early-Onset Alzheimer's Disease in a Large Kindred with an E280A Presenilin-1 Mutation." *Journal of the American Medical Association* 277 (1997): 793.

Martyn, C. N. "Geographical Relation Between Alzheimer's Disease and Aluminum in Drinking Water." *Lancet* 8629 (1989): 59.

Martyn, C. N., et al. "Aluminum Concentrations in Drinking Water and Risk of Alzheimer's Disease." *Epidemiology* 8 (1997): 281.

McLachlan, D. R., et al. "Risk for Neuropathologically Confirmed Alzheimer's Disease and Residual Aluminum in Municipal Drinking Water Employing Weighted Residential Histories." *Neurology* 46 (1996): 401.

Medical Tribune (June 18, 1988). "HRT Shown to Reduce Risk of Alzheimer's Disease."

Mortimer, J. A. "Brain Reserve and the Clinical Expression of Alzheimer's Disease." *Geriatrics* 52 (1997): S50.

Paganini-Hill, A., et al. "Estrogen Deficiency and Risk of Alzheimer's Disease." *American Journal of Epidemiology* 140 (1994): 256.

Pailler, F. M. "Aluminum in Alzheimer's Disease." *Presse Medicale* 24 (1995): 489.

Pericak-Vance, M. A., et al. "Complete Genomic Screen in Late-Onset Familial Alzheimer's Disease." *Journal of the American Medical Association* 278 (1997):1237.

Post, S. G., et al. "The Clinical Introduction of Genetic Testing for Alzheimer's Disease: An Ethical Perspective." *Journal of the American Medical Association* 277 (1997): 832.

Potocnik, F. C. V., et al. "Zinc and Platelet Membrane Microsensitivity in Alzheimer's Disease." *South African Medical Journal* 87 (1997): 1116.

Pratico, D., et al. "Increased F2-Isoprostanes in Alzheimer's Disease: Evidence for Enhanced Lipid Peroxidation in Vivo." *FASEB Journal* (Federation of the American Societies of Experimental Biology) 12 (1998): 1777.

Raiha, I., et al. "Alzheimer's Disease in Finnish Twins." *Lancet* 347 (1996): 573.

Rogaeva, E., et al. "Evidence for an Alzheimer's Disease Susceptibility Locus on Chromosome 12 and for Further Locus Heterogeneity." *Journal of the American Medical Association* 280 (1998): 614.

Rosenberg, R. N. "Genetic Factors for the Development of Alzheimer's Disease in the Cherokee Indian." *Archives of Neurology* 53 (1996): 997.

Roses, A. D. "Alzheimer's Disease: The Genetics of Risk." *Hospital Practice* (July 15, 1997): 51–68.

Rozzini, R., et al. "Protective Effect of Chronic NSAID Use on Cognitive Decline in Older Persons." *Journal of the American Geriatric Society* 44 (1996): 1025.

Schofield, P. W., et al. "An Association Between Head Circumference and Alzheimer's Disease in a Population-Based Study of Aging and Dementia." *Neurology* 49 (1997): 30.

Skoog, I., et al. "15-Year Longitudinal Study of Blood Pressure and Dementia." *Lancet* 347 (1996): 1141.

Small, G., et al. "Diagnosis and Treatment of Alzheimer's Disease and Related Disorders: Consensus Statement of the American Association for Geriatric Psychology, the Alzheimer's Association, and the American Geriatrics Society." *Journal of the American Medical Association* 278 (1997): 1363.

Small, G., et al. "Predictors of Cognitive Change in Middle-Aged and Older Adults with Memory Loss." *American Journal of Psychiatry* 152 (1995): 1757.

Snowdon, D. A., et al. "Linguistic Ability in Early Life and Cognitive Function and Alzheimer's Disease in Late Life: Findings from the Nun Study." *Journal of the American Medical Association* 275 (1996): 528.

Somova, L. I., et al. "Chronic Aluminum Intoxication in Rats: Dose-Dependent Morphological Changes." *Methods and Findings in Experimental Clinical Pharmacology* 19 (1997): 599.

Stephenson, J. "More Evidence Links NSAIDs, Estrogen with Reduced Alzheimer's Risk." *Journal of the American Medical Association* 275 (1996): 1389.

Stephenson, J. "Researchers Find Evidence of a New Gene for Late-Onset Alzheimer's Disease." *Journal of the American Medical Association* 277 (1997): 775.

Stewart, W. F., et al. "Risk of Alzheimer's Disease and Duration of NSAID Use." *Neurology* 48 (1997): 626.

Tang, M. X., et al. "The APOE-4 Allele and Risk of Alzheimer's Disease Among African Americans, Whites, and Hispanics." *Journal of the American Medical Association* 279 (1998): 751.

Tang, M. X., et al. "Effect of Estrogen During Menopause on Risk and Age at Onset of Alzheimer's Disease." *Lancet* 348 (1996): 429.

Taussig, I. M., and M. Ponton. "Issues in Neuropsychological Assessment for Hispanic Older Adults: Cultural and Linguistic Factors," in *Ethnicity and the*

Dementias, Gwen Yeo, Ph.D., and Dolores Gallagher-Thompson, Ph.D., eds., Bristol, PA: Taylor and Francis, 1996.

Teng, E. L. "Cross-Cultural Testing and the Cognitive Screening Abilities Instrument," in *Ethnicity and the Dementias,* Gwen Yeo, Ph.D., and Dolores Gallagher-Thompson, Ph.D., eds., Bristol, PA: Taylor and Francis, 1996.

Van Rhijn, A. G., et al. "Dietary Supplementation with Zinc Sulphate, Sodium Selenite, and Fatty Acids in Early Dementia of Alzheimer's Type." *Journal of Nutritional Medicine* 1 (1990): 259.

White, L., et al. "Prevalence of Dementia in Older Japanese-American Men in Hawaii." *Journal of the American Medical Association* 276 (1996): 955.

Wu, W., et al. "Genetic Studies on Chromosome 12 in Late-Onset Alzheimer's Disease." *Journal of the American Medical Association* 280 (1998): 619.

Xu, H., et al. "Estrogen Reduced Neuronal Generation of Alzheimer Beta-Amyloid Peptides." *Nature Medicine* 4 (1998): 44.

Yaffe, K., et al. "Estrogen Therapy in Postmenopausal Women: Effects on Cognitive Function and Dementia." *Journal of the American Medical Association* 279 (1998): 688.

CHAPTER 6. THE DIAGNOSTIC DILEMMA

American Psychiatric Association. *The Diagnostic and Statistical Manual of Mental Disorders, 4th edition.* Washington, D.C., 1994.

Chong, J. K., et al. "Automated Microparticle Enzyme Immunoassay for Neural Thread Protein in Cerebrospinal Fluid from Alzheimer's Disease Patients." *Journal of Clinical Laboratory Analysis* 6 (1992): 379.

Coon, D., et al. "The Psychological Impact of Genetic Testing for Alzheimer's Disease." *Genetic Testing* 3 (199): 121.

De la Monte, S., et al. "Increased Levels of Neuronal Thread Protein in Cerbrospinal Fluid of Patients with Alzheimer's Disease." *Annals of Neurology* 32 (1992): 733.

De la Monte, S., et al. "Neuronal Thread Protein Over-Expression in Brains with Alzheimer's Disease Lesions." *Journal of the Neurological Sciences* 113 (1992): 152.

De la Monte, S., et al. "Profiles of Neuronal Thread Protein Expression in Alzheimer's Disease." *Journal of Neuropathology and Experimental Neurology* 55 (1996): 1038.

De la Monte, S., et al. "Characterization of the AD7C-NTP c DNA Expression in Alzheimer's Disease and Measurement of a 41-kD Protein in Cerebrospinal Fluid." *Journal of Clinical Investigation* 100 (1997): 3093.

Finkel, S. I., et al. "Behavioral and Psychological Symptoms of Dementia: A Consensus Statement on Current Knowledge and Implications for Research and Treatment." *The American Journal of Geriatric Psychiatry* 6 (1998): 97.

FitzSimon, J. S., et al. "Response of the Pupil to Tropicamide Is Not a Reliable Test for Alzheimer's Dementia." *Archives of Neurology* 54 (1997): 155.

Gambert, S. R. "Is It Alzheimer's Disease?" *Postgraduate Medicine* (June 1997): 42.

Graff-Radford, N. R., et al. "Tropicamide Eyedrops Cannot Be Used for Reliable Diagnosis of Alzheimer's Disease." *Mayo Clinic Proceedings* 72 (1997): 495.

Growdon, J. H. "Pupil Dilation to Tropicamide Is Not Specific for Alzheimer's Disease." *Archives of Neurology* 54 (1997): 841.

Ham, R. J. "Dementia: Diagnosis and Management in the Elderly." *Consultant* (April 1997): 1021.

Holyroyd, S., et al. "Attitudes of Older Adults on Being Told the Diagnosis of Alzheimer's Disease." *Journal of the American Geriatric Society* 44 (1996): 400.

Holzman, D. "Value of Eyedrop Test for Alzheimer's Disputed." *Medical Tribune* (May 21, 1998).

Kinoshita, J. "Progress in Predicting Alzheimer's Disease." *BrainWork* (Nov./Dec. 1997).

Klata, L. A., et al. "Incorrect Diagnosis of Alzheimer's Disease." *Archives of Neurology* 53 (1996): 35.

McCarten, J. R. "Recognizing Dementia in the Clinic: Whom to Suspect, Whom to Test." *Geriatrics* 52 (1997): S17.

McKhann, G., et al. "Clinical Diagnosis of Alzheimer's Disease: Report of the NINCDS/AA Work Group, Dept. of HHS Task Force on Alzheimer's Disease." *Neurology* 34 (1984): 939.

McKinney, M. "Easy Screen Helps Detect Alzheimer's." *Medical Tribune* (April 16, 1998).

Morrow, D. "Stumble on the Road to Market: Haste Makes Problems for Creator of Alzheimer's Test." *New York Times* (March 5, 1998).

National Instititute on Aging/Alzheimer's Association Working Group. "Apolipoprotein E Genotyping in Alzheimer's Disease." *Lancet* 347 (1996): 1091.

Pratico, D., et al. "Increased F2-Isoprostanes in Alzheimer's Disease: Evidence for Enhanced Lipid Peroxidation in Vivo," *FASEB Journal* [Federation of the American Societies of Experimental Biology] (1998) 12: 1777.

Robinson, B. E. "Guidelines for Initial Evaluation of Memory Loss." *Geriatrics* (Dec. 1997): 30.

Roses, A. D. "Alzheimer's Disease: The Genetics of Risk." *Hospital Practice* (July 15, 1997): 51.

Russell, T. B. "Dementia in the Elderly: Is It Alzheimer's?" *Patient Care* (Nov. 15, 1996): 18.

Sano, M., et al. "A Standardized Technique for Establishing Onset and Duration of Symptoms of Alzheimer's Disease." *Archives of Neurology* 52 (1995): 961.

Scinto, L. F. M., et al. "A Potential Noninvasive Neurobiological Test for Alzheimer's Disease." *Science* 266 (1994): 1051.

Small, G. W., et al. "Diagnosis and Treatment of Alzheimer's Disease and Related Disorders." *Journal of the American Medical Association* 278 (1997): 1363.

Solomon, P. R., et al. "A Seven-Minute Screening Battery Highly Sensitive to Alzheimer's Disease." *Archives of Neurology* 55 (1998): 349.

Stephenson, J. "Alzheimer's Disease Experts Advise a 'Wait for the Data' Response to New Diagnostic Test." *Journal of the American Medical Association* 277 (1997): 870.

Teng, E. L., et al. "The Cognitive Abilities Screening Instrument (CASI): A Practical Test for Cross-Cultural Epidemiological Studies of Dementia." *International Psychogeriatrics* 6 (1994): 45.

Tierny, M. C., et al. "Prediction of Probable Alzheimer's Disease in Memory-Impaired Patients: A Prospective Longitudinal Study." *Neurology* 46 (1996): 661.

University HealthSystem Consortium and the U.S. Dept. of Veterans Affairs. "Dementia Identification and Assessment: Guidelines for Primary Care Practitioners." (March 1997).

Yong-Yao, X., et al. "Characterization of Thread Proteins Expressed in Neuroectodermal Tumors." *Cancer Research* 53 (1993): 3823.

CHAPTER 9. THE OTHER DEMENTIAS

American Heart Association. "Memory-Robbing Disorder Detected in One of Three Stroke Survivors." *Stroke* press release (Jan. 8, 1998).

Blakeslee, S. "Kentucky Doctors Warn Against a Regional Dish: Squirrels' Brains." *New York Times* (Aug. 29, 1997).

Brown, P. "Risk of Bovine Spongiform Encephalopathy ('Mad Cow Disease') to Human Health." *Journal of the American Medical Association* 278 (1997): 1008.

Dawson, E. B., et al. "Effect of Ascorbic Acid Supplementation on Blood Lead Levels." *Journal of the American College of Nutrition* (1997) 16:480/Abstract 42.

Dealberto, M. J., et al. "Breathing Disorders During Sleep and Cognitive Performance in an Older Community Sample: The EVA Study." *Journal of the American Geriatric Society* 44 (1996): 1287.

Espinel, C. H. "De Kooning's Late Colors and Forms: Dementia, Creativity, and the Healing Power of Art." *Lancet* 347 (1996): 1096.

Expert Roundtable. "Late-Life Depression: How to Make a Difficult Diagnosis." *Geriatrics* (March 1997): 37–50.

Gray, G. E. "Nutrition and Dementia." *Journal of the American Dietetic Association* 89 (1989): 1795.

Grubb, N. R., et al. "Chronic Memory Impairment After Cardiac Arrest Outside Hospital." *BMJ (British Medical Journal)* 313 (July 20, 1996): 143.

McKhann, G. M. "Heart Bypass Surgery: Effects of Memory and Other Neurological Implications." *BrainWork* (July-Aug. 1997).

Meyer, J. S., et al. "Randomized Clinical Trial of Daily Aspirin Therapy in Multi-Infarct Dementia." *Journal of the American Geriatric Society* 37 (1989): 549.

Moller, J. T., et al. "Long-Term Postoperative Cognitive Dysfunction in the Elderly ISPOCD1 Study: International Study of Post-Operative Cognitive Dysfunction." *Lancet* 351(9106) (1998): 857.

National Commission on Sleep Disorders Research. "Wake Up America: A National Sleep Alert" (Jan. 1993).

National Institute of Health. Depression Awareness, Recognition, and Treatment (D/ART) Program.

New York Times (Dec. 14, 1997). "Ban on Cattle and Sheep Is Extended to All Europe."

Ross, G. W., et al. "Frequency and Characteristics of Silent Dementia Among Elderly Japanese-American Men: The Honolulu–Asia Aging Study." *Journal of the American Medical Association* 277 (1997): 800.

Small, G. "Differential Diagnosis and Early Detection of Dementia." *American Journal of Geriatric Psychiatry* 6 (suppl. 1) (1998): S26.

Taragano, F. E., et al. "A Double-Blind, Randomized, Fixed-Dose Trial of Fluoxetine vs. Amytriptyline in the Treatment of Major Depression Complicating Alzheimer's Disease." *Psychosomatics* 38 (1997): 246.

Taylor, J. L., et al. "Assessment and Management of 'Sundowning' Phenomena." *Seminars in Clinical Neuropsychiatry* 2 (1997): 113.

Trachtenberg, D. E. "Getting the Lead Out." *Postgraduate Medicine* 99 (March 1996): 201.

Zisook, S. "Depression in Late Life." *Postgraduate Medicine* (Oct. 1996): 143–72.

CHAPTER 10. THE NEW ALZHEIMER'S TREATMENTS

Albert, S. M., et al. "Participation in Clinical Trials and Long-Term Outcomes in Alzheimer's Disease." *Neurology* 49 (1997): 38.

Aldridge, D. "Music Therapy and the Treatment of Alzheimer's Disease." *Journal of Clinical Geropsychology* 4 (1998): 17.

Alzheimer's Association. "From Test Tube to Treatment: The Rigorous Road of Drug Testing." *Advances in Alzheimer's Research* (Fall 1996).

American Family Physician (Oct. 1994). "Support Groups May Help Patients with Early Alzheimer's."

American Psychiatric Association. *Practice Guideline for the Treatment of Patients with Alzheimer's Disease and Other Dementias of Late Life.* APA, Washington, D.C., 1997.

Bauer, U. "Ginkgo Biloba Extract in the Treatment of Arteriopathy of the Lower Limbs: A 65-Week Study," in *Rokan Ginkgo Biloba: Recent Results in Pharmacology and Clinic.* Berlin/New York: Springer-Verlag, 1988.

Beck, C. "Psychosocial and Behavioral Interventions for Alzheimer's Disease Patients and Their Families." *American Journal of Geriatric Psychiatry* 6 (1998): S41.

Beck, C. "Improving Dressing Behavior in Cognitively Impaired Nursing Home Residents." *Nursing Research* 46 (1997): 126.

Becker, R. E., et al. "Effects of Metrifonate on Cognitive Decline in Alzheimer Disease: A Double-Blind, Placebo-Controlled, Six-Month Study." *Alzheimer Disease and Associated Disorders* 12 (1998): 54.

Beyersdorfer, P., and D. Birkenhauer. "The Therapeutic Use of Pets on an Alzheimer's Unit." *Alternative Medicine Journal* (March 1994): 16.

Branch, D. R. "Slow-Release Physostigmine Improves Cognition in Alzheimer's." *Family Practice News* (Feb. 1, 1997).

Brown, D., et al. *Clinical Applications of Natural Medicine: Dementia and Age-Related Cognitive Decline.* Seattle: Natural Product Research Consultants, 1997.

Burgio, L. "Interventions for the Behavioral Complications of Alzheimer's Disease: Behavioral Approaches." *International Psychogeriatrics* 8 (suppl. 1) (1996): 45.

Burgio, L., et al. "The Effects of Changing Prompted Voiding Schedules in the Treatment of Incontinence in Nursing Home Residents." *Journal of the American Geriatrics Society* 42 (1994): 315.

Crook, T., et al. "Effects of Phosphatidylserine in Alzheimer's Disease." *Psychopharmacology Bulletin* 28 (1992): 61.

Cummings, J. L. "Metrifonate: Overview of Safety and Efficacy." *Pharmacotherapy* 18 (1998): 43.

Cummings, J. L., et al. "Metrifonate Treatment of the Cognitive Deficits of Alzheimer's Disease: Metrifonate Study Group." *Neurology* 50 (1998): 1214.

Cutler, N. R., et al. "Safety and Tolerability of Metrifonate in Patients with Alzheimer's Disease: Results of a Maximum Tolerated Dose Study." *Life Sciences* 62 (1998): 1433.

DeFeudis, F. V. *Ginkgo Biloba Extract: Pharmacological Activities and Clinical Applications.* Paris/New York: Elsevier, 1991.

Dubreuil, C. "Therapeutic Trial of Acute Cochlear Deafness: Comparative Study with Ginkgo Biloba Extract and Nicergoline," in *Rokan Ginkgo Biloba: Recent Results in Pharmacology and Clinic.* Berlin/New York: Springer-Verlag, 1988.

Ernst, R. L., et al. "Cognitive Function and the Costs of Alzheimer's Disease." *Archives of Neurology* 54 (1997): 687.

Ferris, S. H., and M. S. Mittelman. "Behavioral Treatment of Alzheimer's Disease." *International Psychogeriatrics* 8 (suppl. 1) (1996): 87.

Flanagan, N. "The Clinical Use of Aromatherapy in Alzheimer's Patients." *Alternative and Complementary Therapies* (Nov.–Dec. 1995): 377–80.

Funfgeld, E. W., and D. Stalleicken. "The Clinical Effect of Ginkgo Biloba Extract in the Case of Cerebral Insufficiency Documented by Dynamic-Brain-Mapping: A Computerized EEG Evaluation," in *Rokan Ginkgo Biloba: Recent Results in Pharmacology and Clinic.* Berlin/New York: Springer-Verlag, 1988.

Haguenauer, J. P., et al. "Treatment of Disturbed Equilibrium with Ginkgo Biloba Extract: A Multicenter Double-Blind Study vs. Placebo," in *Rokan Ginkgo Biloba: Recent Results in Pharmacology and Clinic.* Berlin/New York: Springer-Verlag, 1988.

Hindmarch, I. "Activity of Ginkgo Biloba Extract on Short-Term Memory," in *Rokan Ginkgo Biloba: Recent Results in Pharmacology and Clinic.* Berlin/New York: Springer-Verlag, 1988.

Hofferberth, B. "The Efficacy of EGb 761 in Patients with Senile Dementia of the Alzheimer Type: A Double-Blind, Placebo-Controlled Study." *Human Psychopharmacology* 9 (1994): 215.

Itil, T. M., et al. "The Pharmacological Effects of Ginkgo Biloba on the Brain in Comparison to Tacrine." Presented at the New Clinical Drug Evaluation Unit meeting of the National Institute of Mental Health, May 1996.

Kanowski, S., et al. "Proof of Efficacy of Ginkgo Biloba Special Extract EGb 761 in Outpatients Suffering from Mild to Moderate Degenerative Dementia of the Alzheimer Type or Multi-Infarct Dementia." *Pharmacopsychiatry* 29 (1996): 47.

Kawas, C., et al. "Treating Alzheimer's Disease: Today and Tomorrow." *Patient Care* (Nov. 15, 1996): 62–83.

Kleijnen, J., and P. Knipschild. "Ginkgo Biloba for Cerebral Insufficiency." *British Journal of Clinical Pharmacology* 34 (1992): 352.

Knapp, M. J., et al. "A 30-Week Randomized Controlled Trial of High-Dose Tacrine in Patients with Alzheimer's Disease." *Journal of the American Medical Association* 271 (1994): 985.

Knasko, S., and A. Gilbert. "Emotional State, Physical Well-Being, and Performance in the Presence of Feigned Ambient Odor." *Journal of Applied Social Psychology* 20 (1990): 1345.

Knopman, D. S. "Metrifonate for Alzheimer's Disease: Is the Next Cholinesterase Inhibitor Better?" *Neurology* 50 (1998): 1203.

Knopman, D. S., and J. C. Morris. "An Update on Primary Drug Therapies for Alzheimer's Disease." *Archives of Neurology* 54 (1997): 1406.

LeBars, P., et al. "A Placebo-Controlled, Double-Blind Randomized Trial of an Extract of Ginkgo Biloba for Dementia." *Journal of the American Medical Association* 278 (1997): 1327.

Lebuisson, D. A., et al. "Treatment of Senile Macular Degeneration with Ginkgo Biloba Extract: A Preliminary Double-Blind Study vs. Placebo," in *Rokan Ginkgo Biloba: Recent Results in Pharmacology and Clinic*. Berlin/New York: Springer-Verlag, 1988.

Lethem, R., and M. Orrell. "Antioxidants and Dementia." *Lancet* 349 (9060) (1997): 1189.

Logsdon, R. G., and L. Teri. "The Pleasant Events Schedule-AD: Psychometric Properties and Relationship to Depression and Cognition in Alzheimer's Disease Patients." *The Gerontologist* 37 (1997): 40.

Maurer, K., et al. "Clinical Efficacy of Ginkgo Biloba in Dementia of the Alzheimer Type." *Journal of Psychiatric Research* 31 (1997): 645.

Meyer, B. "A Multicenter Randomized Double-Blind Study of Ginkgo Biloba Extract vs. Placebo in the Treatment of Tinnitus," in *Rokan Ginkgo Biloba: Recent Results in Pharmacology and Clinic*. Berlin/New York: Springer-Verlag, 1988.

Morris, J. C., et al. "Metrifonate Benefits Cognitive, Behavioral, and Global Function in Patients with Alzheimer's Disease." *Neurology* 50 (1998): 1222.

Peck, P. "ERT May Help Women with Alzheimer's Disease." *Family Practice News* (Nov. 15, 1996).

Peck, P. "Merry Walker Enables Alzheimer's Improvement." *Family Practice News* (Feb. 1, 1998).

Pettegrew, J. W., et al. "Clinical and Neurochemical Effects of Acetyl-L-Carnitine in Alzheimer's Disease." *Neurobiology of Aging* 16 (1995): 1.

Raskind, M. "A Research Agenda for Disruptive Behaviors in Alzheimer's Disease: A Combined Biomedical and Behavioral Approach." *International Psychogeriatrics* 8 (suppl. 1) (1996): 53.

Rich, J. B., et al. "Nonsteroidal Anti-Inflammatory Drugs in Alzheimer's Disease." *Neurology* 45 (1995): 51.

Rogers, J., et al. "Clinical Trial of Indomethacin in Alzheimer's Disease." *Neurology* 43 (1993): 1609.

Rogers, S. L., et al. "A 24-Week Double-Blind, Placebo-Controlled Trial of Donepezil in Patients with Alzheimer's Disease." *Neurology* 50 (1998): 136.

Sano, M., et al. "A Double-Blind Parallel Design Pilot Study of Acetyl-Levocarnitine in Patients with Alzheimer's Disease." *Archives of Neurology* 49 (1992): 1137.

Sano, M., et al. "A Controlled Trial of Selegiline, Alpha-Tocopherol, or Both as Treatment for Alzheimer's Disease: The Alzheimer's Disease Cooperative Study." *New England Journal of Medicine* 336 (1997): 1216.

Santo Pietro, M. J., and F. Boczko. "The Breakfast Club: Results of a Study Examining the Effectiveness of a Multi-Modality Group Communication Treatment." *American Journal of Alzheimer's Disease* (May/June 1998): 146.

Scherder, E., et al. "Effects of Peripheral Tactile Nerve Stimulation on Affective Behavior of Patients with Probable Alzheimer's Disease." *American Journal of Alzheimer's Disease* (March/April 1998): 61.

Schneider, L. S., et al. "Effects of Estrogen Replacement Therapy on Response to Tacrine in Patients with Alzheimer's Disease." *Neurology* 46 (1996): 1580.

Schnelle, J. F., et al. "Prompted Voiding Treatment of Urinary Incontinence in Nursing Home Patients." *Journal of the American Geriatrics Society* 37 (1989): 1051.

Sikora, M., and R. Sikora. "Ginkgo Biloba Extract in the Therapy of Erectile Dysfunction." *Journal of Sex Education and Therapy* 17 (1991): 53.

Skolnick, A. A. "Old Chinese Herbal Medicine Used for Fever Yields Possible New Alzheimer's Disease Therapy." *Journal of the American Medical Association* 277 (1997): 776.

Spagnoli, A., et al. "Long-Term Acetyl-L-Choline Treatment in Alzheimer's Disease." *Neurology* 41 (1991): 1726.

Tabloski, P., et al. "Effects of Calming Music on Level of Agitation in Cognitively Impaired Nursing Home Residents." *Alternative Medicine Journal* (March 1995): 27.

Tariot, P. N. "Evaluating Response to Metrifonate." *Journal of Clinical Psychiatry* 59 (suppl. 9) (1998): 33.

Teri, L., and D. Gallagher-Thompson. "Cognitive-Behavioral Interventions for Treatment of Depression in Alzheimer's Patients." *The Gerontologist* 31 (1991): 413.

Teri, L., et al. "Behavioral Treatment of Depression in Dementia Patients: A Controlled Clinical Trial." *Journal of Gerontology* 52B (1997): P159.

Tucker, M. E. "Nicotine Patch May Help Cognition in Alzheimer's." *Family Practice News* (July 1, 1996).

Vaccaro, F. J. "Application of Operant Procedures in a Group of Institutionalized Aggressive Geratric Patients." *Psychology and Aging* 3 (1988): 22.

Van Rhijn, A. G., et al. "Dietary Supplementation with Zinc Sulphate, Sodium Selenite, and Fatty Acids in Early Dementia of the Alzheimer's Type." *Journal of Nutrition Research* 1 (1990): 259.

Vesper, J., and K. D. Hansgen. "Efficacy of Ginkgo Biloba in 90 Outpatients with Cerebral Insufficiency." *Phytomedicine* 1 (1994): 9.

Woods, D. L., et al. "Effect of Therapeutic Touch on Disruptive Behaviors of Individuals with Dementia of the Alzheimer's Type." *Alternative Therapies* (July 1996) 2:4:95.

Worcester, S. "Alzheimer's Disease Patients on Donepezil Often Need Less Care." *Family Practice News* (Sept. 1, 1997).

CHAPTER 12. BEFORE YOU DO ANYTHING ELSE, TAKE CARE OF YOURSELF

Alzheimer's Association. "Caregiver Stress: Signs to Watch Out For. Steps to Take" (1995).

Alzheimer's Association. "Hidden Heroes of Alzheimer's Disease: Survey Documents the Love and Labor of Alzheimer's Disease Caregiving" (1996).

Beck, C. K. "Psychosocial and Behavioral Interventions for Alzheimer's Disease Patients and Their Families." *American Journal of Geriatric Psychiatry* 6 (1998): S41.

Begany, T. "Caring for the Caregiver." *Patient Care* (Nov. 15, 1996).

Brown, D. "Family Caregiver Snapshot." *Caregiving* (Jan. 1997).

Coyne, A. C., et al. "The Relationship Between Dementia and Elder Abuse." *American Journal of Psychiatry* 150 (1993): 643.

Dick, L. P., and D. Gallagher-Thompson. "Cognitive Therapy with the Core Beliefs of a Distressed, Lonely Caregiver." *Journal of Cognitive Psychology* 9 (1995): 215.

Dippel, R. L. "The Caregivers," in *Caring for the Alzheimer Patient* (3rd ed.), R. L. Dippel and J. T. Hutton, eds., Amherst, NY: Prometheus Books, 1996.

Erickson, N., and S. Williams. "The Alzheimer's Association," in *Alzheimer's Disease: A Handbook for Caregivers* (3rd ed.), Ronald Hamdy, M.D., et al., eds., St. Louis: Mosby, 1998.

Family Caregiver Alliance. "Caregivers at Risk" (1993).

Family Caregiver Alliance. "Selected Caregiver Statistics" (1995).

Gallagher-Thompson, D. "Direct Services and Interventions for Caregivers," in *Family Caregiving: Agenda for the Future,* Marjorie Cantor, ed., San Francisco: American Society on Aging, 1994.

Gallagher-Thompson, D., and H. M. DeVries. "'Coping with Frustration' Classes: Development and Preliminary Outcomes with Women Who Care for Relatives with Dementia." *The Gerontologist* 34 (1994): 548.

Gallagher-Thompson, D., and D. V. Powers. "Primary Stressors and Depressive Symptoms in Caregivers of Dementia Patients." *Age and Mental Health* 1 (1997): 248.

Gallagher-Thompson, D., and A. Steffen. "Comparative Effects of Cognitive-Behavioral and Brief Psychodynamic Psychotherapies for Depressed Family Caregivers." *Journal of Consulting and Clinical Psychology* 62 (1994): 543.

Gallagher-Thompson, D., et al. "Development and Implementation of Intervention Strategies for Culturally Diverse Caregiving Populations." *Handbook of Dementia Caregiving Intervention Research,* R. Schultz, ed., New York: Spring Press. In press.

Gallagher-Thompson, D., et al. "Family Caregiving: Stress, Coping, and Intervention," in *Handbook of Clinical Geropsychology,* Michael Hersen and Vincent Ban Hasslet, eds., New York: Plenum Press, 1998.

Gallagher, D., et al. "Prevalence of Depression in Family Caregivers." *The Gerontologist* 29 (1989): 449.

Haisman, P. *Alzheimer's Disease: Caregivers Speak Out.* Fort Myers, FL: Chippendale House Publishers, 1998.

Kaplan, C. P., and D. Gallagher-Thompson. "Treatment of Clinical Depression in Caregivers of Spouses with Dementia." *Journal of Cognitive Psychology* 9 (1995): 35.

Kiecolt-Glaser, J., et al. "Chronic Stress and Immunity in Family Caregivers of Alzheimer's Disease Victims." *Psychosomatic Medicine* 49 (1987): 523.

Kiecolt-Glaser, J. K., et al. "Slowing of Wound Healing by Psychological Stress." *Lancet* 347(8993) (1996): 56.

Knight, B. G., et al. "A Meta-Analytic Review of Interventions for Caregiver Distress: Recommendations for Future Research." *The Gerontologist* 33 (1993): 240.

Lancaster, M. "Caregiver Education and Support," in *Alzheimer's Disease: A Handbook for Caregivers* (3rd ed.), Ronald Hamdy, M.D., et al., eds., St. Louis: Mosby, 1998.

Li, L. W., et al. "Social Support and Depressive Symptoms: Differential Patterns in Wife and Daughter Caregivers." *Journal of Gerontology* 52B (1997): S200.

Mittelman, M. S., et al. "A Family Intervention to Delay Nursing Home Placement of Patients with Alzheimer's Disease." *Journal of the American Medical Association* 276 (1996): 1725.

Polich, T. M., and D. Gallagher-Thompson. "Preliminary Study Investigating Psychological Distress Among Female Hispanic Caregivers." *Journal of Clinical Gerontology* 3 (1997): 1.

Raloff, J. "Stress Undercuts Flu Shots." *Science News* (April 13, 1996).

Schultz, R., ed. *Handbook of Dementia Caregiving Intervention Research.* New York: Spring Press. In press.

Small, G. "Diagnosis and Treatment of Alzheimer Disease and Related Disorders: Consensus Statement of the American Association for Geriatric Psychiatry, the Alzheimer's Association, and the American Geriatrics Society." *Journal of the American Medical Association* 278 (1997): 1363.

Steffen, A., et al. "Distress Levels and Coping in Female Caregivers and Non-Caregivers with Major Depressive Disorder." *Journal of Clinical Gerontology* 3 (1997): 101.

Teri, L., and D. Gallagher-Thompson. "Cognitive-Behavioral Interventions for Treatment of Depression in Alzheimer's Patients." *The Gerontologist* 31 (1991): 413.

Thompson, L., and D. Gallagher-Thompson. "Practical Issues Related to Maintenance of Mental Health and Positive Well-Being in Family Caregivers," in *The Practical Handbook of Clinical Gerontology,* Laura Carstensen, et al., eds., Thousand Oaks, CA: Sage Publications, 1996.

Zeiss, A., et al. "Self-Efficacy as Mediator of Caregiver Coping: Developing and Testing an Assessment Model." *Journal of Clinical Geropsychology,* in press.

CHAPTER 13. A PRACTICAL INTRODUCTION TO LOVING CAREGIVING

Adler, G. "Driving and Dementia: Dilemmas and Decisions." *Geriatrics* 52 (suppl. 2) (1997): S26.

Bell, V., and D. Troxel. *The Best Friends Approach to Alzheimer's Care*. Baltimore: Health Professions Press, 1997.

Brown, D. (ed.). *Caregiving* newsletter, Tad Publishing Co., P.O. Box 224, Park Ridge, IL 60068; (847) 823-0639.

Christensen, D. "Test Can Help Evaluate Driving Ability of Demented Patients." *Medical Tribune* (June 18, 1998).

Cox, D. J., et al. "Evaluating Driving Performance of Outpatients with Alzheimer's Disease." *Journal of the American Board of Family Practice* 11 (1998): 264.

Davies, Helen, and Michael Jensen. *Alzheimer's: The Answers You Need*. Forest Knoll, CA: Elder Books, 1998.

Davis, Robert with Betty Davis. *My Journey into Alzheimer's Disease*. Wheaton, IL: Tyndale House, 1989.

Devanand, D. P. "Behavioral Complications and Their Treatment in Alzheimer's Disease." *Geriatrics* 52 (suppl. 2) (1997): S37.

Dippel, R. L., and J. T. Hutton (eds). *Caring for the Alzheimer Patient: A Practical Guide* (3rd ed.). Amherst, NY: Prometheus Books, 1996.

Dowling, J. R. *Keeping Busy: A Handbook of Activities for Persons with Dementia*. Baltimore: Johns Hopkins University Press, 1995.

Edwards, A. J. *When Memory Fails: Helping the Alzheimer's and Dementia Patient*. New York: Plenum Press, 1994.

Forster, J. "When Do You Take Away the Car Keys?" *Patient Care* (Nov. 15, 1996): 41.

Fox, G. K., et al. "Alzheimer's Disease and Driving: Prediction and Assessment of Driving Performance." *Journal of the American Geriatric Society* 45 (1997): 949.

Glaser, V. "Managing Behavioral Problems in Alzheimer's Disease." *Patient Care* (Nov. 15, 1996).

Gray-Davidson, F. *The Alzheimer's Sourcebook for Caregivers: A Practical Guide for Getting Through the Day*. Los Angeles: Lowell House, 1996.

Gruetzner, H. *Alzheimer's: A Caregiver's Guide and Sourcebook*. New York: John Wiley & Sons, 1992.

Gwyther, Lisa. *Care of Alzheimer's Patients*. The Alzheimer's Association, 1985.

————. *Home Is Where I Remember Things.* Duke University Alzheimer's Family Support Center, 1997.

Haisman, P. *Alzheimer's Disease: Caregivers Speak Out.* Fort Myers, FL: Chippendale House Publishers, 1998.

Ham, R. J. "After the Diagnosis: Supporting Alzheimer's Patients and Their Families." *Postgraduate Medicine* (June 1997): 57.

Hamdy, R., et al. *Alzheimer's Disease: A Handbook for Caregivers.* St. Louis, MO: Mosby-Year Book, 1998.

Hodgson, H. *Alzheimer's: Finding the Words, A Communication Guide for Those Who Care.* Minneapolis: Chronimed Publishing, 1995.

Hodgson, H. *The Alzheimer's Caregiver: Dealing with the Realities of Dementia.* Minneapolis: Chronimed Publishing, 1998.

Hoffman, S. B., and M. Kaplan. "Problems Encountered in the Implementation of Dementia Care Programs." *American Journal of Alzheimer's Disease* (July/Aug. 1998): 197.

Mace, N., and P. Rabins. *The 36-Hour Day: A Family Guide for Caring for Persons with Alzheimer's Disease, Related Dementing Illness and Memory Loss in Later Life.* New York: Warner Books, 1991.

Valle, R. *Caregiving Across Cultures.* Washington, DC: Taylor and Francis, 1998.

CHAPTER 14. WHEN YOU CAN NO LONGER COPE WITH
   DAY-TO-DAY CAREGIVING

The Alzheimer's Association. "Selecting a Nursing Home with a Dedicated Dementia Unit."

Dippel, R. L., and J. T. Hutton. *Caring for the Alzheimer's Patients* (3rd ed.). Amherst, NY: Prometheus Books, 1996.

Forster, J. "Legal and Ethical Dilemmas in Alzheimer's Care." *Patient Care* (Dec. 15, 1996): 44.

Gray-Davidson, F. *The Alzheimer's Sourcebook for Caregivers.* Los Angeles: Lowell House, 1996.

Hamdy, R., et al. *Alzheimer's Disease: A Handbook for Caregivers.* St. Louis: Mosby-Year Book, 1998.

Mace, N., and P. Rabins. *The 36-Hour Day: A Family Guide to Caring for Persons with Alzheimer's Disease, Related Dementing Illness, and Memory Loss in Later Life.* New York: Warner Books, 1991.

Phillips, C. D., et al. "Effects of Residence in Alzheimer Disease Special Care Units on Functional Outcomes." *Journal of the American Medical Association* 278 (1997): 1340.

Rovner, B. W., et al. "A Randomized Trial of Dementia Care in Nursing Homes." *Journal of the American Geriatric Society* 44 (1996): 7.

Stern, Y., et al. "Predicting Time to Nursing Home Care and Death in Individuals with Alzheimer's Disease." *Journal of the American Medical Association* 277 (1997): 806.

Ulla, E., et al. "Special Care Units Are Efficient in Respite Care of Demented Patients," in *Research and Practice in Alzheimer's Disease,* B. Vellas, et al., eds., New York: Springer Publishing, 1998.

CHAPTER 16. THE NEW SCIENCE OF STAYING MENTALLY SHARP—FOR LIFE

Belles, M., et al. "Silicon Reduces Aluminum Accumulation in Rats: Relevance to the Aluminum Hypothesis of Alzheimer Disease." *Alzheimer Disease and Associated Disorders* 12 (1998): 83.

Benton, D. "The Impact of Long-Term Vitamin Supplementation on Cognitive Functioning." *Psychopharmacology* 117 (1995): 298.

Bernard, M. A., et al. "The Effect of Vitamin B12 Deficiency on Older Veterans and Its Relationship to Health." *Journal of the American Geriatric Society* 46 (1998): 1199.

Bilkei-Gorzo, A. "Neurotoxic Effect of Enteral Aluminum." *Food and Chemical Toxicology* 31 (1993): 357.

Bliwise, D. L. "Is Sleep Apnea a Cause of Reversible Dementia in Old Age?" *Journal of the American Geriatric Society* 44 (1996): 1407.

Dealberto, M. J., et al. "Breathing Disorders During Sleep and Cognitive Performance in an Older Community Sample: The EVA Study." *Journal of the American Geriatric Society* 44 (1996): 1287.

Deijan, J. B., et al. "Vitamin B_6 Supplementation in Elderly Men: Effects on Mood, Memory Performance, and Mental Effort." *Psychopharmacology* 109 (1992): 489.

Domingo, J. L., et al. "Effect of Various Dietary Constituents on Gastrointestinal Absorption of Aluminum from Drinking Water and Diet." *Research on Community Chemistry, Pathology, and Pharmacology* 79 (1993): 377.

Duggan, J. M., et al. "Aluminum Beverage Cans as Dietary Source of Aluminum." *Medical Journal of Australia* 156 (1992): 604.

Forbes, W. F., and N. Agwani. "A Suggested Mechanism for Aluminum Biotoxicity." *Journal of Theoretical Biology* 171 (1994): 207

Forster, D. P., et al. "Risk Factors in Clinically Diagnosed Presenile Dementia of the Alzheimer Type: A Case–Control Study in Northern England." *Journal of Epidemiology and Community Health* 49 (1995): 253.

Gilbert, S. "Researchers Develop Techniques to Battle Forgetfulness." *New York Times* (Oct. 7, 1997).

Gold, M., et al. "Hearing Loss in a Memory Disorders Clinic: A Specially Vulnerable Population." *Archives of Neurology* 53 (1996): 922.

Goleman, Daniel. *New York Times* (Feb. 26, 1996).

Gordon, B. *Memory: Remembering and Forgetting in Everyday Life.* New York: Mastermedia, 1995.

Gray, G. "Nutrition and Dementia." *Journal of the American Dietetic Association* 89 (1989): 1795.

Hendrie, H., et al. "Alcohol Intake and Cognitive Function in the Elderly." *Journal of the American Geriatrics Society* 44 (1996): 1158.

Hindmarch, I. "Activity of Ginkgo Biloba Extract on Short-Term Memory," in *Rokan Ginkgo Biloba: Results in Pharmacology and Clinic.* Berlin/New York: Springer-Verlag, 1988.

Holzman, D. "Estrogen May Protect Cognitive Function in Older Women." *Medical Tribune* (April 16, 1998).

Jacobs, D. M., and M. X. Tang. "Cognitive Function in Nondemented Women Who Took Estrogen After Menopause." *Neurology* 50 (1998): 368.

Jacqmin, H., et al. "Components of Drinking Water and Risk of Cognitive Impairment in the Elderly." *American Journal of Epidemiology* 139 (1994): 48.

Kawas, C., et al. "Treating Alzheimer's Disease: Today and Tomorrow." *Patient Care* (Nov. 15, 1996): 62–83.

Khalsa, Dharma Sing. *Brain Longevity.* New York: Warner Books, 1997.

Kleijnen, J., and P. Knipschild. "Ginkgo Biloba for Cerebral Insufficiency." *British Journal of Clinical Pharmacology* 34 (1992): 352.

Lautenschlager, N. T. "Risk of Dementia among Relatives of Alzheimer's Disease Patients in the MIRAGE Study: What Is in Store for the Oldest Old?" *Neurology* 46 (1996): 641.

LeBars, P. L., et al. "A Placebo-Controlled, Double-Blind Randomized Trial of an Extract of Ginkgo Biloba for Dementia." *Journal of the American Medical Association* 278 (1997): 1327.

Martyn, C. N. "Geographical Relation Between Alzheimer's Disease and Aluminum in Drinking Water." *Lancet* 8629 (1989): 59.

Martyn, C. N., et al. "Aluminum Concentrations in Drinking Water and Risk of Alzheimer's Disease." *Epidemiology* 8 (1997): 281.

McDonough, E., et al. "Protective Factors in Alzheimer's Disease: A Review," in *Research and Practice in Alzheimer's Disease,* B. Vellas, et al., eds., New York: Springer Publishing, 1998.

McLachlan, D. R., et al. "Risk for Neuropathologically Confirmed Alzheimer's Disease and Residual Aluminum in Municipal Drinking Water Employing Weighted Residential Histories." *Neurology* 46 (1996): 401.

Medical Tribune (May 21, 1998). "Lifelong Exercise May Help Ward Off Alzheimer's Disease."

Medical Tribune (Oct. 10, 1996). "Prolonged Stress May Lead to Memory Loss."

Medical Tribune (June 18, 1998). "Smoking May Lead to Cognitive Decline Dementia."

Meyer, J. S., et al. "Randomized Clinical Trial of Daily Aspirin Therapy in Multi-Infarct Dementia." *Journal of the American Geriatric Society* 37 (1989): 549.

Modern Medicine. "Black Tea Protects Against Coronary Heart Disease and Stroke" (May 1996).

Perrig, W. J., et al. "The Relation Between Antioxidants and Memory Performance in the Old and Very Old." *Journal of the American Geriatric Society* 45 (1997): 718.

Pope, H., and D. Yurgelun-Todd. "Residual Cognitive Effects of Heavy Marijuana Use in College Students." *Journal of the American Medical Association* 275 (1996): 521.

Rogers, S. "Is It Senility? Or Chemical Sensitivity?" *Townsend Letter for Doctors and Patients* (May 1993).

Schardt, D., and S. Schmidt. "Fear of Forgetting." *Nutrition Action Healthletter* (May 1997): 6.

Small, G., et al. "Predictors of Cognitive Change in Middle-Aged and Older Adults with Memory Loss." *American Journal of Psychiatry* 153 (1995): 1757.

Somova, L. I., et al. "Chronic Aluminum Intoxication in Rats: Dose-Dependent Morphological Changes." *Methods and Findings in Experimental Clinical Pharmacology* 19 (1997): 599.

Sorensen, H., and J. Sonne. "A Double-Blind Study of the Effects of Ginseng on Cognitive Function." *Current Therapeutic Research* 57 (1996): 959.

Stephenson, J. "More Evidence Links NSAID, Estrogen Use with Reduced Alzheimer's Risk." *Journal of the American Medical Association* 275 (1996): 1389.

Tang, M. X., et al. "Effect of Estrogen During Menopause on Risk and Age at Onset of Alzheimer's Disease." *Lancet* 348 (1996): 429.

West, M., and J. Grafman. "Train Your Memory." Cognitive Neurosciences Section, National Institute of Neurological Diseases and Stroke, 1998.

Winter, A., and R. Winter. *Brain Workout: East Ways to Power Up Your Memory, Sensory Perception, and Intelligence.* New York: St. Martin's Press, 1997.

Yaffe, K., et al. "Estrogen Therapy in Postmenopausal Women: Effects on Cognitive Function and Dementia." *Journal of the American Medical Association* 279 (1998): 688.

Permissions

In chapter 2, the ten warning signs of Alzheimer's disease have been adapted with permission of the Alzheimer's Association, Chicago, Illinois.

In chapter 3, the Functional Assessment Staging (FAST) scale and the Global Deterioration Scale are reprinted with permission of Barry Reisberg, M.D., of the Aging and Dementia Research Center at New York University Medical Center.

In chapter 7, the American Psychiatric Association's diagnostic criteria for Alzheimer's have been adapted from DSM-IV with permission of the APA.

In chapter 12, the material on cognitive therapy has been adapted with the permission of David Burns, M.D.

In chapter 13, the material dealing with the Best Friends™ approach to Alzheimer's caregiving has been adapted with permission from *The Best Friends Approach to Alzheimer's Care,* by Virginia Bell, M.S.W., and David Troxel, M.P.H. ©1997 by Health Profession Inc., Baltimore. Best Friends™ is a trademark owned by Health Profession Press.

In chapter 13, the "6 R's" of caregiving is reprinted from *The 36-Hour Day,* by Nancy L. Mace, M.A., and Peter Rabins M.D., M.P.H. © 1991, Warner Books.

In chapter 13, the material excerpted from *My Journey into Alzheimer's Disease* by Robert Davis © 1989 is used by permission of Tyndale House Publishers, Inc. All rights reserved.

In chapter 16, the memory assessment quiz has been adapted with permission from the Center for Science in the Public Interest, publisher of *Nutrition Action HealthLetter,* 10 issues for $24.00 from CSPI, 1875 Connecticut Ave., N.W., Suite 400, Washington, D.C. 20009.

Index

About the Authors

Michael Castleman, M.A., is "one of the nation's top health writers" *(Library Journal)*. He is the editorial director of Alzheimers.com, the most comprehensive Alzheimer's Web site for the general public. He is also the author of eight previous consumer health books, most recently *Nature's Cures* (1996), *An Aspirin a Day* (1993), and *The Healing Herbs* (1991). Winner of numerous awards for excellence in journalism, he has taught medical writing at the University of California at Berkeley's Graduate School of Journalism and has contributed articles to dozens of magazines, among them *Reader's Digest, Family Circle, Redbook, Glamour, Psychology Today, Self, New Woman, American Health for Women, Prevention, Healthy Living, Natural Health, Walking, Men's Health, Men's Fitness, Men's Journal,* and *Playboy*. He lives in San Francisco with his wife and their two children.

Dolores Gallagher-Thompson was completing her Ph.D. in psychology at the University of Southern California in the late 1970s, when her aging mother, who lived in New York, had a series of small strokes that left her unable to take care of herself. Gallagher-Thompson became her mother's caregiver, both in New York and long-distance from California. This experience inspired her to devote her professional career to helping caregivers cope with the enormous demands and stresses of dementia caregiving. Now a clinical geropsychologist, Dr. Gallagher-Thompson is an associate professor in the department of psychiatry and behavioral sciences at Stanford University Medical School, one of the associate directors of the Stanford/VA Alzheimer's Research Center, and codirector of the Older Adult and Family Research and Resource Center at the VA Palo Alto Health Care System. She is the author of more than a hundred research papers on caregiving and coeditor (with Gwen Yeo, Ph.D.) of *Ethnicity and the Dementias* (Taylor and Francis, 1996). Her research focuses on programs designed to reduce caregiver stress and depression. She lives in Los Altos, California, with her husband, who is also a psychologist.

After receiving his M.D. in 1972, MATTHEW NAYTHONS juggled work as an emergency room physician in California with world travel as an award-winning photojournalist for *Time, Newsweek,* and *National Geographic,* covering such subjects as the fall of Saigon, the Jonestown massacre, and the Centers for Disease Control. In response to the horrors he witnessed while photographing the 1979 Cambodian refugee exodus, Naythons formed International Medical Teams, which brought medical care to refugees on the Thai-Cambodia border. In 1989, he founded the RxMedia group in Sausalito, California, which produced *The Power to Heal,* a photojournalistic look at health, healing, and medicine around the world. In 1992, he founded Epicenter Communications, which produces photojournalism books, multimedia projects, and books about new media, including the first guide to health information on the Internet (The Internet Health, Fitness and Medicine Yellow Pages). Epicenter's two online health divisions, NetHealth and NetMed, have produced such popular consumer websites as Alzheimers.com, Depression.com, and Diabetes.com.

Since January 1999, Naythons has served as publisher and Vice-president of editorial for PlanetRx, an online pharmacy and health-care destination.